George Henry Lewes

Aristotle: A Chapter from the History of Science

Including Analyses of Aristotle's Scientific Writings

George Henry Lewes

Aristotle: A Chapter from the History of Science
Including Analyses of Aristotle's Scientific Writings

ISBN/EAN:

Printed in Europe, USA, Canada, Australia, Japan

Cover: Foto ©berggeist007 / pixelio.de

More available books at **www.hansebooks.com**

ARISTOTLE.

WORKS BY THE SAME AUTHOR.

THE LIFE OF GOETHE. New Edition, partly rewritten. 1863.

STUDIES IN ANIMAL LIFE. With Coloured Frontispiece and other Illustrations. Crown 8vo. 5s.

THE PHYSIOLOGY OF COMMON LIFE. With Illustrations. 2 vols. 1859.

SEASIDE STUDIES AT ILFRACOMBE, TENBY, SCILLY ISLES, AND JERSEY. With Illustrations. Second Edition. 1860.

THE BIOGRAPHICAL HISTORY OF PHILOSOPHY: FROM THALES TO THE PRESENT DAY. Library Edition. 1857.

ARISTOTLE:

A CHAPTER FROM

THE HISTORY OF SCIENCE,

INCLUDING

ANALYSES OF ARISTOTLE'S SCIENTIFIC WRITINGS.

BY

GEORGE HENRY LEWES.

LONDON:
SMITH, ELDER AND CO., 65, CORNHILL.
M.DCCC.LXIV.

[*The right of Translation is reserved.*]

Nam de famosis philosophus solus Aristoteles cum sua familia vocatus est judicio omnium sapientum, quoniam ipse omnes partes philosophiæ digessit secundum possibilitatem sui temporis, sed tamen ad finem sapientiæ non pervenit.—ROGER BACON: *Opus Majus*, p. 4, Venet., 1750.

Noi siamo qui tra noi discorrendo familiarmente per investigar qualche verità ; io non avrò mai per male, che voi mi palesiate i miei errori, e quando io non avrò conseguita la mente d'Aristotile, riprendetemi pur liberamente, che io ve ne avrò buon grado. — GALILEO GALILEI: *Dialoghi*, XI., 128, *Opere*, Milano, 1811.

Bur.—Volete che Platone sia un ignorante, Aristotile sia un asino, e quei che l'hanno seguitati sieno insensati, stupidi, e fanatichi ?
Fra.—Figlio mio, non dico che questi sieno li pulledri, e quelli gli asini, come voi volete ch'io dica ; ma come vi dissi da principio, lì stimo eroi de la terra, ma che non voglio credergli senza causa, nè ammetterli quelle proposizione de le quali le contradittorie come possete aver compreso, se non siete a fatto cieco e sordo, sono tanto espressamente vere.—GIORDANO BRUNO: *De l'infinito Universo*, Op. Ital., II., 67, Leipzig, 1830.

PREFACE.

THE conception of evolution as the law of life, and consequently as the law of Humanity, a conception which links the Present indissolubly with the whole Past, and gives to the study of history a new and deeper significance, is the creation of our age. By a venial, yet fatal error, Catholicism separated itself from the traditions of ancient thought; with equal exclusiveness, Protestantism opposed the great labours of the Middle Ages; and the philosophy of the 18th century in turn rejected both, shouting the watchwords of Progress and Enlightenment, as if these words were then heard for the first time. All piety towards the Past was gone.

With clearer vision the leading minds of the 19th century have attempted a reconciliation by accepting the positive, and rejecting the negative tendencies of all schools. History has consequently been studied with increasing ardour, and with ever-widening aims. Nor is it only the development of national life which History is summoned to investigate. Everywhere questions of origin and development have become paramount. The history of our globe, and the development of animal life, are debated with a fervour which would have been incomprehensible a century ago. Even the anatomist is no longer contented to display what the tissues *are;* he must also trace their origin, and show how they *became* what they are.

The origin and development of Science are questions of high interest, and fortunately admit of being handled even by those who would shrink from the gigantic difficulties of a History of the Sciences. I have been for many years preparing myself to attempt a sketch of the Embryology of Science, so to speak,—an exposition of the great *momenta* in scientific development; and the present volume is the first portion of such an exposition, which I publish separately because in itself it forms a monograph, and because I may never live to complete the larger scheme.

As a monograph it has not, I believe, been forestalled. Numerous and exhaustive as are the works devoted to Aristotle's moral and metaphysical writings, there is not one which attempts to display, with any fulness, his scientific researches. The only considerable treatise which touches on this ground,[*] is strictly confined within the limits of Natural History.

Although Aristotle mainly represents the science of twenty centuries, his scientific writings are almost unknown in England. Casual citations, mostly at secondhand, and vague eulogies, often betraying great misconception, are abundant; but rare indeed is the indication of any accurate appreciation extending beyond two works, the *De Animâ*, and the *History of Animals*. The absence of translations is at once a cause and a sign of this neglect. Of the 15 treatises analyzed in the present volume, only the two just named have been translated,

---

[*] J. B. MEYER: *Aristoteles Thierkunde, Ein Beitrag zur Geschichte der Zoologie, Physiologie, und alten Philosophie.* Berlin, 1855.

and one of these appeared after my work was written.* Nor would translations be of much help to the ordinary student, unless illuminated by an ample commentary, such as would place him at the requisite point of view for appreciating these ancient monuments of scientific labour. I have endeavoured to furnish such a point of view, as far as the limits and the object of my work permitted.

Instead of following the usual plan of weaving together various passages scattered through widely different works, which thus presents a succinct, systematic, and often false outline of the doctrines, I have analyzed the separate treatises, given the doctrines precisely as Aristotle gave them (illuminating them when necessary and possible from other sources), and have never distorted them into modern formulæ, nor eliminated from them their essential or incidental absurdities. This latter point is of some importance. Most expositions of Aristotle's doctrines, when they have not been dictated by a spirit of virulent detraction, or unsympathetic indifference, have carefully suppressed all, or nearly all, the absurdities, and only retained what seemed plausible and consistent. But in this procedure their historical significance disappears. Writing as an historian, not as a partisan, I have allowed the errors and the crudities to take their rightful place beside the plausibilities and truths; thus preserving, as far as may be, the historical colouring derived from the inherent weakness of early Science, and the individual weakness of Aristotle.

* There is, indeed, a version of all Aristotle's works, by Thomas Taylor, in 10 vols. 4to. But there are two reasons for considering this as practically non-existent: first, its rarity, only a very few copies having been printed; secondly, and chiefly, the translator's imperfect knowledge of science. I speak of the work only from report; but from what I have seen quoted, I believe the report does him substantial justice.

That I have not been unmindful of what my predecessors in all ages have done towards the elucidation of various points, will be apparent from the notes, of which it is only needful to say, that all citations made at secondhand have been scrupulously acknowledged, and all references not thus acknowledged may be accepted as the results of my own research. It is eminently desirable that the growing practice of secondhand citation should be discouraged; since our native infirmity renders us all sufficiently liable to error, without our taking on ourselves the responsibility of other men's carelessness or of their misrepresentations.

Readers who have but small interest in the details of Biology, may perhaps object to my having sometimes—especially in the notes—wandered from the broad path, into the windings and obscure alleys whither only a certain class will care to follow. Let me plead in anticipation, that although my own predilections have seduced me into adding details for the sake of a class, I have not sacrificed any general interest to such predilections, but merely given these details in addition.

The first draught of this volume was completed in February, 1862. The rewriting was finished in July, 1862; but fresh researches, and many revisions, have retarded its publication.

THE PRIORY,
January, 1864.

CONTENTS.

CHAPTER		PAGE
I.	THE LIFE OF ARISTOTLE	1
II.	THE DAWN OF SCIENCE	24
III.	ANCIENT SCIENCE	45
IV.	THE METAPHYSICAL AND SCIENTIFIC METHODS	65
V.	PLATO'S METHOD	101
VI.	ARISTOTLE'S METHOD	108
VII.	ARISTOTLE'S PHYSICS, METEOROLOGY, AND MECHANICS	122
VIII.	ARISTOTLE'S ANATOMY	154
IX.	ARISTOTLE'S PHYSIOLOGY	171
X.	GENERAL PRINCIPLES OF BIOLOGY	182
XI.	ANTICIPATION OF MODERN DISCOVERIES	197
XII.	LIFE AND MIND: *DE ANIMÂ*	221
XIII.	ON THE SENSES	246
XIV.	ON MEMORY, SLEEP, DREAMS, AND LONGEVITY	256
XV.	"THE HISTORY OF ANIMALS"	269
XVI.	"ON THE PARTS OF ANIMALS"	292
XVII.	ON GENERATION AND DEVELOPMENT	325
XVIII.	CONCLUSION	376
	INDEX	383

ARISTOTLE.

CHAPTER I.

THE LIFE OF ARISTOTLE.

§ 1. It is difficult to speak of Aristotle without exaggeration: he is felt to be so mighty, and is known to be so wrong. History, surveying the whole scope of his pretensions, gazes on him with wonder. Science, challenging these separate pretensions, and testing their results, regards them with indifference; an indifference easily exasperated into antagonism by the clamorous urgency of unauthenticated praise. It is difficult to direct the opposing streams of criticism into the broad equable current of a calm appreciation; because the splendour of his fame perpetuates the memory of his failure; and to be just we must appreciate both. His intellect was piercing and comprehensive; his attainments surpassed those of every known philosopher; his influence has only been exceeded by the great founders of Religions; nevertheless, if we now estimate the product of his labours in the discovery of positive truths, it appears insignificant, when not erroneous. None of the great germinal discoveries in science are due to him, or to his disciples. His vast and active intellect gave an impulse to philosophy, and for twenty centuries held the world in awe. Then came a change; the long-murmuring spirit of rebellion grew strong enough to dethrone him. Ages of servility had raised him to an unexampled eminence; in the tumult of revolution this pedestal became a pillory. When the Arabs kill a lion, their released terror vents itself in insults on the harmless corpse: they kick, and spit upon, and apostrophize in sarcasms the helpless image of their former dread. It was thus with the great lion of Stagira. Men who a few years before would have burned a presumptuous critic for daring to think that the great teacher could be wrong, were now laughing to scorn the method and conclusions of the rejected sophist.[1]

Our task is twofold: we shall constantly have to bear in mind the relative (or historical) and the absolute (or scientific) aspect which his achievements present; never permitting our natural and justifiable admiration for the effort, to disguise our appreciation of its result; nor, conversely, permitting our contempt or disregard of the result, to mislead us into an unjust depreciation of the effort. "It is the destiny and glory

---

[1] The virulence with which some of the reformers attacked him is at times amusing. A good example is RAMUS: *Scholarum Physicarum libri octo*, 1565 (which I only know at second hand). Less virulent, but not less decided, is the antagonism of NIZOLIUS: *De veris Principiis et vera Ratione Philosophandi contra pseudo Philosophos*, Parma, 1553. He complains indignantly of the Greeks being followed, " perinde ac si essent oracula quædam Delphica, aut arcana divinitus revelata, quæ nullo pacto falsa esse possent," and he compares Aristotle to the cuttlefish escaping in a cloud of ink—perhaps the earliest example of this now threadbare comparison. LEIBNITZ thought this treatise worth republishing, and wrote a preface to it; see TIRABOSCHI: *Storia della Litteratura Italiana*, 1812,, VII. 44, where he truly says that if NIZOLIUS is right in combating the Peripatetics, he is less happy in the attempt to replace them. A more formidable antagonist is TELESIO, whose work, *De Natura Rerum juxta propria Principia libri novem*, Naples, 1586, I shall have to quote hereafter. Even more virulent is PATRIZIO (see Note 9). GIORDANO BRUNO, though relentless towards the peripatetics of his day, is more respectful to Aristotle. The same must be said of GALILEO and DESCARTES; and notably of TAURELLUS, in his attack on CÆSALPINUS, punningly entitled *Alpes Casæ, hoc est A. Cæsalpini monstrosa et superba Dogmata discussa et excussa*, Frankfort, 1650. No longer worthy of more than a passing glance is BASSO: *Philosophiæ Naturalis adversus Aristotelem libri XII.*, Elzevir, 1649, though once

of the anatomist of Stagira," says Isidore St. Hilaire,[2] "to have had before him simply precursors and after him only disciples." In yielding our most ample tribute, we must be careful to make that tribute generously just: we must hold the balance fairly, weighing the failures with the successes. In an attempt so delicate, I cannot pretend to have preserved the balance; but I can affirm that it has been my constant aim; and I wish that I could be certain of so expressing myself as to prevent readers from misconstruing either the praise or the blame which will have to be pronounced. The risk must be run; both praise and blame must be expressed without reticence. Piety towards the Past demands of us to be ready with our gratitude for all good work; and an equal piety towards the Present commands us to beware of an exaggeration which would convert panegyric of the departed into insults against the living. It is the glory of Science to be constantly progressive. After the lapse of a century, the greatest teacher, on reappearing among men, would have to assume the attitude of a learner. His point of view would no longer command the whole field of knowledge. The very seed sown by himself would have sprung up into a forest to obscure the view. But we who rejoice in the grandeur of the forest must not forget by whom the seeds were sown. His heritors, we are richer, but not greater than he. "The similitude which many have fancied between the superiority of the moderns to the ancients, and the elevation of a dwarf on the back of a giant, is altogether false and puerile. Neither were they giants nor are we dwarfs; but all of us men of the same standard, and we the taller of the two

---

highly prized. Campanella I have not read. Gassendi is an uncompromising adversary (see Note 18). If we except the two great luminous intellects Galileo and Descartes, the inferiority of these adversaries to the man they attack is so conspicuous that nothing but sympathy with their revolutionary fervour can make them tolerable.

[2] Isidore Geoffroy St. Hilaire: *Histoire Générale des Règnes Organiques*, Paris, 1854, I. 19.

by adding their height to our own: provided always that we do not yield to them in study, attention, vigilance and love of truth, for if these qualities be wanting, so far from mounting on the giant's shoulders, we throw away the advantage of our own stature by remaining prostrate on the ground."[3]

§ 2. The ancient biographies of Aristotle have been gathered by BUHLE into the first volume of his valuable but unfinished edition of the *Opera Omnia*. Meagre in detail, and of suspicious authenticity, these are all that moderns have to rely on for the facts of Aristotle's career. And as I was aware, from previous experience, that the whole race of compilers is far from trustworthy, and that little confidence is to be placed in an ancient compiler (though to moderns it generally seems as if anything written in Greek must have a peculiar authenticity, even nonsense wearing an august air in that language), it occurred to me that perhaps the mere registration of the dates at which these several biographies were compiled, might amply justify scepticism as to their accuracy. All ancient writers, except, perhaps, Thucydides, are uncritical in their reception of facts. Even in our own critical age, as it is rashly called, we find it extremely difficult to ascertain the truth respecting celebrated persons; so powerful is the mythical tendency, and so fungus-like the rapidity with which lies are propagated. But the ancients had not risen to the conception of what constitutes evidence; they were as credulous as children; and accepted almost any marvel which was narrated gravely.

What then are the dates, or thereabouts? Aristotle was born B.C. 384. DIOGENES LAERTIUS, whose narrative is the fullest, the best, and the most generally followed, was born, at the earliest, nearly six centuries later—*i.e.* A.D. 200; and it is even supposed that he was as late as Constantine. The next on our list is AMMONIUS (if the work be really his), who comes

---

[3] This fine passage is quoted from LUDOVICUS VIVES by DUGALD STEWART.

eight centuries after his hero, in A.D. 460; and that these eight centuries have not been profitably employed in sifting tradition, and bringing it nearer to accuracy, may be gathered from a single detail noticed by BUHLE,[4] that Aristotle is made a pupil of Socrates, who died just fifteen years before the Stagirite was born. The nearest biographer, in point of time, is DIONYSIUS of Halicarnassus (B.C. 50), and this gives a gap of three centuries; moreover, one meagre page comprises all he has to say. HESYCHIUS was born A.D. 500—nearly nine centuries too late; the date of SUIDAS is uncertain, but probably not earlier than the eleventh century of our era.

These writers contradict each other on separate points. What means have we for deciding between them? They may have had contemporary documents as their authorities; but what guarantee have we for the accuracy of these documents? It is but just three hundred years since SHAKSPEARE was born; throughout this period he has been prized, and written about; compilers have done their worst upon this subject; yet what do we authentically know of his life? above all, what value do we attach to the earliest biography, that by ROWE?

If, therefore, modern scholars have pieced together the various details traditionally preserved about Aristotle, we

---

[4] " Quis enim Ammonium credat tam absurdum, ut Aristotelem per tres annos Socratis, qui diu ante mortuus esset, discipulum, eundemque Alexandri in itinere per Asiam usque ad Indos comitem fuisse, temere asseruerit ? " BUHLE : *Arist. Opera*, I., 51. It has been suggested that instead of SOCRATES we should read the school of Socrates; but there was no such school. Mr. BLAKESLEY, by a plausible emendation, suggests XENOCRATES as the name which by corruption has become SOCRATES. This, however, ill accords with the statement of AMMONIUS; nor have we any evidence that Xenocrates taught till many years afterwards. During the revision of this chapter there has fallen in my way a copy of the Greek text of Ammonius, from the Library of St. Mark's at Venice, now first published by Dr. ROBBE: *Vita Aristotelis ex codice Marciano Græce nunc primum edita*, Lugd.-Batav., 1861, which gives the same reading as the old Latin translation, previously our only guide. Here is the passage: ἐτῶν δὲ γενόμενος ἑπτὰ καὶ δέκα, τοῦ Πυθοῖ θεοῦ χρήσαντος αὐτῷ φιλοσοφεῖν παρ' Ἀθηναίοις, φοιτᾷ Σωκράτει, καὶ συνῆν τὸν, μέχρι τελευτῆς αὐτοῦ χρόνον ὀλίγον ὄντα.

may accept their narrative as the best which is now procurable, though with no firm reliance on any side when separate points are under discussion. I shall not, therefore, occupy the reader's time with discussions, where decisive evidence is necessarily deficient; but tell the story, by using at my own discretion the narratives given in the latest and most authoritative treatises,[5] leaving the unprofitable task of weighing imponderable evidence to those who delight in such ingenuities.

§ 3. Stagira—which, BŒCKH says, should correctly be written Stageiros—was a town in Northern Greece, on the western coast of the Strymonic Gulf (now called the Gulf of Contezza) just where the coast begins to take a southerly bend. Its situation has been compared with the southern part of the Bay of Naples. Immediately south, a promontory, like the Punta della Campanella, and nearly in the same latitude, runs out in an easterly direction, thus effectually screening the little town and its harbour, Capros, from the stormy squalls of the Ægean. Stagira is said to resemble Sorrento, not only in the general disposition of its coast lines, but also in the terraced windings of its multitudinous orange and lemon groves.[6]

§ 4. In this picturesque seaport, Aristotle was born, B.C. 384, that is, exactly one century after the birth of Herodotus; one century before the foundation of the Alexandrian library, and the execution of the Septuagint version of the Scriptures; and two centuries before the death of Philopœmen, "the last of the Greeks," when the Achæan league dissolved before the Roman power, and Greece merged her splendid existence in the dependence of a Roman province.

---

[5] BUHLE, I., 80–104. RITTER: *History of Philosophy, trans. by Morrison*, 1839, III. BLAKESLEY: *Life of Aristotle*, 1839. STAHR, art. *Arist.* in *Dictionary of Greek and Roman Biography*, 1844. BRANDIS: *Aristoteles seine Academischen Zeitgenossen und nächsten Nachfolger*, 1853. ZELLER: *Die Philosophie der Griechen*, 1860, II.

[6] BLAKESLEY: *Op. cit.*, p. 12.

His father, NICOMACHUS, was a physician and an Asclepiad; but whether he had any better claim to the honour of descent from Æsculapius than so many others who usurped the title,[7] or simply belonged to the famous guild, cannot now be determined. It is certain that he was a physician of repute, attached to AMYNTAS II., the father of the Macedonian PHILIP. The fact of his profession, coupled with the fact of Stagira being on the sea-coast, may have been of moment in determining his son's studies in the direction of physiology and marine zoology. There is indeed a passage in GALEN, often quoted, which affirms that among the Asclepiads children were taught dissection, just as they were taught reading and writing, thus becoming as familiar with anatomy as with the alphabet. But this must be accepted with a large handful of salt; for, as we shall see presently, the Asclepiads, and Aristotle himself, were very imperfectly acquainted with anatomy. The statement, however, even in its exaggeration, points to the important fact that anatomy was not neglected, but formed one part of the boy's education; and this isolated fact sums up all we know of that education.

§ 5. It is unknown how long he remained at Stagira before accompanying his father to the court of AMYNTAS, at Pella, where he learned to know and ingratiate himself with PHILIP, who was hereafter to befriend him. Everything at this epoch is conjecture, and conjecture may amuse, but cannot instruct.

§ 6. At the age of seventeen he lost his father. This is the next isolated fact which has been recorded, and it is important. He thus became his own master, with the command of a large fortune; a perilous condition to most youths the temptation to squander his fortune in frivolous dissipation must have been great, and could only be withstood by an unusual seriousness of mind, or unusual felicity in his social connections. So plausible is the supposition that a youth

---

[7] See HARLESS: *De Medicis Veteribus "Asclepiades" dictis*, a work only known to me at second hand.

thus circumstanced will be ruined, that idle gossip, which always flits about a celebrated name, invented a story of his having wasted his means, and having been reduced to sell drugs for a subsistence; a story which, however, found refutation even among the ancients, and is wholly irreconcilable with the known facts of his subsequent career.

He was young, ardent, ambitious, rich. Athens, the glory of the world, though her political sun was setting, the luminous centre of Philosophy and Art, beckoned to him, as Rome and Florence beckon to the students of our day. PLATO taught there, and might admit him to the groves of the Academy. To listen to this " old man eloquent," was a rare attraction, and naturally it drew him to Athens. Arrived there, he found that PLATO was absent. Awaiting the great teacher's return, he qualified himself for discipleship by three years of arduous study. Had he squandered his wealth in dissipation, as the babblers reported, he could not have collected the treasure of books which he is known to have bought; for in those days it was almost as costly to create a library of books as in our own to create a gallery of pictures.[8] To collect books and to read them are not always the same thing. With him they were one; and PLATO, alluding to the extraordinary passion he displayed, called him " the reader." His writings show how diligently he had studied all accessible literature; and it is to his punctilious quotation

---

[8] According to GELLIUS, he paid for the works of SPEUSIPPUS alone three Attic talents, that is about 700*l.* of our money, a sum not to be spared out of the profits of drug-selling unless by a merchant prince. In our own days 1,000*l.* has been paid for a rare edition of an Italian poet; but *that* was merely the avidity of a collector's furor backed by the wealth of an English nobleman. Curious details on the price of books in the Middle Ages may be read in MURATORI : *Dissertazione sopra l'antichità Italiane*, Diss. XLIII. Compare also HEEREN : *Geschichte der Classischen Litteratur im Mittelalter*, Werke, 1822, IV. In our days of cheap literature—cheap, because we have cheap paper, and that because we wear linen instead of woollen clothes—these details seem to render the darkness of the dark ages more intelligible.

of his predecessors that we are greatly indebted for the preservation of many fragments of ancient thought. So little justice is there in Bacon's sarcasm, that like an Eastern despot he strangled his rivals in order to reign peaceably.[9]

§ 7. When Aristotle came to Athens the splendour of her life was fast departing, and near at hand was the towering greatness of Macedon, so soon to overshadow her on the plains of Chæroneia. The sun was setting on the Age of Pericles, and was rising on the Age of Alexander. For sixty years PERICLES had ceased to thunder from the bema; had ceased to communicate his agitating stimulus to art and politics; had ceased to adorn the beautiful city with

---

[9] Aristotle's precepts, no less than his practice, answer this accusation. See *Metaph.*, II., 1, 995; *De Cælo*, I., 10, 279; and *De Anima*, I., 1. BACON simply echoed PATRIZIO, whose enmity was virulent and avowed, and who declares that one cause of this hatred was the abuse which Aristotle heaps on the writers from whom his best ideas are stolen. PATRITII: *Discussionum Peripateticarum tomi quatuor*, Bâle, 1581, from which learned but untrustworthy work some moderns have largely drawn. The first volume contains a life and a list of the extant works, with an account of all the Peripatetics. In the third book there is a valuable collection of the passages in which *A.* refers to his own writings; a collection subsequently used and expanded by RITTER, but without the acknowledgment due in such a case. The second volume gives an exposition of the points of *agreement* between the doctrines of *A.* and Plato, and the older writers. In the third volume the points of *difference* are noted. In the preface he complains of the insults to philosophers (p. 291-2), and sarcastically adds that there is no mention of HIPPOCRATES. (Some moderns, coupling this supposed silence with the silence of THUCYDIDES, have argued that Hippocrates lived after Aristotle; but the fact is that Hippocrates *is* mentioned, and in the *Politics* there is a sketch of his views on climate.) In the fourth volume PATRIZIO gives full expression to his antagonism. GIORDANO BRUNO, in spite of his own opposition to the peripatetic system, speaks with measureless contempt of PATRIZIO as " un sterco di pedante Italiano che ha imbrattati tanti quinterni con le sue discussione peripatetiche," and vows that he has not understood the Stagirite, but only read and reread him " cucito, scucito e confeiito con mill' altri greci autori amici e nemici di quello, et al fine fatta una grandissima fatica non sola senza profitto alcuno, ma etiam con un grandissimo sproposito." *De la Causa Principio et Uno* (*Opere Ital.*, Leipzig, 1830), I., 250. PATRIZIO had many admirers and imitators; a notable one is BASSO (see Note 1). I have not had the courage to extend my wanderings further through this rubbish of denunciation and criticism heaped up by the iconoclasts.

his munificence and taste. SOPHOCLES and EURIPIDES were gone; and the grand and pathetic drama they had unfolded to applauding thousands, had fallen into the hands of CHÆREMON, CLEOPHON, and THEODECTES (the last the friend of Aristotle), whose efforts to make rhetoric supply the place of poetry pointed unmistakably towards decline. ARISTOPHANES no longer laughed at the absurdities, and scourged the corruptions of his time, in riotous and reckless farces, which too often wilfully misrepresented persons and ideas essentially wise and noble. No great prose writer except XENOPHON remained; not one poet of eminence.

But if a sunset, it was still a glorious sunset, with some splendour of the after-glow. Great memories swelled ambitious minds. Powerful vibrations were still felt from Salamis, Marathon, and Platæa. ISOCRATES upheld the renown of Athenian eloquence; and the greater DEMOSTHENES was preparing for his matchless displays. PRAXITELES was at work upon statues, the very copies of which were for centuries to be the despair of artists. SCOPAS, the sculptor of the immortal Niobe and the Venus of Milo, had enchanted the Athenians with his Furies. DIOGENES, with drastic energy, despised the citizens from his tub. The schools were crowded with listeners to many teachers. In every direction there was intellectual activity and social ferment. A young, keen intellect would find there abundant stimulus.

§ 8. As years ripened his intelligence, and free intercourse with eminent men procured him the advantages and opportunity of display, Aristotle gradually won for himself a foremost position. He came there a raw ambitious youth, not only with the disadvantages of inexperience, but with those disadvantages of accent and manner which, in the eyes of supercilious Athenians—the Frenchmen of antiquity—made him seem almost a barbarian. These, however, he soon modified. One fact recorded of him—that he was somewhat given to foppery in costume—implies an eager sensitiveness to approbation, which would have directed his attention to anything provincial in his air. Keen, witty, logical, and learned, he was a brilliant talker, and in that city of talkers could hold his own with the best; not even refraining from controversy with his great master. Without pretending to decide the much vexed question of his ingratitude towards PLATO, I must express my own disbelief in the accusation; although it is very credible, and by no means derogatory to him, that, differing from his master in cast of mind, as well as on certain fundamental points of philosophy, he should often, during the seventeen years they were together, have been seduced into warm, and sometimes irritating, discussion with one whom, on the whole, he considered as the noblest of thinkers. All opposition is apt to be construed as an offence; and if Aristotle's criticisms and allusions to Plato are not always remarkable for their judicial calmness, they have never any approach to irreverence. Often in antagonism—how could this sincerely be avoided?—he is never in hostility to Plato. Indeed, in the *Ethics*, he complains of the necessity of attacking doctrines held by "dear friends," adding— "It is our duty to slay our own flesh and blood where the cause of Truth is at stake, especially as we are philosophers; loving both, it is our sacred duty to give the preference to Truth." It is a timidity unworthy of a noble mind to shrink from intellectual opposition as an offence against friendship, and to suppress convictions for fear of misconstruction.

§ 9. Aristotle remained twenty years at Athens. During seventeen of these years, Plato was first his master, and then his friend. His health was, like that of most ardent brainworkers, delicate. He was short and slender in person; he had small eyes, and an affected lisp. Somewhat given to sarcasm in conversation, he made, of course, many enemies. On hearing that some one had vituperated him in his absence he humourously said, "If he pleases, he may beat me too—*in my absence.*" His heart was kind, as was manifest in certain acts, and is expressed in this saying, "He who has many friends has no friends," which profoundly touches the very core of the subject, and may be paired off with this other saying of his, "A friend is one soul in two bodies." When asked how we should behave towards friends, he said, "As we should wish them to behave towards us."

Advancing age and development, no less than the decidedly scientific bias impressed upon his studies, necessarily caused him to take up an independent position with respect to Plato, who had little taste for physical science, and whose intellect naturally withdrew from those very subjects to which his young rival was, by nature and early bias, strongly determined. Without absolutely opening a rival school, Aristotle gradually gathered round him a circle of admirers, and began, during the last years of his Athenian residence, to give lectures.[10]

§ 10. Among the listeners was HERMIAS, the tyrant (or ruler) of Atarneus, and to him, by invitation, Aristotle went, on quitting Athens, after Plato's death. His companion on this journey was XENOCRATES, the best loved of Plato's disciples. What was the object of their visit? It has been conjectured that HERMIAS invited them to frame a political constitution. The scheme, if such it were, was frustrated by the assassination of Hermias, and the fall of Atarneus into Persian hands. The two philosophers escaped to Mytilene, carrying with them PYTHIAS, the adopted daughter of their friend and patron; and Aristotle subsequently married her, out of compassion for her defenceless position, and respect for the memory of his murdered friend. Worthy of special reprobation, as indicating the peculiar infelicity with which calumny often selects its

---

[10] The story of his having practised medicine at this time, which is founded on his interest in that art, is refuted by his express statement in the work, *De Divinatione*, I., 463, that in medicine he was only one of the laity, though accustomed to philosophize upon it.

points of attack, is the fact that his friendship for HERMIAS, and generosity towards PYTHIAS, furnished the cruel thoughtlessness of scandal with its bitterest accusations. Here once more may be seen how in this life men are punished for their virtues; as a set-off, perhaps, to the rewards which often crown their vices. So little reliance can be placed on these ancient scandals, that some call PYTHIAS the daughter, and others the concubine, of HERMIAS. It is, perhaps, a slight objection to both these assertions that HERMIAS was an eunuch.

§ 11. To the memory of Hermias he raised a statue at Delphi, with an inscription; on which act was founded a charge of impiety. Nor was the memory of Pythias, who died after giving birth to a daughter, less honoured by the grateful husband. In his will he enjoined that her bones should be laid beside his own.

§ 12. He had not long been at Mytilene before he received from PHILIP of Macedon the magnificent offer to undertake the charge of the young ALEXANDER. From this it is evident that his reputation, while at Athens, must have been considerable. To Macedon he went. His princely pupil was then fourteen: young enough to receive a determining bias, old enough to revere the intellectual force which impressed that bias. The respectful love which men of fine intellect and generous sympathies so gladly give to their first instructors is well expressed in the saying of ALEXANDER, that he honoured Aristotle no less than his own father; for if to the one he owed life, to the other he owed that which made life valuable.

That the tutor and pupil might promenade in the cool shade during the hours of instruction, Philip caused a gymnasium to be built in a grove; and even so late as the days of Plutarch, the traveller might still see the shady walks (περίπατοι) with their stone seats for resting-places. Aristotle remained seven years in Macedon; but only four of these were given to the education of the prince, who at eighteen became Regent. Thus while DEMOSTHENES was thundering against the ambition of PHILIP, who claimed for Macedon the hegemony of Greece, Aristotle was stimulating and enlarging the mind of ALEXANDER, who was soon to carry the silver shields of Macedon from Syria to Egypt, from Candahar to the Indus, and from the Indus to the Persian Gulf. Popular fiction makes the great teacher accompany the great conqueror on this splendid expedition; and one regrets that this is a fiction. There was, indeed, other work for Aristotle to do, which the life of camps would hardly have advanced. Still the expedition would have been a vast experience for him; and his observing mind could not have beheld that varied, shifting panorama without great result. To have passed with the conquering hosts to Tyre; to have witnessed the foundation of Alexandria; to have lived through the agitations of the day at Arbela, when the countless hosts of Darius were assembled on the plain beneath the Koordish mountains, and there were slaughtered like sheep; to have witnessed the successive subjection of Babylon and Susa, of Persepolis and Ecbatana; and finally to see the young Dionysus, maddened with the insolence of success, cut off suddenly in his youth; these were grand experiences which one regrets to think were lost to Aristotle.

§ 13. Although, as I said, the relation between master and pupil lasted only four years, the relation of friendly counsel on the one side, and magnificent gratitude on the other continued. Had it not been for Alexander's princely aid, Aristotle's enormous collections could not have been made. The aid is unexampled. It is said, but not on trustworthy authority, that Alexander presented him with the sum of eight hundred talents, which represents nearly two hundred thousand pounds of our money. Few critical readers will believe that; and SCHNEIDER, in his edition of the *Historia Animalium*, quotes with approbation the estimate of a predecessor, who calculates that the whole revenue of Macedon would not have furnished such a sum. Still if we make liberal deductions, and strike off two thirds of this sum, it leaves a splendid surplus. The enormity of the exaggeration points to an enormous sum. Add to this the statement of PLINY, that Alexander gave orders to his hunters, gamekeepers, fishermen, and bird-catchers to furnish the philosopher with all the material he might desire—an order which at once placed several thousand men at his service.[11] But at the same time remember it is PLINY who makes the statement, and for untrustworthiness of statement he cannot easily be surpassed; so that even here an immense exaggeration may be suspected; and to sum up, remember that although Aristotle must have had a large collection of materials before he could have written his work on animals, Humboldt declares that there is no trace in that work of any acquaintance with animals first known through Alexander's expedition.

§ 14. After an absence of twelve years, B.C. 355, Aristotle reappeared in Athens. He found the Academy already occupied by his friend XENOCRATES; so that some other place had to be sought where he might open a school. This he found at the Lyceum, a gymnasium in the vicinity of the temple of Apollo Lykeios, founded by Pisistratus, and embellished by Pericles. It was the most splendid of the Athenian gymnasia, consisting of a mass of edifices surrounded with gardens, avenues, and a sacred grove. It had its spacious courts with porticos, theatres for professors, covered promenades, baths, an arena for wrestling matches, and a stadium for footraces. The walls were adorned with paintings; the gardens and walks were furnished with seats. But we must not suppose, as many suppose, that this establishment was placed

---

[11] Alexandro Magno rege inflammato cupidine animalium naturas noscendi, delegataque hac commentatione Aristoteli, summo in omni doctrina viro, aliquot millia hominum in totius Asiæ Græciæque tractu parere jussa, omnium quos venatus, aucupia, piscatusque alebant; quibusque vivaria, armenta, alvearia, piscinæ, aviaria in cura erant; ne quid usquam genitum ignoraretur ab eo."—PLINY: *Hist. Nat.*, VIII., 16.

under the direction of Aristotle, or that he had any voice in its affairs. He simply received permission to teach in the morning and evening at the *peripatos*,[12] a permission which was the more acceptable because the shady walks offered facilities to his accustomed habit of walking to and fro during the delivery of lectures. The name of Peripatetics is commonly supposed to have been given to his disciples on account of this habit; but as, according to the testimony of THEOPHRASTUS and LYCON, the lecture-place itself was named ὁ περίπατος, the locality probably gave the title to his school. This suggestion is countenanced by the practice in other cases; for we find the schools designated by the places where they were founded, unless when some peculiarity in doctrine gave the title: thus the Academy, the Porch, the Garden, Megara, and Cyrene, severally gave names to schools; but never was a name borrowed from some casual peculiarity in the mode of lecturing. Moreover, Aristotle was by no means singular in this practice of promenading while he taught.

§ 15. For thirteen years he continued teaching, and composing his immortal treatises; powerfully impressing the crowd of eager disciples, but probably regarded with angry suspicion by the patriots, owing to his connection with ALEXANDER. And now came the electric shock, shaking Athens to her foundations, and agitating her with tumultuary hopes: the Great Conqueror was no more! At once, and with exultant energy, the anti-Macedonian party took the lead in public affairs. Aristotle necessarily was in peril; for although, in truth, his life had been blameless of political intrigue, and no colourable accusation could be raised against him on that score, if only because he was excluded from political influence;[13] yet as a foreigner, a philosopher, and a friend of Macedon, he was trebly odious to the political

---

[12] MATTER: *Hist. de l'école d'Alexandrie*, Paris, 1840, I., 30.

[13] This political attitude is conspicuously set forth in Mr. CONGREVE's introduction to his edition of the *Politics*, London, 1855.

leaders; and a pretext for accusation was raised on a ground where such pretexts are always easily raised and are always dangerous—irreligion. He was accused of blasphemy, and of paying divine honours to mortals. And who were these mortals he had honoured? His friend and his wife. The charge may seem frivolous; but too well he knew the temper of the multitude to hope that the absurdity of the charge would be a guarantee for his safety. Mobs seldom reason, rarely examine. The blameless life and lofty soul of SOCRATES had been no defence against the charges of MELITUS; and Aristotle quitted Athens, "not to give the Athenians a second opportunity of committing a sacrilege against philosophy."

§ 16. He retired to Chalcis in Euboea. There he wrote an elaborate defence of his conduct, and exposed the calumnies circulated about him. But his health, always delicate, and severely tasked by unremitting study, rapidly gave way. The Athenians, on his refusal to appear in answer to the summons of the Areopagus, deprived him of citizenship, and all the honours that had been conferred upon him. An idle sentence of death was passed; but nature had already written that sentence in terms that were not idle. He died in the sixty-third year of his age, B.C. 322, only a few months before the great orator, DEMOSTHENES, also an exile.

§ 17. His will, which may be read in DIOGENES LAERTIUS, tells of his thoughtful kindness. His daughter PYTHIAS, his son NICOMACHUS, his adopted son NICANOR, and his concubine HERPYLLIS, are all duly provided for, and some of his slaves are emancipated, others rewarded.

§ 18. The purposes of this History render it unnecessary to enter upon the vexed question of the authenticity of the various writings which have passed under his name, had I the scholarship which could justify such a digression. The curious reader will easily find abundant material on this and all cognate points. We have here rather to consider the nature of his achievements. The first thing which must strike every one is their encyclopædic extent, unrivalled in the history of literature. In all branches of science then cultivated he was proficient. He wrote on Politics, giving the outlines of two hundred and fifty-five constitutions; even the little treatise on that subject, which is still extant, is thought to be one of the very best works yet written, and Dr. ARNOLD, who knew it by heart, declared that he found it of daily service in its application to our own time. His Ethics, Rhetoric, and Logic are still by many held to be authoritative and unsurpassed. His Metaphysics would of itself suffice to found a great renown. His fragments on Poetics is perhaps the most valuable of all ancient critical writings. And as if these were not titles enough, we must now add the several scientific works which form the special object of this volume; these embrace Physics, Astronomy, Zoology, Comparative Anatomy, and *Psychology. With Sir W. HAMILTON, we may say: "His seal is upon all the sciences, and his speculations have mediately or immediately determined those of all subsequent thinkers." HEGEL, though of a less fervid temperament, expresses himself with greater emphasis: "He penetrated into the whole universe of things, and subjected its scattered wealth to intelligence; and to him the greater number of the philosophical sciences owe their origin and distinction." [14]

§ 19. Such an intellectual phenomenon must always excite astonishment. Let us form what opinion we may of his philosophy, we cannot withhold our admiration of the vigour and comprehensiveness of his mind. Nor is this his only claim. He is admirable for the intense urgency of his mind in seeking *scientific* explanations of phenomena, at a period when such explanations were novelties; and for the dominant inductive tendency which led him on all subjects to collect the facts before reasoning on them. The contrast he presents to PLATO

---

[14] HEGEL: *Vorlesungen über die Gesch. der Philos.*, 1833, II., 298.

in this respect is as much to his advantage as the contrast in respect of literary power is to his disadvantage.[15] PLATO was the most artistic of philosophers, and, among men of great eminence, one of the worst of investigators; not, assuredly, from deficient power, but from his disastrous misconception of Method. In spite of a certain loitering diffuseness of style, and an oppressive circumstantiality in refuting trivial considerations, no one before PLATO, no one since, has managed the extremely difficult art of dramatic debate on philosophic topics with such commanding success; and in consequence of this fascinating art, aided by the union of dialectical subtlety with mystical yearnings, a subtlety which seems to give a hope to mysticism, and a warrant to transcendentalism, no one has exercised a more pernicious influence on culture. The charm of the artist has immortalized the vices of the thinker.[16]

With Aristotle the case is different. His Method although imperfect, as we shall shortly see, was not utterly wrong, but wrong only in one important particular; in direction it was wholly right. It was a Method which required development, and was not like that of PLATO, one upon which rational philosophy was impossible. But as an artist, Aristotle is simply

---

[15] The contrast is felicitously presented by MAURICE in the following passage: "The student passing from the works of Plato to those of Aristotle is struck first of all with the entire absence of that dramatic form and that dramatic feeling with which he has become familiar. The living human beings with whom he has conversed have passed away. Prodicus, Protagoras, and Hippias, are no longer lounging upon their couches amidst groups of admiring pupils; we have no walks along the walls of the city, no readings beside the Ilissus, no lively symposia giving occasion to high discourses about love, no Critias recalling the stories he had heard in the days of his youth, before he became a tyrant, of ancient and glorious republics; above all, no Socrates forming a centre to those various groups. Some little sorrow for the loss of so many clear and beautiful pictures will be felt, perhaps, by every one, but by far the greater portion of readers will believe that they have ample compensation in the precision and philosophical dignity of the treatise for the richness and variety of the dialogue."—*Moral and Metaphysical Philosophy*, 1850, I., 162.

[16] *See* Chap. V., "PLATO'S METHOD."

without rank; and as a writer, with submission be it said, he is many degrees removed from excellence. This opinion will probably excite surprise; let it be, therefore, more circumstantially explained. In works like the Politics, Poetics, Ethics, and Rhetoric,—works which from their subject do not severely task the writer's powers of *composition*, in the artful distribution of materials,—he is intelligible, and sometimes epigrammatic, although without charm. But where more severely tasked, and where he is called upon to marshal numerous facts and ideas for effective presentation, so as to shape arguments into culminating sequence, his composition is rambling, scattered, and confused. There is little illustration, and no side-lights of suggestion. The want of artistic composition renders this absence of illustration a serious defect. When a writer's composition is good there is less need of illustration, or (to use a favourite word with the Florentine Platonists) *collustration*. But there are few writers who understand this art; and Aristotle understood it not at all. In studying his works, and especially in attempting to reproduce their arguments, this defect has been painfully forced upon my notice; and when we read praises of his style, supported by the great authority of CICERO, we must admit the inference that *he* referred to works which are no longer extant, and that moderns are awed by the majesty of Greek type. Whatever may be the excellencies of Aristotle's diction (and these few moderns can pretend to appreciate), the defects of his composition are not matters of opinion, but of demonstration.

§ 20. It is not consistent with my design to follow the course of Aristotelian influence through the commentaries of ALEXANDER of Aphrodisias, PORPHYRY, IAMBLICHUS, PROCLUS, THEMISTIUS, SIMPLICIUS or PHILOPONUS—which I only know through extracts liberally given by scholars; and this knowledge has excited in me the liveliest desire *not* to read more. Nor can we follow the splendid train of the Renaissance in which figure ARGYROPYLUS, GAZA, PHILELPHUS, GEORGE of Trebizond, POLITIAN, HERMOLAUS BARBARUS, LAURENTIUS VALLA and REUCHLIN, some of whom will be laid under contribution as we proceed. The history of Aristotle is for many centuries the history of learning. In the 17th century the tide completely turned. It is true that at the close of the 16th CASAUBON (1590) and at the opening of the 17th DU VAL (1619) published complete editions of the works, which, to judge by the reprints,[17] must have been rapidly sold. But these were the last efforts of expiring energy. The revolt against Authority which characterized that century, was necessarily directed against the thinker whose authority had been most servilely accepted.[18] Nor can I find mention of a single edition after that by DU VAL. During the whole of the 18th century there was no edition of the complete works, not even a reprint; and only an occasional edition of the Poetics and Ethics. BUHLE'S undertaking (1791-1800) was thwarted by the burning of Moscow, in which all his collected materials were destroyed.

§ 21. A reaction began at the close of the 18th which has gained strength in the 19th century. LESSING called attention to the Poetics by his own luminous comments. SCHNEIDER by his edition of the *History of Animals* (1812)— which, alas! is even yet the only tolerable edition for the use of naturalists, and is very defective—gave an impulse to the

---

[17] BUHLE, I., 229-30.
[18] HEGEL : *Gesch. der Philos.*, II., 416. It is worthy of remark that in 1624 appeared the work of GASSENDI : *Exercitationum paradoxicarum adversus Aristoteleos libri VII.*, in which, among other propositions, he maintains these four : quod apud *A.* innumera deficiant—immensa superfluant—immensa fallant—innumera contradicant. In the September of the same year the Parliament of Paris, which in the 13th century had declared some of A.'s works to be heretical (See ROGER BACON'S indignant protest, *Opus Majus*, Venet. 1750, p. 10 ; compare also JOURDAIN : *Recherches sur les anciennes traductions Latines d'Aristote*, Paris, 1843), issued an edict that on *pain of death* no opposition against the approved doctrines of the ancients should publicly be taught. The struggle had become a death struggle.

study of the biological works. FÜLLEBORN, BUHLE, and TENNEMANN, in their histories of philosophy, began to assign him his legitimate position; but it was HEGEL who first spoke of him with enthusiasm and commanding authority.[19] From this time he began once more to be considered as the profoundest of thinkers, whose works emphatically challenged the attention of philosophers. Sir W. HAMILTON, in this country, also lent his powerful aid in the revival, and ROSMINI, in Italy, with more reserve, called attention to his significance.[20]

Meanwhile scholars have not been idle. BRANDIS and BEKKER were commissioned by the Berlin Academy to produce a complete edition. For three years these patient scholars courageously toiled over the manuscripts in Italy, France, and England, and the result appeared in BEKKER's edition (Berlin, 1831-40, since reprinted at Oxford), and in the work by BRANDIS already cited (Note 5). A complete edition was printed in 1832 by TAUCHNITZ in sixteen volumes, and in 1843 by WEISSE in one volume, neither of them highly esteemed; and in 1847 DIDOT began an excellent edition in four volumes, edited by BUSSEMAKER, still incomplete.[21] Of separate treatises the editions have been too numerous to be specified here.

§ 22. Activity so energetic, after so long a period of neglect, was naturally prompted and accompanied by a tendency to over-estimate the works; and the danger now is lest the reaction go too far. HEGEL and Sir W. HAMILTON have

---

[19] Lord MONBODDO in his *Ancient Metaphysics*; HARRIS in his *Philosophical Arrangements*; and THOMAS TAYLOR in various works, were enthusiastic enough, but they spoke with no authority.

[20] ROSMINI: *Aristotele esposto ed esaminato.* " Poiche le questioni che giaceino nella filosofia aristotelica sono vitali per l' uman genere, e la grandezza e l'importanza di queste restituirà sempre ad Aristotele un gran peso d'autorità." —p. 14 of the Milan edition, 1855.

[21] This, and BUHLE's, are the editions I have used ; but for general convenience in reference I have given Bekker's pagination as nearly as possible.

done their best to impress on fluctuating public opinion the conviction that not only was Aristotle a thinker of vast power, but of present worth : not only great in his own time, but anticipating the truths of all time. CUVIER, ISIDORE ST. HILAIRE, DE BLAINVILLE, and JOHANNES MÜLLER, drawing after them crowds of obedient disciples, have spoken of his scientific works as if they were on a level with the science of our day, claiming for him some of the most curious discoveries of modern research.

<blockquote>
Certes il ne méritait
Ni cet excès d'honneur, ni cette indignité ;
</blockquote>

and it will be the task of the following chapters to show that both the past neglect and the modern deification need revision. One point only requires to be noticed at present. It is, that among his modern eulogists will be found biologists, politicians, and metaphysicians, but no astronomer, no physicist, no chemist. In other words, in those sciences which have advanced to the positive stage, and in which the rigour of proof reduces Authority to its just position, his opinions are altogether disregarded; whereas in those sciences in which, from their complexity and immaturity, the influence of Authority and the delusive promises of the Subjective Method still gain acceptance, his *dicta* are cited as those of a puissant investigator.

CHAPTER II.

THE DAWN OF SCIENCE.

§ 23. IN one sense, the dawn of Science is coëval with the dawn of human intelligence. Introduced to this mysterious universe naked and helpless, man is early forced to gain some understanding of its relations to him. At first all is dim sensation. To this succeeds a slowly organized classification of elementary experiences. The great forces of Nature are everywhere at work, everywhere manifesting themselves in manifold and intermingling motions, which he must appreciate, and intellectually disentangle, as far as they directly concern him. This is simple knowledge. Science, which is a higher sublimation of this knowledge, begins when the forces of Nature are appreciated in their relations to each other; and in its highest flights all personal relations are merged in a grand disinterestedness. At first man stands before "the roaring loom of Time," gazing in helpless perplexity at the movements of the infinite shuttles, ignorant of the movements which may be beneficent, and of those which may be destructive to him. But he cannot remain thus. His necessities soon change this attitude of wonder into an attitude of inquiry. The objects which he sees are of pressing importance; he must observe them attentively that he may adapt their powers to his purposes. The preservation of his daily existence depends on the accuracy with which he observes, classifies, and infers the properties of objects—their order of co-existence and succession. He has to find his friends and his foes amid the multitude of forces which surround him. None immediately announce their qualities; each has to be carefully watched and tested; the dearest friend suddenly proving the direst foe under very trifling changes of conditions. Then come intellectual needs; above all, the imperious desire for an explanation. The spontaneous activity of his growing intellect urges him to make out some scheme by which the various phenomena may be bound together. He begins to link the known and accessible on to the unknown and inaccessible; he animates the universe; interprets all he sees by all he feels.

Thus Philosophy emerged from Knowledge. As civilization advanced, Knowledge became more extensive and precise, Philosophy more ambitious in its sweep. Arts arose, which preserved and extended the common fund of Knowledge, transmitting it as a priceless heirloom. Those great nations which duly cherished this heirloom, and increased its store, magnified their existence, and became the glory of our race. Those nations which neglected it, perished, or continued barbarous—that is, comparatively helpless and miserable.

§ 24. Although in this sense Science may be said to be coëval with man, the sense in which moderns employ the word carries a more restricted meaning. To measure the ground; to measure the seasons and the length of days; to cure a disease or dress a wound; to plough the soil and garner the harvest; to guide a fragile bark along a perilous coast by the aid of the Pleiades, or "sailing stars;" to know that fire burns, liquids evaporate, and metals fuse—these are among the early experiences of the race, but they are not Science. They are the preparatory materials—items of that Common Knowledge which the energy of man, as he advances to maturity, developes into Science.[1] Science, as we now understand the word, is of later birth. If its germinal origin may be traced to the early period when Observation, Induction, and Deduction were first employed, its birth must be referred to that comparatively recent period when the mind,—rejecting the primitive tendency to seek in *supernatural agencies* for an explanation of all external phenomena,—endeavoured, by a systematic investigation of the *phenomena themselves* to discover their *invariable order and connection*. The separation of Science from Knowledge was effected step by step as the Subjective Method was replaced by the Objective Method: *i. e.*, when in each inquiry the phenomena of external nature ceased to be interpreted on premisses suggested by the analogies of human nature. We shall presently state more explicitly the character of these Methods (§ 31); to prepare the way for a thorough appreciation of them, is the purpose of the ensuing paragraphs.

§ 25. The history of human development shows that there are three modes by which we conceive phenomena; and there are only three. The second being a transition from the first to the third, we might, in strictness, admit of only two distinct modes of conception. The first of these supposes that the order and succession observed in phenomena, is due to the influence of *outlying agencies*—powers which are *super* natural, above the objects, not belonging to them. The second supposes that the order of phenomena is due simply to properties inherent in the objects themselves, which properties are realities, and form part of the *nature* of the objects. Obviously, things must either be conceived as, by nature, passive or active; if passive, they can only be moved by superior powers, independent of them; if active, they possess in themselves the conditions of their activity. Thus on one

---

[1] To make clear the distinction between Science and Common Knowledge would carry us too far; it will be discussed in the Prolegomena to the History of which the present volume forms a chapter.

of two fundamental assumptions, respecting the activity of objects, rests every possible explanation we can frame of the mysteries around us.

§ 26. The attitude of mind which is based on the first of these assumptions is that which is common to all primitive theories. It characterizes what AUGUSTE COMTE names the Theological Stage in human development. On this assumption, all phenomena not of the simplest and most familiar kind are referred to the agency of invisible powers, spirits, deities, or demons. To these powers, and not to any activity inherent in the objects themselves, the changes in phenomena are assigned. It is the will of some spirit which moves the objects. As this idea of will originates in the analogies of human volitions influencing human actions, the same capriciousness and variability which characterize human actions are supposed to characterize external phenomena. Much more caprice would be attributed to the gods, because we do know something of human motives—greed, anger, and love; but we do not know why Zeus sends a storm in harvest-time, or burns his own temple with lightning, or kills a pious man by the side of a blasphemer. *Variableness* is predicated of all successions of phenomena, save those of such frequent occurrence, that expectation of their being found to vary is finally extirpated.

§ 27. In direct contrast to this is the scientific attitude, based upon the second of the two assumptions just rehearsed. It never could have obtained acceptance in the early stages of our development. It implies a certain advance of culture and great familiarity with the orderliness of Nature. Before men could refer the changes they observed to the influence of properties inherent in the objects, a strong conviction must have arisen that the order of succession in phenomena was *not* variable, but fixed. *Invariableness* would inevitably lead to the conception of all changes being due to the relations between the various properties of objects—first, by discrediting the interference of an external *will*, which is essentially incalculable ; next, by disclosing that there was really no need of anything but the recognized or recognizable properties of objects to account for all changes.

The conviction that objects are not by nature inert, passive, acted on only by outlying, supernatural agencies, grew up slowly with the slowly-growing perception of the essential invariableness of phenomena whenever the conditions are the same. In our day, reliance on the stability of created things is unshakeable. The idea of variability is banished from external phenomena, and admitted only by one school with reference to internal phenomena. Whenever a change does not take place in accordance with our previsions, we never suppose the failure to be owing to the caprice of Nature, or to some *outlying* power; we at once conclude the presence of ·some interfering condition, some relation which we have overlooked.

Not only is the primitive conception of variability banished for ever, but in its banishment is included that of *externality*. Causation is now assumed to lie within, and not without, the circle of phenomena. Science, withdrawing from all speculation where it can find no adequate evidence, and where its methods are inoperative, refrains from inquiry as to ultimate causes, and says nothing respecting the mystery of creation ; in dealing with created objects, and with natural phenomena, it presupposes no variableness in their order of succession and co-existence. Thus the clergyman who told the farmer that it was useless to pray for rain till the wind changed, had embraced the scientific view, and had learned to distrust appeals against the order of Nature, because that was not a variable order. In earlier days this man would have considered the direction of the wind quite insignificant, and would have believed that prayer was likely to determine a change in the weather by determining a change in the will which regulated it.

To the mind of men in the primitive, theological stage, the sun was a god driving a chariot of fire, the moon a goddess and a huntress. So difficult was it to escape these personifications that we find remnants of this Polytheism even in the teaching of the Christian Church, which assigned to every planet its tutelary angel.[2] The scientific mind replaces these gods and angels by laws of nature, according to which the planets move by forces similar, and under conditions similar to those observed in all other moving bodies. It having been discovered that the orbit of the planets is an ellipse, NEWTON demonstrated on dynamical principles that a body *could* only move in such an orbit in virtue of two forces, the variations of which are in a reciprocal ratio with the vector—the one force being centrifugal, the other centripetal. Thus the law of gravitation dethroned the arbitrary agencies. Though in itself not more intelligible than the action of the gods, this law has the supreme advantage of linking astronomical and terrestrial phenomena into general harmony, and admitting of a systematic co-ordination of all observed facts. Besides this, it gets rid of the presumed *variability* in the agency, and leads to the careful study of the inevitable order; instead of encouraging attempts, by prayers, supplications, invocations, or the sacrifices of animal life, to persuade the inevitable order to alter its course.

§ 28. These two sharply opposed modes of conceiving phenomena, one of which aims at penetrating the mysteries of existence, and explaining the external order by knowledge of the ultimate causes, the other of which aims only at detecting the exact relations of co-existence and succession which determine that order, without any hope of knowing the ultimate causes: these two modes require some intermediate transitional mode which will enable the mind to pass from the one to the other. Such a transition is effected in the Metaphysical stage, which agrees with the theological inasmuch as it

---

[2] " Le Père Schot, jésuite, a écrit qu'en 1660 on voyait à Rome la *Basilique des Sept Anges Gubernateurs des Planètes.*"—SAVERIEN : *Hist. des Progrès de l'Esprit Humain*, Paris, 1775, p. 222.

also assumes a knowledge of the ultimate causes, and assumes that these causes are *in essence* independent of the objects.[3] But it differs from the theological in discarding the idea of these agencies being *variable;* by this it forms the passage to a scientific conception. In the place of deities it assumes abstract entities. Thus by gradual modifications the personal agency becomes an impersonal agency, the deity an abstraction, and this in turn becomes more and more material, as we see in the succession of 1, Spirit; 2, Entity; and 3, Fluid or Ether.

Although the entities which are assumed as the ultimate causes of change are neither the objects themselves, nor properties of the objects, they are assumed to be *inseparable* from the objects and *invariable* in their agency. It is thus they form an easy transition to the more purely objective conception of laws. For example, the Vegetal Soul, which is supposed to be the cause of all the phenomena observed in plants, is not a plant, nor a property of the plant, nor the resultant of the plant's many properties; it is an existence *sui generis*, in virtue of which the plant *is*. At the same time this Vegetal Soul is exclusively limited to the plant; it has no other form of existence; it exists only under the conditions of plant-life. And when the biologist patiently traces out these conditions, the metaphysician willingly accepts them, simply protesting against the supposition that the life of the plant is due to nothing more than the mutual action and reaction of the properties inherent in the molecules composing the plant; he asserts that, over and above these, there is the Vegetal Soul, arranging the molecules and directing their forces.

§ 29. Such are the three modes of conceiving the course

---

[3] " Le caractère fondamental des conceptions métaphysiques est d'envisager les phénomènes indépendamment des corps qui nous les manifestent, d'attribuer aux propriétés de chaque substance une existence distincte de la sienne."— COMTE: *Cours de Philosophie Positive*, 1835, II., 446.

of nature which will everywhere be found curiously interwoven amid the web of human history. Each has been predominant at certain epochs. Each has had a potent influence on our culture. But it is obvious that after the mind has passed through its earlier stages of development, progress is seriously impeded by theological and metaphysical explanations of natural phenomena. Whether such explanations are now desirable in any other department of inquiry, is a question which need not here be agitated; it is certain that they are obstacles to the progress of science. The theological explanation is an obstacle, because instead of stimulating the mind to a close and reverent study of the truths revealed in Nature, it directs the attention to whatever has been *assumed* respecting the will and purpose of deities, *supposed* to be manifested in phenomena. The metaphysical explanation is an obstacle, because it withdraws attention from the close scrutiny of facts, and deludes the mind with unverified, unverifiable assumptions.[4]

When an epidemic fever wasted the Grecian camp, the cause was at once assumed to be Apollo's wrath. Had not the Deity been angered, the people would not have been punished. What had angered him? Surely it must have been the insult offered to his priest? Acting on this natural inference, the Greeks bethought them how to appease this wrath. In the Crimea our troops also suffered from fever; we bethought ourselves of the ventilation and drainage: an idea which to the Greeks would have appeared not only inefficacious, but impious. On the Palatine Hill, the Romans erected a Temple to the Goddess of Fever. We build fever-hospitals, and our form of prayer is a dose of quinine.[5]

---

[4] "Nous devons examiner la nature par tous les moyens que fournissent l'observation et l'expérience; et non leur supposer des principes sur lesquels l'esprit se repose et croit avoir tout fait lorsqu'il lui reste tout à faire."— VICQ D'AZYR: *Discours sur l'Anatomie. Œuvres*, 1805, IV., 15.

[5] To a mind even moderately trained in the use of evidence and logical connection, ancient superstitions are absolutely inconceivable. What, for

So long as diseases were conceived to be the products of supernatural agency, their cure was properly sought in invocations, sacrifices, prayers and charms, rather than in the study of the organism, and an accurate acquaintance with the properties of objects. And although it is true that reliance on supernatural appeals never wholly excluded reliance on all natural means that were known, the quinine being administered as well as the prayer, yet the mere fact that men conceived the order of phenomena to depend upon a mutable will, was an obstacle to the thorough and patient study of natural means. No sooner was it understood that diseases were the results *inseparable* from certain conditions of organic substances, and that under similar conditions the action of these substances was *invariable,* than the mind recognized the necessity of relinquishing a vain reliance on invocation, and gave its severe attention to the study of objects, and the conditions of health and disease.

§ 30. The theological, metaphysical, and scientific explanations have three different *criteria,* or guarantees. The guarantee of the first is sacerdotal. A conclusion is held to be certain, if it is conformable with the doctrines of which the priesthood is the interpreter. Those doctrines, being received as indisputable, form the standard of all truth. The guarantee of the second is somewhat less absolute; it admits of question, because it is based on reason, not on faith; nevertheless, any conclusion which can be logically deduced from general doctrines accepted by metaphysicians is held by them to be demonstrated. To the theologian it is enough if he can adduce a text. To the metaphysician it is enough

---

example, can we suspect to have been the grounds on which the Druids believed that in any perilous juncture they could be guided by the writhings of a dying man ? They seized some innocent wretch, plunged a knife in his breast, " à ce coup mortel ce misérable tombant à la renverse, on augurait de l'événement à venir en observant les circonstances de sa chûte, les convulsions de différentes parties de son corps, et le rejaillissement de son sang."—*Histoire Littéraire de la France,* by the Benedictines of St. Maur, 1733, I., 28.

if he can deduce his proposition from "clear and distinct ideas."

The guarantee of science is in the *verification of experience*, direct or indirect (§ 64). It distrusts the validity of *à priori* conclusions, or of any explanations drawn *solely* from general ideas of Nature's order, unless those general ideas have themselves been rigorously demonstrated to be *necessities of thought*, or to *represent the observed order*, (§ 63 *a*). What must be, or may be, has to give place to what is. The general doctrines of Science are never, like those of Theology and Metaphysics, conceived to be final. However firmly fixed at present, they may be shaken tomorrow by a new discovery. Moreover, in the general doctrines of Science, while one portion is understood as beyond dispute until the horizon of knowledge is enlarged, another portion is admitted to be more or less hypothetical and approximative. In every case Science welcomes scrutiny and scepticism; its final guarantee is conformity with fact. Its general doctrines have been slowly elaborated, verified step by step, and therefore, to a considerable extent, they represent the actual facts, and are not arbitrary assumptions founded on slight analogies, or conclusions deduced from unverified premisses.[6]

The contrast between the metaphysical and scientific guarantee is that the verification which both need is by the one disregarded and by the other emphatically put forward. While both the metaphysicist and the physicist draw conclusions from their general doctrines, the one is contented with logical symmetry, the other demands the confrontation with fact. The ancient astronomers believed in the uniformity of the celestial revolutions, and in the circularity of their orbit.

---

[6] " Expliquer un phénomène se réduit toujours à faire voir que les faits qu'il présente se suivent dans un ordre analogue à l'ordre de succession d'autres faits qui sont plus familiers, et qui dès lors semblent être plus connus."—BARTHEZ : *Nouveaux Élémens de la Science de l'Homme*, Paris, 1816, I., 8.

On subjective grounds this belief is not only logical, but irresistible. How, as M. Biot remarks,[7] could men imagine these movements to be variable, which were seen to be performed in perfect freedom, and in periods rigorously constant, no obstacle being suspected? How could such movements be accelerated or retarded, being, as they were, eternal, and due to neither impact nor resistance? From this assumption of uniformity, the circularity of the orbit was a necessary conclusion. The logical chain was perfect. It so completely fettered the mind as almost to bar the way against the admission of the truth. Kepler had difficulty in accepting his own discovery, when indubitable proofs revealed that the orbit of Mars was not circular, and consequently that its velocity was not uniform, but subject to periodical variations. Thus nothing could be more plausible, considered à priori, than the ancient theory; nevertheless, no sooner were adequate means of Verification applied to the theory than the whole fabric tumbled down like a house of cards.

§ 31. I have thus endeavoured to characterize the three modes of speculative inquiry by which in all ages men have explained the facts of nature; these modes, as Auguste Comte profoundly saw, constitute the necessary evolution of speculative thought. To get rid of the equivoque which lies in the phrases theological and metaphysical, we may group all three under the Subjective and Objective Methods, their tendencies being thus characterized: the Subjective draws all explanations of external phenomena from premisses directly suggested by consciousness; it identifies the external order with the internal order. Obviously, this is the primitive method. When in the early days of our development we find ourselves face to face with phenomena, the order of which we do not understand, we satisfy the irresistible impatience which demands an immediate explanation, by

---

[7] Biot: Études sur l'Astronomie Indienne et Chinoise, 1862, p. 58.

assuming that the objects are moved as we are moved. We feel that our own actions are determined by our volitions, by the mysterious something within us; and we assign a similar cause to the motions of external objects. Quite otherwise is it with the Objective Method. This arises out of a more extensive and precise knowledge of the objects, familiarity with which gradually reveals something of their order of co-existence and succession. As such knowledge accumulates, it irresistibly pushes aside the interpretation which was originally drawn from consciousness. It reveals the cosmical order more and more as a system not measurable by the analogies of human personality. Under the light of this knowledge men cease to suppose anger behind the violence of a storm, or prophecy in the gloom of an eclipse. The savage who thinks the watch is alive, can only be made to relinquish this subjective hypothesis by acquiring positive knowledge of the properties of steel springs and the actions of a mechanism; but no sooner is this objective knowledge acquired than he ceases to have recourse to the analogies of his own nature for an explanation.[8]

The Subjective Method claims direct knowledge of the nature of things and the ultimate causes of all changes. The Objective Method by looking *at* things, assuming the position of simple spectator, renounces all hope of ever penetrating the mysteries of existence, of ever knowing the intimate essence of things, and only hopes to detect the invariable order of co-existence and succession. The one claims a knowledge of "noumena," the other a knowledge of the laws of phenomena.

---

[8] The influence of the Subjective Method is constantly traceable in commercial and other enterprises rashly undertaken by men in the confidence that facts will bend to their desires. A man sees great advantage to himself *if* events take a certain direction; and he believes that this direction will be taken because he greatly desires it. The more objective mind sets aside its wishes and tries to calculate the chances of the direction from a knowledge of the external conditions.

§ 31 a. It is evident, therefore, that since the Subjective Method arises from our ignorance, and the Objective from our positive knowledge, there can have been no period in the history of our race in which either Method obtained exclusive acceptance. Even the earliest and most ignorant tribes must have so far familiarized themselves with certain phenomena as to have explained them without reference to the deities spontaneously invoked in less familiar cases. The observed properties of the things themselves were deemed sufficient for the immediate production of the changes, so that by availing himself of these properties man was often able to modify the course of phenomena according to his needs. After learning that unless the wood were dry even his fetish could not make it burn, he soon came to fix attention on the dryness, and to cease invoking his fetish. On the other hand, the most advanced European nations, although they have frankly assumed the scientific attitude with respect to most cosmical phenomena, still retain in their systems a large admixture of theological and metaphysical conceptions.

The rise of the Objective or Scientific Method is a late event in the history of man, if we consider it not in isolated fragmentary efforts, but as a *systematic and conscious attitude of mind*. A late and glorious event, of which no trace is visible in the early civilizations. The dawn of this new era in which Nature was investigated without reference to supernatural agencies, but solely with the view of deciphering her alphabet, and reading her own sacred writing, is to be sought in Italy. It was the Greeks, and especially the Italian Greeks who commenced this revolution. In saying this I am not unmindful of the opinion, held by many learned scholars, that the East was the cradle of Science. It is not a subject that can be adequately discussed here; nor can I pretend to the erudition requisite for its discussion. But leaving the subject in worthier hands, there is one general consideration which to my mind carries conviction.

We have no evidence whatever that the Egyptians, Assyrians, Persians, or Hindoos, conceived the true scientific Method; and there is positive evidence that they could not have had the scientific knowledge often attributed to them, simply because they had not the Instruments by which such knowledge is attained. They had not the requisite Mathematics; they had not the Instruments. Unless facts are accurately known, laws must remain obscure. But accuracy in the knowledge of facts, that is to say, scientific accuracy, depends on instruments of *measurement* and *calculation*. Science is pre-eminently quantitative, *i. e.*, dependent on exact appreciations of quantities of time, space, and force; and hence its progress is intimately connected with the perfection and application of Instruments of measurement and calculation. Wanting these, the East necessarily wanted scientific knowledge.

Not only am I compelled to follow those scholars who discredit the claims of the East to any initiation of the era of science, but I should also question the claim, more commonly allowed, of the Egyptians as astronomers. That they made numerous observations, and amassed some of the preparatory material, is admissible, without involving any assent to their scientific claim. It would be difficult to show that they had mastered any of the initial conceptions. We read, indeed, of priests, relieved from toil, devoting their leisure to study; but what was the nature of that study? We hear of their careful observations and their enormous annals, on which point exaggeration is traditional: HIPPARCHUS speaks of the Assyrians having continuous records for 270,000 years; DIODORUS says the Chaldeans claim for their observations an antiquity of myriads of years; and " MARTIANUS CAPELLA adopts a statement that astronomy had been practised in secret by the Egyptians for 40,000 years before it was divulged to the rest of the world."[9] If this were true it would only the

---

[9] LEWIS: *Historical Survey of the Astronomy of the Ancients*, 1862, p. 264.

more decisively refute their pretensions; since to have observed the heavens for forty thousand years, and not discern a single astronomical law, proves them to have been without the rudiments of exact Science. Indeed, when we reflect that they had not discovered one of the fundamental laws of motion, and were unacquainted with trigonometry, it is obvious that they were without exact knowledge, and without the means of obtaining it.[10]

The Egyptians made observations which were sufficiently accurate for many of their needs, but not for science. And no sooner do we pass from Astronomy to the other sciences than discussion ceases. No one thinks of assigning the origin of Dynamics, Optics, Acoustics, Anatomy, &c., to the East. It is undoubtedly to the Greeks that we must look for these; as it is to them that we must look for the systematic adoption of Method. The researches of the Pythagoreans on the vibrations of bodies are the earliest researches in Physics which were conceived in a scientific spirit.[11] By the development of the mighty instrument of *calculation*, and by their stedfast constancy in investigating the causes of phenomena irrespective of theological bias, this wonderful people began that intellectual movement which in

---

[10] " À la réserve du gnomon, tous les instrumens astronomiques sont des inventions des Grecs. Nul autre peuple n'a produit aucune observation qui méritât ce nom."—DELAMBRE: *Hist. de l'Astronomie Ancienne*, 1817, I., p. 20. Compare also MONTUCLA: *Histoire des Mathématiques*, 1768; and MUSSENBROECK: *Cours de Physique Expérimentale*, par SIGAUD DE LA FOND, Leyden, 1769, I., p. 23. On the astronomy of the Hindoos see BIOT: *Études sur l'Astronomie Indienne et Chinoise*, 1862, p. 47, where it is proved that the Greeks were the parents of Hindoo science.

[11] " Pendant que les Etrusques torturaient et défiguraient la Nature pour faire coincider les phénomènes qu'ils observaient avec leurs idées mythologiques, et que les Grecs tournaient leurs plus grands efforts vers les problèmes métaphysiques qui surpassent les forces humaines, les habitans du Midi de l'Italie cultivèrent les sciences de l'observation, suivaient la méthode expérimentale, et contribuaient aux progrès de la géométrie et de l'arithmétique. Les recherches des Pythagoriciens sur les vibrations des corps sont les plus anciennes expériences de physique qui soient parvenues jusqu'à nous."—LIBRI: *Histoire des Sciences Mathématiques en Italie*, Paris, 1838, I., 28.

modern times has achieved conquests more glorious than the dreams of poets.

§ 32. Observe the significance of the fact that the Greeks gave us Mathematics. Of all sciences this is the one which most rigorously typifies the true Method. In it there is no place for the supernatural. It admits no outlying agencies. It fixes the mind on relations, and only on relations. By so doing it coerces the mind to maintain the strictly scientific attitude, namely, the most watchful solicitude respecting accuracy, both in data and conclusions. Much has been written about the superior certainty of Mathematics; but this does not, I conceive, result from the simplicity of its symbols, nor from the simplicity of the ideas involved; since it is obvious that we may employ very simple symbols and very clear ideas, yet arrive at very uncertain and very absurd conclusions.[12] The superior exactness and certainty of Mathematics are due to the fact that no hypothesis is allowed to stand for more than an hypothesis; no deduction takes its place as a datum until it has been demonstrated. Whereas in all other sciences the mind has great difficulty in restraining its impatience, and is thus induced to employ unverified data, and to rely on unverified deductions; but whenever the data and the deductions have been rigorously verified, the truths of Physics and Chemistry are as *certain* as those of Mathematics.

There is a second important element in scientific research for which we are indebted to the Greeks: the systematic employment of Scepticism; without which, indeed, research would be vain, and a true Method impossible. The Greeks, unwilling longer to acquiesce in traditional dogmas,

---

[12] " Une proposition tout à fait absurde peut être extrêmement précise, comme si l'on disait que la somme des angles d'un triangle est égale à trois angles droits ; et une proposition très certaine peut ne comporter qu'une precision fort médiocre, comme lorsqu'on affirme que tout homme mourra."— COMTE: *Cours de Philosophie Positive*, 1830, I., 103.

early saw that if Observation and Reason were to be the guides in investigation, these guides, being fallible, required perpetual vigilance. "Men who desire to learn," said ARISTOTLE, "must first learn to doubt; for science is only the solution of doubts:"[13] an aphorism, novel in those days, in our own a truism.

That the Greeks imperfectly practised the scepticism which they inculcated, will be seen by and by. In their eagerness to explain phenomena they were far too ready to accept observations which had not been controlled, and deductions which had not been verified. Nevertheless it is their immortal glory to have recognized the *necessity* of proof; and this recognition was itself consequent upon their ceasing to interpret phenomena as the direct results of supernatural agencies. HIPPOCRATES, amid much that is preposterous in the eyes of modern science, exhibits the new spirit which was then guiding inquiry. Let us cite an example. Speaking of a disease which was attributed to a god, he remarks, "For my part I think this disease comes from a god just as others do; and that there are no diseases more divine or more human than others. Each disease comes according to natural laws; none has any other origin."[14]

§ 33. A fortunate union of temperament with culture enabled this wonderful people to range through Nature in pursuit of the true relations of things, without perplexing themselves by fictions imagined respecting outlying agencies, essentially mysterious. The mysteriousness was not denied; it was simply set aside, removed from the sphere of scientific thought. The Greek had a free, independent spirit, adventurous, rebellious, curious; and boldly doubting, sought a

---

[13] *Metaph.*, III., 1. Compare *Phys.*, I., 2. ἔχει γὰρ φιλοσοφίαν ἡ σκέψις.
[14] HIPPOCRATES: *De Aëre, Aquis, et Locis.* CVII., Ed. CORAY, Paris, 1800, I., 100. ἐμοὶ δὲ καὶ αὐτέῳ δοκέει ταῦτα τὰ πάθεα θεῖα εἶναι, καὶ τ' ἄλλα πάντα, καὶ οὐδὲν ἕτερον ἑτέρου θειότερον, οὐδὲ ἀνθρωπινώτερον, ἀλλὰ πάντα θεῖα· ἕκαστον δὲ ἔχει φύσιν τῶν τοιουτέων, καὶ οὐδὲν ἄνευ φύσιος γίγνεται.

solution of his doubts in his own way. He refused submission to established doctrines. He would accept neither priest nor philosopher as his oracle. Without directly contradicting the priest, he boldly erected his own Academy beside the Temple.

Both their weakness and their strength aided the Greeks in this new enterprise. For it was a weakness in them that they had little sympathy with that sense of the Infinite which characterizes some other eminent nations. This is visible in their Art: an Art matchless in clearness and proportion, in the beauty of arrested lines, and the repose of symmetrical simplicity; but having none of those finer issues which escape into the sublimity of Christian Art. Greek Art is a lute, not an organ.

ARISTOTLE is a striking illustration of this excellence and this defect. He seems utterly destitute of any sense of the Ineffable. There is no quality more noticeable in him than his unhesitating confidence in the adequacy of the human mind to comprehend the universe; a quality obviously connected with the defect just mentioned. He never seems to be visited by misgivings as to the compass of human faculty, because his unhesitating mind is destitute of awe. He has no abiding consciousness of the fact deeply impressed on other minds, that the circle of the Knowable is extremely limited; and that beyond it lies a vast mystery, dimly recognized as lying there, but also recognized as impenetrable. Hence the existence of Evil is no perplexity to his soul; it is accepted as a simple fact. Instead of being troubled by it, saddened by it, he quietly explains it as the consequence of Nature not having correctly written her meaning. This mystery which has darkened so many sensitive meditative minds with anguish, he considered to be only bad orthography (§ 107).

Although ready enough to recognize the fallibility of men, he nowhere, that I remember, expresses a conviction of the inherent fallibility of reason. His contemporary, the author of *Ecclesiastes*, passionately declared that all science was vanity. Nor was this merely the dejected expression of his own sense of miserable failure; it was the serious conviction of human infirmity. Not only had *his* efforts failed, all men would fail, because the task was greater than human strength. Such doubts never assailed the Greek. Great as his failure was, he had little suspicion of it, and no suspicion of human frailty. Where he knew that his insight fell short, he was assured that the gaze of his successors would penetrate. For the race, if not for himself, he had regal pretensions.

§ 34. This royal confidence powerfully aided the development of Science. It gave the stimulus to research, and made inquiry adventurous. Yet it also exercised in one respect a retarding influence. It prevented due circumspection. It caused scepticism to stop half-way. It relied too securely on logical deduction; and accepted evidence without cross-examination. A little more distrust, a more modest hesitation, might have prevented that precipitancy to which alone many errors were due.

But if this confidence had its drawbacks, it had also its incitements. It led to the laborious study of Nature, merely with a view to knowledge for the sake of knowledge, and not with a view to Religion, nor the interests of Commerce. Science acquires her dignity, and her supreme power, from her noble disinterestedness. Although her researches even in the remotest regions are always finally beneficent among our daily uses, although the abstract speculations of geometers determine the satisfaction of our vulgar needs, it is not with this view that researches are undertaken. Use is secondary and derivative; the primary object is elucidation of the Truth. All Truth is beneficent; but her seekers desire to behold the serene splendour of her face, and not themselves to reap the benefits which spring up on her track.

§ 35. This attitude was first assumed by the Greeks. Their

philosophers were content to seek wisdom as the one great object, without directly subordinating their search to Religion or to Use. In doing so they incurred serious peril. They were assailed by the ridicule and persecution which await all innovators. ARISTOPHANES only gives expression to public hatred and to public scorn, in ridiculing and misrepresenting the physical inquirers of his day—men said to occupy themselves in

> Walking on air and contemplating the sun.

The attempt to explain Nature, without reference to the gods, very generally drew on philosophers the accusation of impiety. Nor was this prejudice confined to the vulgar and unthinking; it was shared and avowed by SOCRATES. The repugnance which, in early life, caused him to relinquish physical inquiries, was, as we learn from Xenophon, repugnance at the idea of excluding the constant agency of the gods, and the consequent destruction of moral feelings connected with this agency. The same thought has, in all ages, roused the bitter hostility of theologians, against the scientific attitude, as one essentially irreligious.[15] This hostility has gradually grown feebler, and is now entirely restricted to narrow or imperfectly cultivated minds. The change has been effected partly by the irresistible progress of Science with her triumphant demonstrations, and partly by a deeper philosophy, which has disclosed that Science can only destroy false explanations, which it is for our welfare to have destroyed. No single truth can be shaken by Science. If in her own path she detects certain truths, these must necessarily be harmonious with all other truths. We must learn to welcome all, and to *prove* all.

Even those bigoted minds which still regard with alarm the steady advance of Science, must admit the fact of its

---

[15] "Illos omnes Deum aut saltem Dei providentiam tollere putant, qui res et miracula per causas naturales explicant aut intelligere student."—SPINOZA; *Tractatus Theolog.-Politicus*, vi. *Opera*, III., 86. Ed. BRUDER, Leipzig, 1846.

advance, the greatness of its victories, the triumph of its Method, and the certainty of its continuing to extend its empire. In minds of larger culture, or of less jealous narrowness, there is a complete cessation of the old antagonism ; a gradual approximation is being made between theology and science, and a more candid recognition of their mutual claims in regard to the grand religious and moral ideas which must ever determine the movement of society.

§ 36. The object of this chapter has been to show why the Greeks are to be regarded as the originators of Science, strictly so-called, and why this History takes note of no earlier people. Other peoples amassed details of knowledge, manifested intellectual activity, invented useful arts; but it is in the Greek writers that we must seek the inauguration of the scientific epoch. It is in them that, for the first time, appears the systematic effort to ascertain the relations of things objectively, *to detect the causes of all changes as inherent in the things themselves*, and to reject all supernatural or outlying agencies.

The Greeks began, but only began, this revolution. They carried it but a little way. Their explanations were generally inaccurate, owing to causes which will be set forth in the next chapter; and the eclipse which for several centuries darkened the day that had thus brightly dawned, was owing chiefly to the energetic revival of that very theological spirit from which the illustrious Greeks had emancipated themselves.

CHAPTER III.

ANCIENT SCIENCE.

§ 37. Two thousand two hundred years have passed since ARISTOTLE began his scientific investigation of Nature, and during two thousand of these years his writings were regarded as the purest and most copious fount of knowledge. Then came a revolution; and during the two hundred years which succeeded that revolution, almost everything we now dignify by the name of scientific truth, saw the light. The earlier discoveries were but as preludes to the great achievements of modern research; nor do those early discoveries form more than an insignificant item in the mass of ancient science. How can this failure of twenty centuries be accounted for? And why were the ancients so strikingly eclipsed by the moderns?

§ 38. In subsequent pages of this History we shall have to enumerate the causes which prolonged the infancy of Science from the days of ARISTOTLE and ARCHIMEDES to those of KEPLER and GALILEO. At present we have to consider how it was that the Greeks and Romans, in spite of the splendour of their genius, made such slight progress in the discovery of physical laws. In Art, Literature, and Philosophy they have legislated for the world. In Science, they are without authority. Vainly have scholars struggled against this verdict; vainly have they striven to keep up a superstitious reverence for the profundity of ancient writings by audacious announcements of "anticipations of modern discoveries."[1] The candid student is quickly disabused; he learns that this profundity is indistinctness, the anticipation purely verbal. Interesting these ancient writings must ever be: not as surpassing, or even approaching, the depth and grandeur of some modern works; not as anticipating the results of modern labour; but as brilliant points in the dimness of the Past, by which the story of human development may be deciphered; and as lessons, wherein may be read the results of yielding to that natural impatience which urges us to outstrip by guesses the tardy conclusions of experience. The failure of ancient efforts thus assumes an impressive interest, far exceeding the interest excited by a discovery of accordance between the old thought and the new. It suddenly lights up the study of ancient writings, rescuing them from the dilettantism of scholarship, and placing them among the serious archives of progress.

§ 39. There is tolerable unanimity as to the fact of the ancient failure, but uncertainty and indistinctness as to its cause. The failure is generally assigned to a complete dis-

---

[1] See, for example, IDELER: *De Meteorologia veterum Græcorum et Romanorum*, Berlin, 1832. He considers that Aristotle originated the undulatory theory of light, because the generation of light by motion is compared with the generation of sound! SCHWEIGGER maintains that in the ancient myths were embodied the shattered and misunderstood fragments of a science which existed in a remote antiquity. In the myth of the Dioscuri, for example, he reads a perfect appreciation of the two electricities. *Ueber die älteste Physik und den Ursprung des Heidenthums aus einer misverstandenen Naturweisheit*, 1823. These views, of which BACON gave a fanciful anticipation in his *New Atlantis*, and BAILLY a more elaborate sketch in his *Lettres sur l'Origine des Sciences*, Paris, 1777, have been further developed by KARL FISCHER: *Beiträge zur Urgeschichte der Physik*, 1833. The notion is not more extravagant than that of DEMOCRITUS and ARISTOTLE having anticipated modern physical discoveries, which is not unfrequently put forward. See especially DUTENS: *Origines des Découvertes attribuées aux Modernes*, 1796. The hardiest of recent assertors of the profundity and accuracy of Aristotle's physics is M. BARTHÉLEMY ST. HILAIRE, to whom the public is deeply indebted for several free and vigorous translations. See the Introduction to his *La Physique d'Aristote*, 1862.

regard of Observation and Experiment, together with a "fondness for abstract reasoning." The amount of truth in this charge depends upon the sense in which it is interpreted. Taken absolutely it might be impugned by a defender of the old philosophy on two different counts. He might reply that men may amass great wealth of observation, perform numerous experiments, and carefully abstain from abstract reasoning (if *that* be a merit), without reaching the explanation of a simple physical law. He might affirm, and affirm truly, that the ancients did observe, did perform experiments, and did employ the Inductive Method, which indeed was systematically proclaimed by ARISTOTLE with a precision and an emphasis unsurpassed by BACON himself.

§ 40. The cause commonly assigned, therefore, lends no illumination. As a general statement, it is too vague in its truth, and may be so erroneously interpreted as to pass from a truism into a falsism. Let us seek something more precise. A survey at once close and comprehensive detects the existence of two causes: a *psychological* and an *historical* cause. The first lies in the nature of the Method pursued; the second lies in the condition of knowledge at the period. On the Method pursued by the ancients, no satisfactory issues *could* have been reached, even had it been backed by the stored-up wealth of modern research: on such a Method failure inevitably followed, precisely as it follows the efforts of moderns whenever they employ it. Nor, on the other hand, is it less certain that had the ancients clearly conceived and rigidly adhered to that Method which alone issues in fruitful results, their achievements, splendid in comparison with what actually was achieved, would still necessarily have been slight, because there was no stored-up-material to form the basis of extensive discovery. Science is a growth. The future must issue from seeds sown in the past. The bare and herbless granite must first be covered with mosses and lichens, if from their decay is to be formed the nidus of a higher life.

No magnificent vegetation springs up at once; it emerges gradually from the accumulated stores of former epochs. From the small beginnings and successive growths of knowledge there emerges a more comprehensive and more complex Science. The advance is not simply one of *addition*, but of new *development*—a development rendered possible by the addition; just as the addition of a new tissue raises the organism to a higher possibility of functional power. The truth sought in one age as a goal becomes a starting-point to the age which follows; the discovery which was the passionate aim of one man, and conferred on him lasting glory, becomes to his successors a mere instrument of new research.

No one who reflects on the actual condition of any science, will fail to notice the complicated connection of all the sciences. The perfection of one demands illumination from all. Not only are the movements of the stars incomprehensible before the laws of Mechanics are established, but even a fact so simple as the transit of a star cannot be ascertained until after it has been illuminated by optics, barology, and thermology. The position of a star has to be estimated with reference to the laws of aberration and refraction of light, which in turn are affected by the laws of atmospheric density, which again depend on laws of temperature. The very telescope with which the star is observed is itself the product of advanced science.

This connection of the sciences points to a simultaneous growth, and a slow growth. Therefore in the early ages, before a large mass of established truth had been accumulated, before instruments had been invented, and when discoveries which were to be the instruments of research were still unsuspected, it almost was impossible for any mind, however great, to give a scientific explanation of any class of phenomena; all that could be done was to suggest some happy hypothesis, or to work out some small point of special value. Some few minds were contented with this humble effort; but the majority, especially of philosophers, were too impatient; and unable to rest without some explanation, trusted confidently to the Subjective Method, because the Objective Method *could* not then have been constantly applied, so as to satisfy their intellectual cravings.

§ 41. Before we can explain the failure of the ancients we must rightly appreciate the influence of two different and concurrent causes, methodological and historical. Those writers who, to my knowledge, have treated this subject *ex professo*, have entirely overlooked the historical cause, confining themselves to a specification of the defects in the ancient Method. Nor does it seem to me that they have been successful in very distinctly marking the sources of failure, even with respect to Method. They have felt the defects rather than assigned a philosophical explanation of them. An exception must be made in favour of Dr. WHEWELL, who has brought his views on the philosophy of science to elucidate this very question; with what success we will presently inquire. The general mode of viewing the failure is typified in PLAYFAIR's celebrated Dissertation prefixed to the *Encyclopædia Britannica*, and we may content ourselves with a scrutiny of its arguments.

§ 42. After comparing ancient with modern physics, PLAYFAIR thus delivers his verdict: "Extreme credulity disgraced the speculations of men who, however ingenious, were little acquainted with the laws of nature." Why were they so ignorant? Because "unprovided with the great criterion by which the evidence of testimony can alone be examined. Though observations were sometimes made, experiments were never instituted; and philosophers who were little attentive to the facts which spontaneously offered, did not seek to increase their number by artificial combinations."

PLAYFAIR is inaccurate in saying that no experiments

were instituted, and that observations were only occasional; but this historical error is insignificant beside the methodological error of assuming that the chief source of the ancient failure was the absence of experiment. What is Experiment? what its function? Its function obviously is to supplement Observation, or rather to *direct* it, by making it definite, precise, in cases where to the unassisted observer the facts are indefinite and confused. Experiment, by varying the circumstances which usually accompany the phenomena, endeavours to disengage the conditions which are *coincident* from the conditions which are *causally related*. Hence it has been happily defined "une observation provoquée." Instead of contenting itself with the ordinary course of phenomena, it produces a definite disturbance of that course by artificial means. Observation tells us in the gross that atmospheric air which has been inspired by an animal, and then expired, is more or less damaged for further respiration. Experiment tells us definitely what have been the changes undergone by the gaseous constituents of air. Observation gives us the fact with great certainty, but without precision; Experiment adds nothing to the certainty, but renders the fact precise, and quantitatively appreciable. Although Experiment is an instrument of immense importance, it is one which derives all its value from the mind directing it. Used at haphazard, its results are fortuitous. The example of the alchemists should teach us how little it effects in incompetent hands; that example discloses experimental investigations wandering into paths more eccentric, and arriving at conclusions more preposterous than ever seduced an ARISTOTLE or an ARCHIMEDES. Experiment is an art, and demands an artist.

§ 43. Moreover PLAYFAIR's misconception may be answered on other grounds. He would not deny that Astronomy, Anatomy, Zoology, and Botany are sciences; he would not deny that the ancients failed to discover the laws of these sciences; yet he would be forced to admit that in these sciences his "grand criterion," Experiment, has scarcely any place, however humble. The astronomer cannot disturb the ordinary course of the stars; he must observe and calculate. The anatomist and zoologist must likewise observe and describe. These operations were performed by the ancients; yet they failed. Immense stores of observation were accumulated, but they were of little value. If it be said that the Greeks may have observed and experimented, yet did not observe correctly, nor experiment skilfully, the statement is true, but unenlightening. Our inquiry is, Why was this so?

§ 44. As if imperfectly satisfied with his explanation, PLAYFAIR next tries the effect of rhetoric. "Experience in those days was a light which darted a few tremulous and uncertain rays on some small portions of the field of science; but men had not acquired the power over that light which now enables them to concentrate its beams, and to fix them steadily on whatever subject they wish to examine. This power," he adds, as if he were speaking of something definite, "is what distinguishes modern physics, and is the cause why later philosophers, without being more ingenious than their predecessors, have been infinitely more successful in the study of nature."

Stripped of all metaphor this means that the ancients failed because they did not bring the results of their research in many directions to elucidate each special inquiry. But unless those results had been truths, their concentration would have only been a complication of error. And our inquiry is, Why were these results imperfect? Why were the separate sciences so barren? To this PLAYFAIR gives no answer. If, indeed, we place ourselves at that elevation which brings twenty centuries under our eye, from which point of view all details are merged in a general mist, and only the broad failure becomes visible, we may say with truth, that deficient

Observation was the origin of the failure. But such a truth is barren of instruction. To make it fruitful we must rear it in the soil of History; we must trace the actual struggles of Science, and learn there what were the causes of this imperfection. Had the Greeks observed truly, they must have succeeded; the fact of their failure proves that some radical defect existed: a defect of completeness, or a defect of Method. Can we discover that defect?

§ 45. It is the exceptional merit of Dr. WHEWELL to have seen the necessity of a distinct answer to this question, and to have proposed an answer which claims to be at once definite and philosophical. It is given in the section on the "Cause of the failure of the Greek Philosophy" in his History.[2] He first points out the common error of supposing that this cause lay in neglect of facts. The Greeks, he assures us, did not disregard experience, did not spin their philosophy purely from their own minds. "The disregard of experience is a phrase which may be so interpreted as to express almost any defect of philosophic method, since coincidence with experience is requisite to all theory." He adds that ARISTOTLE not only insisted on experience as the foundation of science, but "also stated in language much resembling the habitual phraseology of modern schools that particular facts must be *collected;* that from these, general principles must be obtained by *induction;* and that these principles, when of the most general kind, are axioms"—an assertion we shall see amply justified in our sixth chapter.

After referring to the large collection of facts, and the ingenuity of their classification, to be found in Aristotle, he remarks: "Since, as we have before said, two things are requisite to science—Facts and Ideas; and since, as we have seen, Facts were not wanting, we are naturally led to ask, were the ancients deficient in Ideas? was there a want among

---

[2] WHEWELL: *History of the Inductive Sciences*, 3rd ed., 1857, L, 54.

them of mental activity, and logical connexion of thought?" The answer is foreseen. Undue mental activity is the standing reproach against them.

§ 46. Having thus surveyed the elements of the question, and having found that the defect sought could be neither owing to absence of Facts, as is commonly alleged, nor to absence of Ideas, Dr. WHEWELL concludes that "the defect was that though they had in their possession Facts and Ideas, the *Ideas were not distinct and appropriate to the Facts.*"

§ 47. An obvious answer to this solution is that it merely restates, in other words, the case of failure. In saying that the Ideas were not distinct and appropriate to the Facts, he simply says that the Facts *were* wrongly interpreted, not *why* they were so. Answering this criticism, he affirms that his explanation, over and above the case of failure, points out the one special direction, out of several, in which the Greeks went wrong. "They did not fail because they neglected to observe facts; they did not fail because they had not ideas to reason from; but they failed because they had not the right ideas in each case. And as long as they were wrong in this point, no industry in collecting facts, or ingenuity in classing them and reasoning about them, could lead them to solid truth."

§ 48. It is many years since this explanation was first propounded, but I find myself still unable, after long meditation, to see either the precision it claims, or accuracy in the premises from which it is deduced. I must venture therefore to consider it under both aspects. With respect to the first it should be observed that "distinct and appropriate Ideas" have a peculiar position in the author's philosophy, which may be appreciated through the following passage:—

"The Greeks in their physical speculations fixed their attention upon the wrong aspects and relations of phenomena;

and the aspects and relations in which the phenomena are to be viewed in order to arrive at scientific truths, may be ranged under certain heads, which I have termed Ideas : such as Space, Time, Number, Cause, Likeness. In every case there is an Idea to which the phenomenon may be referred so as to bring into view the Laws by which they are governed; this Idea, I term the *appropriate Idea* in such a case; and in order that the reference of the phenomena to the Law may be clearly seen, the Idea must be *distinctly* possessed. Thus the reason of Aristotle's failure in his attempts at mechanical science is that he did not refer the Facts to the appropriate Idea, namely Force, the Cause of Motion, but to relations of Space, and the like; that is, he introduced *geometrical* instead of *mechanical* Ideas."

§ 49. That many special errors may be referred to such a cause is admissible. A writer so conversant with science and its history as Dr. WHEWELL, would not propound an explanation which was destitute of confirmatory examples; but he will admit that, unless the explanation be generally applicable, it will not serve our purpose; and it would be easy to cite abundant examples of unequivocal failure which cannot be referred to the indistinctness or inappropriateness of the Ideas. When the orbit of the planets was held to be circular, and their motion uniform, the appropriate and distinct Ideas of Space and Time were not less vividly present to the mind of ARISTOTLE, than they were to the mind of KEPLER, when he held the orbit to be elliptical, and the motion variable. Again, ARISTOTLE's failure in Biology is not less conspicuous than his failure in Mechanics; yet the ideas of Final Cause, Likeness, and Vitality, which are said to be the ideas appropriate to this science, were assuredly possessed by him with a distinctness unsurpassed in modern times. In the course of the ensuing pages many glaring errors of the Greeks will have to be noticed; and the reader will see how few of them can be referred to the cause assigned by Dr. WHEWELL.

§ 50. Instead of conceiving that the Greeks failed to detect the laws of equilibrium and motion because their Ideas of pressure, resistance, momentum, &c., were indistinct, it seems to me more consonant with History to conceive that these Ideas were gradually evolved from the precise appreciation of the Facts of equilibrium and motion. Thus, what Dr. WHEWELL considers to be primary, fundamental, I hold to be secondary and derivative. The appropriate Ideas said to determine the progress of discovery are, I conceive, themselves perfected—brought into distinctness—during the progress of discovery, and cannot properly be applied as Instruments until some progress has been achieved. To use the very illustration of our author—" The Idea of Likeness could not be applied so as to give rise to a scientific classification of plants till considerable progress was made in studying the general relations of vegetable form and life."[3] However, as this is a point in which our views on science are widely at variance, I shall not further moot it here.

§ 51. If it were admitted that the one determining cause of the failure was the absence of distinctness and appropriateness in the Ideas, a philosophic historian would still be called upon to explain this absence. The reason why the Greeks viewed phenomena under wrong relations, and why the moderns viewed them under right relations, would stand in need of explanation. Thus Dr. WHEWELL's reply to the question, Why did the Greeks fail? is wanting in precision, to say the very least; and we may now proceed to consider the want of accuracy in the premises on which his conclusion is founded.

§ 52. He affirms that the Greeks were not wanting in Facts, nor deficient in Ideas. The statement is delusively equivocal. In strict language, neglect of facts *was* the cause of failure; and it is inaccurate to say that the Greeks were

---

[3] *History of Scientific Ideas*, 1858, II., 115.

not strikingly deficient in them. Anatomy, for example, is a science which consists in the accurate appreciation of visible facts. It demands nothing but patience in dissection and correctness in description. This science the Greeks professed; they expounded the facts of animal organization, and their failure was extensive, minute, surprising. Can we say there was not neglect of facts here?

§ 53. Although it may be justifiable to answer vague allegations respecting the ancient contempt of observation, by pointing out the large accumulation of facts from which the Greeks drew their data, and by quoting their emphatic recognition of the Inductive Method, it is equivocal to claim for them such an appreciation of facts as warrants the assertion that their failure did not arise from deficient observation. It is true that they observed; it is not true that they observed adequately. It is true that they invoked experience; it is not true that they invoked it sufficiently. They very imperfectly appreciated the nature of evidence; they were careless both as to the quantity and quality of the facts.

§ 54. Nor is the assertion that they were fully possessed with Ideas less equivocal. Undoubtedly, they exhibited immense intellectual energy, but their Ideas were for the most part inductions carelessly obtained from facts which had never been verified; consequently the ingenuity and activity of their theories only exhibit mental energy, careless whether its constructions rest on granite or on shifting sand. It will be seen hereafter that they were not less regardless of Verification in the region of ideas than in facts; and therefore, although we cannot say that they were deficient in facts or ideas, meaning by deficiency entire absence, we must avow them to have been deficient in both, meaning by it, insufficiency. This was not due to want of power, but to want of Method. They observed and reasoned, but observed badly, and reasoned precipitately.

§ 55. There are three modes of investigation: Observation, Induction, Deduction. To be fruitful, these must all be rigorously subordinated to Verification. Before each new step can be safely taken, the facts must be verified, the induction verified, and the deduction verified. At any one of these stages error may creep in; unless these doors are securely barred, no success is certain. Imperfectly observed facts, imperfect inductions and deductions, constantly betray men of science in our own day; and more constantly betrayed the Greeks, because the Greeks were less alive to the dangers. Our sole superiority consists in this: we have an ampler basis of demonstrated and colligated truths, and a keener sense of the sources of error. They were careless and credulous, where we are circumspect and sceptical. They were confident and precipitate in induction; and when an argument was verbally consistent it had an excellent chance of being accepted as an accurate representation of the order of nature.

§ 56. Abundant illustrations will present themselves in the course of the following pages; meanwhile let this example suffice. The ancients maintained that the velocity of a falling body is proportional to its weight. This is an opinion naturally suggested by an unverified survey of the phenomena; and in those days no one thought of verifying what was *primâ facie* plausible; no one thought of ascertaining whether a heavy body did fall more rapidly than a lighter body. The fact was assumed on the faith of such experiences as the fall of a stone and a feather. When GALILEO denied the fact, he was ridiculed by the Aristotelians. When he sought to bring it within the range of Verification, by dropping bodies of different weights from the leaning tower of Pisa, so powerful was the old prejudice that it was unshaken even by the simultaneous sound of these bodies ringing on the pavement. The Aristotelians, from having so long neglected Verification, had come to disbelieve in its teaching.

§ 57. To affirm that the Greeks wanted neither Facts nor

Ideas is therefore manifestly equivocal. For the purposes of Science they wanted both; that is, they wanted true facts and true ideas. Such facts as they had, seldom sufficed for their inductions, and their deductions were seldom confronted with reality. In a word, they failed because they had not a clear conception of the true Method, and wanted the aid of the proper Instruments. The true Method came into use only after the baffled ingenuity of many generations had disclosed the futility of every other, and partial success had cheered men on the difficult but certain path. Each step on that path made it easier for followers. The Greeks had no predecessors. With the impatience of active intellects they attempted to build before the accumulation of building materials had furnished the means, and before Architecture had furnished a Method. "The ancients," says Bacon, "proved themselves, in everything that turns on wit and abstraction, wonderful men. But as in former ages, when men sailed only by observation of the stars, they could indeed coast along the shores of the old continent, or cross a few of the Mediterranean seas; but before the ocean could be traversed, and the new world discovered, the use of the mariner's needle, as a more faithful and certain guide, had to be found out."[4] Unhappily the ancients were ill-content to creep along the coasts, and slowly collect the wealth to be found there. They hoped to traverse the great ocean without the guide of a compass. That guide is Verification.

§ 58. In the absence of this important principle, the interpretation of nature can be but mere guesswork, sometimes right and sometimes wrong, but without a standard of right or wrong. The complexity of phenomena is that of a labyrinth, the paths of which cross and recross each other; one wrong turn causes the wanderer infinite perplexity. Verification is the Ariadne-thread by which the real issues may be found. Un-

---

[4] Bacon: *Works*, by Spedding and Ellis, 1858, IV., 18.

happily, the process of Verification is slow, tedious, often difficult and deceptive; and we are by nature lazy and impatient, hating labour, eager to obtain. Hence credulity. We accept facts without scrutiny, inductions without proof; and we yield to our disposition to believe that the order of phenomena must correspond with our conceptions.

Verification, the alpha and omega of research, of which Experiment is the potent handmaid, was so little understood by the ancients, that it found neither employment in their practice, nor recognition in their philosophy. I do not, of course, mean that they never verified their facts or conclusions; only thus could they have acquired any accurate knowledge. I mean that they rarely set about Verification with a distinct consciousness that such a process was an indispensable part of true investigation. The great HIPPARCHUS and the illustrious ARCHIMEDES are individual examples of true scientific inquiry, and their success was their reward. But few ancients can be named beside these. Even in a science founded so much on calculation as Astronomy we see a deplorable deficiency of any due recognition of Verification. Thus when ERATOSTHENES conceived the felicitous idea of measuring an arc of the meridian by the sun's distance from the zenith of Alexandria on the solstitial day, conceiving that on the same day the sun was exactly in the zenith of Syene, he never thought of verifying his basis, never ascertained whether Alexandria and Syene were, in fact, due north and south of one another. Yet this is what no modern astronomer would neglect. Had ERATOSTHENES taken this preliminary trouble he would have found that Syene is to the east of Alexandria, and must have measured his arc by other points. In future chapters we shall notice ARISTOTLE framing theories, more or less ingenious, upon premises which a very moderate scrutiny would have detected to be utterly erroneous; and we may compare this facile acquiescence in unverified facts with the laborious solicitude of a HALLER, sacrificing one hundred and ninety animals to establish the basis of his theory of Irritability,[5] or with the patience of a MÜLLER, devoting two years of almost daily observation to the generative organs of reptiles and birds.[6] These great investigators knew the futility of theorizing so long as facts remained unverified. They knew the perpetuity of error and disputation when unchecked by peremptory fact.[7]

§ 59. We have thus gradually disclosed the *psychological* cause of the ancient failure. It was this defect of Method which prevented successful research. The ancients flagrantly disregarded the principle of Verification, both in the region of facts and the region of ideas; neither recognizing its necessity as a matter of teaching, nor employing it with any rigour and system in practice. To this source every one of their errors may be traced. Every error may be shown to have arisen from reliance on unproved facts, precipitate inductions, or mere phrases reasoned from as if they

---

[5] HALLER: *Mémoires sur la Nature sensible et irritable des parties du corps animal*, Lausanne, 1761, I., 4. He complains of his contemporaries for not taking due precautions. "Ils ne font que peu, ou point, d'expériences, et ce qui est plus dangereux encore, ils leur substituent des analogies auxquelles ils donnent la même force." In the preface to the 8th vol. of his *Elementa Physiologiæ*, he finely says: "Lætus exitum video immensi operis: qui ab annis retro triginta et sex majorem partem vitæ meæ in id unum impendi. Numerosos libros eo fine legi: animalia pene innumera incidi, et mortua et imprimis viva, ut motus animales eorumque causas perciperem. . . . Longum id tempus non suffecit tamen ut omnia ipse, et satis accurate, et satis repetito viderem; fuerunt quæ nunquam, fuerunt quæ non satis iterato viderim." This was the spirit which made him one of the great legislators of science in his day.

[6] MÜLLER: *Bildungsgeschichte der Genitalien*, 1830. Comp. also VULPIAN et PHILIPEAUX: *Recherches Expérimentales sur la régénération des nerfs* in the *Mémoires de la Société de Biologie*, Paris, 1859, I., 382, where, noticing the small amount of facts they adduce after so many experiments, they add, "on en trouvera les raisons dans le contrôle rigoureux auquel nous avons soumis nos observations, parceque, *nous défiant de nous mêmes, et soulevant àpropos de chaque fait des objections*, nous n'acceptions comme réellement démonstratives que les expériences qui ne pouvaient laisser place à aucun doute." No ancient would have understood such scruples; all moderns will applaud, if they have not the patience to imitate them.

[7] For example, the disputes of physicians continued through centuries respecting the share in diseases due to an acid state of the blood, before any one had ascertained the fact of free acid existing in the blood at all.

were demonstrated truths. And to this source, likewise, may all the errors of moderns be traced.

The last sentence seems to raise a doubt as to the propriety of bringing against the ancients a charge to which the moderns are confessedly open. But it is with steady purpose that I identify the psychological cause in both cases. The human mind has not changed. The cause of error is everywhere the same. In modern times this cause must be very active, since we see unequivocal evidence of its effects. The superiority we have over the ancients arises from our having learned in the study of science to distrust the facile procedure of the mind when left to its native impulses. We have learned the art of investigation. Often failing in its application, we, at any rate, recognize its methods. The ancients imperfectly understood that art; and since the art could only have emerged gradually in the growth of Science, we are brought to the second or *historical* cause of the ancient failure. The psychological cause lies deep in human nature, and is not less operative in our days than of old, whenever it is disengaged from the influences of the historical cause; that is, whenever the mind acts free from the control of acquired knowledge and acquired tendencies. A long training of the mind in scientific investigation has induced a firm reliance on scientific Method. This represses the spontaneous impatience and credulity natural to the untrained intellect. We have acquired the habit of Verification in a long experience of the dangers incurred by its neglect. We have learned to view Metaphysics with such distrust as not unfrequently to misconceive the value of abstract principles.

§ 60. It thus appears that if we can explain the failure of the ancients by their disregard of Verification, we have still to explain why they disregarded so important a principle, and why moderns have both recognized and employed it. The explanation is simple and has already been sketched (§ 40). Science is the attempt to interpret the phenomena of nature; and this interpretation borrows light from the general illumination of discovery. But men cannot, or at least, they will not, await the tardy results of discovery; they will not sit down in avowed ignorance. Imagination supplies the deficiencies of Observation. A theoretic arch is thrown across the chasm, because men are unwilling to wait till a solid bridge be constructed. The mind, as BACON says, "has a yearning which makes it dart forth to generalities that it may have something to rest in; and after a little dalliance with experience becomes weary of it." The early thinkers, by reason of the very splendour of their capacities, were not less incompetent to follow the slow processes of scientific investigation, than a tribe of martial savages to adopt the strategy and discipline of modern armies. No accumulated laws, no well-tried methods existed for their aid. The elementary laws in each department were mostly undetected. And with this poverty in material, with this absence of acquired skill, and this native precipitancy of judgment, acting on the ambition to interpret nature, it is not wonderful if they chose the *à priori* road, neglecting the laborious Inductive road which had not then been proved to lead to great results. History tells how the theories established in one generation become the starting-points of successors. The laws, so difficult to discover, become, when discovered, familiar facts ready for the tyro's use. NEWTON, with all his genius, would not have detected the law of gravitation had not KEPLER and GALILEO preceded him; nor could they have made their discoveries had not Greek mathematicians supplied the means. It was by the bold and happy identification of celestial with terrestrial physics that the great thinkers of the seventeenth century made physical Astronomy an exact science, making it a part of Mechanics, explaining its phenomena by those very Laws of Motion which were proved to regulate the phenomena of terrestrial bodies.

The growth of discovery is slow, and man is naturally impatient. Herein, as before hinted, lies the explanation of the preference for the Subjective Method. Not until that method had been tried by successive generations, and found to lead to no discovery, was it relinquished for the more modest and difficult method which experience proved to be the true one. And this relinquishment was gradual. The great results obtained in the 17th century naturally fixed attention on the method by which they were reached. From that time to the present there has been an ever-increasing extension of the method. And that this has been determined by the accumulations of Knowledge is evident when we reflect that the Subjective Method is co-extensive with our ignorance. It is the tendency of all positive knowledge of objects gradually to displace the subjective fictions by which the blank of ignorance was at first filled up. Thus with the growth of knowledge Metaphysics, which once reigned supreme, has given place to Science in all but a few departments of inquiry. It will be the task of this History to set forth the various stages of this progress and their causes. For the present it is enough to note how the existence of a mass of accurately-appreciated facts has determined the *general* acceptance of that Method on which alone the mass may be largely increased, and the true laws of phenomena discovered. The amazing rapidity of scientific progress in the last half century, compared with the slowness of its progress in early times, is clearly due to the facilities afforded by what may be called the historical conditions—the state of knowledge out of which the progress issued.

To resume: The cause of the ancient failure was primarily a defect of Method; and the continuance of this cause, which lies deep in human nature, was due to the imperfect condition of Knowledge. At no time was the right Method wholly disregarded, but the predominance of the false Method kept it in a state of feeble subjection. As knowledge slowly advanced, this predominance slowly diminished; and at the present time the relative positions are changed; the false Method is still employed, and in certain inquiries preserves its supremacy; but the existence of a vast body of scientific doctrine, and the rapidly increasing extension of the scientific spirit, prove that the true Method is at length predominant.

CHAPTER IV.

THE METAPHYSICAL AND SCIENTIFIC METHODS.

§ 61. THE conclusion arrived at in the preceding chapter requires that some specific account should be given of the two rival Methods, Subjective and Objective, which for so many centuries have struggled for mastery. I shall here confine myself to the metaphysical phase of the Subjective Method. Since the days of BACON it has been a standing reproach against the Greeks and the Schoolmen that they wasted fine intellects in metaphysical disputes, prolonged the infancy of philosophy by forsaking the plain paths of observation for the wilderness of abstract speculation, and failed to make any considerable advances towards true knowledge, because they engaged in the hopeless endeavour to solve problems insoluble by man. There is a sense in which this reproach is just. There is also a sense in which it is profoundly unjust. Those who perceive only the former, cannot understand why those who perceive the latter should still persist in relying on their baffled pretensions, and should declare that the historical fact of incessant failure is no convincing reason for ultimate despair.

The great battles of Humanity are never fought in vain. Supposing it to be granted that energy and ingenuity have been flung away upon problems essentially insoluble, the efforts of Metaphysics have not been without fruit. Apart from the valuable experience gained respecting the nature of the problems attacked, there has been the far greater gain of clear insight into the true Method, which discloses what problems are insoluble, and why they are so. For it is a great, though frequent error, to suppose that all metaphysical problems are beyond our power, and that many physical problems are not so. The vanity of Metaphysics lies in its Method, not in its aims. The same Method is no less disastrous in Physics. How little force there is in the declamations against that "fondness for abstract reasonings" supposed to have led the ancients astray from the path of observation, may be appreciated on remembering that the Chaldeans observed the heavens for centuries without learning more astronomy than would equip an old almanack-maker; and that many modern astronomers, instead of confining themselves to observation, are exclusively occupied in calculation and abstract reasoning, some of them being scarcely able to recognize a star in the heavens.

§ 62. The fundamental ideas of modern science are as transcendental as any of the axioms in ancient philosophy. Who will say that the Law of Causation, or the Laws of Motion, although *suggested* by experience, and found to be *conformable* with it, do not transcend it? These are τὰ μετὰ τὰ φυσικά. Take the formula: "Motion is necessarily rectilinear and uniform." This is purely ideal. Our experience, when closely examined, is never of uniform and rectilinear motions, but always of motions accelerated or retarded, and more or less divergent. But the curve of a projectile is explained as the resultant of the resistance of the air, and the attraction of the earth acting upon a body which is conceived to be in uniform and rectilinear motion; and this conception itself is derived from the law of inertia, in other words from the law of causation, that no change (of velocity or direction) can take place without a cause. Thus the uniformity of undisturbed rectilinear motion is an *abstraction*. But it is gained objectively—it is abstracted from facts accurately observed, and is verified by undeviating conformity with facts. In like manner the Law of Inertia is an abstraction; it so far transcends all experience as to seem in flagrant contradiction to daily experience which shows us that bodies in motion gradually cease to move, without any cause of the cessation being apparent. The law asserts that a body in motion will move for ever with undiminished velocity, *unless* acted upon by some external cause. This assertion obviously goes beyond the possibilities of experience. We know no body that is not acted upon. The thing does not exist. Nevertheless the law is irresistible. No sooner is it understood than it is accepted without qualification. And the reason of this is that it rigorously fulfils every condition of Verification. Considered in its ideal aspect—(as a mere abstraction)—it is seen to be in conformity with what may be termed the *Ideal test*, namely, that its negative is unthinkable. I mean, of course, unthinkable by us, not by the ancients, who held that bodies moved and ceased to move from internal causes. Considered in its phenomenal aspect—(as an expression of observed facts)—it is seen to be in conformity with the *Real test*, namely, that by experimentally diminishing all the known causes of resistance to a body we proportionately diminish its retardation; from whence we conclude that if all resistance were abolished all retardation would disappear; and thus we establish by experiment a truth which transcends the limits of experience.

§ 63. It is not a difference in the problems so much as a difference in the Methods, which distinguishes ancient from modern investigation. Compare the *Physics* of ARISTOTLE with the *Principia* of NEWTON, and this becomes immediately apparent. In the latter we find metaphysical abstractions, but not the metaphysical Method. The formulas are gained objectively, not subjectively: they are accurate *descriptions of the observed order in phenomena;* they are moulded on realities; they were abstracted from objects, and have been rigorously *verified* according to the Ideal and Real tests. The formulas of Aristotle are not more transcendental, but they want the guarantee of Verification. On confronting them with the accurately observed order of phenomena we find them to be at variance with that order, or unrelated to it. Formed upon incomplete or unverified data, often upon slight analogies and verbal resemblances, they are inaccurate as descriptions. When he deduces his theorems of circular movement from the idea of the circle as the most perfect form, he has neither the justification of conformity with observed phenomena, nor of conformity with the ideal criterion. The two ideas of perfection and motion are not *co-ordinates;* they admit of no equation.

If an à *priori* proposition conforms to the Ideal Test, that is to say, if its negative is unthinkable, or absurd, we accept it as subjectively true. When we say that under similar conditions similar causes *will* be followed by similar effects, the truth of the proposition is irresistible, although its absolute conformity with fact can never be established, being, as it is, a proposition respecting the future. Its negation being really unthinkable, its positive truth is irresistible. On the other hand, when Galileo supposed, with the ancients, that the velocity acquired by a falling body, at any point, must be proportional to the *space* through which it had fallen; this *à priori* idea, though very distinct and plausible, did not withstand the Ideal Test, since its negation *was* thinkable, and there was the equally distinct idea of the velocity being proportional to the *time* by which to oppose it. Then came the necessity for Verification; and the criterion in this case was obviously that which we have named the Real Test. By this criterion he learned that his first conception was erroneous, and, although the conception which replaced it was not more intelligible, it had the supreme advantage of being a more accurate description of the order of nature.

The Ideal Test was recognized by Aristotle and Des-

CARTES, when they advanced it as a principle of the logic of Science, that on *passing beyond the region of sense we are to rely on what is possible*.[1] In all verifiable cases we dare not be confident that an explanation is true because its truth seems possible. Our conceptions of possibility are too contingent to form a secure ground of deduction. Thus, to GALILEO, it seemed possible that velocity must be proportional to space, because, in so conceiving it, he had not distinctly visible to his mind *all* the elements of the problem ; in other words, all the possibilities. On the application of the Real Test he found that the seeming possibility was a fiction. He might have suspected this on the application of the Ideal Test, for the negation of the proposition, "velocity is proportional to space," is perfectly conceivable. Indeed, in such cases Possibility requires to be submitted to the twofold verification, and cannot therefore of itself furnish an ultimate test.

§ 63 a. We are thus brought round to the simple rule which Science inscribes on the pediment of her temple :—*No formula admissible unless verifiable ; none admitted, except as an hypothesis, until verified ;* the Verification having two different criteria : one, conformity with the positive laws of thought; the other, conformity with the observed order of phenomena.

This rule at once distinguishes the soluble from the insoluble problems, by furnishing the tests to which they must con-

---

[1] *Meteor*, I., vii., 343. "Concerning things which escape the perception of our senses, we consider them to be sufficiently demonstrated when we have shown them to be possible: περὶ τῶν ἀφαντῶν τῇ αἰσθήσει νομίζομεν ἱκανῶς ἀποδεδεῖχθαι κατὰ τὸν λόγον, ἐὰν εἰς τὸ δυνατὸν ἀναγάγωμεν." DESCARTES refers to this as representing his own views : *Principia Philosophiæ, Pars quarta*, § cciv. ; he adds the important qualification : " quod equidem verum esse libentissimè concedo, satisque à me præstitum esse putabo, si tantum ea quæ scripsi talia sint ut omnibus naturæ phenomenis accuratè respondeant." This is in accordance with KANT's excellent remark that, "Irrthümer entspringen nicht allein daher weil man gewisse Dinge nicht weiss, sondern weil man sich zu urtheilen unternimmt ob man gleich nicht Alles weiss was dazu erfordert wird."—*Untersuchungen über die Deutlichkeit der Grundsätze.* Werke, 1838, I., 100.

form. In transcendental questions the test is ideal. No question within the sphere of natural phenomena is too vast for human capacity, or too subtle for human ingenuity, if it can be brought within the range of Verification, direct or indirect; and all questions are insoluble so long as they remain outside this range. A year ago (1860) it would have been as idle to speculate respecting the metals which now exist in the sun's atmosphere, as respecting the change of a luminiferous vibration into a sensation of light — both questions were hopelessly insoluble because both lay outside the sphere of Verification. No sooner did the brilliant discoveries of KIRCHOFF and BUNSEN[2] disclose a means of Verification (Spectrum analysis), than the question became strictly scientific. In like manner, if ever the means of establishing an equation between motion and sensation be detected, we shall be able to recognize the sensation of light to be the correlated form of the force previously existing as vibrations of the luminiferous medium; and we shall trace the re-appearance of this force in the motion of muscular contraction, just as in physics we see motion passing into heat, and heat re-passing into motion, or into electricity.

§ 63 *b*. That the ancients and the schoolmen spent themselves on insoluble problems, is true; but it is not the capital charge against them. Their grand mistake was the employment of a Method on which *all* problems were insoluble, and

---

[2] "Nos connaissances positives par rapport aux astres sont nécessairement limitées à leurs phénomènes géométriques et mécaniques, sans pouvoir nullement embrasser les autres recherches physiques, chimiques, physiologiques et même sociales que comportent les êtres accessibles à tous nos divers moyens d'observation."—COMTE : *Cours de Philos. Positive*, 1835, II., 9. Compare also pp. 11, 13. This seemed justifiable at the time it was written, although perhaps there was even then an unphilosophical absoluteness in asserting the necessary limitation of knowledge, since WOLLASTON and FRAUNHOFER had discovered the "lines" which form the basis of the new means of verification. It is quite *possible* that we shall one day indirectly verify physical, chemical, and even biological propositions concerning the planets, as we have already verified their magnitudes, distances, orbits, and times of revolution. But until the means of Verification are detected, such problems are insoluble.

which rendered their explanations of ordinary phenomena as fruitless as their speculations about noumena and efficient causes. Instead, therefore, of indulging in declamations against their verbal quibbles and pursuit of metaphysical abstractions, we may inquire why verbal quibbles should so long have deluded them, and why the pursuit of metaphysical abstractions seemed to them the pursuit of noblest wisdom. To ascertain this we must appreciate their Method, in contrast with the Method of Science.

§ 64. Science is that *co-ordination of facts which describes the order of co-existence and succession in phenomena*. It classifies facts, bringing the particular facts under general heads, co-ordinating them into theories which have all the exactitude compatible with our means.

§ 64 a. What is the meaning of Fact? Nothing seems easier to define, until we try; on trial, the task is perplexing because of the ambiguities of language. In philosophical and in vernacular usage, an antithesis is implied between Fact and Idea (or Theory), which fades into vagueness on examination. Facts are commonly understood to relate exclusively to sense—to the objective world—to phenomena existing externally, and *per se*. Ideas, on the contrary, relate to consciousness—to the conceptions we form of external things. The sweetness of an apple is a fact when the quality on which it depends is considered apart from our sensation; an idea when considered as a part of our experience. Facts might thus be defined the *order* of phenomena; Ideas, or Theories, our *conceptions* of that order. In this sense there can be no false facts, but only false ideas.

Could such distinctions be consistently maintained it might be well. But they cannot. The psychologist knows how shadowy and artificial are these pretended limits. His analysis discloses that facts are indissolubly ideal—the appearances of things to us, not the things *per se*, and that so far from any fact being the unadulterated image of its object, the conditions of our consciousness are necessarily mingled with it. Moreover his analysis shows in the simplest fact an inextricable blending of *inference* with sensation. A fact may be defined as a bundle of inferences tied together by one or more sensations. Take a case so simple as the sight of an apple on the table. All that is here directly certified by consciousness is the sensation of a coloured surface; with this are linked certain ideas of roundness, firmness, sweetness, and fragrance, which were once sensations, and are now recalled by this of colour, and the whole group of actual and inferred sensations clusters into the fact which is expressed in "there is an apple." Yet any one of these inferences may be erroneous. The coloured object may be the imitation of an apple in wood or stone; the inferences of roundness and solidity would then be correct, those of sweetness and fragrance erroneous; the statement of fact would be false. Or the object seen may be another kind of fruit, resembling an apple, yet in important particulars differing from it. Or the object may not exist, and our perception may be an hallucination. Thus a case seemingly so simple may furnish us with the evidence that Facts express our conception of the order in external things, and not the unadulterated order itself. Should the accuracy of any particular fact happen to be of importance—and in Science all facts are important—we must verify it, before accepting it. How is it verified? By *submitting each of its constituent inferences to the primordial test of Consciousness.* The test with regard to objects within range of sense is obviously the reduction of inference to sensation. The test with regard to axioms, or general principles transcending sense, is conformity with the laws of thought (§ 62); when we have thus verified a fact we have attained the highest degree of certitude.

§ 65. The mental vision by which in Perception we see the *unapparent* details—*i. e.* by which sensations formerly co-existing with the one now affecting us are reinstated under the form of ideas, which represent the objects—is a process closely allied to Ratiocination, which also presents an *ideal series* such as, if the objects were before us, would be a series of sensations, or perceptions. A chain of reasoning is a chain of inferences, which are *ideal presentations* of the details now *unapparent to sense*. Could we realize all the links in this chain, by placing the objects in their actual order as a visible series, the chain of reasoning would be a succession of perceptions, and would cease to be called reasoning. The path of the planets is seen by reason to be an ellipse; it would be perceived as a fact if we were in a proper position, and endowed with the requisite instruments to enable us to follow the planet in its course. Not having this advantage, we infer the unapparent points in its course, from those which are apparent. We see them mentally. In like manner, suppose a human body is discovered under conditions which suggest that it has been burned, but without sufficient indication of the cause, *i. e.* the facts antecedent to the burning. Some one suggests that these unapparent facts are those of Spontaneous Combustion. Our greater familiarity with the facts of combustion in general, and with the facts of the animal organism, enables us to *see* that this explanation is absurd; we mentally range the supposed objects before us, and see that *such* an order of co-existences and successions is in contradiction to all experience; we cannot see what the actual order was, but see clearly that it was not *that*.

Correct reasoning is the ideal assemblage of objects in their true relations of co-existence and succession. It is seeing with the mind's eye. Bad reasoning results from overlooking either some of the objects, or their relations; some links are dropped, and the gap is filled up from another series. Thus the traveller *sees* a highwayman, where there is truly no more than a sign-post in the twilight; and a philosopher, in the twilight of knowledge, *sees* a pestilence foreshadowed by an eclipse.

These considerations may elucidate the real meaning to be

assigned to Facts, which are sometimes taken to express the order of external things, and sometimes our conception of that order—our *description* of it; just as sound means both the vibrations of the air, and our sensation of them. There is a general tendency to use the word Fact for a final truth. "This is a fact not a theory" means, "this is an indisputable truth, not a disputable *view* of the truth." But if, as we have seen, Facts are inextricably mingled with Inferences, and if both Perception and Reasoning are processes of *mental vision reinstating unapparent details*, and liable to error in the inferences, it is clear that the radical antithesis is not between Fact and Theory, but between *verified and unverified Inferences*.

§ 66. The antithesis between Fact and Theory is untenable, for the same statement may be either a fact or a theory, without any change in its evidence. It is a fact that the earth is globular. It is a fact that this globe is an oblate spheroid. It is a fact that its orbit is elliptical. No one doubts that these are facts, no one doubts that they are theories. Shall we say that they were theories until they were verified, when they became facts? This will not extricate us; since all facts require verification before they are admitted as truths; up to that point they are not less inferential than theories.

I see an apple now falling, and I see an apple which has fallen. These are two facts which ordinary language will not suffer us to call theories. Now consider two theories which ordinary language suffers us to call facts: namely, that all apples when unsupported will fall, and that the spaces fallen through will be as the squares of the times. These are two theories of extreme generality, which are far more indisputable than the facts we have contrasted them with. They carry such certainty that no mind having the requisite preparation can for a moment hesitate in assenting to them. They are inferences which are necessities. Whereas the inferences involved in the facts before named may very easily be erroneous. The falling object may not be an apple; the apple found at the foot of the tree may not have fallen, but have been plucked and placed there. Thus doubt is permissible; and if the facts carried any importance we should be bound to verify the accuracy of our inferences. No doubt is permissible in respect to the two theories, because the inferences on which they rest have already been rigorously verified. They carry none of those possibilities of error which we know may be carried by individual experiences; all such possibilities have been eliminated in the establishment of the general truth. Should any individual experience seem in contradiction with a thoroughly verified theory, should a hundred individual experiences contradict it, our confidence would suffer no disturbance; we should at once assign them to the interference of some *condition not included in the formula.* That condition might be wholly undiscoverable, but we should be certain that the laws of nature were invariable; and our experience of disturbing influences is sufficiently extensive to invoke them in every apparent exception to a law. If it happened that two magnets placed side by side impressed on a particle of iron a velocity greater, or less, than the sum of the velocity due to each magnet acting separately, and if this were to occur a thousand times, we should not doubt the truth of the law that the velocity is proportional to the force, but should attribute this exception to some exceptional condition, such as the influence of one magnet on the other. The reason is simple: the law has been rigorously verified; the absence of any exceptional condition has not been verified, whereas the presence of such a condition is suggested by manifold experiences in analogous cases.

§ 67. Failing thus to discover any valid antithesis between Fact and Theory, we must look upon the ordinary distinction as simply verbal. Shall we express it by the terms Description and Explanation, implying that a Fact describes the order of phenomena, and a Theory interprets that order? For many purposes this would suffice. Yet on examination we shall find that an Explanation is only a fuller Description: more details are introduced, greater precision is given, the links in the chain which are unapparent to sense, are made apparent to reason; but the essential mystery is untouched; successions are enumerated, but causation escapes. Thus in the description of falling bodies, greater fulness and precision of detail are given when the unapparent links are added, and the law of attraction is introduced as the explanation. In like manner the description of an event, say the destruction of a house by a fire, acquires greater fulness and precision of detail when the apparent details are completed by some eye-witness who saw the fire break out, and explains it by this enumeration of details. In each case the objects are ranged in their order, and are *seen* thus; but in each case many objects are not seen, many intermediate links are overlooked, or are undiscoverable; and the causal nexus is for ever undiscoverable. Thus it is that explanations are descriptions, and descriptions are explanations, facts are theories, and theories facts. Science is the explanation of nature; the systematic co-ordination of the facts of co-existence and succession.

§ 68. It is beyond the purpose of this chapter to specify the means by which facts and theories are verified. Enough that whether they be simple or complex, particular or general facts, they only amount to descriptions of the external order. What is termed the explanation of a phenomenon by the discovery of its cause, is simply the completion of its description by the disclosure of some intermediate details which had escaped observation. The phenomenon is viewed under new relations. It is *classed*. It is no longer isolated, but linked on to known facts: as when the ascent of a flame, and the descent of an apple are seen to be particulars of one general fact.

We learn that chlorine is a gas having a strong "tendency" to unite with hydrogen; that is to say, we have discovered this among its several relations. But the tendency is only manifested in sunlight. The two gases may be mingled together in darkness, and will not there unite if they are left together. Admit a ray of light, and the gases rush together with a loud explosion. So far we can *describe*. If we desire to *explain*, we must seek the intermediates; we must bring the particular facts under some general fact, and thereby detect the unapparent antecedent named cause. Shall we seek this intermediate in a "repulsive force," which we assign to the darkness, and which would forcibly separate the two gases? On the Metaphysical Method this would be legitimate, and metaphysicists might accept the explanation. On the Scientific Method it would at once be condemned, because it does not bring the *unknown into visible relation with the known*, but into *imaginary relation* with *an imagined fact*. Darkness is itself a negation, and its repulsive force a fiction without basis. Let us turn to Light, which is more or less known. Do we know anything of it which enables us to class this effect on the two gases under the same head as other effects? We believe that it is ethereal undulation of a specific velocity, and we may infer that the transference of this velocity to the atoms of the gases causes them to rush together. We cannot produce this combination by any other known velocity, consequently we are not able rigorously to assert that it is motion and *no* other cause which effects the change; but we have so many evidences of chemical change produced by motion, *i.e.* by heat and light and electricity, that it is difficult to assign any other cause. Now let us suppose this proved. What has been done? The obvious order has received an addition to its description by the recognition of an unapparent detail. If our senses were sufficiently acute we might see the vibration of light transferred to the gaseous atoms, we might see them quivering and rushing together; we might see them liberated from the ethereal vibrations (heat), which had kept them in a more expanded condition, and which now produce the explosion. But that is all we should see; the mystery of their new union, the nature of the forces, would be veiled from us, and our explanation would still be no more than a description of the order in phenomena.

§ 68 a. To this illustration from science let one be added from ordinary life. A man stumbles on the prostrate body of a girl. There is blood on the ground; a gash in her throat; a razor lies on the trampled mud. These appearances suggest unapparent details. He sees that the girl has been murdered; recognizes the razor as belonging to her brutal stepfather; and at once explains the presence of the corpse by inferring that the girl was murdered by her stepfather. This description of the order of events, this mental vision of unseen occurrences, may be correct. Another man looking from a distant window may have seen the murder committed; seeing the facts which the other only inferred. But both are describing an order of events in which there is large inference, and both may be in error. The first witness infers that the girl was murdered; she may have committed suicide. The second witness verifies the truth of the inference respecting the murder; but the inference respecting the identity of the stepfather needs confirmation. One relies on the fact that the razor belongs to the stepfather, and that this man has frequently maltreated the girl: but the razor may be the property of another man, or may have been used by another purposely to mislead suspicion. The eye-witness, again, infers that the man seen from the window was the stepfather, and no other: infers this from certain visual sensations; but the murderer may have resembled in general aspect the stepfather. Suppose that the accused is able to prove on unexceptionable evidence, that at the very hour named, he was many miles away from the spot; this would at once set aside all the criminating evidence founded on the inferences of the eye-witness. By thus sifting the facts, confronting inferences with the actual order of things, justice and science arrive at their verdicts.

The digression we have just made discloses that whatever may be the convenience of language, Fact and Theory, Description and Explanation, admit of no essential separation. The only vital antithesis is between verified and unverified inferences. We are thus once again brought to the iteration of the important principle that Verification is the alpha and omega of philosophy; and that it is by the vigilant solicitude for Verification, and the comprehensive delicacy of the means employed in it, that Science asserts her superiority over Metaphysics.

§ 69. The metaphysician and metaphysicist pretend to co-ordinate facts with all the rigour of a physicist; but they admit facts which have not withstood the preliminary test, and facts which are not amenable to that test. This disregard and misapprehension of the test are due to overweening confidence in the validity of reason. Ideas are accepted, unchallenged, as the correct representatives of the external order. "There is one basis of science," says DESCARTES, "one test and rule of truth, namely, that whatever is clearly and distinctly conceived is true."[3] A profound psychological mistake. It is true only of *formal* logic, wherein the mind never quits the sphere of its first assumptions to pass out into the sphere of real existences; no sooner does the mind pass from the internal order to the external order, than the necessity of verifying the strict correspondence between the two becomes absolute. The Ideal Test must be supplemented

---

[3] " Hac igitur detectâ veritate simul etiam invenit omnium scientiarum fundamentum: ac etiam omnium aliarum veritatem, mensuram ac regulam ; scilicet, quicquid tam clarè ac distinctè percipitur quam istud verum est." He afterwards qualifies this by adding " when the idea involves existence." SPINOZA, implicitly in the *Ethics,* and explicitly in his letter to OLDENBURG, assumes the same criterion. Compare, also, his tract, *De emendatione intellectus,* § 108. Indeed, it is the only ground on which Metaphysics can be justified.

by the Real Test, to suit the new conditions of the problem. "Reason is the Absolute," says SCHELLING, "and all the objections against this proposition spring from our tendency to regard things, not as they are in Reason, but as they appear."[4] Again: "It is a fundamental belief that not only do things exist independently of us, but that our Ideas so completely correspond with them that there is nothing in the things which is not in our Ideas." HEGEL, in the introduction to his Logic, comes upon the question, "What is truth? In ordinary language we name the concordance of an object with our conception of it, truth. In philosophical language, on the contrary, truth is the concordance of the meaning with itself (*übereinstimmung eines Inhalts mit sich selbst*). And this sense has also penetrated our vernacular, for we speak of a true friend, meaning thereby one whose actions correspond with the idea of friendship."[5] And he scornfully characterizes Empiricism as seeking truth in Experience instead of in Thought (*statt in dem Gedanken selbst das Wahre zu suchen*.)[6] It is on such principles that the modern German Philosophy has reproduced the ambitious but inane attempts of Scholasticism. Hegel's disciples avow that "since the Whole is ideally in the Mind, the *I* has only to yield itself to its *I-hood*, in order to see the Absolute in itself as there immediately given."[7] The curious results of yielding to the *I-hood* are familiar to all those who have toiled through modern German philosophy.

Let us for one moment pause to consider how HEGEL applies this method to the elucidation of Matter and Spirit.

---

[4] SCHELLING: *Zeitschrift für speculative Physik*, II., Heft. II., 3,

[5] *Hegel's Philosophie in wörtlichen Auszügen*. Von FRANZ und HILLERT: Berlin, 1843, p. 27.

[6] HEGEL: *Encyclopædie der philos. Wissenschaften*, § 37, Heidelberg, 1830, p. 44.

[7] FRANZ und HILLERT: *Op. cit.* XII. The original must be added: "Denn da im Geiste idealiter das Ganze ist, so hat sich das Ich nur seiner Ichheit zu begeben, um in sich selbst das Absolute anzuschauen welches sich unmittelbar darbietet."

,The substance or essence (*substanz*) of Matter, he says, is Gravity; that of Spirit is Freedom. But Matter is only heavy inasmuch as it tends to a centre. It is composite; its very existence is external to itself—*sie besteht ausser einander*. Thus the essence of matter consists in the search for an unity which would be its destruction."[8] Now, supposing we accepted these strange propositions, does not the inquirer at once perceive that such subjective manipulations can be of no assistance in the search for external relations?

§ 69 *a*. But the errors of a DESCARTES or a HEGEL, not to mention the thousand broad and subtle intellects which have pursued similar paths, are not to be disposed of by a sentence. History reveals the completeness of the failure; but Philosophy demands an exposition of its cause. I have already indicated that cause in general terms, and will endeavour to complete that indication.

First, let us consider the futility of deciding upon the external order, by subjective scrutiny—of passing from formal logic into the sphere of concrete objects—without being careful to apply the Real Test. Oxygen and nitrogen are two colourless gases; abstract Logic assures us that out of two negatives we cannot educe a positive; out of two colourless gases, therefore, Logic tells us that we can get no colour by their union. But what is the fact? We pass from the subject to the object; we bring the two gases into union; and the nitrous acid which results has a deep orange colour. The application of the Real Test, the verification of our deduction by the confrontation with reality, discloses an imperfection in that deduction, which, subjectively, could not have been suspected. And if, in so simple a case, the objective facts are not in accordance with the subjective deduction, how much more urgent is the demand for Verification in highly complex

---

[8] HEGEL: *Philos. der Geschichte*, 1849, p. 22. Comp. also *Encyclop. der philos. Wissen.*, § 262.

cases, physiological or psychological, not to mention the favourite themes of Metaphysics?

And yet it is obvious that the truths of formal logic are unimpeachable. But they lose their guarantee in passing beyond their sphere. The laws of Rational Mechanics are none the less certain, because in Practical Mechanics the effects of friction and the inevitable imperfection of materials cause us to modify our calculations. But the results of applying the laws of Rational Mechanics without due consideration for the disturbing causes would be disastrous. It is the same in speculation. No sooner do we pass beyond the region of abstractions, than we must at every step assure ourselves of the truth of our inferences by the confirmation of reality. This necessity metaphysicians have overlooked. Logical dependence was the sole test they sought. A conclusion was pronounced valid if it could be shown to be " involved in the idea " which was formed of the facts; but *how* that idea itself had been formed, or how far it was verifiable, was disregarded. The uniform velocity of the planets was involved in the idea of their circular orbit, which again was involved in the idea of the circle as the most perfect form. The variable velocity of the planets is equally involved in the idea of their orbit being elliptical; but this idea was not gained by deduction from the idea of perfection; it was gained by an abstraction from the observed order of phenomena: it was a verifiable and verified inference. The one conclusion was purely metaphysical, the other purely scientific.[9]

§ 70. Unless we adopt the Platonic conception of Ideas, and suppose that our *à priori* notions are independent of

---

[9] ROGER BACON is worth quoting here : " Duo enim sunt modi cognoscendi, scilicet per argumentum et experimentum. Argumentum concludit et facit nos concludere quæstionem, *sed non certificat* neque removet dubitationem, ut quiescat animus in intuitu veritatis, nisi eam inveniat via experientiæ ; " and comparing the man who argues about the properties of fire with the man who tests them, he adds, " sed assumpta experientia combustionis *certificatur animus et quiescit in fulgore veritatis*."—*Opus Majus*, Venet., 1750, p. 336.

experience, it is obvious that the Metaphysical Method violates the first principles of research. If experience is the basis of even abstract knowledge—the abstract notions being elicited from concrete facts—experience will be the test of all knowledge. This is not the place to re-open the discussion respecting the origin of knowledge. Those who hold that the mind is furnished with ideas derived from a source independent of experience, and not therefore amenable to it, must nevertheless confine themselves strictly within the sphere of such ideas, and not include in it the facts only given by experience. DESCARTES, who started from universal doubt, refusing to admit anything but what was demonstrably true, very soon wandered into error, because his criterion of truth was simply subjective; whereas another criterion was no less indispensable directly he passed from the region of ideas to the region of facts. Thus, in assigning the pineal gland as the seat of the soul, he says, " The reason which persuades me that the soul can have no other seat is that I consider all the other parts of the brain are double, and that thought is single; and *one can easily conceive* that the images are collected in this gland by means of the animal spirits."[10] What he can easily conceive, he at once unsuspectingly accepts to be the truth; any confirmation of this view by the application of the Real Test he deems superfluous. Here, as throughout, he falls into the common mistake of metaphysicians. KANT truly says " it is the fate of human reason in speculation to build as rapidly as possible, and only when the edifice is completed to examine the solidity of its foundations."[11] And the source of such carelessness he finds in this, that knowledge often consisting in the analysis of our conceptions, we are led to pay exclusive attention to them, rather than to their origin.

§ 71. That the vital distinction between Metaphysics and

---

[10] DESCARTES: *Traité des Passions*, art. 32. *Œuvres*, ed. SIMON: Paris, 1844, p. 519.
[11] KANT: *Kritik. Einleitung*, § III., p. 9.

Science is less the nature of their problems than the nature of their Method, which finally determines what problems are soluble and how they can be solved, may be shown from two sides. Many of the fundamental principles of Science are, as we have already seen, principles which transcend experience, although rigorously conformable with it. They are necessary truths, in the sense that the mind having once understood the terms of their enunciation cannot conceive the propositions otherwise; they conform to the Ideal Test, and cannot be made matters of direct observation. The law of causation, and the law of inertia, are not measurable and demonstrable in the same way as the law of refraction is measurable and demonstrable. No physicist ever thought of proving the former by experiment; no physicist would accept the latter unless it had been experimentally verified. Hence KANT has proposed to form a separate science, *physica pura* or *rationalis*, of those propositions which usually form the introduction to Physics.[12]

But the reason which most imperatively forces us to regard Method as the primary and cardinal distinction, I take to be this: a theory may be transferred from Metaphysics to Science, or from Science to Metaphysics, simply by the addition or the withdrawal of its verifiable element. Thus the law of universal attraction becomes pure Metaphysics if we withdraw from it the verifiable specification of its mode of operation. *Withdraw* the formula " inversely as the square of the distance and directly as the mass," and Attraction is left standing a mere " occult quality." Indeed the Cartesians reproached it with being such an occult quality, and stigmatized it as a revival of Aristotelianism. On the other hand, *add* this verifiable formula to the " inherent virtue " of the old metaphysicists, and the result is a strictly scientific proposition.

---

[12] KANT: *Kritik. Einleitung*, and compare also his very remarkable treatise *Metaphysische Anfangsgründe der Naturwissenschaft. Werke.* V., where these propositions are elucidated.

§ 72. And how is this transference from Metaphysics to Science effected? Obviously by the precision of our description, the *intercalation of facts in their proper order*, facts which previously had been unsuspected, or had not been seen in that order. It is a common mistake to suppose that Science deals solely with facts, and Metaphysics with ideas. Both deal largely with both. The difference lies in the *authenticity* of the Method by which the facts are collected, and co-ordinated. There is abundance of well authenticated facts which nevertheless form no Science because their co-ordination has not been effected; they are bricks awaiting the architect. It is certain, for example, that the cervical vertebræ of all mammals (with two or three exceptions) are seven in number; the long-necked giraffe has the same number as the short-necked hog, or mole. The same uniformity, however, is not found in other vertebræ. The giraffe has 14 dorsal and 20 caudal vertebræ; the mole has 13 dorsal and 10 caudal. Indeed, the varieties are no less striking in the other portions of the spinal column, than the uniformity is in the neck; and these varieties suffice to refute the suggestion which has been propounded respecting the mystic influence of the number seven; a suggestion not only metaphysical in its principle, but faulty in its disregard of the fact that in some mammals the cervical vertebræ are not seven in number, in the sloth, for example, they are nine. Although we are at present without a reason, without an explanation, we carefully preserve the facts; they are not science yet; they may become science by co-ordination with other facts. If we attempt to co-ordinate them, we class them first under the general fact of Type. All the mammals are related: probably by kinship, remote ancestry; certainly by those organic resemblances which constitute Type. Passing to more special considerations, and asking why the cervical vertebræ have varied so little from the ancestral type, and why the dorsal, lumbar, and caudal have varied so much, we are led to seek the conditions of variation;

when these have been ascertained, we may be able to co-ordinate them, and then we shall have a scientific explanation why mammals have seven cervical vertebræ, neither more nor less. The metaphysician instead of waiting for such facts proceeds to solve the difficulty by invoking the influence of Number, or perhaps of Final Causes.

§ 72 a. The spontaneous tendency to invoke a Final Cause in explanation of every difficulty is characteristic of metaphysical philosophy. It arises from a general tendency towards the impersonation of abstractions which is visible throughout History. We animate Nature with intentions like our own. We derive our ideas of Cause, and Force, from our own experience of effort; and the changes we observe are interpreted as similar in origin to the changes we effect. This leads to the Fetichism of savages and children; to the Polytheism of more advanced intelligence; and, by a gradual refinement in abstraction, to the Metaphysics and Transcendental Physics of later days. We first impersonate the causes as Deities; we next eliminate more and more of the personal elements, leaving only abstract Entities; we finally reduce these Entities to Forces, as the general expression of Properties or Relations; e. g., the Force of gravity is only the abstract expression of the fundamental relation which matter universally manifests. All matter is heavy; all masses attract other masses; this property is as universal and fundamental as that of impenetrability; we abstract it as gravitation or attraction (§ 74 c). In this gradation the Will first disappears; next the independent Existence; leaving finally, an abstract expression of observed order. In the final stage we recognize that what was assumed to be an independent something, regulating phenomena, moulding them according to *its* nature, is only an impersonation of the order in phenomena, the statement in abstract terms of the very facts themselves. Thus, observing the facts of organic growth and development, physiologists have attributed them to the agency of a Plastic Force (*vis formativa, Bildungstrieb*), which moulds the heterogeneous materials into definite shapes. If, however, we seriously consider what this Plastic Force can be, *apart* from the phenomena, we are quickly led to perceive that it is only a name assigned to the observed order, a generalized expression of the facts, which has been personified, according to a well-known tendency.

§ 72 *b*. Of this kind is the impersonation of a Vital Principle, which has played so conspicuous a part in speculation, and which has been endowed with many imaginary attributes, among them that of controlling chemical agency. What is it, in a last analysis? All the visible facts of life are generalized in an abstract expression; this abstract expression is personified; this personification is endowed with attributes; and we then believe firmly that over and above the facts observed there is an *independent* Principle regulating these facts, calling them into existence, and impressing on them a definite direction; in other words, besides the organism and its functions, the organs and their acts, we believe in the existence of a mysterious something, an Entity inhabiting the organism, fashioning its organs, and directing its acts. Did we not know that the mechanism of a watch was arranged by man, and that its activities depended on the properties of matter, placed in certain relations of interdependence, we should believe in the existence of a Watch-principle, fashioning springs, wheels, and escapements, and regulating their activities. But knowing the fact, we recognize the purely ideal existence of such a Principle; and in like manner we can conceive that what we imagine to be a Vital Principle, anterior and independent in the organism, is really nothing but our generalized expression, abstracted from the mutually-dependent facts.

§ 72 *c*. It is the same with all the other numerous impersonations of abstract ideas. They are collected from the observed order, and interpreted according to the analogies of our personality; then the facts from which they were abstracted are gradually dropped out of sight, until only the abstraction remains. When this has been done, we have great difficulty in not believing that they exist independently of the facts—that our subjective separation corresponds with an objective separation—and we therefore make them the starting-points of investigation without reference to the facts. This is the basis of Metaphysics.

§ 73. Having thus endeavoured to understand the nature of Metaphysics, and the reason why it necessarily formed the first explanations of philosophy, we may now glance at the influence of Language in abetting the spontaneous tendency. "All the first attempts to comprehend nature led to the introduction of abstract conceptions, often vague, indeed, but not therefore unmeaning, such as *motion and velocity, force and pressure, impetus and momentum* ($\dot{\rho}o\pi\dot{\eta}$). And the next step in philosophizing necessarily was to endeavour to make these vague abstractions more clear and fixed, so that the logical faculty should be able to employ them securely and coherently. But there were two ways of making this attempt; the one by examining the words only and the thoughts which they call up; the other by attending to the facts and things which bring these abstract terms into use. The latter, the method of *real* inquiry, was the way to success; but the Greeks followed the former, the *verbal* or *notional* course, and failed." [13] Not the Greeks alone, but all metaphysicians, metaphysicists, and metaphysiologists, have followed this course, and consistently followed it, when they have once adopted the belief that the order in ideas necessarily represents the order in external things. The pivot of Science is precisely the Verification of this assumed correspondence.

Moreover, aiding and abetting this tendency in the mind to accept ideas as exact representations of things, there is the tendency to assume that distinct names represent distinct

---

[13] WHEWELL: *History of the Inductive Sciences*, 1857, I., 27.

facts, so that to analyse the meaning of words is held equivalent to analysis of the things represented. Psychology has made a great advance when it has learned to question these primitive assumptions, an advance which was scarcely suspected in ancient philosophy. The theory of Language was little understood, and nations familiar with no language but their own could hardly have been on their guard against verbal fallacies. When ARISTOTLE commences an investigation he is careful to enumerate what other men have said on the subject, and the meanings which are attached to certain words. In this he is imitated by most moderns, but with a difference: while they display even greater servility to the mere opinion of authoritative writers, they own no servility to the current meanings of words; if they are careful in defining their expressions, it is in order to be understood; whereas Aristotle defined them in order to expound the facts they resumed. "The propensity to seek for principles in the common usages of language," says Dr. WHEWELL, "may be discovered at a very early period. Thus we have an example of it in the saying of Thales, when he was asked, What is the *greatest* thing? He replied *Place*; for all things are *in* the world, and the world is *in* it. In Aristotle we have the consummation of this mode of speculation. The usual point from which he starts is that *we say* thus or thus, in common language. Thus, when he has to discuss the question whether there be in any part of the universe a Void, or space in which there is nothing, he first inquires in how many senses we say that one thing is *in* another. He enumerates many of these: we say the part is in the whole, as the finger is *in* the hand; again, we say the species is in the genus, as man is included *in* animal; again, the government of Greece is *in* the king; and various other senses are described, but of all these the *most proper* is when we say a thing is *in* a vessel, and generally *in place*." [14]

---

[14] *Op. cit.*, p. 29.

§ 74. The Method which has led to success in every department of inquiry, and a success proportional to the rigour of its employment, does not, as many suppose, lead us to rely solely or mainly on observation, to the neglect of ideas, but to rely solely on those facts and ideas which have withstood the tests of Verification, and have received their "Hall mark" from the Goldsmith's Company (§ 62). This Method at once eliminates many of the objects of metaphysical research, rejecting them because not verifiable. The primary requisition of Science is that, apart from the hypothesis which colligates the facts, and is understood to be only an hypothesis (§ 74 a), every detail in its Descriptions (Explanations) shall have been confronted with the observed order in things. It thereby renounces, as beyond its scope, all inquiry into noumena, or essences, confining itself to phenomena and their order of co-existence and succession. Metaphysics, believing that what *we think* necessarily corresponds with what *Nature is*, endeavours, by analysis of the ideas of existence and cause, to gain a clear understanding of them. Its Method demands only the one criterion of logical dependence; and so long as it keeps within transcendental limits, this criterion is the only possible one. In passing from formal logic to physical inquiry, a new set of conditions is entered upon, and the test of conformity with fact becomes imperative.

Owing to the impatience excited by metaphysical pretensions, there has of late years arisen a desire to banish the word "cause" from inductive philosophy; but the word is useful, and it *cannot* be banished. All that can be done is to mark out clearly the meaning assigned to it in science, namely, that of *unconditional antecedence*. The metaphysical conception of a cause, the *producer* of effect, needs limitation. We can know nothing of the final nexus. When we say that heat produces expansion, we simply express the observed facts, that one heated body brought near a colder body begins to *con-*

tract, and the colder simultaneously begins to *expand;* nothing new has been *produced;* a mutual change in the condition of the two bodies has resulted in the *transference* of so much motion (heat, expansion) from one body to another.

Hence, rigorously speaking, we must limit even the conception of *necessary sequence*, which is held to express all that is known of causation. There is no *following* of effects from causes; but, as Sir JOHN HERSCHEL more truly says, the causes and effects are *simultaneous*. If a bar of antimony and bismuth, in contact, be heated, a current of electricity is said to be produced; yet if a fine wire be introduced between the extremities, the wire becomes heated, and no electricity is manifested. Is the heat a cause of electricity in the metals, and this electricity a cause of heat in the wire? Which is cause, and which effect? Both or neither. Again: bring a magnet within a certain distance of a needle and the needle rushes towards it. Here the magnet is said to produce motion by its attraction, which is the cause—antecedent—of the effect. Our minds demand such artifices: we abstract one detail from a complex description, that is, we *abstract the attraction* and view it by itself, considering it as the *cause* or antecedent of the motion which succeeds it in our conception; and similarly we *abstract the motion*, viewing it by itself, and consider it as the effect, or consequent of the attraction. But however indispensable, such language is merely an artifice. No separation actually exists. There is not *first* attraction, and *subsequently* motion; the two are simultaneous. In like manner, we say the earth's attraction *causes* the weight of the apple; but the weight *is* the attraction: they are two aspects of one unknown reality.

§ 74 *a*. Although admitting the utility of the word Cause, thus explained, Science disclaims all attempts to penetrate the secrets of causation. It seeks only the phenomenal and relative. It recognizes the constant presence of the Unknowable, as something real though inaccessible; but while admitting the mystery it makes no effort to transcend the already vast limits of the Knowable. So readily does it restrict itself within the relative and phenomenal that it accepts hypotheses which are themselves unverifiable and which even seem absurd if in any way they facilitate the more accurate co-ordination of facts. This is a paradox; but it is significant. The first person who grasped its significance I believe to be COPERNICUS. In the preface to his immortal work he says of the heliocentric hypothesis, "It is by no means necessary that hypotheses should be true, nor even seem true, it is enough if they *reconcile calculation with observation.*" [15] The hypotheses of geometry are manifestly of this kind; no one believes in the existence or possibility of a line without breadth. The hypotheses of atoms, and of an attractive force inherent in molecules, are beyond all reach of proof. They are metaphysical ideas, and find a place in Science simply because they facilitate calculations and the exposition of facts. The metaphysical Method would employ them as bases for the deduction of facts, would argue from them as if their nature were known and their truth indisputable. But Science, which concerns itself only with facts and their observed order, in its indifference to the undiscoverable nexus binding the facts into this order, allows any hypothesis respecting that nexus, provided some convenience of colligation or exposition belongs to it. Nay it even adopts contradictory hypotheses when they suit convenience. For example, we adopt the hypothesis that the gravity of bodies above the superficies of the earth is inversely as the squares of their distances from the earth's centre. It is because this hypothesis reconciles calculation

---

[15] COPERNICUS : *De Revolutionibus Orbium cælestium.* "Neque enim necesse est eas hypotheses esse veras, imo ne verisimile quidem, sed sufficit hoc unum, si calculum observationibus congruentem exhibeant." I do not remember where I found this striking passage. To a similar effect, though less explicit, DESCARTES : *Principia, pars IV.*, § 1 and 204.

with observation that we accept it, knowing all the while that the absolute relation may possibly be different. But in the theorem of falling bodies we adopt a contradictory hypothesis, that is, we assume the action of gravity to be *the same at all distances;* because the heights to which bodies can be carried above the surface of the earth are so trifling compared with the length of the earth's semi-diameter, as to be disregarded in our calculation. If we never had occasion to pass beyond terrestrial phenomena this theorem would perfectly satisfy all our needs; yet we know that it is false; but it has the relative truth demanded for our purposes; and we have no better assurance of the truth of universal attraction. So indifferent is Science to the absolute truth of ideas; so anxious about their relative truth! The reverse is the case with Metaphysics. It cannot be indifferent to absolute truth; if its ideas are false, all deductions drawn from them are vitiated. See the contrast in an example: whether comets be said to make their appearance in consequence of the anger of a deity, or in consequence of the law of gravitation, the explanation in either case rests on the assumption of an ultimate cause acting in the manner described; but in the one case the truth of the assumption is all important, in the other it is indifferent. Unless the anger of a deity be actually in operation, the first explanation is wholly irrelevant and must lead to irrelevant conclusions; but the second explanation preserves all its value provided that the path of the comet be *observed* to be precisely the curve which accords with the assumption of a gravitating force. Let this curve be verified, according to the known law, and we are supremely indifferent respecting the truth or error of our ideas as to the force of which the *law* is known. How clearly NEWTON saw this appears in the following declaration: " What I call attraction may be performed by impulse, or by some other means unknown to me. I use that word here to signify only in general *any force* by which bodies tend towards one another, *whatever be the cause."* In truth the cause is in itself unknowable, and it is solely the law of its action with which Science is concerned. Given the law—*i.e.* the verifiable statement of the observed order—and the cause is known in all the fulness possible or desirable for human needs. Suppose that an angel were discovered in the centre of the sun *drawing* the planets; this discovery would at once displace our hypothesis of attractive force inherent in the molecules of matter; but it would make no alteration in our formula of the law; the drawing would still take place with an inverse quadratic power, and all our calculations would remain unshaken. A new band would tie our facts together, but the facts would present an unchanged order.

§ 74 *b.* One other aspect of causation, rarely appreciated, remains to be noticed. While it is important to understand that causes—in the metaphysical sense—cannot be known, and that all inquiry into their ultimate nature is waste of ingenuity, not less important is it to understand that our limitations in this direction are no greater than those placed by our necessary ignorance of matter, and of *all* noumena. All knowledge is phenomenal. Apart from the phenomena, we know no more of Matter than we know of Force. But phenomena we know; and we are also said to know their *laws*, when we have rigorously ascertained the exact order of their co-existence and sequence. Observing falling bodies with the requisite precision, we find that the space fallen through is invariably proportional to the square of the time. This is a law; and other laws are known as accurately as the properties of the bodies themselves. But we are not content with these laws; we desire to know the *cause*. What is it which forces bodies to fall, and to fall in this order? We name it the force of gravity; but the name brings no extension of knowledge. *In itself* the cause remains unknown; but we already know it in its positive characters, or modes of action, as fully as we can know Matter. Both Force and

Matter are abstractions. They stand on similar ground: as essences equally inaccessible, as phenomena equally accessible.

Considered solely in reference to falling bodies, the general fact (law), that they fall through spaces proportional to the squares of the times, gains no additional illumination from an ascription of the cause, since all we know of this cause is the law of its action. But although the cause, named gravity, is merely an abstraction, yet it enables us to class under the same head, to interpret by the same laws, many phenomena besides those of falling bodies. By this force we explain the figure of our globe and its flattened poles, the orbit of the moon, the movements of all planetary masses, the precession of the equinoxes, and the ebb and flow of the tides. Thus, although causes, or forces, are abstractions, the great and obvious advantage to philosophy of such abstractions needs not be emphasized. Their danger lies in our tendency to forget that they are introduced into our calculations solely as unknown agents acting through known laws; a forgetfulness which leads us to postulate more of them than has been disclosed through the laws. If once anything is assumed of Force, which has not already been verified in fact, we incur the same danger as when we assume properties in a substance which have never been recognized in it.

An immense gain to philosophy, and the dissipation of an incalculable amount of vague theorizing, must result when men have firmly fixed in their minds the true conception of Force as a mere abstraction which only has reality for us through its demonstrated Laws. People will cease to talk glibly of nerve-force, vital-force, &c., in explanation of phenomena not yet reduced to law; they will understand that only such effects as can be deduced from the known laws may be predicated of the unknown forces. Without being called upon to give up the advantages of having such abstractions as that of Force, they will escape the danger of metaphysical reliance on such generalized expressions.

Thus once again the principle of Verification shows itself as our firmest guide and our best consolation. Knowledge may be limited to phenomena, causes may be hidden from us, as all ultimate existence is hidden, for the ground of existence must transcend knowledge so long as Being and Knowing are not one; but within the sphere of positive knowledge a sufficient basis may be laid, resting on three separate stages: 1st, the observation of phenomena (facts); 2nd, the observation of their order of co-existence and succession (laws); 3rd, the determination of the abstract forces from which the order results as a calculable consequent (causes).

§ 74 c. In the foregoing section no notice has been taken of the great question mooted in philosophy respecting the existence of Force as an Entity independent of Matter; for in truth whether we believe in two distinct existences (Force an *Ens*, and Matter an *Ens*), or believe that Force is only the abstract expression for the dynamical relations of Matter (§ 72 a), in either case the principles are equally valid; since the realist must admit that Force can only be investigated in its positive characters, or laws; and the nominalist holds that beyond these laws there is nothing to investigate. In each case the limitation to phenomena imperatively calls for Verification and condemns Metaphysics.

§ 75. Metaphysics is the *co-ordination of unverified facts*. Science is the *co-ordination of verified facts*. That confirmation which the one sees in Logic, the other sees in Observation. The metaphysical tendency is the *spontaneous* tendency; the scientific caution is an acquired caution. Hence not only is the metaphysical tendency active in all the early epochs of speculation, both of the race and the individual, but is with great difficulty repressed even in the highly-trained intellect of an advanced period. It may be traced in the speculations of philosophers whom we should never think of classing among metaphysicians. LAMARCK abounds in illustrations. For instance, he argues that a Polype cannot have Sensibility, because that "would be contrary to the laws of organization, and to the plan which Nature is obliged to follow in all her works."[16] No ancient speculator was ever more adventurous; to deduce a fact from the idea of "a plan which nature is obliged to follow," in lieu of ascertaining what the fact is, what plan she *does* follow, is pure metaphysics. Elsewhere he explains the variety in organisms as due to two causes: one of these is the metaphysical *pouvoir propre de la vie*, which tends incessantly to form complex organisms, and to perfect them; the other is the modifying influence of external circumstances.[17]

Nay, even NEWTON, the exalted type of the scientific intellect, occasionally yields to the metaphysical tendency, as may be seen in his account of the *Vis Inertiæ*, or in the following query at the close of the *Optics:*[18] "It seems probable to me that God in the beginning formed matter in solid, massy, hard, impenetrable, moveable particles, of such size and figures, and with such properties and in such proportions to space, as most conduced to the end for which He formed them; and that the primitive particles being solids are incomparably harder than any porous bodies compounded of them, even so very hard as never to wear or break in pieces: no ordinary power being able to divide what God made one in the first creation." It is noticeable how NEWTON, with his usual caution, advances this as what to him seems probable; an ancient would have advanced it as a fact beyond dispute. Yet why probable? What proof can there be, except such metaphysical proof as is to be found in the easiest

---

[16] LAMARCK: *Histoire des Animaux sans Vertèbres*, Paris, 1835, I., 105.
[17] *Ibid.*, I., 114.
[18] NEWTON: *Works*, ed. HORSLEY, 1782, IV., 260.

ᵗmode of conceiving an order of things wholly removed from any possible knowledge?

Newton's query is, however, simply an hypothesis, and is made to prove nothing. This cannot be said of many hypotheses now current, especially those in what Berzelius sarcastically calls the "physiology of probabilities." No one who scrutinizes the science of our day can fail to perceive how ready men still are to accept phrases for explanations, and guesses for facts. Long before these pages are yellow with age, men will have learned to look upon much that is now taught in the schools respecting the oxidation of the tissues, and the like, with a pity akin to that which is bestowed on the physiology of Aristotle or Van Helmont. It will then be noted that this explanation—the oxidation of tissues—was presented without the guarantee of a single direct observation, that it was based on inferences, none of which were verified, and that it was a phrase used to cloak our ignorance, much as the "nervous fluid" was used a few years ago.[19]

§ 76. Let it be noted, on the other hand, that many objections are raised against ideas and expressions, which though metaphysical are perfectly justifiable. For example, Laplace in stating the first law of motion says that a body at rest does not contain within itself any reason for moving in one direction rather than in another.[20] This seems to Auguste Comte a metaphysical, and therefore vicious, conception,[21] the principle of "sufficient reason" being odious to him. How, he asks, could we be assured that "there was no reason" for the deviation? what can we know of it except from experience? In this criticism, it seems to me that his antagonism against

---

[19] Cuvier said he could not believe in the existence of a fluid which no one had demonstrated; instead of acknowledging the propriety of this caution, Lamarck scornfully retorted that, on similar grounds, physicists would be forced to abandon the magnetic fluid (*Hist. des Animaux sans Vertèbres*, I., 189). Not long afterwards they did abandon it.

[20] Laplace: *Exposition du Système du Monde*, 6th ed., 1836, I., 275.

[21] Comte: *Cours de Philosophie Positive*, 1830, I., 557.

metaphysics has led him too far. If we replace the word "reason" by the word "condition," the formula will run thus, "a body remains at rest, because there is no condition present which would cause it to move;" and such a formula is every way unexceptionable. If we are asked how we can be assured of this, we reply, The axiom of general causation, founded on universal experience, assures us that no change can take place unless the conditions of change be present. I cannot agree in the assertion that "all these pretended explanations resolve themselves into nothing but repeating in abstract terms the very fact itself, and saying that bodies have a natural tendency to move in a right line, which was precisely the proposition to be proved." What is here called the fact itself is never a matter of experience; there are no motions in a straight line absolutely perceived by us; the "natural tendency" is an abstraction, an idea, guaranteed by observation and calculation (§ 62), but deduced *à priori* from the law of causation. The "principle of sufficient reason" fulfils all the requisites of the *à priori* method. It conforms to the Ideal Test, namely, that its negation is inconceivable, or absurd. Whereas the principle of "perfection" by which ARISTOTLE infers that all movements are naturally circular—a principle by COMTE placed on a level with that of the "sufficient reason"—does not conform to this test. We can as readily conceive its negation as its affirmation; in other words, the laws of thought, which represent universal experience, do not force us to conceive undisturbed motion as circular, but they do force us to conceive it as uniform and rectilinear.

I have thus endeavoured to make clear the characteristics and defects of the Metaphysical Method in contrast with the characteristics of the Scientific Method, and shall have frequent opportunities in the course of this History of invoking and illustrating what may be called the supreme law of all research —the principle of Verification. No one familiar with History will consider that too much importance is here assigned to Method; few will consider that its true characteristics have hitherto been adequately expounded even by those who have specially treated of it. The principles of Inductive and Syllogistic Logic have indeed been amply expounded; but the supreme law (with its two criteria, Ideal and Real), has been taken for granted, rather than articulately expressed, and has very often been wholly overlooked. Hence the iterated insistance on it in these pages, "car les hommes ont encore plus besoin de méthode que de doctrine, d'éducation que d'instruction." [22]

---

[22] COMTE: *Cours de Philosophie Positive*, 1835, II., 225.

CHAPTER V.

PLATO'S METHOD.

§ 77. HAVING chosen Aristotle as the representative of Ancient Science, it is unnecessary for me to expound the doctrines of his various precursors; yet on many accounts it is desirable to sketch the outlines of the Method adopted by his great master and rival PLATO, indicating how far it was metaphysical, and how far scientific; not only that we may thereby gain clearer insight into the condition of ancient thought, but also that we may be more just to the Stagirite, by estimating the kind of science which satisfied the mind of his illustrious teacher.

The name of PLATO is still surrounded with the respect due to a great genius and a great renown. It is true that this respect often degenerates into servility, because here, as elsewhere, the admiration of the few becomes the exaggeration of the many, and genuine enthusiasm is echoed in loud lip-homage. But no amount of exaggeration, or of insincerity, ought to make us unjust to the noble faculties which inspired these excesses. I do not myself pretend to share the sympathy and admiration for Plato's philosophy, which has undoubtedly been felt in all ages by many wise and beautiful souls. He had great qualities, and has greatly influenced men; but our admiration for his dramatic power, dialectical skill, and moral elevation ought not to blind us to the defects of his teaching, and above all to the disastrous tendency of his method. A general estimate of Plato is not within the scope and purpose of this History; and in the present chapter we have to consider him solely with reference to Science; an aspect, it must be confessed, in which he is seen to great disadvantage.

§ 78. In the *Phædo* he has sketched the history of his studies. He tells us how in youth he was eager to learn all about the causes of things, but found to his disappointment that his efforts left him no wiser. One day he heard a person reading from a book of ANAXAGORAS, in which it was declared that " Mind was the cause and orderer of all things." This filled him with delight. He at once accepted its truth. " And I considered with myself that Mind orders all things and disposes each as it will be best for it. If any one, then, desire to discover the cause of any phenomenon, how it is produced, and how it perishes, he must ascertain in what way it is best for it to exist or act. From this it follows that a man should consider only what is most excellent and best." With such a clue to the mysteries of nature ANAXAGORAS, he thought, could enlighten him not only as to whether the earth were flat or globular, but also as to the cause of its being so, showing that it is better for it to be what it is; and, " if he should say it is in the centre, he would explain why it is better in the centre." To his great disappointment, he found ANAXAGORAS adducing simple physical reasons, instead of the teleological reasons which he had expected. Such a teacher could no longer allure him. A new course opened. Wearied with contemplating things as they are, he bethought him that men in studying an eclipse of the sun look at its image reflected in the water, lest they should become blind by gazing directly at the sun. " It seemed to me, therefore, that I ought to have recourse to reasons, and in them to contemplate the truth of things. Thus always adducing the reason which

I judge to be strongest, I pronounce that to be true which appears to me to accord with it; those which do not accord with it I deny to be true."[1]

In this frank avowal of the Subjective Method he takes no precautions and offers no guarantee for the solidity of the grounds upon which he judges one reason to be stronger than another. Between the caprices of imagination and the rigours of demonstration he offers no criterion. And the disastrous consequences of this oversight are visible in every page of the *Timæus*, where the idea of a Best, to which Nature is made to conform, leads him into extravagances such as would be incredible unless their origin were known.

§ 79. Above the world of fleeting phenomena, he conceived a world of permanent existences. These were Ideas. With these, and these only, was Science properly concerned. The visible phenomena are diagrams for the convenience of reason. The great value of Science consists in its withdrawal of the soul from the contemplation of phenomena, and its insistance on the contemplation of pure essences. " If geometry compels the soul to contemplate real existence it does concern us; but if it only forces the changeful and perishing upon our notice it does not concern us. . . . Science is pursued solely for the sake of knowledge."[2]

He ridicules the notion of Astronomy, as practised by astronomers, being capable of making the soul look upwards; and says it positively makes the soul look downwards. " I

---

[1] PLATO: *Phædo*, p. 90, ed. *Bekker*, Berlin, 1817: ἔδοξε δή μοι χρῆναι εἰς τοὺς λόγους καταφυγόντα ἐν ἐκείνοις σκοπεῖν τῶν ὄντων τὴν ἀλήθειαν . . . . καὶ ὑποθέμενος ἑκάστοτε λόγον ὃν ἂν κρίνω ἐρρωμενέστατον εἶναι, ἃ μὲν ἄν μοι δοκῇ τούτῳ ξυμφωνεῖν τίθημι ὡς ἀληθῆ ὄντα . . . ἃ δ᾽ ἂν μή, ὡς οὐκ ἀληθῆ. He overlooks the fact so felicitously expressed by BACON that the mind may be an unequal mirror to the rays of things—" instar speculi inæqualis ad radios rerum, qui suam naturam naturæ rerum immiscet, eamque distorquet et inficit."

[2] PLATO: *Republic*. Translated by DAVIES and VAUGHAN, Cambridge, 1852. One of the rare translations from the Greek which may be used with confidence.

cannot conceive that any science makes the soul look upwards unless it has to do with the real and invisible. It makes no difference whether a person stares stupidly at the sky, or looks with half-shut eyes upon the ground; so long as he is trying to study any sensible object I deny that he can be said to have learned anything, because no object of sense admits of scientific treatment. Since this fretted sky is still a part of the visible world we are bound to regard it, though the most beautiful of visible things, as far inferior, nevertheless, to those true revolutions which real velocity and real slowness, existing in true number and in all true forms, accomplish relatively to each other, carrying with them all that they contain: which are verily apprehended by reason and thought, but not by sight. Therefore we must employ that fretted sky as a pattern or plan to forward the study which aims at those higher objects."

Further on, he says, "Whenever a person strives by the help of Dialectics to start in pursuit of every reality by a *simple process of reason independent of all sensuous information*, never flinching until by an act of pure intelligence he has grasped the *real nature of good*, he arrives at the very end of the intellectual world." There is more of the same kind in this 7th book of the *Republic*, but no more need be cited here.

§ 80. Let us now glance at a few of the results to which this Method led him. We open the *Timæus*, and learn that the Universe was generated as an animal, with a soul, because that was best.[3] Whatever is generated must necessarily have body, and be visible no less than tangible. Nothing can be visible without Fire, nothing tangible without a Solid, nothing solid without Earth. Thus the first step in creation was the production of two elements. But it is impossible for two things to cohere without the intervention of a third. A bond

---

[3] PLATO: *Timæus*, ed. Bek., p. 27.

is necessary, and of all bonds the most beautiful is that which as nearly as possible unites into one both itself and the things bound.[4] Had the substance of the universe been a superficies without depth, one medium or bond would have sufficed; but as it was a solid, and solids are never one only, but always joined by two bonds, therefore the Creator placed Water and Air between Fire and Earth. These are the Four Elements, and the reason has been given why they are only four.

The elements are fashioned into a perfect sphere, because the sphere is the most perfect of figures, and most resembles itself. Although this universe was made an animal, it was made becoming and congruous; hence it had neither eyes nor ears, there being nothing external for it to see and hear; no lungs, for it needed not respiration; no digestive organs; no secretory organs; no feet, for its motion is peculiar, namely, circular, and circular motion requires no feet, since it is not progression.

§ 81. The mathematicians having discovered the five regular solids, PLATO naturally made great use of them in his cosmology. Four of them were represented by the four elements—the Earth was a Cube, Fire a Tetrahedron, Water an Octahedron, and Air an Icosahedron. This left the fifth, the Dodecahedron, without a representative, accordingly it was assigned to the universe as a whole.

The Creator, having thus shaped the visible universe, and distributed souls over the earth, the moon, and other unnamed places,—and having commissioned the younger gods (*dii minores*) to construct man,—retired to his repose.

It is needless to add that PLATO never thinks of offering any better reason for these propositions than that they are by him judged sufficient. If one of his hearers had asked him why water might not be a cube, and air an octahedron—or

---

[4] δεσμῶν δὲ κάλλιστος ὃς ἂν αὐτὸν καὶ τὰ ξυνδούμενα ὅτι μάλιστα ἓν ποιῇ.

what proof there was of either being one or the other—he would have replied: "It is thus I conceive it. This is best."

§ 82. Let us proceed. The universe, we learn, has a soul which moves in perpetual circles. Man also has a soul which is but a portion thereof, consequently it also moves in circles. To make the resemblance more complete, man's soul is also enclosed in a spherical body—namely the head. But the gods foresaw that this head, being spherical, would roll down the hills and could not ascend steep places; to prevent this, a body with limbs was added, that it might be a locomotive for the head. And as the foreparts are more honourable and regal than the hind parts, the gods made man's locomotion chiefly progressive.

§ 83. As may be anticipated, the anatomical and physiological conclusions to which such a Method leads are not in strict agreement with inductive science. Thus we find the liver described[5] as "compact and smooth, shining and sweet, though somewhat bitter; and the reason is that the thoughts falling on it from the intellect, as on a mirror, might terrify it by employing a bitterness akin to its nature; and threateningly mingle this bitterness with the whole liver, so as to give it the black colour of bile; or, when images of a different kind are reflected, sweetening its bitterness, and giving peace to that part of the soul which lies near the liver, giving it rest at night, with the power of divination in dreams. Although the liver was constructed for divination, it is only during life that its predictions are clear; after death its oracles become obscure, for it becomes blind."

Even more surprising is the description of the intestines. They are, he says, on the left side for the purpose of acting like a sponge to keep the surface of the liver bright and clear, and capable of reflecting the images of the soul.

§ 84. In a modern such ideas would not appear profound.

---

[5] *Op. cit.*, p. 100.

I have not cited them for the poor pleasure of holding up a great name in the light of ridicule; but to show how even a great intellect may unsuspectingly wander into absurdities, when it quits the firm though laborious path of inductive inquiry. "The dove cleaving the thin air," to use the happy illustration of KANT, "and feeling its resistance, might suppose that in airless space her movements would be more rapid. Precisely in this way Plato thought that by abandoning the sensuous world, because of the limits it placed to his understanding, he might more successfully venture into the void space of pure intellect."[6] It is not in Science only that PLATO is misled by his Method. The same confidence in deduction from unverified premisses vitiates his teaching in every other department of inquiry, moral and political; but in Science his errors are more patent, because his statements admit of a readier, and less equivocal, confrontation with fact.

---

[6] KANT: *Kritik. Einleitung*, § *III.*, 1790, p. 8.

CHAPTER VI.

ARISTOTLE'S METHOD.

§ 85. THE contrast between the Master and the Pupil is nowhere more emphatic than in Method. Aristotle may be truly styled the father of the Inductive Philosophy, since he first announced its leading principles; and announced them with a completeness and precision not surpassed by BACON himself. There is, indeed, a radical defect in his conception of Method, but it is a defect not less visible in the *Novum Organum*, and is common to all the systematic expositions of Method that have yet been published. This defect is the absence of the due recognition of Verification. All writers implicitly recognize Verification as the inseparable attendant of Observation, Induction, and Deduction; but they do not explicitly, and emphatically, assign to it the primary importance it should have; they do not trace in its neglect the cause of every failure. Overlooking this defect, men have expressed surprise at the unquestionable fact that ARISTOTLE and BACON failed egregiously in scientific research, in spite of their conception of scientific Method; and this failure has sometimes been made a ground for denying the value claimed for Method. But the seeming contradiction disappears on close examination. The failure is then traced to a radical imperfection in the Method. A discrepancy is disclosed between the principles which Aristotle and Bacon implicitly taught, and the principles they actually employed.

§ 86. We will first inquire what those principles were. In direct opposition to PLATO, who, denying the validity of the senses, made intuitions the ground of all true knowledge, Aristotle sought his basis in sensuous perception. Anticipating BACON, he affirmed that it was wiser to dissect the complex phenomena of sense than to resolve them into abstractions—"melius est naturam secare quam abstrahere." [1] His reliance was on Experience and Induction: the one furnishing the particular facts, from which the other found a pathway to general facts—or laws.[2] Without sensation thought is impossible.[3] PLATO held that the deceptions of sense justified scepticism of all sense-knowledge (ἀπατῆς μεστὴ ἡ διὰ τῶν ὀμμάτων σκέψις). Aristotle, more correctly, taught that error did not arise from the senses being false media, but from the wrong interpretations we put on their testimony. Manifold deceptions may thence arise; but each sense speaks truly so far as it speaks at all.[4] It is from sense we gain the knowledge of particulars. It is from Induction we gain the knowledge of universals. Agreeing with Plato that Science is only concerned with universals, he affirmed that these could only be reached through Experience.

§ 87. This is the corner-stone of the experience-philosophy or "Empiricism," so often urged as a reproach against Aristotle.[5] HEGEL boldly denies the charge. Science regards the accusation as an eulogy. Unhappily, even by Aristotle, experience was too frequently neglected and too carelessly interrogated. The vigilance of scientific scepticism was wanting. Yet at times he seems thoroughly impressed with the necessity

---

[1] BACON: *Nov. Org.*, 41.
[2] ἐπαγωγὴ δὴ ἡ ἀπὸ τῶν καθέκαστα ἐπὶ τὰ καθόλου ἔφοδος. *Topic*, I., 10. See also *Anal. Post.* I., 31; *Hist. Animal.* I., 6.
[3] οὐδὲ νοεῖ ὁ νοῦς τὰ ἐκτὸς μὴ μετ' αἰσθήσεως ὄντα. *De Sensu*, VI., 445; *De Anima*, III., 8, 432.
[4] *De Anima*, III., 3; *Metaph.*, IV., 5; and elsewhere.
[5] Even so late as SCHLEIERMACHER, who urges it in his History of Philosophy.

of securing his basis before attempting to build. "Let us first understand the facts, and then we may seek for their causes."[6] There are many passages in which he distinctly disapproves of the fatal tendency to eke out deficiencies of observation by mere guesses, and to rely on those guesses as on observations. Of such passages four may here be given :—

I. Speaking of the parthenogenesis of bees, he says, "There are not facts enough to warrant a conclusion, and more dependence must be placed on facts than on reasonings, which must agree with facts."[7]

II. Speaking of Hybridity, after noticing the opinions of his predecessors, and even suggesting an *à priori* argument himself, he says, "But such a proof is far too abstract and empty (κενῆς). For reasons not drawn from the inherent principles of things (τῶν οἰκείων ἀρχῶν) are empty, and only seem to explain them, just as only those are geometrical proofs which are deduced from geometrical principles ; so also in all other sciences. The empty argument seems potent, but is powerless."[8]

III. Speaking of those who held a certain astronomical view, he says, they did so because their thoughts were not directed to the phenomena and the discovery of the causes, but they endeavoured to make the phenomena correspond with their opinions.[9] And still more strongly in this passage : "These philosophers, treating of phenomena, say things which by no means correspond with the phenomena, the cause of this being that they have not rightly conceived first principles, but reduce everything to certain prescribed notions (πρός τινας δόξας ὡρισμένας), and they persist in these in spite of all contradiction, as if they were in possession of true principles, as if these ought not rather to be educed from the phenomena."[10]

---

[6] *De Part.*, I., 1, 639.
[7] *De Gener. Animal.*, III., 10, 760.   [8] *Ibid.*, II., 8, 748.
[9] *De Cœlo*, II., 13, 293. Compare also *ibid.*, p. 294.
[10] *Ibid.*, III., 8, 306.

IV. "The reason why men do not sufficiently attend to the facts is their want of experience. Hence those accustomed to physical inquiries are more competent to lay down the principles which have an extensive application; whereas others who have been accustomed to many assumptions without the confrontation of reality, easily lay down principles, because they take few things into consideration. It is easy to distinguish those who argue from facts and those who argue from notions."[11]

§ 88. Instead of distrusting knowledge derived through the senses, and placing unhesitating reliance on knowledge derived from intuitions, he declared that ideas are nothing but the products of reason. Reason separates, by abstraction, the particular objects from their general relations, *i. e.* those relations which these objects have in common. Anticipating modern Psychology, he taught, confusedly indeed, and not always consistently, that intelligence is a late development. The understanding is built up from sensuous materials. Each particular sensation gives rise to a sensuous state, and the permanence of this state is Memory. From memory arise, first, *distinctions;* and finally, after many repetitions, *experience;* from experience a pathway leads to Science, that pathway being Induction. PLATO taught that all knowledge was reminiscence—a revival of pre-existent Ideas. From any one Idea we can arrive at all others, owing to the logical connexion existing between them. In direct contradiction to this, Aristotle maintained that complete knowledge could only arise out of complete experience; and he significantly points out the danger of the Platonic Method, which neglects facts, and rashly concludes a general proposition from a few particulars.[12]

§ 89. In indicating the way we are to arrive at general

---

[11] *De Gen. et Corr.,* I., 2, 316. Compare also *De Partibus,* IV., 5, 679.
[12] *De Gen. et Corr.,* I., 2.

truths, he expresses himself with a precision unsurpassed by moderns. "We must not," he says, "accept a general principle from logic only, but must prove its application to each fact, for it is in facts that we must seek general principles, and these must always accord with the facts."[13] Nor, while thus insisting on Observation, was he wholly without a perception of the value of that aid to inquiry, which is usually supposed to be a modern invention, I mean Experiment. He did not, indeed, see its importance as moderns have seen it; for, not rightly apprehending the necessity of Verification, he failed to apprehend the true purpose of Experiment, which is simply a means of verifying the accuracy of data, and conclusions hypothetical or theoretical. But he refers to it, and even to vivisection, often enough to mislead a modern worshipper into the belief that this great instrument of scientific research was distinctly recognized by him. Here are a few of the passages I have noticed.[14]

He refers to the experiment of tying or removing the right testis of the male, previous to congress, in disproof of the hypothesis that the sexes are derived from the right and left testes.[15] He refers to the experiment of removing the eyes from young birds, to show that these organs are capable of being reproduced, a capability not observed in adult birds.[16] Although he places the seat of motive power in the heart, yet he refers to the experiment of removing the heart from tortoises, after which they still continue for some time to move;[17] and to prove that the nutritive soul is contained in the centre, he refers to the insects whose heads and limbs

---

[13] *De Animal. motione*, I., 698. Δεῖ δὲ τοῦτο μὴ μόνον τῷ λόγῳ καθόλου λαβεῖν, ἀλλὰ καὶ ἐπὶ τῶν καθίκαστα καὶ τῶν αἰσθητῶν, δι' ἅπερ καὶ τοὺς καθόλου ζητοῦμεν λόγους, καὶ ἐφ' ὧν ἐφαρμόττειν οἰόμεθα δεῖν αὐτούς.

[14] M. BARTHÉLÉMY ST. HILAIRE has pointed out several others in the introduction to his work *La Météorologie d'Aristote*, Paris, 1863.

[15] *De Gener. Animal.*, IV., I.

[16] *Ibid.*, IV., 6.

[17] *De Resp.*, XVII., 479.

may be removed without destroying their vitality. The fact is incorrectly stated. The separated head will live almost as long as the body; and I have often found the hinder part of a triton live and move for hours after its separation from the body.[18]

§ 90. Since then, it appears that Aristotle very distinctly recognized the cardinal principles of the Baconian philosophy, why, it will be asked, has the world credited BACON with a great reform in the very attacks he made on Aristotle? The answer is simple. Bacon did not attack the Method which Aristotle *taught;* indeed, he was very imperfectly acquainted with it. He attacked the Method which the followers of Aristotle *practised.*

The further question may be raised, Why these followers practised a Method so unlike the one their master taught? Because, unhappily, Aristotle himself had set them the example. He did so from the two causes already explained in our third chapter: 1° the initial weakness in his Method, namely, the insufficient part assigned to Verification, and 2° the inevitable immaturity of all scientific ideas at such an era; these made him depart from his own precepts, and led him a deluded captive through the labyrinth of metaphysical conjecture. It is to these causes that BACON's failure must also be ascribed; for grandly as he traces the various streams of error to their sources, he is himself borne along by these very streams, whenever he quits the position of a critic, and attempts to investigate the order of nature for himself.

§ 91. Aristotle's failure was inevitable. We have seen that, even on the supposition of his having mastered the true Scientific Method, he could not *continuously* have applied it in an epoch when the elementary laws had still to be discovered. The native impatience of the human mind disdains that fortitude of resignation which is implied in rejecting

---

[18] STILLING narrates that a frog lived, hopped about, and defended itself, for an hour after removal of its heart, and the *whole* of its viscera. *Untersuchungen über die Functionen des Rückenmarks,* 1842, p. 38.

all but verified facts and verified conclusions, at an epoch when the means of verification are little understood.

In future chapters we shall see how little Aristotle recognized the absolute importance of Verification; how little he troubled himself to ascertain the accuracy of the facts he so laboriously collected; how little he discriminated between perfect and imperfect inductions; how little he perceived the lurking fallacy of analogical reasoning; in a word, how little he understood the nature of proof. This is what was meant by saying that his Method was imperfect at its base. In the Prolegomena, I shall explain the immense importance which must be assigned to Hypothesis; and that, so far from the true philosopher being called upon to renounce hypotheses, he is called upon to be incessantly inventing them, if he would enlarge the boundaries of our horizon; but he must distinctly understand that, until rigorously verified, an hypothesis is only a guess, which may be a sublime truth, or may be an absurd error. Hypothesis, like everything else, must be proved, or held as a mere thread, which for convenience sake may tie the facts together until a better be discovered. It must never form a basis of deduction. This Aristotle did not distinctly understand, although he is said to have invented the theory of proof. Let us see what that theory was.

§ 92. Science is the co-ordination of facts (§ 64), the reduction of particular facts to general facts. "As this can only take place through an induction of universals from particulars, proof must first lie in the correctness of the induction; and when these universals have been attained, and a deduction is made from them to some new particulars, proof lies in the correctness of this deduction. There is, however, an initial difficulty: all knowledge rests upon antecedent knowledge. We see this in induction and in demonstration; the one arriving at a conclusion from particulars *already known;* the other starting from a conclusion *already known.*" PLATO evades this difficulty by referring all knowledge to reminiscence. This explanation Aristotle rejects. He affirms that demonstration rests upon universals which are *in their nature* better known[19] (or, let us say, more certainly apprehended); whereas induction rests on particulars, which are better known *to us.* The basis of Science is therefore an Inductive Syllogism.

It is necessary to appreciate clearly this distinction between knowledge of universals and knowledge of particulars. He affirms that, although sensation is the origin of all knowledge, the first ideas awakened in the soul consist of *general* ideas. Thus a man seeing a body at a distance has at first only the general idea of *substance;* on approaching nearer, and observing that it moves spontaneously, he has the less general idea of an *animal.* On approaching still nearer, he recognizes the kind of animal, by recognizing many of the particulars which distinguish it as *kind;* and he thus gains a particular idea, in lieu of his first general idea. In this way the mind advances from the universal to the particular. The infant at first calls every man papa, and every woman mamma; afterwards it learns to discriminate individuals.

The fallacy here is patent. It confounds an *indefinite* with a *generalized* conception. It is a fallacy which leavens ancient speculation.

§ 93. Since proof rests on universals, perception, which is concerned only with particulars, can give no science. Nay, if we could perceive that a triangle has the sum of its angles equal to two right angles, we should still be forced to seek for a proof of it (ἐζητοῦμεν ἂν ἀπόδειξιν), otherwise we should have no knowledge of it.

---

[19] This very important distinction in his philosophy was completely misunderstood by the schoolmen, who, as Mr. ELLIS pointed out, were misled by the ambiguity of the Greek dative, *notius naturâ*, to suppose that *notius naturæ* was meant, as if Aristotle contrasted Nature's knowledge with our own. BACON fell into this error: *Works* by ELLIS and SPEDDING, 1857, I., 137. The same mistake is made by ROGER BACON: *Opus Majus,* Venet., 1750, p. 46.

If the question be asked *why* we must seek this proof of what has already been perceived, Aristotle answers: "Because only particulars can be perceived, and science is of universals." In another work (for hitherto I have been drawing from the *Analytics*), he judiciously remarks that it is absurd to seek for a proof of that which is clearly known, and for which all the conditions of a correct perception are present.[20] But even the universal must be obtained through induction from perceptions. He says that if we were in the moon, and the earth, coming between us and the sun, deprived us of light, we should have no knowledge of the cause of darkness; we should see that the moon was dark, but not why it was dark. It is true that, from frequent observation, we might find out the cause by detecting the universal; since *out of numerous particulars the universal becomes evident* (ἐκ γὰρ τῶν καθέκαστα πλειόνων τὸ καθόλου δῆλον). But, he adds, the universal has the preference, because it makes evident the cause. We do not understand a phenomenon until we can demonstrate its cause by a syllogism, showing that it necessarily follows from some general principle. Hence syllogism is the true scientific instrument; and as the syllogism proceeds from the general to the particular, it must be better known in its nature than the particulars it has to prove.

There is no need to enter more minutely here into Aristotle's Logic. The reader may find it analysed with great care by BIESE,[21] and more briefly in most histories of philosophy. The foregoing paragraphs contain all that is essential as regards Method.

§ 94. It is clear that this conception of proof is one which inevitably tends to make investigation metaphysical and *à priori*. In spite of his recognition of the importance of observation and induction, he conceived universals as better

---

[20] *Phys.*, VIII., 3. Compare *Metaph.*, IV., 4.
[21] BIESE: *Die Philosophie des Aristoteles in ihren inneren Zusammenhange*, Berlin, 1835-42.

known than particulars. It was therefore inevitable that he should practically rely on universals to the neglect of particulars, care more about syllogisms than observations; and whenever the universals (general ideas) happened to be true, the reliance was secure. Unfortunately these universals were very often false, still oftener irrelevant; and as no criterion of their truth or relevancy was furnished by the syllogism, the reliance proved disastrous. By his theory of proof he placed the Ideal Test above the Real Test: this is metaphysical. Hence in his writings we see little of the patient circumspection of Verification; we see only the impatient facility of Deduction from assumptions which have not been confronted with reality.

§ 95. It was this which led him and all the ancients to waste so much effort in the pursuit of causes. Science was supposed to be the knowledge of causes; not the knowledge of laws, or the order of succession and co-existence, but of causes which were knowable entities.

He recognized four different kinds: the *formal*, or substantial; the *material;* the *motor*, or efficient; and the *final*. A word of explanation on each of these may be of service.

I. The *formal cause*, or *essence*, known under the scholastic titles of "quiddity" and "substantial form," is what may be called the *raison d'être* of a thing. Although form cannot be disjoined from substance in fact, it can in thought,—and that was enough for the ancients. We still preserve the idea in such phrases as, the essence of good government consists in reconciling order with progress; or, the essence of a circle consists in the equi-distance of every point in the periphery from the centre.[22] The substantial form, in short, is that

---

[22] " En contemplant les choses nous voyons qu'elles sont différentes entr'elles, et que chacune a quelque chose de particulier qui la distingue des autres : c'est ce qu'on appelle *l'essence* d'une chose, qu'on définit *ce qui fait qu'une chose est ce qu'elle est.*"—S'GRAVESANDE: *Intro. à la Philosophie*, Leyden, 1737, p. 5. This is strictly Aristotelian, and explains the phrase by which Aristotle defines the formal cause :—ἡ οὐσία καὶ τὸ τί ἦν εἶναι. The phrase is not gramma-

which makes a thing to be what it is. N.B.—The distinction between the *essence of a thing* and the *essence of our conception of a thing* had not then been admitted into philosophy.

II. The *material cause—causa materialis*—ἡ ὕλη καὶ τὸ ὑποκείμενον—is the matter itself, conceived apart from its form. Under all the varieties of things we recognize something which exists as the *subject* of these varieties; for example, the substance of the soul is something distinct from its phenomena.

III. The *motor cause*—efficient cause—ἡ ἀρχὴ τῆς κινήσεως—which plays so great a part in scholasticism, is a conception necessarily added to the two first-named causes, since these alone will not explain movement or change. But inasmuch as change is incessant, there must be some principle of change. Nature is not self-moved; we must, therefore, assume a Prime Mover, himself immoveable.

But even thus we fail to account for the phenomena of this changing universe. What is it which determines each particular movement to be that and not another? What is it which causes the harmony, regularity and beauty of the world? Obviously a fourth cause :—

IV. The *final cause*—τὸ οὗ ἕνεκα καὶ τἀγαθόν. This gives to every movement an aim, and a benevolent aim. The good of each and the good of all is the final cause of every change.[23]

---

tically explicable. See TRENDELENBURG's edition of the *De Animâ*, 1833, pp. 192-471 ; or ZELLER: *Philosophie der Griechen*, 1860, II., 147.

[23] " Finis vero est, quo res tendit. Finium alii præoptati, alii consequentes. Præoptati ejus generis sunt, ut valitudo quæ medicamentis et deambulatione comparatur. Consequentes vero ejus generis sunt, ut medicatio et deambulatio:-primum enim valetudinem, deinde ea quæ valitudini faciunt quærimus."— HERMOLAUS BARBARUS: *Compendium scientiæ naturalis ex Aristotele*, 1547, *Lib.* I., p. 6. I cannot quote from this once renowned and now forgotten scholar, without remarking that, although he occupies a prominent place in the correspondence of scholars during the latter part of the 15th century, and was thought by ERASMUS to be a " divine man," whose name could never die, he has so completely passed out of sight that most Encyclopædias and Biographical Dictionaries do not even mention him. The notices in TIRABOSCHI: *Storia della Litt. Ital.*, 1807, VI.; in HEEREN: *Geschichte der classischen Litteratur*

§ 96. It is apparent, on the most casual inspection, that no one of these causes can be verifiable; no one of them is susceptible of any stronger guarantee than that of a certain logical concordance in the assumptions we make respecting them; but inasmuch as they pass beyond the sphere of ideas, and claim to represent external realities, the Real Test is indispensable; yet it cannot be applied. Such conceptions are, therefore, utterly unscientific. Nevertheless the slow evolution of Science has not altogether disengaged itself from their trammels. Even in the present day there are not wanting men of eminence who firmly uphold the validity of final causes, and believe teleological argument to be an instrument of research. This is owing to the lingering influence of the Subjective Method, and is seldom met with in astronomy, physics, or chemistry. The Objective Method teaches that it is idle to assign a final cause, unless we believe that we have, or can have, authoritative knowledge of what actually were the Creator's intentions; and such knowledge Science modestly disclaims. It endeavours to co-ordinate facts; assumptions respecting the intentions of the Creator are not verifiable; if we accept them as we accept other transcendental conceptions, they can only be an unknown quantity in our calculation. The futility of the teleological argument may be seen in this, that until we have discovered the law of succession, until the facts are co-ordinated, the assumption of a final cause brings with it no illumination; and when the law has been discovered, the addition of the final cause brings no increase of knowledge.

§ 97. By the imperfection of his Method, no less than by the condition of culture at the time, Aristotle was, therefore, practically a metaphysician, assuming, without misgiving, the

---

im *Mittelalter*, II. (*Werke*, 1821-8, V.); and in CORNIANI : *I secoli della Litt. Ital.*, 1818, III., are all obviously at second hand, drawn probably from that marvellous torso of Italian erudition, MAZZUCHELLI: *Gli scrittori d'Italia*, 1758, vol. II., parte I., 256. A good account of him is given in JOHNSON : *Life of Linacre*, 1835. SCALIGER speaks of him as " incomparabilis doctrinæ, divinæ probitatis."—*Contra Cardanum*, 1557, Exerc. clvii.

validity of all principles that were clear and logically consistent, no matter if they were merely verbal propositions, wholly without correspondence in fact. He argued from these principles, and only scrutinized the *logical dependence* of his deduction, instead of scrutinizing the principles themselves, and the verification of his conclusions. Thus, from the assumption that the circle is the most perfect form, he deduced the conclusion that the motion of the planets must be circular. From the assumption that the centre is the "noblest place," he deduced the conclusion that the heart, being central, must be the seat of the noblest faculty—the soul. And in this path his disciples unhesitatingly followed.

Although History is bound to record the disastrous results which issued from the imperfect conception and imperfect practice of the Objective Method, not less is it bound to testify to the greatness of the revolution which that Method inaugurated. Aristotle's claim to our veneration is that he produced an organon of science. It was a gigantic creation; and for centuries was regarded as the perfect organon. This book it was which opened the subject, and which for centuries was thought to have closed it. We, instructed by a fuller wisdom, may point out its deficiencies, and perceive how they hampered as much as they aided true investigation. The errors and excesses of his followers threw strong light on his defects. But we must not suffer these defects to obscure the real greatness of his achievement. His noblest title is that of Father of the Inductive Method. He first made men aware of the paramount importance of Fact, and taught them to seek explanations of phenomena on the Objective Method.

His followers were fascinated by his defects. Hence the revival of Science was accompanied by the most energetic protests against Aristotelianism, as being the despotic obstacle to all true research; and ROGER BACON expressed a feeling which afterwards moved many minds, when he said that if he had the power he would burn all the works of the Stagirite, since the study of them was not simply loss of time but multiplication of ignorance.[24]

---

[24] Si haberem potestatem supra libros Aristotelis, ego facerem omnes cremari ; quia non est nisi temporis amissio studere in illis, et causa erroris, et multiplicatio ignorantiæ.—ROGER BACON: *Opus Majus*, JEBB's preface, p. v. Yet in spite of this outbreak every page is studded with citations from Aristotle, of whom he everywhere speaks in the highest admiration.

After writing this note I found JOURDAIN in his erudite work, *Recherches sur les anciennes traductions latines d'Aristote*, 1843, p. 386, giving a rational explanation of ROGER BACON's words: " En s'exprimant ainsi, il ne voulait sans doute pas parler des ouvrages d'Aristote ainsi que Jebb paraît le croire, mais simplement des versions latines sur lesquelles la foule des étudiants s'exerçait." The virulent style in which Bacon speaks of these translations renders this explanation highly probable. And indeed on referring again to JEBB's preface I think this was his interpretation also, although ROGER BACON's latest biographer, CHARLES: *Roger Bacon, sa vie, ses ouvrages, et ses doctrines, d'après des textes inédits*, 1861, p. 103, and MILMAN: *History of Latin Christianity*, 1855, VI., 477, have understood the passage as I have given it in the text.

CHAPTER VII.

ARISTOTLE'S PHYSICS, METEOROLOGY, AND MECHANICS.

§ 98. ALTHOUGH modern Science includes ideas not less *transcendental* than those included in ancient Science, and employs the *à priori* or deductive Method with almost equal confidence, the resemblance is only superficial. If similar ideas are invoked they are ideas reached by a different route, having a different guarantee, and occupying a different position in the system of thought. In modern science they are the highest generalities of accurate, quantitative research. Often transcending the limits of actual experience, they are always founded on experience, and are strictly conformable with all we know or can think. As abstract expressions of the observed order of nature they are liable at any moment to be displaced in favour of expressions more accurate. They serve as guides and starting-points in research. They are not believed in as absolute existences. In ancient science they were held to be absolute existences, which it was the primary object of research to find, and which, when disclosed to the imagination, required no confrontation with reality. The ancients studied phenomena to discover the realities underlying phenomena; the moderns study phenomena to detect the order of their co-existences and successions.

§ 99. It is deeply significant of the importance of Method that, although Aristotle and his followers were in the main metaphysical in their researches, they failed in their attempts to establish the transcendental ideas of Physics, not less signally than in their attempts to discover special laws. The reason is that their Method was subjective; whereas even the laws of transcendental physics are discoverable solely by the objective Method. It is also noticeable that, although the ancients had formed the conception of the Indestructibility of Matter, they failed to take the step which now seems so easy, the Indestructibility of Force. *Ex nihilo nihil fit* was an axiom applied only to Matter. While no one thought that new matter could be produced, every one believed that force could be produced where no force pre-existed. The idea had not arisen that each manifestation of force was a devolution from some other already in existence.

The conception of the Indestructibility of Force—with its consequence "the Correlation of Forces" (or, more accurately, the correlations of Force), is modern. It is now so obvious that no physicist disputes it, whatever may be his views of the *nature* of Force—whether he believes it to be an Entity, or a Relation (§ 72 a). There is indeed some difficulty in keeping this conception steadily before the mind, and this arises from the two conditions under which Force is apprehended, conditions which are antagonistic to Sense, though transcendentally identical. These are the statical and dynamical conditions—*i.e.*, Force as *tension*, and Force as *vis viva*. According to sensuous perception, these are antagonistic, and mutually exclusive; and correspond with the two fundamental conditions of matter, namely, Rest and Motion. According to transcendental ideas, they are identical: as *tension* disappears, *vis viva* reappears; and what seems lost as *vis viva* is found to be restored in *tension*. Tension is not the less force because of its equilibrium; matter is not the less active because it is at rest.

What is called the *passive*, or static, condition of bodies is a pure abstraction, a fiction framed for our convenience, a necessary fiction, but directly at variance with what is disclosed by objective inquiry. The idea of absolute inertness—inactivity—is a figment; it is correlative with the idea of all activity being due to some *outlying* agency, some existence apart from, and controlling bodies. It arose from the metaphysical view of Nature which interpreted subjective distinctions as objective realities, and thus separated Motion from the Moving Body, because such abstractions were possible in thought, and convenient in speech. The abstraction became personified as an independent Force (§ 72 a). In Mechanics we also make this abstraction, and conceive bodies as passive; nor is there any impropriety in doing so, for Mechanics deal only with abstractions. Elsewhere we recognize the fiction, and we conceive Motion not as a *thing*, but as a *relation:* "a change of situation in reference to bodies conceived as at rest,"[1] though the bodies are *known* not to be at rest. Thus in a moving ship, only those bodies are said to move which change their position in the ship. But this ship, thus conceived to be at rest, is moving through the sea; the sea moves with the earth round its axis; the earth moves round the sun; the sun moves through space. Thus we pass on in our analysis, till finally we arrive at *fixed points*, from which absolute motion may be considered. We *imagine* space without limit, motionless, penetrable by matter. It is to the parts of this imaginary space that we refer the positions of bodies, and conceive those bodies to be in motion when they correspond with successive portions of this space. This is the ultimate effort of abstraction. All we know of motion is change of position; such changes are necessarily relative; absolute motion is therefore unknown; and consequently Rest must be equally unknown.

§ 100. To cite another example:—The transcendental idea of *uniformity* in Nature, which is so completely interwoven

---

[1] LAPLACE : *Exposition du Système du Monde*, I., 269. On the relativity of our conceptions of Motion and Rest, compare KANT : *Neuer Lehrbegriff der Bewegung und Ruhe, Werke*, 1839, V., 279. Compare also his *Anfangsgründe der Naturwissenchaft, erstes Hauptstück*, V., 320.

with modern speculations, was by no means clearly conceived by Aristotle. We shall presently find him maintaining that action and reaction are not *always* equal. We shall find him satisfied with the conclusion, based on extremely superficial observation, that some male animals have teats, others not ; that lions have only one cervical vertebra, although dogs, in all other respects so similar in structure, have several. HERSCHEL has noticed how the Stagirite obstructed the progress of astronomy by not identifying celestial with terrestrial mechanics, but laying down the principle that celestial motions were regulated by peculiar laws, thus placing them entirely without the pale of experimental research, while at the same time the progress of mechanics was impeded by the assumption of natural and unnatural motions.[2]

The remark is just, and yet, although a clear conception of the principle of uniformity would have prevented such an error, we must not forget that the principle itself was really disclosed by vast experiences of uniformity ; that is to say, the idea was obtained inductively. In our day the principle is so familiar that we imagine it must have been an easy step to generalize from terrestrial to celestial mechanics. Yet neither KEPLER, the bold, nor GALILEO, the far-seeing, had the courage to make such a generalization. KEPLER assumed that there was some distinct force operating in planetary motions ; and it was for the same purpose that DESCARTES invented his vortices. Even NEWTON, as will be seen hereafter, was very timid in extending terrestrial to celestial laws ; and AUGUSTE COMTE goes so far as to consider the extension of gravitation *beyond* our solar system to be very rash, unless understood to be simply a conjecture founded on analogy.[3] This seems to me ultra-scepticism. It is true that we have at present no proof that gravitation extends beyond our own system ; but neither have we the shadow of an indi-

---

[2] HERSCHEL : *Discourse on Natural Philosophy*, 1830 (294).
[3] COMTE : *Cours de Philos. Positive*, 1835, III., 254.

cation to the contrary, and gravity is so indissolubly bound up with our conception of matter that we cannot think of the stars being material without at the same time thinking of them in relations of gravity. Direct proof to the contrary would, of course, rectify this belief, but until that is furnished, the idea of matter without gravity is unthinkable.

§ 101. He who is ignorant of Motion, says Aristotle, is necessarily ignorant of all natural things. Much as he has written about Motion, it is very significant that he should not have contributed the smallest item even to what we now call the metaphysics of the subject.[4] Not only was he entirely in the dark respecting the Laws, he was completely wrong in his conception of the *nature* of Motion. He thought it was a something superadded; an "energy" which was opposed to that of Rest. He thought that every body in motion naturally tends to rest. We have learned to identify the two; we have learned that Rest is not a mere privation, not a mere negation, but one aspect of the positive energy of Force (*tension*, not *vis viva*); for we have learned that Rest is only Equilibrium, and *that* is the action of equal and opposing forces, *i. e.*, tension.

The ancients all conceived Rest as something essentially different from Motion, different in nature, not simply in quantitative amount. They believed the earth to be at rest; we no longer believe this of the sun. We have measured the velocity of the earth which seems to be at rest, and have learned to regard motion simply as a change of relation.

In justice to Aristotle, however, we should remember that these ideas are of late development. Even MUSSENBROEK could only conceive Motion and Rest as two attributes or properties of bodies. He thought that Motion was by no means

---

[4] In writing this I was little prepared to find a modern contradictor; yet M. BARTHÉLEMY ST. HILAIRE asserts that he knows no work in the whole range of philosophy wherein the theory of motion has been treated "avec plus d'étendue ni plus de solidité."—*La Physique d'Aristote*, 1862, I., p. lxiv. His idolatry leads him to make many such surprising assertions.

necessary to bodies, since a body might rest eternally in the place once given it by the Creator.[5]

§ 102. Aristotle has been compared with NEWTON on the ground that both make a theory of motion the basis of Physics. But the comparison is unjust; the reaction it provokes against Aristotle leads to a misconception of his real greatness by the application of a false standard. While it is true that both deliver a theory of motion, it is certain that Aristotle had mastered none of the elements out of which a true theory could be constructed, whereas Newton had not only mastered the elements, but also the laws, which constitute a theory as magnificent in reach as it is fruitful in result.

§ 103. The physical writings of Aristotle still extant are the eight books of *Physics*, the four books *On the Heavens*, the two books on *Generation and Corruption*, with the *Meteorology*, and the *Mechanical Problems*. The contents of these works very slightly correspond with their titles, according to modern conceptions. The sciences which we class under the heads of Physics and Astronomy are in no sense represented in them. There is no attempt to sketch the laws of Statics, Dynamics, Optics, Acoustics, Thermotics, or Electricity. There is nothing beyond metaphysical disquisitions suggested by certain physical phenomena; wearisome disputes about motion, space, infinity, and the like; verbal distinctions, loose analogies, unhesitating assumptions, inexpressibly fatiguing and unfruitful. They have furnished matter for centuries of idle speculation, but few beams of steady light to aid the groping endeavours of science. We cannot say that on every point he is altogether wrong; on some points he was assuredly right; but these are few, isolated, without bear-

---

[5] MUSSENBROEK: *Cours de Physique Expér. et Mathématique*, 1769, I., 71. His predecessor ROHAULT had a clearer view, and defined Motion as " the successive application of a body to the different parts of those bodies which are immediately about it." Rest, therefore, became " the continual application of that body to the same parts of those bodies which are about it and immediately touch it."—*System of Natural Philos.*, by CLARKE, 1735, I., 39.

ing on the rest of his speculations, and without influence on research. I shall therefore analyse these works much more rapidly and briefly than the works on Biology.

I.—*The Work on Physics.*[6]

§ 104. In *Book I.*, after briefly laying down the rules of Method, he examines the opinions of his predecessors. This has an historical interest, but science nowadays is somewhat indifferent to criticisms on Being, or the various meanings which may be attached to the word. Nor will any but metaphysicians trouble themselves with the celebrated principle of Contraries, once so fruitful in disputation. He says truly enough (Chap. II.) that the early speculators erred because insufficient experience led them into a wrong path; but his own conception of the right path turns out not a whit less misleading.

There are, he says, three principles: Matter, Form, and Privation. In every phenomenon we can distinguish the substance and its form; but as the form can only be one of two Contraries, and as only one of these two can exist at each moment, we are forced to admit the existence of a third principle—Privation—*to account for the contrary which is absent.* Thus a man must be either a musician or a non-musician; he cannot be both at the same time; and that which prevents his being one of these is the privation of the form.[7]

Another conclusion reached, after some difficulty, is that Motion really exists.

---

[6] PRANTL has added a German translation and useful notes to his edition of the text. Leipzig, 1854. And during the revision of these sheets there has appeared a French version by BARTHÉLEMY ST. HILAIRE : *La Physique d'Aristote*, Paris, 1862, in two volumes, with a long preface and a paraphrase. The version seems excellent.

[7] " Voilà cette théorie fameuse de la matière et de la forme si souvent reprochée à Aristote, et que l'on critiquera sans doute plus d'une fois encore. Pour moi, je la trouve simple et vraie."— BARTHÉLEMY ST. HILAIRE, I., p. xxviii.

§ 105. In *Book II.* he presents his definition of Nature. After some confused and vacillating explanation, he arrives at the conclusion that Nature is the principle of Motion and Rest. Those things are called natural which are self-moved. He then enters upon the four causes, which we have already expounded (§ 95). These comprise Nature: for everything has substance, everything has form, everything has motion, everything has an end or aim.

§ 106. In the eighth chapter of this Book there is a discussion on final causes, which is too interesting to be passed over. He first argues against those who hold Chance to be a cause of phenomena. "What, it has been said, is to prevent nature from acting without an aim, and without any reference to the Best (μὴ ἕνεκά του ποιεῖν μηδ' ὅτι βέλτιον)? Why should not Zeus rain from necessity (ἐξ ἀνάγκης), and not to make the corn grow? Since the vapour, rising upwards, must become cold, and vapour chilled is water, which would descend as rain; and, because this has happened, the corn has grown. Again, if the corn in a granary is ruined by the rain, we cannot say that the final cause of the rain was the ruin of the corn, but that this ruin was accidental (τοῦτο συμβέβηκεν). What, then, prevents the organs of animals from being formed in a similar way? The teeth are produced necessarily; those in front are sharp and capable of tearing the food; those behind are broad, and capable of grinding it. They are not there for these ends, but these ends simply coincide with their existence (συμπεσεῖν). And so of all other organs. Thus, those things which happen to be constituted as if they were made for an express purpose persist, and are preserved because the conditions permit; but those of which this is not the case have perished, or will perish." [8]

Having thus stated the argument with great impartiality,

---

[8] ὅπου μὲν οὖν ἅπαντα συνέβη ὥσπερ κἂν εἰ ἕνεκά του ἐγίνετο, ταῦτα μὲν ἐσώθη ἀπὸ τοῦ αὐτομάτου συστάντα ἐπιτηδείως· ὅσα δὲ μὴ οὕτως ἀπώλετο καὶ ἀπόλλυται.

he proceeds to answer it as follows:—" That this should be the case is impossible, and for this reason: these things, and all things naturally generated, are *always*, or *mostly*, so generated. On the contrary, this is never seen in spontaneous or accidental cases. Thus, it does not seem to be accidental, or coincidental, when much rain falls in winter; but it does seem so when it occurs in the dog-days. Nor is it accidental when great heat occurs during the dog-days; but it is so during winter. If, therefore, such occur, either as an accident or with a view to some purpose, and if it is impossible to say the phenomena are accidental, it is clear they must occur with some end in view. But since all things are thus in nature—as even those admit who speak of these things—there must necessarily be a final cause of these things which in nature exist, or are produced."

Considering the reputation of Aristotle as a logician, this is, perhaps, one of the feeblest arguments ever put forth on this subject, which has elicited many.[9] Had he confined himself to the proposition first announced, namely, that constant uniformity of adaptation to an end implies a design, whereas accidental adaptations are only occasional, there would have been some force in the argument; but his illustrations betray the confusion of his ideas.

§ 107. He goes on to specify the obvious illustrations used by the advocates of final causes, in the acts of animals, and in the structure of plants, concluding that "there must be some cause for everything which exists, or is produced." But Nature is to be considered under two aspects—Matter and Form. Now form being an end, and all the rest being arranged with reference to it, we may call the form the final

---

[9] Opinions differ. M. Barthélemy St. Hilaire, always ready with his enthusiasm, thinks this argument "une magnifique apologie de la nature." Aristotle himself, on one occasion, sees through the absurdity of always seeking final causes (§ 401).

cause. Error is, however, possible both in Nature and in Art. A grammarian may be betrayed into an error of spelling, a physician into administering a wrong potion. Similar errors may exist in Nature. Monstrosities are Nature's faults in orthography.

§ 108. In *Book III.* we have his celebrated definition of Motion as the passage from *potential* existence to *actual* existence. "Motion is the energy of what exists in power, so far as existing. It is the act of a moveable which belongs to its power of moving."

Before studying motion it is necessary to come to a clear understanding of Infinity, since motion is continuity, and as such infinitely divisible; therefore the Infinite must first be studied. Then again as Motion implies both Space and Time, these also must be studied. What Aristotle has to say on these transcendental questions the curious reader must find out for himself; it would occupy too much space, and too unprofitably, to reproduce it here. I will rather call attention to the long persistence of the metaphysical fallacy which kept up discussions on such subjects as the existence of space as anything more than a relation. The fallacy (§ 69) is, that whenever man can form clear ideas, not in themselves contradictory, these ideas must of necessity represent truths of nature.[10] Hence when we conceive body, we conceive it as existing *in* something, which contains it (*i. e.* body as filling space), we are led to believe that this *all-container* must itself have an objective existence. The idea will not withstand criticism. An equal necessity can be shown for something to contain the container. As we cannot pursue this reduction *ad infinitum*, we must stop somewhere; why not, therefore,

---

[10] " Jusqu' à présent nous n'avons traité que de l'idée du vuide; il faut maintenant que nous fassions voir qu'il n'est pas impossible qu'il existe dans le monde un vuide étendu ; ce qu'on peut démontrer facilement d'après l'idée que chacun peut se former du vuide; *car on peut supposer que tout ce qui se conçoit clairement et qui n'emporte aucune contradiction avec soi, existe.*"—MUSSENBROEK: Cours de Physique, I., 82.

stop at Substance, of which we know something, rather than go on to Space, of which we know nothing?

The argument of J. BERNOUILLI, cited by MUSSENBROEK with approval, is a specimen of metaphysical trifling quite worthy of Aristotle. "Before the creation of the world there was nothing existing, except God. If this universal vacuity was not repugnant to Creative Wisdom, we cannot suppose it repugnant to his Wisdom if there are now many vacant spaces between existing bodies." Out of similar "suppositions" and "clear ideas," metaphysicians have built many systems; systems, but no science.

§ 109. Instead of wearying the reader with discussions about Space, let me detach from Aristotle's fourth book the theory of projectiles, interesting in itself, and also because it gives us the first glimpse of a conception of Inertia.

He argues that *in vacuo*, Motion is impossible. In a void there can be no difference of place; and motion implies difference of place. He then adds that projectiles continue moving after the original motor ceases to be in contact with them, "either, as some say, by reaction (διʼ ἀντιπερίστασιν), or by the motion of the moved air, which is more rapid than that of the natural tendency of the body to its proper place."[11]

"*In vacuo*, on the contrary, there will be nothing of the kind, no body can have motion there unless it be carried and supported as in a chariot." How the chariot is to be moved in vacuo, he does not explain; yet he started from the position that no motion was possible in vacuo. "Moreover," he adds, "no one can say why in vacuo a body once set in motion should ever stop; since why rather here than there? Consequently it must either remain in necessary rest, or—if in motion—in endless motion, unless some stronger interferes."

---

[11] Compare also *lib.* VIII., chap. X., 267, where the same explanation is given. GALILEO's masterly refutation of this may be seen in his *Dialoghi, Giornata Seconda* (*Opera*, Milan, 1811, XI., 344).

§ 110. On many accounts this is an interesting passage. He had by no means overlooked the fact of the *resistance* of air, since he compares it with the resistance of water. Yet the air is made to keep up rather than destroy the motion of a projectile. He had, also, as we see, got a glimpse of Inertia—at least, as regards bodies *in vacuo*. But it never occurred to him to connect the two ideas, and make inertia keep up the continuity of motion, and resistance of the air destroy the motion.[12] He was forced to seek for some *continuous external motor* to account for continuous motion; "the pulses of the moved air" was the first cause which presented itself, and was accepted at once. Whereas had he (and succeeding philosophers) steadily conceived the so-called Law of Inertia—that is to say, the transcendental Law of Causation, that every *change* demands a cause,—he would have perceived that continuous motion was motion unchanged—would have perceived that *no* external cause was needed for such continuity, but was only needed to arrest, deflect, accelerate, in a word *change* the motion. The pulses of air might thus have been conceived as retarding the motion, deflecting it, or accelerating it—and by Verification he would have ascertained which of these conceptions was correct. But in no sense could the pulses of air have been conceived as causing the simple continuance of motion, since continuance implied that there was nothing to cause change.

§ 111. The succeeding *Books* (V.—VIII.) are mainly devoted to Motion. It is divided into *absolute*, *partial*, and *accidental* motions—phrases much cherished by scholasticism, which fed on phrases as the fabled chamæleon fed on air. By accidental motion is not meant motion occurring without a known cause, but motion which has reference to the "accident" or attribute of a thing. Thus when we say "a musician walks" we speak of an accidental motion; since it is not the

---

[12] As Des Cartes did. See his *Principia Philos.*, pars II., c. xxxviii.

musician which walks, but the man in whom being a musician is the "accident."

Partial motion is when we say of a sick man that he is cured. In truth this motion of cure concerns only his diseased organ, and not the whole man himself.

Absolute motion is that in which the object moves entirely, as when we say "a man walks" because his whole body changes its place.

In the theory of motion five elements are involved: the motor, the moved, the direction of movement, the starting-point, and the goal. It is from the last that motion receives its special designation. Thus the corruption of a body is its movement towards non-existence, although it must necessarily start from existence. In like manner the movement of generation is a movement towards existence, though starting from non-existence.

§ 112. A little of this kind of philosophy will doubtless suffice for all readers. They can easily imagine how fertile such principles must have been in verbal disputation, how sterile in any other result. Yet this is the system which has been compared with NEWTON's!

There are three Categories of Motion laid down:— 1. Quantity; 2. Quality; 3. Place. On these he rings the changes. When a body increases or diminishes, there is the "motion of quantity." When the body changes its quality without changing its quantity—as in becoming hot or cold—there is "the motion of quality." When a body merely changes its place, there is locomotion, or the "motion of place."[13]

§ 113. Motion in space, from an external motor, is of four

---

[13] HERMOLAUS BARBARUS thus compendiously states it: "Motus autem est ejus rei, quæ movetur, fluens atque inchoata perfectio. Quæcunque verò moventur, aut spatium percurrunt (ut ea quæ loco mutantur), aut quantitatem transferunt (ut ea quæ auctantur minnunturque), aut qualitatem (ut ea quæ calefiunt frigefiuntque), aut aliquid hujuscemodi nanciscuntur."—*Compendium Scientiæ Naturalis ex Aristotele*, 1547, *Lib. I.*, p. 8.

kinds:—Traction, Impulsion, Translation, and Rotation. To these all changes may be referred. Thus Compulsion (ἔπωσις) is an Impulsion (ὦσις) in which the motor *accompanies* the body which it moves; and Repulsion (ἄπωσις) is an Impulsion which does not accompany the moved body. Projection is the impress of a more violent movement than the body would naturally have, and lasts until this "natural motion" regains the upperhand. Expansion is repulsion, Contraction is traction.

This analysis may be carried further; we may reduce both translation and rotation under the heads of traction and impulsion. Thus the body may be accidentally moved, or be *in* some body which is moved, or be *on* that body; that which carries may itself be carried, either because it is drawn, or pushed, or rolled. Rotation is obviously constituted by traction and impulsion.

§ 114. There are two great classes of movements—1st, the natural; and 2nd, the violent, or unnatural. These belong to all bodies. Fire ascends, and a stone descends, by natural movement. A stone may be made to ascend, but this is owing to violence; some external motor causes it to ascend; by its natural movement the stone would never rise, but always fall. For a similar reason fire may be made to descend; but left to its natural movement it will only ascend.

§ 115. Translation being the first of movements, and being reducible to circular, linear, and mixed, the question arises: Which of these is the most perfect? which represents the infinite, continuous, uniform motion of the First Mover? Not the mixed, since that is a combination of the two others. Not the linear, since a straight line is necessarily finite, and if a body were to move eternally along it, there must be a *return*, which would produce contrary movements, and moments of repose, which would be solutions of continuity. The circular therefore alone remains: in the circle there is no solution of continuity: the motion may be eternal in it.

This demonstration of circular movement as the most perfect, played a conspicuous part in peripatetic philosophy. Yet the reader sees at once how entirely it is removed from reality, how purely verbal its basis, how utterly unscientific. The same may be said of all the ideas expounded in the *Physics;* and we need bestow no more time upon them.

II.—*The work on the Heavens.*[14]

§ 116. The title of this work, *De Cœlo*, was not given by its author. It raises in the modern reader an expectation which will not be fulfilled of finding in it astronomical views. Its subject-matter is very much that of the *Physics;* indeed the two works may be considered as parts of one treatise.

§ 117. In *Book I.* substance is treated as a continuity of three dimensions, divisible on all sides. Bodies are determined by motion; but every motion is either straight or circular, or else a compound of the two. Circular motion is movement round a centre; straight motion is either upwards or downwards. That is named upwards which goes *from* the centre; that is named downwards which goes *to* the centre.

The qualities of bodies which correspond to these forms of Up and Down are Levity and Gravity. These are not relative but absolute; they belong to the bodies themselves. In a subsequent passage (*Book IV.*) Aristotle objects to the early philosophers that they conceived these contraries of Up and Down as simple relations, without determining what Levity and Gravity were in themselves. He maintains that Earth by nature tends downwards, and has absolute gravity; Fire, on the contrary, tends upwards, and has absolute levity. The former underlies the firm and solid; the latter rises above, and swims over the elements. Those bodies which move in circles can be neither heavy nor light, since they

---

[14] PRANTL has given an edition of this also, with a German translation, followed by the little treatise *On Generation and Corruption.* Leipzig, 1857.

cannot be moved *from* or *to* a centre, either by natural, or unnatural motions.

§ 117 a. The profound difference between such ideas and the ideas of modern science must be obvious. Instead of trying to ascertain the law of gravitation, that is to say, its proportional relations, a verbal definition of the *nature* of gravitation is given, without any guarantee for the accuracy of the definition. No illumination can issue from such a source, nor from the subsequent demonstration that an infinite body is impossible, consequently there can be no infinite gravity, no infinite levity.

§ 118. We have learned that the weight of bodies is not an *absolute quality* inherent in the particles, but the *relation* existing between the particles and the centre of the earth, a relation which varies with the variation of the distance. But this conception could not have been formed until it had been disclosed in the phenomena of celestial mechanics. It was otherwise with the conception of positive levity. The ordinary phenomena of terrestrial physics might have disclosed to Aristotle the error of supposing bodies to have positive levity. EPICURUS clearly saw through the fallacy of imagining that Fire ascended in virtue of its levity. " No body," says Lucretius,[15] " can by its own force tend upwards ; flame descends when left to its own nature, as we see in lightning, falling stars, and the descending beams of the sun which reach the earth."

§ 119. In *Book II.* there is much profitless discussion of the Contraries in Space, Right and Left, and the like. It is to be observed that he regards these not as *relative*, but as *positive;* thus in Book IV. he distinctly says that Up and Down, Right and Left, are fixed by nature, and are not

---

[15] LUCRETIUS : II., v., 184, seq. "Nullam rem posse sua vi corpoream sursum ferri, sursumque meare." The idea of a positive Levity continued to reign so long that even in 1755 we find Dr. SAMUEL CLARKE elaborately refuting it. See notes to ROHAULT'S *System of Natural Philosophy*, I., 99.

simply relations to us: οὐ μόνον πρὸς ἡμᾶς. After this discussion he advances the proposition that whatever exists exists for its own end. The energy of God is immortality: this is eternal life. The Godlike must consequently have eternal motion, and as the Heaven is Godlike it must contain bodies eternally moving in circles. Why are not all bodies of this nature? Because it is necessary, when a body moves in a circle, that there should be a fixed and motionless centre; such a centre is the earth. By a similar course of argument, it is proved that there must be a contrary to this earth; namely fire. But the positive is prior to the privative, and heat is prior to cold. Now, Rest and Gravity are said to be privations of Motion and Levity. The apparent contradiction in thus making fire prior to earth is reconciled by PRANTL somewhat *more Germanico*. He sees in it a deep ontological meaning, that out of the co-existence of two contraries a deeper metaphysical priority for one of the two may be evolved, and precisely for this of fire.[16]

Leaving this dainty morsel to the palates of metaphysicians, we may consider the important detail that when Aristotle speaks of Rest and Cold as *privations*, he is not to be understood as meaning *negations*. In his system privatives are positives (§ 104). Hence the solid earth is conceived as privative in respect of fire; gravity is privative in respect of levity.

§ 120. "The necessary form of the Heaven," he says, "is a circle; for this form is the most suitable to its substance, and is the first in nature: τοῦτο γὰρ οἰκειότατόν τε τῇ οὐσίᾳ καὶ τῇ φύσει πρῶτον." Substance can be *known*, then? Yes, but you must not ask how the knowledge is acquired. He proceeds to demonstrate his proposition at length; but we need not follow. The stars attract us. "It is most rational to conceive the stars as constituted of that substance in which they

---

[16] See PRANTL: *ad locum*, p. 298.

have their orbit." Why? The answer is intensely significant. "Because we have said already that there was something which by its very nature was moved in a circle: ἐπειδὴ ἔφαμέν τι εἶναι ὃ κύκλῳ φέρεσθαι πέφυκεν." Should any doubt arise respecting the high rationality of such a conclusion, the doubt will be silenced by the axiom that " everything necessarily arises from that *in* which it is." Thus as the stars move *in* circles they must be formed out of circles.

§ 121. The dynamical theory of heat, which in our day has received something approaching to a demonstration, and has led to the questionable hypothesis that the heat of the sun is produced and constantly renewed by the shock of planetary masses against it, gives a curious interest to the following passage, which an uncritical admirer might regard as an anticipation. "The heat and light of the stars are evolved from the friction of their bodies against the air; for motion naturally produces heat, even in wood and stones; and still more must this be the case with bodies which are nearer to fire; and air is nearer to fire, as may be concluded from the heat of arrows which become so heated that sometimes their lead is melted; and when they are heated the air surrounding them must be heated also. Motion through the air generates heat. Of the Upper bodies, each is moved in its own circle, so that it does not become hot, but the air surrounding it is made hot, and there hottest where the sun is. We must conclude, therefore, that the stars are neither made of fire nor moved in fire."

§ 122. Anything like a connected view of his astronomical opinions must be deferred until we come to the early history of astronomy; here we may content ourselves with one more characteristic detail, namely, his proof of the stars being spherical. "They are by nature incapable of being self-moved; and as nature never does anything irrational or purposeless (οὐδὲν ἀλόγως οὐδὲ μάτην), it follows that to the body incapable of self-movement she would give the form which is the least moveable; now the sphere is the least moveable, since it has no instruments by which to move : διὰ τὸ μηδὲν ἔχειν ὀργάνον πρὸς τὴν κίνησιν."

§ 123. In *Book III.* he gives expression to the famous conception of four elements. He defines an element to be that which exists potentially, or actually, in bodies, and cannot be resolved into any other elements. Fire and earth are potentially *in* flesh and wood; otherwise they could never come *out* of flesh and wood. But in fire there is neither actual nor potential flesh or wood; otherwise we should see them produced out of it.

PRANTL thinks it is a striking illustration of the Grecian tendency to neglect facts for ideas that not one among these early speculators ever attempted to ascertain what earth and fire really are. The reproach is scarcely just, for it is difficult to conceive how such an attempt could have been made at that period. The energetic protests against the *à priori* Method which escape from Aristotle in this very book, warrant us in saying that he would have escaped from it had the other Method been open with any prospect of result. He accepted the idea of the elements because it was plausible. There was no suspicion of its accuracy, no known means of verifying it.

Although only four elements are enumerated here, and generally also elsewhere, yet a fifth is often named, the Ether, and a great part assigned to it in his speculations. Critics, however, are far from agreement respecting it. RITTER, HENRI MARTIN and MEYER, for example, maintain the Ether to be a distinct element. BIESE, HUMBOLDT, and ZELLER argue that it wants the cardinal character of an element, the *principle of contraries*. It is neither heavy, nor light; neither hot nor cold; therefore it has no linear, but only circular movement, and is destitute of up and down. One cannot but see that Aristotle's language must be very vacillating or obscure when there can be two opinions on such a point. I think that although his language is lax, his meaning is consistently preserved. There are some unequivocal passages in which Ether is included *generally* among the elements, though it is always marked off from the other four, as standing by itself; the four elements are commonly spoken of because they are the four mundane principles; from them all bodies on our earth and in our atmosphere are derived; whereas the Ether begins where our world ends, and fills the whole of the supramundane space. This view is clearly expressed in the apochryphal treatise *De Mundo*,[17] which may be cited as collateral evidence, showing how Aristotle was understood by the Alexandrians : " Ether is the substance of the heavens and the stars ; so named not because it is of fire, but because of its eternal circular movement. It is an element differing from the four others, not to be confounded with them, because divine." There is, therefore, good reason why the principle of contraries which characterizes the other four should be absent from this element.

§ 124. In *Book IV.* he returns to Gravity and Levity, which are conceived to be at once absolute and relative. " Heavy and light we call that which by nature has the power of being moved; for the two energies there is no name unless it be velocity. Some things are called absolutely heavy, or absolutely light; others only relatively so. Of those which have weight we say some are lighter than others—as wood is lighter than brass."

After objecting to the earlier philosophers for having only considered heavy and light bodies, without inquiring into the nature of Gravity and Levity, he proceeds to define Gravity as absolute in all bodies which tend towards the centre; and Levity as absolute in all bodies which

---

[17] *De Mundo*, II., ed. Bussemaker, p. 628. οὐρανοῦ δὲ καὶ ἄστρων οὐσίαν μὲν αἰθέρα καλοῦμεν, οὐχ ὥς τινες διὰ τὸ πυρῶδη οὖσαν αἴθεσθαι . . . ἀλλὰ διὰ τὸ ἀεὶ θεῖν κυκλοφορουμένην, στοχεῖον οὖσαν ἕτερον τῶν τεττάρων, ἀκήρατόν τε καὶ θεῖον. Compare also III., p. 629, πέντε δὴ στοχεῖα ταῦτα, κ.τ.λ.

tend from the centre. "It is absurd to suppose that there is nothing in the celestial region which corresponds to Upper and Under." He contends against the notion that bodies are light in proportion to the amount of empty space which they contain. Those who reason thus forget, he says, that there must also be less substance, otherwise a large mass of gold would be lighter than a small quantity of fire, since it would contain more empty space.

§ 125. In the *Physics* he argues that *place* is something positive. He here argues that everything has its appointed place, to which it constantly tends: the light bodies belong to the Upper, the heavy bodies to the Lower. "To ask why fire moves upwards and earth downwards, is as if one were to ask why the curable passes into health, and not into whiteness."

§ 126. He inquires into the reason why bodies have different weights under different conditions. In the air a *talent* of wood is heavier than a *mina* of lead; but in the water it is lighter than the lead. The reason is: all things, except fire, have weight; and all things, except earth, have lightness. Consequently earth, and that which contains most earth, must necessarily have weight anywhere; water also must have weight everywhere except in the earth; air also must have weight everywhere except in water and earth. In other words, everything, except fire, in its own place has weight. That even air has weight is proved by the fact that a bladder filled with air is heavier than the same bladder empty. Hence when a body contains more air than water and earth, it is lighter in water than another, but heavier in air; since it will swim on the surface of the water, but not on the surface of the air. Water will sink below everything but earth, and air will rise above everything but fire. Thus we see that the four elements have their four places: fire at the top, earth at the bottom; between the two air and water.

§ 127. He declares that the shape of bodies is not the

cause of their moving up and down; but only the cause of the greater velocity with which they move. He raises the question why flat pieces of brass or lead swim on the surface of water, whereas smaller pieces, if round, long, or pointed, sink; and other substances, as dust, float in air?

The reader here recognizes the problem solved by GALILEO in a masterly manner, both by reasoning and experiment. The solution of Aristotle is, as usual, little more than a restatement of the problem in different words. He begins by saying that every continuity is more or less divisible, and that every body has a more or less penetrating power over it. The easily limited is easily divided; air is more so than water, water more so than earth. And the smaller a body is, the more easily is it divided. The body which has a flat shape remains at the top of the water, because it has a larger quantity of water under it, and this larger quantity is less easily penetrated; but a body of contrary shape sinks because there is a less quantity of water under it to be penetrated.

These are all the topics needful to be noticed in this work until we come to consider his astronomical theories. The two books on "Generation and Corruption" may be passed over; for they are in his most wearisome style of verbal disputation, and contain no scientific views not expressed elsewhere.

III.—*The Work on Meteorology.*[18]

§ 128. This is in many respects one of his most interesting treatises. It has a more directly scientific attitude, and is guided by a more consistently inductive method than either of the works just noticed. No one will be surprised to hear that it very imperfectly corresponds with what in our days is understood by a treatise on Meteorology; nor must we

---

[18] A translation of this work has just appeared by M. BARTHÉLEMY ST. HILAIRE: *La Météorologie d'Aristote*, Paris, 1863.

object to its including questions of astronomy, geology, and chemistry; for at that period the boundaries of the several sciences were not carefully marked. Even at the present time Meteorology, rich in details, is eminently imperfect, aided though it is by instruments of precision, and a vast body of scientific truths which would lend their collustration, were fundamental principles established. In Aristotle, therefore, we can still less expect to find material of value. His observations and theories wear somewhat the aspect of the observations and theories to be found in the works of the early alchemists, as compared with modern chemistry. But although the absolute value of the treatise is insignificant its historical value is considerable, and on this point, therefore, the reader's attention may chiefly be fixed.

The work shows what could and what could not be effected by Observation, when unassisted by Instruments. Aristotle, equally with moderns, makes Heat the chief agent in meteorologic changes. But this is general, *qualitative* knowledge, and Science demands *quantitative* knowledge. Wholly destitute of a measure of heat he could establish no quantitative bases for his reasonings. In like manner he was without a Barometer which could measure the weight of the atmosphere at different times and in different places. He knew that the atmosphere had weight, but was unable to measure that weight. He further wanted an Anemometer by which to measure the velocity of atmospheric currents, and a Hygrometer by which to measure the quantities of vapour. Nor had he any knowledge of Electricity, which also plays a considerable part in meteorologic phenomena. Thus, deprived of all those puissant means of investigation which could make observation precise, we see in his work an example of the genuine commencement of Science, when man is face to face with complex phenomena, the order of which he intensely desires to discover, and finds himself reduced to qualitative observation and to reasoning. Now the remarkable point in Aristotle's treatise is that, standing as he does in the condition of the early pioneers, he does not adopt that primitive theological mode of explanation which we have seen (§ 31) to be generally characteristic of such a condition, but on the contrary, adopts a strictly scientific method, rejecting all theological explanations, and endeavouring to range the phenomena in their natural order. He examines the facts and co-ordinates them to the best of his ability.

§ 128 a. *Books I. to III.* discuss a variety of questions. First the elements are enumerated. These are five; the Ether, which fills supramundane space (§ 123) and is endowed with circular movement, is only alluded to; the four others are fire, air, water, earth, which compose all mundane bodies. He then gives theoretic explanations of shooting stars, comets, the milky way (which he regards as an exhalation from the earth suspended in the air; although DEMOCRITUS had already asserted it to be a cluster of stars), clouds, fogs, dew, hoar-frost, rain, snow, hail, winds, the formation of rivers, the reciprocal changes of sea and land, the saltness of the sea, the nature of winds, and the influence of sun and stars on them, earthquakes (which are compressed winds), thunder and lightning, the rainbow, and meteors.

On these multiform topics his theories, as may be imagined, are mostly wide of the mark, but they often display remarkable sagacity, and bear the stamp of an earnest investigating mind. The large accumulation of facts is very noticeable; but rather, I think, on account of the attitude of mind which impelled him to make such an accumulation, and to insist with so much emphasis on the value of facts, than, as M. BARTHÉLEMY ST. HILAIRE would have us believe, because the facts themselves display any noticeable sagacity. M. St. Hilaire is at great pains, in his commentary, to point out every occasion on which his hero is correct or approaches correctness in facts; but a little reflection reveals that in the majority of such cases the facts are such as lie open to universal observation, implying no merit therefore in the observer, while in no case have they quantitative precision. It is for its method, rather than for its results, that this treatise is remarkable. I shall, therefore, content myself with this general indication.

§ 128 b. *Book IV.* is more in the nature of a chemical treatise, dealing with the elements and their active and passive principles. The hot and the cold are the active, the moist and the dry are the passive principles. This is clear from their definitions, for we call the hot and the cold active because that which coagulates bodies is certainly an active principle; the moist and the dry are passive because they are limited with ease or with difficulty, according to the modifications impressed upon them. The hot unites the homogeneous and separates the heterogeneous; as may be seen in the fusion of metals. The cold unites the heterogeneous; as we see in ice, which is the union of the heterogeneous materials of water. The moist has no natural limit, but readily accepts a limit; the dry, on the contrary, has a natural limit.

From these two active and two passive principles are derived the four unions corresponding with the elements. Thus, Fire is warm and dry; Air is warm and moist; Water is cold and moist; Earth is cold and dry. Each element has its appointed place. Fire and Earth are the two extremes; they are purer and less mixed than the two intermediates, Air and Water. In the gradual development of these elements, there is an ascent from the imperfect to the more perfect. In Water there is Earth; in Air there is Water; in Fire there is Air.

It is needless to follow him in his explanation of the liquefaction and coagulation of bodies, the fusion of metals, the phenomena of putrefaction and digestion, and the temperature of bodies; although his ideas on these subjects reigned almost without dispute for many centuries. We shall here-

CHAP. VII.] METEOROLOGY, AND MECHANICS. 147

after find more fitting occasions for the display of such ideas. At present we must pass on to the Mechanical problems.

IV.—*The Mechanical Problems.*

§ 129. Although it is certain, from his numerous references, that Aristotle wrote a work called *Problems*, scholars dispute how far the work which now passes under that title is genuine, and how many of the problems, thus collected together, were really written by him. On this dispute I cannot venture to offer an opinion. Nor does the question of authenticity acquire any importance for us, since the work certainly represents peripatetic views, and has always been accepted as Aristotelian.

Most of these problems relate to medical and physiological subjects. Those which relate to Music have been learnedly expounded by CHABANON;[19] those which are usually called "mechanical" have been expounded by POSELGER,[20] who maintains that they are not correctly styled "mechanical," being strictly dialectical. It is certain that Aristotle declares it to be his intention to solve *aporia, i. e.* difficulties; but if this was his intention, and if his solution of these was always dialectical, as POSELGER maintains, we may be permitted a doubt whether this be not as great a deviation from scientific procedure as the attempt, with which WHEWELL reproaches him, to solve mechanical problems geometrically. On this point we may remark that Aristotle could not, had he wished it, have furnished strictly mechanical answers, since mechanical science was not then in existence. It is to ARCHIMEDES we owe the foundation of Statics; to GALILEO the foundation of Dynamics. Aristotle could only solve the difficulties he raised with such means as were ready to his hand; and this he did. The whole collection affords interesting proof of his

---

[19] In the *Mémoires de l'Académie des Inscriptions*, 1793, XLVI.
[20] In the *Abhandlungen der mathematischen Klasse der Academie der Wissenchaften zu Berlin*, 1829.

immense curiosity, his ardent desire to interrogate nature, and the misdirected ingenuity with which he answered his own questions.

§ 130. Although he had no systematic knowledge of mechanical laws, he had gained certain glimpses which now seem surprising. The principle of "virtual velocities" was certainly known to him. This has been denied; but GALILEO himself says that he found it in Aristotle, and doubtless alludes to the following passage:—" The same force will raise a greater weight in proportion as the force is applied at a longer distance from the fulcrum, because it then describes a larger circle; and a weight which is farthest removed from the centre is made to move through the greatest space."

§ 131. He also gained a glimpse of the parallelogram of forces. POSELGER thinks his statement of it superior in elegance and precision to that given by KANT. Yet in spite of this, I must still think that Aristotle only gained a glimpse of the law, as he did of the principle of "virtual velocities," since he failed to see its far-reaching importance, and made little or no use of it. In his hands it never became the instrument which it has proved in modern hands; but was neglected for dialectical distinctions and physical hypotheses.

MONTUCLA speaks with supreme contempt of Aristotle's mathematical insight.[21] I cannot presume to offer an opinion on such a point, but I observe that MONTUCLA is apt to speak contemptuously on very slight grounds. Other authorities are more laudatory.[22] An unbiassed opinion is rare, the servility towards great reputations making men eager to interpret the slightest indications as evidences of mastery. This much, at least, is certain, that Aristotle made no advances in mathe-

---

[21] MONTUCLA: *Histoire des Mathématiques*, Paris, 1758, I., 204.

[22] LIBRI: *Histoire des Sciences Mathématiques en Italie*, Paris, 1838, I., 99, notices, as a fact of the highest interest, and one which has escaped notice, that Aristotle employed "des lettres de l'alphabet pour désigner les quantités indéterminées."

CHAP. VII.] METEOROLOGY, AND MECHANICS. 149

matics, and, while he frequently employed mathematical illustrations, he did not apparently devote to the science the attention devoted to other sciences.

§ 132. Of these Mechanical Problems now under notice, MONTUCLA says that they gained a great reputation in those ages, when, to ensure applause, it was enough for the Stagirite to have spoken; but that this applause will not be bestowed by moderns, who must consider the majority of the answers as entirely false, while the first and principal solution is "tout à fait ridicule."[23] Let us consider this. The problem being how a lever, or balance, of unequal arms, could hold in equilibrium unequal weights or forces. "Aristotle seeks it in the marvellous properties of the circle, of which he makes a puerile enumeration, after which he says it is not surprising that a figure so fertile in marvels should produce one in the equilibrium of equal powers." This criticism has been frequently repeated. It is scarcely just. Aristotle mentions, indeed, the wonderful properties of the circle; but not to draw therefrom his mechanical solution so much as to justify the dialectical nature of the problem.

"Those things," he says, "are wonderful which occur according to nature, but of which the cause is hidden; and those also which are effected by art contrary to nature. When anything is effected contrary to nature it presents a difficulty which requires art ($\delta\iota\grave{\alpha}$ $\tau\grave{o}$ $\chi\alpha\lambda\epsilon\pi\grave{o}\nu$ $\mathring{a}\pi o\rho\acute{\iota}a\nu$ $\pi a\rho\acute{\epsilon}\chi\epsilon\iota$ $\kappa a\grave{\iota}$ $\delta\epsilon\widehat{\iota}\tau a\iota$ $\tau\acute{\epsilon}\chi\nu\eta\varsigma$); and the art which resolves such difficulties we call Mechanics. Of this kind are the means by which great weights are moved by small weights, and all other mechanical problems. These are not quite the same as physical problems; nor very different from them, but pertain to both. Mathematics treat of the formal, Physics of the material. The lever presents difficulties of this kind. For it seems absurd ($\mathring{a}\tau o\pi o\nu$) that a great weight should be moved by a force

[23] MONTUCLA, I., 205.

which is itself added to a great weight. We can easily, with a lever, move a weight which we could not move without one. Of all these cases, the circle contains the principle and the cause, and very naturally, since there is no absurdity in something wonderful being derived from something more wonderful. A combination of opposites is the most wonderful of all, and such a combination is the circle. It is constituted by a stationary point and a moving line, which are contraries in nature, and hence it is not surprising if contraries result."

In this proem he is obviously treating solely of the dialectical nature of the problem. He does not pretend to explain the mechanical effect from the wonderfulness of the circle; *that* is explained by the properties of the lever, with which he was not unacquainted, although it is true that he "perplexed himself with loose and inappropriate notions respecting natural and unnatural movements."[24] He says, "A body at the end of a lever has a natural motion in the direction of the tangent, and an unnatural motion in the direction of the radius. The reason why a force acting at a greater distance from the fulcrum moves a weight more easily, is because it describes a larger circle."

§ 133. It would needlessly occupy great space to go through these problems seriatim; many of them consist simply of questions which he does not attempt to answer. A sample or two must suffice.

In the XXth he moots the question, subsequently discussed by BORELLI, MERSENNE, LEIBNITZ, BERNOUILLI, MACLAURIN and others, touching the difference between pressure and percussion. "Why," he asks, "when we place an axe upon wood, and on the axe place a heavy weight, is the wood but slightly indented; whereas if we raise the axe, without the weight, and strike upon the wood, the wood is split, although the *falling* weight is much less than the *resting and pressing*

---

[24] WHEWELL: *History of the Inductive Sciences*, 1857, I., 61.

weight? Perhaps because everything acts by motion (ἤ διότι πάντα τῇ κινήσει ἐργάζεται); and a weight already in motion takes the motion of another more powerfully than a weight at rest? Hence in this case the resting weight acts with no motion; but when moved, its motion is increased with that of the striker." The mind which has once grasped the conception of the measure of force being as the mass multiplied by the velocity finds no difficulty in understanding why the effect of the axe at rest is so much less than that of the axe in motion. But in Aristotle's day this conception was unsuspected; and he could only detect the general fact that velocity increased the effect.

§ 134. In the XXXIInd he asks: "Why a body in motion is more easily moved than the same body at rest—a rolling carriage being more easily moved than when it first begins to move? Is it because it is more difficult to move a weight in a contrary direction? For some part of the moving power must be lost, even though it be swifter, and the impulse in one direction will be slackened by reaction; this also will be the case when the body is at rest; for that which is at rest resists. When a body is in motion, and receives a new impulse in its own direction, it is as if the force and velocity of the moving body had been increased by so much."

It is evident here that he had not fully understood the law of inertia, since he supposes it is only a body at rest which resists; but he was so near the conception of the law of accelerated motion, that we are the more surprised to find him not detecting the old error of supposing the velocity of falling bodies to be proportional to the spaces.[25]

§ 135. In the XXXIIIrd he asks: "Why does a projectile finally come to rest? Is it because the projecting

---

[25] We shall have to consider this hereafter. Meanwhile the reader may look up GALILEO's masterly refutation. *Dialoghi, Giornata Seconda. Opere*, Milan, 1811, XI., p. 478.

power ceases; or because of the reaction; or because the weight of the body overcomes the projecting force? Or is it absurd to ask such a question, the principle being absent (ἀφέντα τὴν ἀρχήν)?"

§ 135. In the XXXIVth he asks: "Why when a body is not self-moved does it continue moving, when the motor neither follows it, nor acts from a distance? Is it not manifest that the first impulse acts upon another body, and this again upon another, and ceases only when this transference can go no further?" The law of inertia is here entirely disregarded; a proof that Aristotle had no steady conception of the law.

§ 136. One more, and we conclude. "Why cannot we throw a very large nor a very small body, but it is necessary there should be a proportion between the mass and the projecting force? Is it because of the necessary reaction against the impelling force? For that which, owing to its magnitude, does not yield, or, owing to its feebleness, does not resist, cannot be impelled. That which is greater than the impelling force does not move—that which is much less, has no resistance."

§ 137. From this summary of Aristotle's Physics it is abundantly manifest that in spite of his acuteness, and his intense desire for knowledge, he had not mastered the initial conceptions of the science. Not simply deficient in the indispensable requisites of quantitative co-ordinated facts which distinguish Science from Common Knowledge, we find him deficient even in the transcendental postulates of Science. Disputes, but no illumination, could proceed from such postulates as the Contraries, Natural and Unnatural Motions, Up and Down, Heavy and Light. These hampered while they flattered the intellect; preventing the labour of real investigation, by the belief that subjective distinctions represented objective facts. Of what avail was it to learn that besides the four elements, Matter has also its contraries—the hot and the cold, the moist and the dry—these being the principles of generation?

§ 138. Such speculations are condemned to the sterile fecundity of disputation, and carry with them no possible enlightenment. I do not say that Aristotle's efforts were in vain. Far from it. The world is the richer for his genius, the wiser from his failures. But he came at a time when the continuous enployment of the Objective Method was next to impossible. He ploughed the unbroken soil, in which others hereafter were to plant the seeds.

The conclusion forced upon us, therefore, is that the neglect into which his physical speculations have fallen is entirely justified. The present has absolutely nothing to learn from them, except the historical lesson to be gained from the spectacle of a gigantic mind struggling along a hopeless path.

Must we say the same of his biological speculations? Let the following chapters furnish a reply.

CHAPTER VIII.

ARISTOTLE'S ANATOMY.

§ 139. THE eulogies lavished on Aristotle, as a biologist, even by men whose own special knowledge might have made them the severest critics, remind us rather of the tone adopted in the Middle Ages, than of the more circumspect and critical language of our own age. "In Aristotle," says CUVIER,[1] "everything amazes, everything is prodigious, everything is colossal. He lived but sixty-two years, and he was able to make thousands of observations of extreme delicacy, the accuracy of which the most rigorous criticism has never been able to impeach." This rhetorical exaggeration is painfully insincere; no one better than Cuvier could have known the worthlessness of Aristotle's observation on all points which were not open to the common eye; but that servility, too common among Frenchmen, which makes them eager to do homage to every established reputation, made Cuvier forget his own knowledge, and bow his head before the blinding splendour of a great renown.

Little less rhetorical is DE BLAINVILLE, who, though notorious for his love of contradiction, dared not whisper a word against "le grand Stagirite." "It is the Natural Sciences," he says,[2] "which owe the most to Aristotle. His plan was

---

[1] CUVIER: *Histoire des Sciences Naturelles*, 1841, I., 132.
[2] DE BLAINVILLE et MAUPIED: *Histoire des Sciences de l'Organisation*, 1847, I., 212.

vast and luminous; he laid the bases of science which will never perish."

ISIDORE GEOFFROY ST. HILAIRE, speaking from less acquaintance with Aristotle's writings, is splendid in eulogy.³ "He is in every branch of knowledge like a master who cultivated that one only. He reaches, he extends the limits of all the sciences, and penetrates to their very depths."

Our own countrymen have been somewhat soberer, although even they have written very surprising eulogies; one of the most amusing being that of the worthy naturalist, MACGILLIVRAY, who discovers that Aristotle not only collected a mass of facts, but "elicited from them general principles, the accuracy of many of which might surprise us, if we did not reflect that in this department, at least, he followed the true method by which the physical sciences have in our own times received so vast an augmentation." [4]

I have indicated the tone by these examples, partly to justify what might otherwise seem a needless severity in pointing out the deficiences of this wonderful man; and partly also to justify the large space devoted to his biological writings. The summary treatment which sufficed in the case of the Physics would, in the case of Biology, have carried no conviction. The reader was prepared to find the Physics altogether valueless, but he is told that in the department

---

[3] ISIDORE ST. HILAIRE: *Histoire Générale des Règnes Organiques*, 1854, I., 18 seq.

[4] MACGILLIVRAY : *Lives of Eminent Zoologists*, Edinburgh, 1834, p. 32. HERSCHEL has lent his powerful countenance to the applause of Aristotle's accuracy of observation : *Discourse on Natural Philosophy* (101). GRANT also : *Lectures on Comparative Anatomy*, in *Lancet*, October, 1833, p. 90. We shall hereafter see with what justice. Counter-statements may occasionally be met with. BUONAFEDE cites the example of BURNET, who drew up a list of Aristotle's " puerilities " :—" Stati sano' disse 'O Stagirita : tu per me sarai sempre un cattivo astronomo, un teologo peggiore, un pessimo fisiologo."— *Della Storia e della Indole di ogni Filosofià*, II., 289 (ed. of Italian Classics, Milan, 1837). And NIZOLIUS, after quoting the assertion of AVERRHOES, that in 1500 years no error had been detected in the Stagirite, replies "non multo pauciora vel falsa vel inutilia vel etiam ridicula ab eodem scripta reperiri."— *De veris principiis et vera ratione philosophandi*, Parma, 1553, p. 6.

of Natural History, Aristotle made important discoveries, anticipated some of the brilliant results of modern research, and laid the " eternal bases " of the Science. Nothing but a detailed examination would suffice to elicit the truth on such points ; and I shrink the less from entering upon these details, because many of them would necessarily find a place somewhere in this History, and this is as good a place as any.

§ 140. Biology has two grand divisions, statical and dynamical: in common language, Anatomy and Physiology. We have only to reflect how knowledge of the laws of life is necessarily dependent on accurate acquaintance with the structure of living beings, in a word, how Physiology is nothing but "animated Anatomy," as HALLER felicitously called it, to perceive the importance of commencing an examination of Aristotle's biological writings, with a view of his knowledge of structure.

§ 141. The extent of his survey is amazing, embracing the whole animal kingdom, from sea anemones to man. But of the accuracy of his knowledge, I am compelled, after long and minute study, to form a very different estimate from what is current among critics and historians.[5] Reading his works by the light of modern discovery, we are apt to credit him with all that his words suggest to us ; we come, indeed, upon numerous inaccuracies, and on many statements which imply gross carelessness ; but whenever his language does not palpably betray him, modern readers insensibly fill out his hints with details from their fuller store. On a superficial examination, therefore, he will seem to have given tolerable descriptions ; especially if approached with that disposition to discover marvels which unconsciously determines us in

---

[5] *E. g.:*—" Les travaux d'Aristote ont fait cesser en grande partie l'ignorance profonde où l'on était sur la structure animale."—LAUTH: *Histoire de l'Anatomie*, Strasbourg, 1815, I., 61. Yet he proceeds in detail to show that Aristotle really knew very little.

our study of ancient writers. But a more unbiassed and impartial criticism will disclose that he has given no single anatomical description of the least value. All that he knew may have been known, and probably was known, without dissection. The casual revelations of the slaughter-house and battle-field, together with the intimations gathered from auguries and embalmments, probably furnished his knowledge of man and the larger animals. I do not assert that he never opened an animal; on the contrary, it seems highly probable that he had opened many. But I am persuaded that he never *dissected* one in the careful systematic style necessary for more than a general acquaintance with the positions of the chief organs. He never followed the course of a vessel or a nerve; never laid bare the origin and insertion of a muscle; never discriminated the component parts of organs; never made clear to himself the connection of organs into systems.

§ 142. In illustration of what was meant by reading his works in the light of modern discovery, let us take the idea of the homologies of the skeleton, which he is said to have originated in a comparison of the fore and hind limbs. The *analogy* was certainly noticed by him. But it is too obvious to have escaped attention. To make it fruitful, to demonstrate that what seemed to be an *analogy*, really was a *homology*, and expressed an identity of composition in the two limbs, it was necessary that this vague idea should be carried into the comparison of bone with bone, muscle with muscle, nerve with nerve, vessel with vessel. Aristotle as may be supposed never attempted anything like this; nor did any one attempt it, till VICQ D'AZYR; and since then, Homology has become an important branch of anatomical research.[6] When we now read Aristotle's vague

---

[6] VICQ D'AZYR : *Mémoires sur les rapports entre les usages et la structure des quatre extrémités dans l'homme et dans les quadrupèdes*, in his *Œuvres*, 1805, IV., 315. Compare OWEN : *On the Homologies of the Vertebrate*

and meagre account, we read into it all that moderns have taught us.

But if, disengaging the mind from such sources of misconception, we inquire what he really did know, we find it amounts to nothing beyond the result of casual and careless inspection. It would be unfair to compare his observation with that of the patient SWAMMERDAMM, or that of LYONET, who accurately describes the four thousand and forty-one muscles of the caterpillar ;[7] but it is strictly just to compare his observation with that of GALEN, whose anatomical knowledge, imperfect as it was, rested upon careful dissection. On such a comparison, his inferiority is not simply inferiority in degree, it is inferiority in kind.

§ 143. Aristotle knew nothing of the muscles, not even of their existence. He knew very little indeed of two or three nerves, and absolutely nothing of the nervous *system*. He did not distinguish between arteries and veins.[8] Thus the three most important parts of the organism, animal, psychical, and vegetal, were wholly hidden from him. Naturally, the less obvious parts were not better known. According to LAUTH, he described well the structure of men and animals, whenever he could observe the entire body, or the body

---

Skeleton, 1848; where, however, the homologies are merely shown in the bony structure, without reference to the soft parts; and an elaborate memoir by GERVAIS: *Comparaison des membres chez les vertébrés*, in the *Annales des Sciences Naturelles*, 1853, p. 21. Since then M. MARTINS has published a curious and striking memoir in the *Mémoires de l'Acad. de Montpellier*, 1857, III., endeavouring to prove that the humerus is identical with the femur, but twisted 180 deg. on its axis, whereas the femur is straight. "Ainsi les systèmes musculaires, artériels et nerveux du bras et de l'avant bras confirment l'idée d'une torsion de l'humérus, car tous sont disposés comme ils le seraient sur un fémur dont les condyles auraient exécuté un mouvement de rotation de 180 deg., la tête restant immobile fixée dans la cavité cotyloïde."—*Archives Générales de Médecine*, Oct., 1858, p. 481.

[7] LYONET : *Traité anatomique de la chenille qui ronge le bois de saule*, La Haye, 1760, p. 584.

[8] He refuted the old error of the head being the origin of the bloodvessels, and rightly assigned the heart as the origin. THIELMANN: *Veterum opinion. de angiol. atque sang. motu*, 1832, p. 28. He also first distinguished the aorta from the vena cava, but went no further.

opened by incisions; but he was without the art of isolating the organs, and he erred in describing them, because to know them properly, we must begin by dissecting them.[9] It is further noticeable that many of his statements are wholly without foundation, in fact, sometimes even without the superficial appearance of it; and as they could not have originated in misinterpretation of observed appearances, they were probably assumed merely to suit his views.

§ 144. After this, it seems idle to consider the oft-mooted question whether he dissected the human body. If the answer should be affirmative, it would be still more damaging to his reputation, since it would render many of his errors unpardonable. But a close scrutiny of the evidence forces a negative answer; and, as opinions seem to be still divided on the subject,[10] we may here examine the evidence.

§ 145. It is now generally accepted as beyond dispute that

---

[9] CONRINGIUS, who denies that Aristotle dissected man, declares he was most expert in the dissection of animals : " ut animalium omnem rem nemo etiam illo vel fusius vel etiam accuratius prosequutus sit."—*Intro. in artem Medicam*, 1687, p. 147. CASTELLI declares Plato and Aristotle to have been supreme anatomists: " præstantissimos anatomicos fuisse."—*De optimo Medico*, 1637, p. 36. It is needless to cite others ; even glaring errors were either defended because Aristotle had put them forth, or, if refuted, were refuted tenderly.
        E perchè egli è Aristotele, besogna
        Credergli, ancorchè dica la menzogna,
is a couplet quoted by REDI.—*Esperienze intorno alla generazione degl' insetti*, in the Florentine ed. of his *Opuscoli*, 1858, p. 191.

[10] As early as 1687, CONRINGIUS pronounced decidedly against it. " Aristoteli, quamvis in brutorum sectionibus peritissimus fuerit, humani tamen corporis insignem adeo notitiam non habuit, si sane partes internas et in ipso corpore delitescentes spectes."—*Op. cit.*, p. 153. On the other hand, BARCHUSEN: *De Medicinæ origine et progressu*, 1723, after citing two or three examples, says: " Hæc et similia abunde probant Anatomen quoque in hominibus ævo Aristotelis institutam, et non Herophilum, quem Tertullianus false appellat dicterio lanium, qui sexcentos exsecuit," p. 127. HALLER, as cited by HARLES, is of the same opinion, which HARLES: *Geschichte der Hirn-und Nervenlehre im Alterthume*, 1801, p. 56, also adopts. SPRENGEL: *Geschichte der Arzneikunde*, 1821, I., 456, is dubious, but inclined to the affirmative. ANTONIO COCCHI is emphatic in the negative, but advances no evidence.—*Discorso intorno l'Anatomia. Opere*, Milan, 1824, I., 29. PORTAL: *Histoire de l'anatomie et de la chirurgie*, 1770, says, " Il y a toute apparence qu'il n'a jamais disséqué des hommes," I., 41.

his predecessor, HIPPOCRATES, never dissected the human body, and the grounds of this opinion are, first, the known feelings of the Greeks respecting the sacredness of the dead; and secondly, the ignorance of human anatomy exhibited in his works.[11] These are also the grounds for a similar opinion in the case of Aristotle.

I.—*The Feeling of the Greeks.*

§ 146. The laws were very stringent respecting immediate burial. In Athens the Demarch who allowed a corpse to remain a single day unburied was subject to a fine of 1,000 drachmas; and victorious generals had been condemned to death because they neglected to bury the slain. The whole of that tragic masterpiece, the *Antigone*, turns upon the sacredness of the dead, and the necessity, higher than imperial commands, of immediate burial. The popular feeling against dissection remains energetic even in our own day; and in future chapters of our History we shall see the struggles of Science against this horror at the very idea of a human body being violated by the scalpel. With the Greeks this feeling was intensified by their belief that the released soul wandered sadly on the shores of Styx during the whole period that the body remained unburied. It is exceedingly doubtful that Aristotle would have braved such feelings merely for the sake of more accurate knowledge of details; doubtful because his was not a fierce rebellious spirit rising against the prejudices of his age; doubtful because the Asclepiads drew

---

[11] See CONRINGIUS: *Op. cit.*, p. 152. BARCHUSEN: *Op. cit.*, p. 126, considers the point doubtful. HALLER has a little paper in his *Opuscula Anatomica*, Gottingen, 1751, p. 133, entitled, " Quod humana corpora secuerit Hippocrates," in which he argues that Hippocrates dissected man and not monkeys, because monkeys were rare and costly in price, and are nowhere mentioned by him. Yet in his oration, " de Amoenitate Anatomes," in the same volume, p. 330, he says—" Audaciores Græci et ingenio ad inquirendam veritatem excitato, ante tempora Ptolemæi Philadelphi, *aut nunquam aut rarissime* hominum corpora adtigerunt." See the whole question satisfactorily argued by GRUNER: *Analecta ad antiquitates medicas*, 1774, p. 98, seq.

their knowledge of anatomy from animals, and were contented with it;[12] and doubtful because he, who nowhere shows any pressing anxiety about the accuracy of the facts he collects, but is quite willing to accept those ready to his hand, would have wanted the powerful fascination which alone can suppress the shuddering repulsion that keeps men from the dissecting-room.

§ 147. The fascination must be strong, for the disgust is powerful. Our senses are affected by the sickening scent of a corrupting body, by the painful sight of bloodstained instruments, and the scattered shreds of a dismembered corpse. There is also a deeper moral disgust, peculiarly affecting to imaginative minds. The spectacle of death is always accompanied by a certain awe. At the bedside, or on the battlefield, no gazer remains unmoved: pity, and a sense of community in death, steal over every mind when unshaken by violent emotions. How much more painful the dissecting-room, where the corpse is untended by affection, and unpitied by strangers! none of the sanctity of death surrounds it; none of the tenderness of love watches over it; none of the ceremonials of respect defend it. There it lies, naked, and alien alike from affection and respect, flung upon a table in oblivious disregard of its having once been the temple of a human life. It is no longer that temple; it is not even a corpse; it has become a *subject*.

---

[12] While in Rome I read, in EMIL BRAUN's *Handbook of the Ruins and Museums of Rome*, 1856, p. 211, a reference to two anatomical figures in the Vatican sculpture gallery, which afforded "a practical contradiction to the widely diffused opinion that the ancients did not found their knowledge of anatomy on the study of the human body." This sent me to the Vatican with some curiosity. As usual, BRAUN was speaking in utter ignorance. The figures show no science. The skeleton of the thorax is extremely rude; the ribs are all anchylosed. The viscera, exhibited in the second figure, seem to have been modelled from memory, and the memory ill-instructed; the heart is egg-shaped, its position vertical, the apex attached to the diaphragm; there is no aorta; no bronchi; the lungs arise immediately from the larynx; there is no pleura; and, in short, the whole representation is contemptible. If BRAUN is right in his conjecture that these figures, " unique of their kind, were probably originally in some temple of Æsculapius," it says little for the Asclepiads.

Yet all these sources of repulsion have been, and daily are, overcome. Men sit patiently for many hours, inhaling the nauseous odours, exploring with their scalpel the winding intricacies of vein and nerve, steadfast, patient, victorious. They have suppressed the suggestions of the scene by firmly fixing their minds on the object of their task. It is not because their sensibilities have become obtuse, but because their power of abstraction has overcome the solicitations of suggestion. They have not become hardened; they have simply learned to concentrate their thoughts upon a definite pursuit. Were it not for this we might wonder that men did not consent to remain for ever unenlightened on the marvels of their organization, rather than acquire the knowledge by so repulsive a route.[13] But the passion for knowledge is imperious. It urges men to surmount all obstacles, to brave the prejudices of others after suppressing their own—to brave human laws, to rob the grave in the dead of night, and pursue their study in secrecy and peril. This passion furnishes the power of abstraction; and hence it is that anatomy has been pursued by poets, theologians, and even women. GOETHE, for example, a nature of the keenest sensibility, who could not bear to look upon SCHILLER dead, even he was an anatomist. HALLER, one of the great anatomists, was early and late a poet of some mark. BOSSUET was not repelled from the study; he wrote an anatomical tractate. ANNA MANZOLINA made those wax preparations of every part of the body which became the pride of Bologna; and for these she had herself

---

[13] " Sans doute il répugne à l'homme de voir d'aussi près son néant, il fuit ce triste spectacle, et il consent à s'ignorer lui même, plutôt que de s'affliger à la vue de tant de misères."—VICQ D'AZYR: *Œuvres*, IV., 229. " Natura mortis horrorem nobis impressit, et contubernio cadaverum nihil tristius est." HALLER: *De amœnitate anatomes. Opuscula*, 1751, p. 327. " To converse with dead and putrid carcases were, one would think, a shocking and odious employment, yet some anatomists dote upon it: and I must own its usefulness has greatly enamoured me with dissection."—BOYLE: *On the Usefulness of Philosophy. Works*, by SHAW. 1738. I., 5.

held the scalpel, "con virile e forte animo, e con incredibile costanza."[14]

§ 148. But Aristotle, wanting the imperious desire, was little likely to have overcome this repulsion, and still less likely to have braved the prejudices of his contemporaries for an object of which he did not rightly estimate the value. It is true that human dissection was practised in Alexandria some centuries later, under the Ptolemies, and the idea is not, therefore, wholly inadmissible that Aristotle *may* have privately dissected.[15] Not wholly inadmissible, yet wholly without evidence. All the evidence runs counter to it. HIPPOCRATES did not, nor did GALEN, four hundred and fifty years afterwards;[16] yet both Hippocrates and Galen had incomparably more need of such knowledge for their purposes than Aristotle had for his. Although Aristotle never once intimates that he had dissected man, and, as we shall see, his mistakes exclude such a supposition, there is one casual sentence which I have met with that might bear this construction:—in the *De Partibus* (I. 5, 645), defending the study against those who despised it, he says:—" We cannot, without great reluctance, behold the parts of which man is composed, such as blood, flesh, bones, vessels, and the like ; but we must regard them as the

---

[14] MEDICI: *Compendio Storico della Scuola Anatomica di Bologna*, 1857, p. 357.

[15] SPRENGEL suggests that he may have done so in Chalcis.—*Gesch. der Arzneikunde*, 1821, I., 456.

[16] This also has been a disputed point; but I consider it conclusively settled by the testimony of GALEN's editor and translator, DAREMBERG, who says that he has repeated every one of Galen's dissections, which has convinced him that only animals were employed. " Galien répète sans cesse qu'il décrit particulièrement le singe comme étant l'animal le plus voisin de l'homme; son seul tort c'est d'avoir presque toujours conçju du singe à l'homme."—*Œuvres de Galien*, Paris, 1854, I., xiv. The resistance of scholars against this truth, when first published by VESALIUS, is singularly like the resistance of theologians to the revelations of Astronomy and Geology. The Galenists first denied the truth of what VESALIUS affirmed ; when public demonstrations rendered this denial ridiculous, they fled for refuge to two explanations—1st, that the text of Galen was corrupt; 2nd, that the human organism had become different since Galen's days.

architect regards the wood, stones, lime, &c., with which he builds." This would furnish a strong presumption were it not contrary to all the other evidence. As it is, I leave it without attempting to weaken it by another interpretation.

II.—*Special Ignorance.*

§ 149. We have his own confession that the internal anatomy of man is the least known, and must therefore be studied in animals.[17] Although this does not imply that nothing was directly known of the internal parts, it very clearly implies that such knowledge was not to be gained through dissection. And the nature of the mistakes he has made points in the same direction.

Some of these errors may indeed admit of a favourable interpretation; for example, he describes the lungs of man as not double, like those of oviparous animals, but single (μονοφυῆ) like the heart;[18] yet elsewhere he says the lungs are always double, though least so in man.[19] Again when he describes the uterus as double, the error is manifest. It is double in the embryo; double in many animals, such as the hare or rabbit; but even in monkeys there is only a trace, which reveals the original separation into two equal halves. In the human female this trace has disappeared. If Aristotle had ever seen an uterus, how came he to make so obvious a blunder? Two explanations are admissible:—1°, either he means the two ovaries (which are always by him undistinguished from the uterus), to represent this twofold nature; or 2°, the uterus which came under his observation may have been one of the rare specimens of abnormal duplicity; from this he may have concluded that normally the uterus was

---

[17] *Hist. An.*, I., 13, 494. ἄγνωστα γάρ ἐστι μάλιστα τὰ τῶν ἀνθρώπων, ὥστε δεῖ πρὸς τὰ τῶν ἄλλων ζῴων ἀνάγοντας σκοπεῖν.

[18] *De Partibus*, III., 7, 669.

[19] *Hist. An.*, I., 13, 495.

double. I think, however, it is more probable that he had never seen one at all; and that his statement is simply an *à priori* conclusion. He thought the uterus was the analogue of the testes, and these being double, the uterus must also be double.[20]

§ 150. Some other statements do not admit such palliation. What are we to think of the assertion that the heart lies higher than the lungs, above them, ἀνωτέρω τοῦ πλεύμονος, where the trachea bifurcates?[21] Could he ever have seen the human kidney, which he describes as *lobed* like that of an ox?[22] It is no answer to say that the kidneys are lobed in the foetus;[23] since all trace of the lobular form disappears about the fifth month, and he is not likely to have examined a foetus younger than this; moreover, he distinctly states it of the adult, not the foetus.

§ 150 *a*. His description of the spleen is inaccurate, though not so glaringly inaccurate as that of the kidney. VESALIUS notices the error of attributing only eight ribs to man, as a proof that he was not speaking from direct inspection.[24]

§ 150 *b*. He speaks of the heart having only three chambers; whereupon LAUTH remarks that he only judged of its structure from the external aspect:[25] an error, since he mentions its septa and its tendons. Those who maintain

---

[20] *De Gen. An.*, I., 3, 716.
[21] *Hist. An.*, I., 14, 495. *De Part.*, III., 6, 669.
[22] *De Part.*, III., 9. 671.
[23] " Je l'ai vu quelquefois formé de huit, plus souvent de six, ou de quatre petits reins de chaque côté."—SERRES: *Précis d'Anatomie transcendante*, 1824, p. 101. It is amusing to find BARCHUSEN apparently citing this very case of the kidney as a proof of Aristotle having dissected man.—*De Medicinæ Origine*, 1723, p. 127, note.
[24] VESALIUS: *Opera Omnia*, ed. BOERHAAVE and ALBINUS, 1725, p. 76. SONNENBURG: *Zoologisch-Kritische Bemerkungen zu Aristot. Thiergeschichte*, Bonn, 1857, p. 5, adopts the convenient hypothesis of a corrupt text in this case, although he knows that the error was repeated by PLINY.
[25] LAUTH: *Histoire de l'Anatomie*, 1815, I., 62. There is an amusing note on this point in the commentary of BLAZIUS to WESSLING'S *Syntagma Anatomicum*, Amsterdam, 1666, p. 150.

that he must have practised human dissection, refer to his mention of the heart not being vertically placed, but inclining a little to the left (§ 898). But we learn from GALEN that this was the vulgar opinion, derived, as he says, from the fact that the beating of the heart is felt under the left breast.[26]

§ 150 c. But perhaps the climax of inaccuracy is to be found in what he says of the brain, namely that it is *bloodless*, and that it does not extend to the back part of the skull, "which is quite empty"—assertions several times repeated. Without insisting on the fact that more blood goes to the brain than to almost any other organ[27] (which Aristotle had no means of knowing), it is enough to say that casual inspection of an uncooked brain reveals the presence of abundant blood, even the white matter being studded with red spots.[28] But in the cooked brain (or in the brain of fish) no such appearance presents itself; whence we conclude that he had never seen the human brain, since he could not have seen it cooked, and in the fresh state its blood is apparent.[29] As to the surprising and unintelligible assertion that there is no brain in the back part of the skull, if it does not prove, as PORTAL remarks,

---

[26] GALEN: *De usu Partium, lib.* VI., ch. 2, p. 415, ed. KUHN, 1822. This opinion he considers to be erroneous, a clear proof that he had not dissected the human body. It should be noted that GALEN conceived the heart as having only two chambers, the ventricles; the auricles were regarded merely as accessories. See DAREMBERG: *Œuvres de Galien*, I., 400.

[27] One-fifth of the whole amount, according to the estimate of HALLER : *Elementa Physiologiæ*, Lausanne, 1762, IV., 141 ; and one-third, according to MALPIGHI: *De Cerebro*, p. 6 in *Opera Omina*, 1686.

[28] " Dum cerebri portiones abscindis, ait, ex Plempio, Mœbius, p. 592, adverte guttulas et punctula sanguinis, in cerebri substantia, et disce Aristotelem non vera docere dum scribit cerebrum nihil venarum in se continere."— BLAZIUS : *in comment. Wessling Syntagma*, p. 214. In his anxiety to defend the Stagirite from so gross an error, BLAZIUS adds: " Ast qua ratione probabunt arterias non æque sanguinem hunc exhibere in dissecto tali cerebro quam venas."

[29] " Donde si raccoglie che Aristotele non anatomizzò mai alcun cadavere umano, e che la sua notomia e la sua crudizione nella storia degli animali fu molto sotto il mediocre."—BUONAFEDE: *Della Istoria e della indole di ogni filosofia*, Milan, 1837, II., 209.

that he had never opened a skull;[30] it proves that he observed carelessly.

§ 150 d. Examples of this glaring kind have been chosen, because mistakes which casual inspection would have prevented are more illustrative than any enumeration of errors on obscurer points. They prove that Aristotle could never have dissected a human subject, perhaps had never seen one laid open; or else they prove that his inspection was careless, his memory treacherous, and his anatomical knowledge extremely superficial.

§ 151. Nevertheless he is said to have made discoveries, and we even read that he first discovered the nerves. The learned HARLES, in his valuable contributions to the history of ancient neurology,[31] has satisfactorily shown that no anatomist before Aristotle had the slightest knowledge of the nerves; no one seems to have suspected the existence of such organs. Every one of the passages which later writers (GALEN included) have cited, prove on close inspection that the words νεῦρον and τὰ νεῦρα refer to tendons, ligaments, aponeuroses, or even muscles, and never mean nerves.

This misleading use of the word was continued long after it had come to be applied to the structures now designated as nerves. GALEN did not escape the confusion, and his successors forgot altogether the original use of the term.[32] It

---

[30] PORTAL: *Histoire d'Anat. et de la Chirurgie*, 1770, I., 42. SCALIGER attempts to palliate this by saying, " tametsi multa medulla est in quibusdam, caput iis magnum adeo, ut inanis esse cavitas videatur;" but SONNENBURG, in citing this passage in his *Zoologish-Kritische Bemerkungen zu Aristoteles Thiergeschichte*, Bonn, 1857, p. 9, truly says that Aristotle expressly declares it to *be* and not to *seem* empty. Moreover, in point of fact, it does not seem empty. SONNENBURG's defence is that by the back part of the head Aristotle meant the neck. It is possible that by ἰνίον neck was meant; but this does not render the passage less inaccurate. The neck is not more empty than the skull.

[31] HARLES: *Versuch einer Geschichte der Hirn-und-Nervenlehre*, 1801, 20-54.

[32] VESALIUS notices the mistake : *Opera*, 1725, p. 13; and KÖHLER: *Aristoteles de Molluscis cephalopodibus*, 1820, p. 4, remarks that even in our own time tendons and nerves have been mistaken for each other, alluding to the tendinous filaments which surround the œsophagus of the Holothuriæ, and which SPIX and others have supposed to be nerves; the real nervous system discovered by MÜLLER lies above these.

still exists in the common language of metaphor. We speak of a nervous arm, nervous courage, and a man of nerve, an unnerved condition, "hardy as the Nemæan lion's nerve."

§ 152. In commencing our inquiry therefore we must begin by distinctly recognizing the fact that when Aristotle uses the word νεῦρον he does not mean nerve;[33] otherwise we shall fall into the error of GALEN, frequently repeated by successors, of attributing to Aristotle the very gross absurdity of deriving all the nerves from the heart.[34] If therefore it be true, as affirmed, that he is the first anatomist by whom the nerves were mentioned, by what name are we to recognize them? By that of πόροι or *ducts* (tubes, canals), this term being employed by him to designate the optic, olfactory, and auditory nerves. GALEN is in error when he attributes this to EUDEMUS and HEROPHILUS.[35]

The word is noticeable; but let not the reader jump to the conclusion that it indicates any knowledge on Aristotle's part of the tubular structure of nerves, first described by LEEUWENHOEK, and made familiar to all Europe by EHRENBERG.[36]

---

[33] See this point conclusively settled in PHILIPPSON: ὕλη ἀνθρωπίνη, Berlin, 1831, p. 12; in HARLES: *Op. cit.*, 65; and in SPRENGEL, I, 456. There are, indeed, a few passages where the word νεῦρον correctly indicates a nerve; but it is evident that in these he mistook the real nature of the part indicated.

[34] An absurdity which CÆSALPINUS undertook to defend: *Peripateticarum quæstionum*, Venice, 1571, *lib. V.*, ch. 3, p. 106, scornfully noticed by TAURELLUS in his attack on Cæsalpinus: *Alpes Cæsæ*, 1650, p. 864. SOMMERING set up the defence that Aristotle wished to indicate "cor mediante cerebro nervorum principium esse:" *De basi encephali*, 1778, p. 8. GALILEO tells a story of having been present when a Venetian anatomist demonstrated that the origin of the nerves was in the brain and not the heart, and then demanded of an Aristotelian what he had to say; whereupon the philosopher, after a pause, replied, "Voi mi avete fatto veder questa cosa talmente aperta, e sensata, che quando il testo d'Aristotele non fusse in contrario, che apertamente dice i nervi nascer dal cuore, bisognerebbe per forza confessarla per vera." — *Opere*, Milan, 1811, XI., 265.

[35] *De libris propriis*, chap. III., cited by DAREMBERG.

[36] LEEUWENHOEK: *Select Works*, II., 303. EHRENBERG: *Beobachtung einer bisher unbekannten Structur des Seelenorgans* in the *Abhandlungen der Akad. der Wissenschaften zu Berlin*, 1834, p. 665. In this memoir Aristotle is credited with the discovery of three cerebral nerves; but no mention is made of his having called them tubes.

On the contrary, he probably observed the readiness with which the semifluid contents can be pressed out of the tough neurilemma, and hence concluded that the nerves were ducts.[37] The tubular structure, of which moderns speak, is that of the seemingly solid fibres which compose the nerves; and this is visible only under the microscope.

§ 153. Although it is certain that Aristotle first called attention to the existence of the nerves which have their origin at the base of the brain, it is very far from certain that he had any suspicion of their being special structures, differing from all other ducts; and it is indisputable that he never classified them with the other nerves. I am therefore disposed to accept the view of PHILIPPSON, that πόροι never meant organs tantamount to "nerves," but simply brain-ducts, in nowise discriminated from other ducts, except by their position.[38] We find the word duct used for the channel of any fluid except blood; it even designates the ureter and the intestine. But I have sought in vain for any intimation that these brain-ducts were special structures. If, therefore, on the one hand, πόρος is a word of very general signification, and, on the other, no special signification is assigned to it when used to designate the optic and olfactory nerves, how can we credit Aristotle with the discovery of these nerves? He described the course of these ducts, not accurately indeed,

---

[37] The idea of the optic nerves being tubes, or ducts, was accepted by AVICENNA and ROGER BACON. I am not aware at what period it was relinquished. VESALIUS declares that he can establish no difference between nerves founded on their being hollow, since he had never yet seen one that was so. —*Opera*, ed. Boerhaave and Albinus, p. 361. In spite of this the opinion continued, and even in WESSLING's *Syntagma*, 1666, the optic nerve is said to be more porous than any other, p. 220. Comp. FABRICIUS ab AQUAPENDENTE : *Opera Omnia*, 1738, I., 193. WILLIS : *Opera Omnia*, Geneva, 1676, I., 111, has no mention of ducts.

[38] PHILIPPSON: ὕλη ἀνθρωπίνη, p. 15-21. TRENDELENBERG also says: "Medici πόρους nervos esse volunt . . . sed ab Aristotele tam angustis terminis circumscripti non sunt. Ductus enim sunt, ut quicunque est finis, conjunctionem et quasi partium commercium adjuverit."—Notes to his ed. of the *De Animâ*, 1833, p. 162. Comp. *ibid.*, p. 396.

but sufficiently to establish his claim to *this* discovery; but he never suspected the part they played in vision and smelling. He thought the optic duct *nourished* the eye.[39] This settles the question. In like manner, although he describes the olfactory and auditory nerves, there is overwhelming proof that he did *not* suppose them to be connected with smelling and hearing.[40]

We conclude, then, that although he knew something of the anatomical distribution of three of the nerves, he knew absolutely nothing of the nervous system; and as he likewise knew very little of the viscera, and of the muscular system nothing,[41] it is clear that his anatomical knowledge was too slight and inaccurate to serve as the basis of sound physiology.

---

[39] *De Gen. An.*, II., 6; PHILIPPSON: *Op. cit.*, 18; HARLES: *Op. cit.*, 113. ROGER BACON says, " nervus tamen iste in quo est hæc via humoris vitrei se diffundit."—*Opus Majus*, p. 203.

[40] HARLES confesses this. Comp. also PHILIPPSON, p. 19.

[41] FABRICIUS ab AQUAPENDENTE was one of the first to make this evident. —*Opera Anatomica*, p. 383.

CHAPTER IX.

ARISTOTLE'S PHYSIOLOGY.

§ 154. To explain the phenomena of Life, without having previously mastered the facts of anatomy, is as hopeless as to attempt an explanation of the action of a watch, in ignorance of springs, escapements, and wheels, merely from seeing it wound up, and hearing it tick. Nothing but vague unassured guesses can be formed. Of this kind is the physiology of Aristotle. All the complex phenomena which are still but imperfectly explained, even now that anatomy is accurately and extensively studied, aided by the minute researches of chemists and physicists, were by him interpreted from superficial observation and *à priori* theories. Observation was necessarily incomplete; the broad gaps left, instead of being filled up by patient research, were bridged over by considerations of Final Causes, or by analogies often fanciful, never verified. Here, as elsewhere, we find him wholly wanting in the vigilance required for testing the accuracy of the data from which he reasoned; and very often employing great ingenuity in attempting to explain a fact which did not exist. We shall meet with many examples; but the following is amusing no less than instructive.

§ 155. " If a woman, suffering from scarlet fever," he says, " look at herself in a mirror, the surface of the mirror will become suffused with a kind of bloody mist;[1] and this mist, if the mirror be quite new, cannot be rubbed off without difficulty." This was doubtless one of the old woman's tales current in his day. He never thought of ascertaining the truth of the statement, but proceeded to explain it, which he does in various ways. "The cause," he says, "is that the eye not only receives the impressions from without, but reacts upon external objects, setting them in motion. The eye is full of blood-vessels, and during the fever, the blood being in commotion and inflammation, the eye, though we cannot detect it, is agitated and feverish; the air is moved by this, and conveys the motion to the surface of the mirror. The polished surface of the mirror is very sensitive to all motions, and hence they become visible upon it."

§ 156. Having gained this glimpse into his mode of interpretation, let us briefly review his opinions on the chief vital phenomena.

The obvious facts of the conversion of food into blood, and of blood into the substance of the body, were early known. But neither the anatomical nor the chemical knowledge necessary to our approximate theory of Digestion were familiar to him; consequently, he did not even suspect the order of changes which are impressed upon food in the mouth, the stomach, and the intestines; still less did he know the influence of the liver, spleen, and lungs, in the final elaboration of the food. He thought that the food passed into the stomach, and was there *cooked* by the animal heat. He understood that food must become liquid before it is assimilable, since blood is its final product. Food is made liquid

---

[1] γίνεται τὸ ἐπιπολῆς τοῦ ἐνόπτρου οἷον νεφέλη αἱματώδης.—*De Insomniis*, II., 459. In the original the occasion is not scarlet fever; the variation, however, leaves the argument unaffected. The idea is repeated, and, as usual, exaggerated by PLINY: "Acrescunt superventu musta, sterilescunt tactæ fruges, moriuntur insita, exuruntur hortorum germina, et *fructus arborum quibus insedere, decidunt*."—*Hist. Nat.*, *VII.*, 13. Even the more sceptical ROGER BACON accepts the notion.—*Opus Majus*, Venet., 1750, p. 65.

in the stomach and intestines, and this liquid *steams up* through the small vessels of the mesentery, which lead to the larger vessels, and thence to the heart: *there* it ceases to be ichor, and becomes blood. Nature acts like an economist, giving the best parts of the food to the noblest parts of the body; as the freemen eat the prime portions, the slaves eat the inferior portions, and the rest is thrown to the dogs, so the nobler organs—flesh and the senses—receive the sweetest, and the baser organs—bones, hair, &c.—receive the bitterest parts. He suspected that the liver and spleen played some part in digestion, but what part he never distinctly stated.

From the heart the veins carry the cooked blood to every part of the body. The veins become smaller and smaller, until they are too small for the passage of the blood; through these, therefore, it can find no egress, only the excretion of moisture (τῆς ὑγρᾶς ἰκμάδος) which we call sweat (ἰδρῶτα), and this especially when the body is warmed and the veins open wider (§ 476).

This latter statement reads very like the modern idea of the blood parting with certain of its principles which ooze through the walls of the capillaries; but such was not really his meaning. He knew nothing of the blood gushing through these capillaries and returning to the heart. He imagined that the vessels terminated in the flesh, and there the blood became flesh. Nor is this idea quite banished yet. Many physiologists imagine—or speak as if they imagined—that the organs are formed *by* the blood; whereas embryology discloses that many organs exist before the blood has appeared. Instead of saying that the organs are formed by the blood, we ought to say they are nourished by it. They draw their material from the organic plasma; and blood, when once it has appeared, is carried by this plasma. It is equally true to reverse the proposition, and say the organs form the blood, since blood is affected by two different influences, one impressed by nutritive material, and one by the organs through which it passes.

§ 157. Although the vascular system was altogether misconceived by him, yet the manifest importance of the blood leads us to expect to find all his theories having an intimate dependence on the heart, which he regarded as the centre of Life, Sensation, Motion, and Heat. It is the great cooking apparatus.[2] The blood, in being cooked, causes an expansion, or steaming, which makes the heart expand, and with it the chest expands. Into the space thus formed the cold air rushes, and by its coldness contracts the chest, which again contracts the heart. These alternate expansions and contractions cause the pulsation of the heart and bloodvessels. The blood is always formed in the heart, never returns there, but is converted into flesh, fat, bones, &c.

As the great source of Heat, the heart must also be the great source of Motion, for heat is motive. Moreover, it is full of tendons, and it is the tendons which move the limbs.

That Aristotle should have made the heart the origin of the tendons (νεῦρα) is a striking example of theoretical anatomy in flagrant contradiction with even casual inspection.

§ 158. On Respiration he has written a separate treatise. In it he complains that his predecessors left unasked the question *why* animals breathe, or else answered it from very insufficient observation. He notices the common error of supposing that all animals respire—an error, by the way,

---

[2] " The *diastole*, or dilatation, is made by the blood boyling or swelling by the *spirits* within it : and so Aristotele's opinion concerning the pulsation of the heart (namely, that it is made by a kinde of ebullition,) is in some sort true. For as in milk set upon fire, and in beere, we see dayly a fermentation, working, or intumescence; so is it in the pulse of the heart, in which the blood, as by a kinde of fermentation work'ng up is distended, and then ebbs or falls down againe."—HARVEY: *Anatomical Exercitations concerning the Generation of Living Creatures*, 1653, I.I., p. 276. By SWAMMERDAMM this idea of the heart as a great cooking centre was retained unhesitatingly. He thought the blood which returned to the heart was that which had not been competent to nourish the body, and returned to be re-cooked—*um aufs neue gekocht zu werden.*— *Bibel der Natur.*, 1752, p. 54 (written a century earlier).

from which few moderns are free—an error which arises from the latitude given to the word "Respiration," used not to designate the act of breathing—an act compounded of two distinct yet dependent processes, inspiration and expiration— but to designate the ultimate fact of an exchange of gases taking place between the blood and the atmosphere. It is superfluous to say that *this* was unknown to Aristotle; the existence of gases was unsuspected. But had he known it, he would have been justified in protesting against the confusion of this *general property* possessed by *all* living tissues, of exchanging carbonic acid for oxygen, with the *special function* of respiration possessed only by a respiratory apparatus of organs. It is only by an abusive laxity of language that we apply one term to acts so markedly distinct as:— 1. The inspiration and expiration of air, in animals with lungs. 2. The muscular movements which wash the gills with water, in some animals with branchiæ. 3. The simple bathing of the whole surfaces with air or water in all other animals.

It is true that in all three, the ultimate fact is the aëration of the nutritive fluid; the exchange of carbonic acid for oxygen. But this *community of end* does not efface the *differences in the functions* by which it is attained. Aristotle knew that there was a community of end, which he thought was a cooling process; and difficult as it is to draw absolute lines of demarcation he was on the whole justified in asserting that Respiration belonged only to animals with lungs. "If fish breathe," he says, "they must expire the air at the same moment that they draw in the water—which is absurd." He thought that no air entered the fish's body: an error, but his proof was not contemptible. If you place an animal under water, he says, bubbles of air will rise. Now, as none rise from fish, it is evident that they contain no air. The existence of air in the water, and the passage of the oxygen from that air into the blood, were unknown to him. GALEN, who knew that the water contained air, also knew that the gills supplied the place of lungs; the little holes, which he supposed them to have, admitted the passage of air, though excluding the water.[3]

If we regard Aristotle's theory of respiration historically, it is admirable. Indeed, no important improvement was made on it until the discovery of the circulation changed the whole aspect of the problem, which the discovery of the gases was still further to modify.[4]

§ 158 a. He thought that the fact of fish dying when removed from the water into the air was a proof that they did not breathe, since they gape like suffocated animals. DIOGENES explained this as due to the fact that fish out of water receive too much air, whereas in the water they have no more than is needful. This Aristotle calls a foolish explanation, and adds, that were it true, we should observe it of terrestrial animals; but who ever saw an animal suffocated because it had too much air?[5] Men fall into such

---

[3] GALEN: *De Usu Partium*, VI., 9, 443, ed. KUHN.

[4] Up to the time of HARVEY the theory remained undisturbed, as may be seen in FABRICIUS ab AQUAPENDENTE: *De Respiratione et ejus instrumentis*, Opera, 1738, p. 161. The absurd criticisms of SEVERINUS: *Antiperipatias de respiratione piscium diatriba*, 1661, shows the immense superiority of the Stagirite. In spite of GALEN and RONDELET (who had shown that fish breathe the air in the water), we find CARDAN, the most learned physician of his age, declaring most positively that fish do not breathe air.—*De varietate rerum*, Lugduni, 1580, *lib. VII.*, cap. xxxvii., p. 289. (The elaborate and interesting work by MORLEY: *The Life of Cardan*, 1854, presents a curious picture of the literary life at that period.)

[5] The reason why fish die out of water is still awaiting an answer. I instituted numerous experiments which disproved the explanation propounded by FLOURENS, namely, that the weight of the leaflets composing the gills differs but slightly from that of water, so that the least movement suffices to float them, by which their surfaces are thoroughly bathed with water. In the air the difference between the weight of the leaflets and that of the air causes the gills to collapse; thus, instead of the leaflets floating free in the air, they are pressed together, and thus an insufficient amount of blood gets aërated: *Annales des Sciences Naturelles*, 1830, p. 5. This, however, is only *one* cause. When I kept the leaflets separated, and their whole surfaces exposed to the air, the fish died almost as rapidly as before; but when I suffered the gills to collapse, and prevented the rapid evaporation from the whole surface of their bodies, the fish lived three times longer than similar fish unprotected. Dr.

errors, he says, because they disregard internal structure, and do not ask what is nature's aim in all she does.

§ 159. Having argued that Life cannot exist without a certain amount of warmth which is necessary for digestion, and that the seat of this source must be the centre, or heart, he remarks that when heat is intense it consumes itself; therefore for its preservation a certain cooling opposition is indispensable. Respiration is the cooling process. Air is best adapted for it, because its lightness enables it to penetrate where water could not find an entrance.[6] This is his teleological explanation; nor is the anatomical explanation much more satisfactory. The air rushes in when the chest expands, but how the air gets from the lungs, which he compares to bellows, into the heart is far from clear. He says that this mechanism is described in another work. I can find no description in the works extant. In one place he says the windpipe goes to the heart; yet elsewhere he rightly says it bifurcates on its entrance into the lungs.

§ 160. He has also written a special treatise on Animal Movements. But when we consider that he was ignorant of nerves and muscles, it is apparent that all his explanations must have wanted a basis.[7] Accordingly in all that he has

---

McDonnell, in his valuable paper on the *Habits and Anatomy of the Lepidosiren* ("Journal of the Royal Dublin Society," 1860), mentions that his Lepidosiren managed to live for seventy-five days out of water, because the slough it secreted prevented the evaporation from the surface of its body. It has lungs, however. Eels live a long while out of water, because their bodies are covered with a mucus which retards evaporation.

[6] Comp. GALEN: *De usu Partium*, VI., 2; and TELESIUS: *De natura rerum*, Naples, 1586, lib. VI., p. 238.

[7] FABRICIUS ab AQUAPENDENTE has argued this point decisively.—*De musculi actione*, p. 400. MEYER: *Aristoteles Thierkunde*, 1855, says FABRICIUS is in error when he attributes to Aristotle the hypothesis of the pneuma moving the bones through the arteries. Yet see § 161. It was distinctly the opinion of TELESIUS: *De natura rerum*, V., 197. ROULIN has given an instructive sketch of the successive hypotheses, in his *Recherches théoriques et expérimentales sur le mécanisme des mouvements* in MAJENDIE'S *Journal de Physiologie*, 1821, I., 209. Long after muscular contractility was discovered, the belief in animal spirits, as necessary to excite that contractility, remained till it was replaced by the

written on this subject there is no attempt at an explanation of the *mechanism* of motion, nothing is said which was not Common Knowledge. There is metaphysical and psychological argument, but no anatomy, no physiology. He says the animal never moves but for some end, its motives being intelligence and instinct; it is always some good which is sought. Appetite says: drink is necessary; sense or reason says: this is drinkable; and we drink. It is with us absolutely as with automata, which move by a very slight movement of their springs which act on other springs. The organs by which animals move are the tendons and bones; these represent the springs and wood of the automata. There is, however, this difference: In the automata the parts are incapable of internal modification, and their action is fatal; but the parts of animals are capable of great modification; the same part may become larger or smaller, and its form may change, under the influence of heat and cold, or some internal cause. Imagination or thought may modify them. The idea of cold or heat, of pleasure or pain, is thus almost the same as the reality: we tremble at the very thought of certain objects.

§ 161. All motion has its origin in the soul, and the agent which is intermediate between soul and body is the pneuma, or spirit, which is placed in the heart. He says that he has elsewhere explained his views on the pneuma; unhappily none of the extant works throw much light on it. He says, however, that it is by nature peculiarly fitted to cause movement.[8]

§ 162. To the vast and important class of phenomena grouped under the sensorial functions, his attention had naturally been much directed; but here again the anatomical basis was wanting. He had not mastered the initial discovery

---

"nervous fluid," which was replaced by "nervous force," or—as I have proposed to call it—*neurility*. TELESIUS was fully aware of the marvel of heavy limbs being moved by so slight a spirit, *tantulus spiritus;* but threw the marvel upon Infinite Wisdom.—*Op. cit.*, p. 197.

[8] Comp. MEYER in preceding note.

that the nervous system formed the sensorial mechanism. Departing from the route which HIPPOCRATES had at least opened, though not with much success, in assigning to the brain the faculty of sensation, Aristotle, on purely *à priori* grounds, placed the seat of sensation in the heart because it was in the centre of the body. He thought it was only because the chief organs of sense are in the head that some philosophers supposed the brain to be the seat of sensation. One argument against such a supposition is that the brain itself is insensible.[9] The heart is in the noblest position, the centre, and must, therefore, have the noblest function; and its relation to the nutritive soul proves it to be the organ of sensation.[10]

§ 163. Having on these grounds assigned this function to the heart, it is noticeable that he never attempts to demonstrate the connection between the heart and the organs of sense, or the phenomena of sensation. It is true that he says "all the senses pass through ducts, πόροι, to the heart;" but he does not show this. The senses of Touch and Taste he asserts to be visibly in connection with the heart: a puzzling assertion which admits, I think, of this theoretical vindication—Touch is the universal sense, possessed even by animals which possess no other; it is consequently directly connected with the Vital Principle, of which the heart is the centre. Taste is the sense next in universality, and for a like reason it must have a direct connection with the heart, which he styles the Acropolis of the body.

---

[9] This is insisted on by CÆSALPINUS: *Peripateticarum Quæstionum*, 1571, lib. V., quæst. 3 and 6. That the brain is the seat of sensation, he says, would be said by none, " nisi is qui crassè hæc contempletur," p. 107. We shall hereafter consider this difficulty (§ 385).

[10] ROGER BACON reconciles the two opinions respecting the seat of the soul, by saying that the sensitive soul has two instruments: one, the heart, being radical and fontal; the other, the brain, being that which is first affected by the Visible Species, and which first distinguishes the operation of the senses. He quotes AVICENNA to a similar effect.—*Opus Majus*, p. 196.

We may also notice that although he argues against the brain as the seat of sensation because it is insensible, he never undertakes to show that the heart is more sensible. The truth is that the *à priori* argument derived from the nobleness of a centre was the argument which coerced his conviction.

§ 164. Since he overlooked the real functions of the brain, we may ask what functions he assigned to it. The answer will probably raise a smile: he declared it was a moderator: its coolness, "for it is the coldest part of the body," serves to temper the great heat of the heart-region. Hence it has no blood sent to it; only to the enveloping membranes is a small quantity sent, in order to temper its coolness. Hence also bloodless animals have no brains, since their moderate heat requires no cooling. GALEN justly criticises this notion of the brain serving to cool the heart; and he also expresses his surprise at Aristotle's opinion that the brain is cold.[11]

It is interesting to consider how the idea was arrived at.[12] Clearly it was not through direct observation, since he had no means of measuring temperature in living animals, and if he judged simply by the touch, the dead brain would not be colder than the liver or kidney. If not arrived at through direct observation, it must have been from *à priori* considerations; thus, believing the brain to be bloodless, he concluded it was cold. (§ 384.)

§ 165. From this survey of the chief vital phenomena we discern that Aristotle's physiology was entirely the physiology of conjecture; it was without one single solid stone to serve as a foundation for future discovery. In the presence of such a result, we ask with surprise, how it comes to pass that biologists of renown can have affirmed that Aristotle laid the

---

[11] GALEN: *De usu Partium*, VIII., 3.

[12] See JOHN DAVY: *Researches Physiological and Anatomical*, 1839, I., 157, for some attempts to estimate the temperature of the brain; but as the experiments were performed on animals recently killed and decapitated, the results are only approximative.

eternal bases of their science, and that his writings are still authoritative to discerning minds. Surely the bases of Biology are to be sought in Anatomy and Physiology? Yet these were entirely unknown to him.

Although I have met the affirmation of enthusiastic eulogists by a confrontation with fact, which may seem to press somewhat hardly against Aristotle, the wish to be perfectly equitable makes me help to restore the balance by pointing out the philosophical generalities which he enunciated, and which arrest the attention of modern students. This will occupy the next chapter.

CHAPTER X.

GENERAL PRINCIPLES OF BIOLOGY.

§ 166. THAT which first led me to study Aristotle's scientific writings was the thrill of surprise on meeting with certain passages seeming to prove that he had arrived at general principles which modern biologists estimate among the most precious results of philosophic speculation. This surprise, and the admiration consequent upon it, were heightened on my learning that not only had he at one bound reached the summits of speculation, but had also actually anticipated some of the startling discoveries of our times. Thus both in speculation and observation he had shown himself a master and a forerunner.

This was my experience; and it is reasonable to presume that it is not unallied to the experience of those eminent investigators who have spoken of Aristotle in terms of extravagant eulogy. In the next chapter we shall have to consider in how far moderns really have been anticipated by the observations of Aristotle. For the present we confine ourselves to the philosophical generalities.

§ 167. There is no disputing the fact that several modern speculative views are to be found very clearly expressed in his writings. But it may reasonably be doubted whether these always had the same significance to him as they have to us;

and the ground of this doubt is chiefly that he did not make the same application of them, nor did he insist upon their importance as luminous guides. An example has already been given (§ 142) in the supposed perception of homologies. Another may be seen in the so-called "law of economy"[1] which declares that Nature everywhere gives to one part what she takes from another. This law, which GEOFFROY ST. HILAIRE fancied was his own discovery,[2] and which he entitled *la loi du balancement des organes*, is very questionable, and would require a vast amount of detailed proof. Aristotle's applications are few and not successful. Thus, he says, Nature cannot give the Bear a tail, because she has used up the earthy material in covering his body with hair; and although there are other hairy animals with tails, yet the law of economy still prevails, since these animals with tails are without flesh on their legs. He overlooks the large amount of bone which coats the cartilaginous plates, when he says "the cartilaginous fish are without bones, because the thickness of their skins has exhausted all the available earthy matter."

§ 168. Another consideration is to be held in view. In the History of Science, as in the growth of an individual mind, it sometimes happens that the earlier speculations are nearer the truth than those which succeed them; accordingly we find certain old ideas which had been discarded as erroneous are reinstated by completer knowledge. On many points we find ourselves, after long wanderings, returned to the ancient starting-place, resuming the forsaken position; but if we occupy this position anew, it is with very different armaments, and we are in no danger of being dislodged by the

---

[1] *De Partibus*, I., 9, 655.
[2] First vaguely expressed in his *Philosophie Anatomique*, 1818, p. 456. It had, however, been explicitly stated by GOETHE in 1807. See his work: *Zur Morphologie*. It was afterwards well stated by BICHAT: *Recherches sur la Vie et la Mort*, 1829, p. 218.

first assailant. The early thinkers sometimes had a correct general view simply because they had not sufficient knowledge of details to obscure the view, or to open another. With fuller knowledge arose many difficulties; in trying to find a pathway through these, the seekers wandered from the old road. We are warranted therefore in questioning the profundity of an ancient speculation, unless it can be shown to have been formed from ample details, and to have been applied extensively to the explanation of particulars.[3]

To give an example: I was formerly much struck with the clear insight Aristotle displayed in avoiding the confusion introduced by later biologists, who make plants *essentially* distinct from animals, and make an *essential* distinction between Life and Mind. But although he placed himself at the loftier point of view which recognizes the identity of Plant and Animal, the identity of Life and Mind, I am now of opinion that he did so by a very simple induction such as a superficial view of the general phenomena would first suggest, but which would have been blurred by more detailed knowledge. He identified plants and animals, but, as we shall see (§ 179), on grounds such as no modern would accept. In like manner he pronounced the sponge to be an animal; and moderns declare this judgment to have been correct. He has not told us what were his grounds; but we may reasonably ask, whether, had he known so much of sponges as OKEN and BURMEISTER, he would have maintained, against them, that sponges were animals? Had he known the grounds upon which psychologists still, for the most part, found an essential distinction between Life and Mind, which they hold to be

---

[3] D'ALEMBERT expresses a similar opinion: " La philosophie moderne s'est rapprochée sur plusieurs points de ce qu'on a pensé dans le premier âge de la philosophie, parcequ'il semble que la première impression de la nature est de nous donner des idées justes que l'on abandonne bientôt par incertitude ou par amour de la nouveauté et auxquelles enfin on est forcé de revenir."—*Sur le Système du Monde. Œuvres*, 1805, XIV., 79.

two not one, would he have maintained their identity? These questions cannot be positively answered; his wonderful sagacity *might* have pierced the fallacies which have misled more instructed minds; but on the whole, highly as I estimate his sagacity, it seems to me most probable that he would not have held his views at a later epoch in History, and with an ampler knowledge of the details.

§ 169. It is not because ancient ideas happen sometimes to agree in expression with our completer knowledge, that we are to assume, as a matter of course, that the ancients really held the opinions we hold. Among their many speculations manifestly erroneous, some few are found to be in seeming conformity with the latest results of research. Are we to assume in the ancients a power of divination rendering research superfluous? or shall we not rather suppose that two or three of their conjectures turn out right by accident, not insight? and even when these opinions were inductions from the facts, are we not justified in suspecting that they were due to the simple conception being unobscured by a multiplicity of details? It may seem ungenerous, by raising these doubts, to deprive the ancients of their credit; but impartial criticism is forced to raise such questions; since otherwise we shall have to accept the dangerous paradox that truths of science may be *divined* spontaneously, and need not therefore be laboriously *sought;* and that the ancients were by some peculiar privilege dispensed from the necessity of accurate knowledge. To state such an opinion is to refute it. Nevertheless the uncritical attitude with which men in general approach ancient authors constantly betrays them into a more or less explicit acceptance of such an opinion. When Galen happens casually to describe flame as ignited air, and says that the rose-tree burns because it contains much of this air, a modern historian reads in these vague phrases a wonderful anticipation of chemical discovery. "Ne dirait-on pas que, *par une sorte d'intuition spontanée*, Galien pressentit la découverte des gaz incandescents, tels que l'hydrogène, l'hydrogène bi-carboné, l'oxyde de carbone, &c. ?"[4]

§ 170. One of the great difficulties in interpreting ancient opinions is to guard against the tendency of reading our fulness of knowledge in their vague expressions. We often find in ancient works the precious metal we have ourselves brought with us; as the Alchemist often unconsciously put into his crucible the gold which he afterwards discovered there with surprised delight. MURATORI[5] mentions that in a very ancient astronomical manuscript there is the figure of a man gazing at the stars through a long tube; a similar representation was noticed by MABILLON in another manuscript; and PORTA in his work on "Natural Magic" (1549) says that at Alexandria a telescope was used to descry ships at a distance. From these facts MURATORI remarks that it would naturally be concluded that the telescope was known to the ancients; but he adds that MARVILLE, VEGETIO, and FABRIZIO, correctly explain the mistake, namely, that these tubes were without glasses, and were used to assist vision by shutting out other objects. A modern, seeing the tube, infers the existence of a telescope; imagination supplies the lenses.[6]

§ 171. Unless we are rigorous in our examination, we shall constantly fall into the error of attributing knowledge to the ancients which they could not have possessed. Thus Aristotle has been credited with the discovery of the vertebral theory. LAUTH, who considers the theory absurd, says—"ce qui doit surprendre davantage, c'est son idée sur les os, qu'il croit provenir de la colonne vertebrale, idée réproduite dans les derniers temps."[7]

---

[4] HOEFER: *Histoire de la Chimie*, Paris, 1842, I., 173. There is much more of the same unhistorical appreciation in this work.

[5] MURATORI: *Dissertazioni sopra le Antichità Italiane*, ed. 1790, XLIV., p. 374.

[6] There is a passage in ROGER BACON describing what might be effected with lenses, which has led many to suppose that he had discovered the telescope; but in a subsequent chapter of this History we shall see that, in truth, he knew nothing whatever about the telescope.

[7] LAUTH: *Histoire de l'Anatomie*, p. 61. Comp. p. 73.

CHAP. X.]   GENERAL PRINCIPLES OF BIOLOGY.   187

Now, the fact simply is that Aristotle described all the bones as connected with the vertebral column. His words are—" The bones, in animals, are all dependent upon one, and are connected together like the veins; nor is any one to be found isolated. The origin of all the bones is the spinal column." [8] A modern reading this may read into it the vertebral theory; but Aristotle had *no* such conception in his mind; his object, moreover, was descriptive, not transcendental, anatomy.

§ 172. In the course of our analyses we shall meet with various examples of such seeming anticipation; and also meet with genuine inductions, really remarkable. Of the latter may at once be mentioned his clear perception of the important morphological law, that *the greater luxuriance of the plant is at the expense of its seed;* hence the more the growth is stunted the more seed will be produced. He has made such frequent use of this principle, and always with such insight, that we cannot question his having thoroughly mastered it.

§ 173. He had also meditated on the progressive complexity of life, and in some respects he is superior to many illustrious moderns who have taught various forms of the doctrine of a chain of created beings; in other words, of a series passing, by insensible gradations, from the simplest to the most complex.

Perhaps the wildest of these was put forth by ROBINET,[9] who supposed minerals to develope into plants, and plants into animals. The scheme of BONNET [10] is less extravagant. He admits that there is no transition between the mineral and the plant; admits that Nature seems to take leaps. From the

---

[8] τὰ δ'ὀστᾶ τοῖς ζῴοις ἀφ' ἑνὸς πάντα συνηρτημένα ἐστὶ καὶ συνεχῆ ἀλλήλοις ὥσπερ αἱ φλέβες· αὐτό δὲ καθ' αὐτὸ οὐδέν ἐστιν ὀστοῦν. 'Αρχὴ δ' ἡ ῥάχις ἐστὶν ἐν πᾶσι τοῖς ἔχουσιν ὀστᾶ.—*Hist. An.*, III., 7, 516.

[9] ROBINET: *De la Nature*, Amsterdam, 1766. I gave an analysis of this rare work in *Frazer's Magazine*, Nov., 1857.

[10] BONNET: *Considerations sur les Corps organisés*, 1768.

plant, however, the chain is unbroken up to man. BUFFON maintains the existence of a series of insensible gradations, conceiving that the whole living universe presents itself as one family,[11] an opinion also adopted by HERDER.[12] TREVIRANUS makes a separate kingdom of the cryptogamic plants and the zoophytes, intermediate between the two kingdoms, vegetal and animal; and LEUCKART[13] thinks the sponges may, perhaps, form such an intermediate kingdom. MECKEL[14] holds that all existing organisms may be modifications, by insensible gradations, of one primitive type: a view recently made popular by the "Vestiges of the Natural History of Creation," and placed on a scientific footing by DARWIN.[15] Noticing the obvious objection that no such gradations are discoverable, but, on the contrary, that very great gaps occur at all parts of this pretended series, LAMARCK remarks that the animal scale only presents its degrees in the principal masses, and not in the species, nor even in the genera,[16] and therefore he rejects the idea of a connected chain. He holds that it is only at their common starting-point that the two grand divisions of organic life, vegetal and animal, are related by the simplicity of their structure. Not only does he deny the "chain of creation," but he holds that even animals do not form a chain; they simply exhibit a *progressive complexity* of organization.[17] In the same spirit GEOFFROY ST. HILAIRE pronounces the "chain" to be a chimera, and substitutes for it his doctrine of "Unity of Composition." SERRES, reproducing the arguments of MECKEL, says that the "missing links" in the chain may all be discovered if we seek them in the life of the embryo. On comparing animals arrived at their complete

---

[11] Quoted by ISIDORE ST. HILAIRE: *Essais de Zoologie Générale*, 1841, p. 78.
[12] *Ibid.*
[13] LEUCKART: *Observationes Zoologicæ*, p. 13.
[14] MECKEL: *Traité d'Anat. Comparée*, Paris, 1828, I., 83.
[15] DARWIN: *Origin of Species*, 1860.
[16] LAMARCK: *Philosophie Zoologique*, 2nd ed., 1830, I., 107.
[17] LAMARCK: *Hist. des Animaux sans Vertèbres*, 2nd ed., 1835, I., 51, 110.

development, we find many and wide differences between them; but if we compared them during their successive stages of evolution, we should see that these differences were preceded by resemblances,[18] that, in fact, comparative anatomy is an arrested embryology, and embryology is a transitory comparative anatomy. AUGUSTE COMTE proposed to fill up the missing links by the imaginative and arbitrary creation of new forms.

§ 174. It would be tedious to enumerate all the shapes this general conception of a connected chain has assumed; always, I think, upon arbitrary and unsatisfactory grounds. The simplest observation concurs with the profoundest, that organic beings are not linked together in a chain nor in a series; and, although it may flatter our propensity to arrange Nature according to our own notions of symmetry and simplicity, the attempt is perpetually frustrated on descending from the lofty region of speculation into that of concrete reality. Nor do the laws of development, in proving that all animal forms may have been developed, by successive modifications, from one original, justify the notion of a series. The image of a tree much better represents the facts than that of a chain. An *ideal* series of Locomotives might be constructed, from the first rude cart or barrow up to the railway carriage and steamboat, which would have quite as much objective reality as the animal series.

§ 175. Aristotle's conception was that of an ascending complexity in vital phenomena from plants to man; and this we may now see in detail.

Instead of the three kingdoms—mineral, vegetal, and

---

[18] SERRES: *Précis d'Anat. transcendante*, 1842, p. 135. The progress of embryology has discredited this striking and plausible generalization, by confirming the views so luminously set forth by VON BAER: *Zur Entwickelungsgeschichte*, 1808, p. 199, and *Nova Acta*, 1826, that the vertebrate type is at the very first constructed differently from that of the invertebrate; and that not only do the analogous organs appear in different successions, but are formed on different plans. See the elaborate memoir by LEREBOULLET: *Recherches d'Embryologie comparée* in the *Annales des Sciences Naturelles*, 1863, XX., 7.

animal—which moderns have borrowed from the alchemists,[19] he made the more philosophical division of 1° the Inorganic, τὰ ἄψυχα, and 2° the Organic, τὰ ἔμψυχα. The distinction between living and non-living beings is broad and palpable; it is obviously of quite another kind from the distinction between plants and animals.[20] But although the line of demarcation is broadly marked, yet Nature passes by ascending steps from one to the other; from the inanimate she passes to animals, through beings which are not indeed to be called animals, yet are so like them that the two are only separated by slight intervals.[21]

§ 176. The first step is that of Plants; which, compared with minerals, may be called animated, but compared with animals seem inanimate. Plants have Life; "for that which nourishes itself, grows, and decays, we call living." An animated body must have a soul, since the soul is the essence and reality of an animated body. It is the first *entelechie*, the reality by which the body becomes active. (§ 215.)

§ 177. The first stage of the soul's activity is that which all living beings have in common, namely, Nutrition, or Vegetal Life, as it has been called since BICHAT.[22] Plants have organs; but as these are limited to the one function of

---

[19] A fact first noticed by ISIDORE ST. HILAIRE: *Hist. des Règnes Organiques*, 1856, II., 6. A fourth kingdom, the atmospheric, was proposed by MUSSENBROEK: *Cours de Physique*, 1769, I., 11.

[20] "J'ai depuis longtemps trouvé plus convenable d'employer une autre division primaire, parcequ'elle est propre à faire mieux connoitre en général tous les êtres qui en sont l'objet. Ainsi je distingue toutes les productions naturelles comprises dans les trois règnes, en deux branches principales—1₀ en corps organisés, vivans; 2° en corps bruts et sans vie."—LAMARCK: *Philosophie Zoologique*, 1831, I., 92. He fancied he was establishing an important innovation, yet his illustrious countryman, VICQ D'AZYR, had already suggested the very same division, *Œuvres*, IV., 18–230. And Aristotle had preceded them by three-and-twenty centuries.

[21] ἡ γὰρ φύσις μεταβαίνει συνεχῶς ἀπὸ τῶν ἀψύχων εἰς τὰ ζῶα διὰ τῶν ζώντων μὲν οὐκ ὄντων δὲ ζώων οὕτως ὥστε δοκεῖν πάμπαν μικρὸν διαφέρειν θάτερον θατέρου τῷ σύνεγγυς ἀλλήλοις.—*De Partibus*, IV. 5, 481.

[22] *Vegetatio* also by the mediæval writers. See ALBERTUS MAGNUS, or HERMOLAUS BARBARUS.

Nutrition, they are designated simply as Upper and Under. They have no Right and Left, these being in relation to locomotion; nor Before and Behind, these being in relation to sensation. The upper and under parts are not the same as in animals; for plants take in nourishment by the roots, and these, therefore, are the upper, representing the mouth of an animal. The roots shoot up from the seed, and may be compared to umbilical veins, since through them the plant is nourished from the earth, as the embryo is nourished from the uterus. The stem shoots perpendicularly and carries nourishment to the fruit and the seed. The leaves protect the fruit, and are permeated with veins, which persist after the leaf is dead. Fruit and seed are one. The pericarp surrounds the seed, which is a kind of secretion from the nutriment; for the plant has no excretions, because its food is digested in the earth; and in lieu of excretions it forms fruit and seed. Plants, being fixed in the soil, have no occasion for the use of various and dissimilar parts: a few simple organs suffice for their simple functions. Nor are they ruled, like animals, by one central Vital Principle, since they live after division, and are reproduced by grafting.[23] But although Plants have a Vital Principle analogous to that of animals, it is not *central*, and cannot receive sensitive impressions,[24] consequently it cannot move. Therefore the first stage of mere nutritive activity is all that the soul developes into in the plant.

---

[23] Grafting, however, can no longer be made a mark of distinction for plants, since it has been successfully effected on animals. BARONIO transplanted the spur of one cock to the comb of another, with complete success. TIEDMANN: *Physiologie de l'Homme*. Paris, 1831, I., 163. HUNTER repeated the experiment with equal success; and recently M. OLLIER has transplanted pieces of bone to various parts of the organism. *Annales des Sciences Naturelles*, 1858, p. 378. Comp. BROWN SEQUARD'S: *Journal de Physiologie*, 1859, pp. 1-169, and 1860, p. 88. It was DUHAMEL who first proved that the growth of bone took place from the periosteum. See his éloge by VICQ D' AZYR: *Œuvres*, I., 150.

[24] See *De Part.*, II., 10; *Hist. An.*, II., 17; *De Somno*, 2; *De Resp.*, 8; *De Motione Animal.*, 9, on the heart as the centre of sensation and thought.

§ 178. Although his views are not clear on the point, he seems to have had his attention arrested by the morphological tendency of plants to develope their organs at the periphery, and of animals to develope theirs at the centre. He, also, as before noticed, mastered the relation between growth and reproduction. The annual plants, he says, use up all their nutritive material to form seeds, as in the cereals. He also notices how the forms of plants are determined by the soil, and that they thrive better from rain than from water poured on them.[25]

§ 179. The second step Nature takes is from plants to Plant-animals, Zoophytes. "There are many marine creatures," he says, "which leave the observer in doubt as to whether they are plants or animals, for they grow on the rocks, and many die if detached." With the exceptions of the Sponges and Sea-anemones, Aristotle was unfortunate in the examples he selected. The Polypes he held to be plants; and he placed several animals having no characteristic of plants in the intermediate class of Zoophytes. For instance, he names the Pinna and the Solen; but the first does *not* die, as he says, when detached from the rock; and the second is not attached to the rock, but burrows in the sand like a mole. Possibly he may designate other animals than those now recognized under these names; yet it is certain that he is referring to some kind of shell-fish, since he says: " The whole class of testaceous animals seem to be plants, in comparison with animals which can move themselves." Nor- is want of locomotion the only sign; he refers also to their want of the organs of sense. "Some of them have flesh, such are Ascidians and Acalephæ; but the Sponge is exactly like a plant."

§ 180. It is interesting to know on what grounds he

---

[25] For fuller details respecting Plants, see WIMMER: *Phytologiæ Arist. fragmenta*, 1838; or BIESE: *Die Philos. des Aristoteles*, 1842, II. The book *De Plantis* is universally acknowledged to be spurious.

decided the nature of the sponges to be animal. For many years eminent naturalists were divided on this point. BAUHIN, RAY, TOURNEFORT, FORSKÄL, TOZZETTI, SPALLANZANI, BLUMENBACH, SPRENGEL, OKEN, and BURMEISTER, held them to be plants; BELON, PEYSONNEL, TREMBLEY, ELLIS, SOLANDER, LINNÆUS, LAMARCK, CUVIER, and DE BLAINVILLE, held them to be animals. The latter opinion is now almost universal. But what is the proof? Mainly the fact that the glairy substance of the sponge is composed of *sarcodic* particles, each having an expansile motion similar to that of the Amœba; this, and the presence of cilia lining their canals, are the principal marks of animal nature;[26] but neither of these could have been known to Aristotle, since they are visible only under the microscope.

The only reason adduced by him is that sponges have sensation. "The proof of this," he says, "is their retracting when they perceive any attempt to tear them from the rock. They also retract when the waves dash violently. There are some people—for example, the people of Torona—who dispute this." Such a passage leads us to doubt whether he did not confound the Polypes with Sponges. No such retraction has been observed in the latter. The old Italian naturalist, IMPERATO,[27] however, describes the sponges accurately enough, and yet he also speaks of their powers of voluntary retraction, which he asserts resides solely in the mucus; but he may be merely repeating the statements of Aristotle and Pliny.

§ 181. The third step taken by Nature is the development of Animals, which arises from an increased activity of the Vital Principle, resulting in sensibility; and with sensibility, desire; and with desire, locomotion. This new soul is

---

[26] DUJARDIN: *Histoire Naturelle des Infusoires*, 1841, p. 305. BRONN: *Die Klassen und Ordnungen des Thier-Reichs*, 1859, I., 9.

[27] IMPERATO: *Dell' Historia Naturale, libri XXVII.*, Naples, 1599, p. 727. " La consistenza di quali è simile a corpo di lano compatta, fistuloso, vestito, e sparso per tutto di muccagine membranosa . . . nella muccagine è propriamente il senso, e la vita, con la virtù di poter ritirarsi in se stessa."

only a more energetic and more complex form of the original Life. The much debated question respecting a line of demarcation between Plant and Animal had not arisen in those days. It is not settled in our own. Where one school sees only a *higher differentiation*, the other sees the avatar of a *new principle* of Life. By the latter, the animal is held to be an organism having another kind of Vital Principle, essentially distinct from that of the plant. Now in so far as a marked difference exists between plants and animals in their organisms and functions, we need a special term to indicate this difference; and thus may call the one vegetal life, and the other animal life, without danger, and with positive advantage. But the same is true of all other differentiations: we need to distinguish infancy from puberty, and puberty from old age. We do not, however, suppose that these three differentiations of one organism are owing to three different principles. We distinguish sensibility from thought; but few psychologists now suppose that sensibility belongs to one vital principle, and thought to another. We call them two manifestations of one Life. In like manner we should regard Vegetal and Animal Life as *differentiated organic energies*, the one a higher development of the other, dependent on a more complex organism.[28] Hence we ought to feel no surprise if, in the earlier forms of each, the two are indistinguishable; and if no boundary line can be drawn between the plant-world and the animal-world. Hence, also, we ought to expect to find—what we do find—that plants sometimes exhibit the manifestations which are thought to be

---

[28] Compare GEGENBAUER: *Grundzüge der vergleichenden Anatomie*, 1859, p. 9. Aristotle's views are thus briefly expressed by HERMOLAUS BARBARUS: *Compendium Scient. Nat.*, 1547, lib. V., p. 43.—" In plantis quidem sola est vegetatio; in iis vero quæ sensu moventur, et vegetatio et sensio cernitur: at homini, et vegetatio et sensus et intellectio est attributa. Quoniam vero inesse non est verisimile tria genera animarum ei, qui est ratione insignitus, putandum est unam, atque eam quidem rationalem, in homine reliquarum tenere potestatem."

exclusively animal; I mean locomotion and obscure traces of sensibility; while, on the other hand, some animals lead an almost vegetal existence, being wholly destitute of locomotion, and having but the faintest traces of sensibility.

§ 182. Aristotle makes man the head of the animal creation. To him belongs the godlike nature. He is preeminent by thought and volition. But although all are dwarf-like and incomplete in comparison with man, he is only the highest point of one continuous ascent. He is the wisest and most thoughtful of animals, but other animals are also endowed with thought. The difference is, that animals only know particular truths, they never generalize, never form abstractions.

In this Aristotle anticipated LINNÆUS and the majority of modern naturalists. Yet there have not been wanting attempts, even in our own day, to separate man from the animal kingdom, and to give him a kingdom to himself as broadly distinguished from the animal, as the animal is distinguished from the vegetal, and the vegetal from the mineral.[29] Still more frequent and more justifiable have been the efforts to found a distinction on intellectual superiority; man being classed as rational, and animals as irrational;[30] a classification which is forced to invoke the

---

[29] ISIDORE ST. HILAIRE: *Hist. des Règnes Organiques*, vol. I., where previous attempts are enumerated. See also QUATREFAGES: *L'unité de l'espèce humaine*, 1861.

[30] "Rationale nullum est præter hominem."—CHARLETON: *Exercitationes de different. et nominibus animalium*, Oxon, 1671, p. 1. He derives our word *Man* from the Anglo-Saxon *mænan*, to think; "cui felicissime alludit Græc. μένος, *animus*, à quo et Latin. *mens* deflexum videtur." This is like PLATO's derivation of ἄνθρωπος, from the faculty of observing what is seen; animals only see, they do not observe.—*Cratylus*, ed. Bekk., Berlin, 1817, p. 37. MAX MÜLLER finds the origin of our word man in the Sanskrit *mann*, a derivative root, meaning to think. "From this we have the Sanskrit *mann*, originally thinker, then man. In Gothic we find both *man* und *mannisks*, the modern German *mann* and *mensch*."—*Lectures on the Science of Language*, 1862, p. 385. PATRIZIO denied all distinctions between rational and irrational, because, according to him, the whole world was rational, having a soul. "Nobis vero dis-

bold hypothesis of DESCARTES, that brutes are mere machines, and have no thought or volition; since in the absence of such an hypothesis, there is the awkward fact that animals reason, and reason in the same way as man, if not so much or so well.

Such is the scheme of an ascending complexity of Life conceived by Aristotle. We shall better appreciate it when his views on Life and Mind have been expounded; but before this can be done, we have to consider a question of some interest, already alluded to, namely, in how far he is to be credited with having anticipated certain modern discoveries.

---

tinctio hæc animi rationalis et irrationalis minime probatur. Nullum enim animum sua natura irrationalem esse existimamus."—*Nova de Universis Philosophia libris quinquaginta comprehensa*, Venet., 1593. *Panarchia, XXII.* (There are really sixty-nine books, instead of fifty, as named in the title.)

CHAPTER XI.

ANTICIPATION OF MODERN DISCOVERIES.

§ 183. ONE of the first remarks which escapes from almost every zoologist of our day, when Aristotle is named, turns on the surprising anticipations of modern discoveries said to be found in his writings. The piercing intellect which could thus foresee results of modern research at a time when Science was wholly without the means and appliances of modern research, is pronounced something marvellous. Marvellous, indeed, the fact would be; unhappily for the lovers of the marvellous and the eulogists of the past, the fact is a misconception. Let me confess that for a long while I shared the belief, and echoed the eulogy. With a view to this History, I carefully collected all the instances of anticipation, intending with them to make a great display in honour of the old Greek. But on submitting them to that rigorous scrutiny which the impartiality of History demands, they turned out to be no marvels at all. The most striking examples may now be cited and examined.

I.—*The Hectocotylus of the Argonaut.*

§ 184. Our first instance is the one most frequently cited. The history of the discovery has been sketched by VERANY and VOGT, from whose pages it may here be repeated. The

Hectocotylus was first described, in 1825, by DELLE CHIAJE,[1] as a parasite upon the beautiful Argonaut, and the more familiar Octopus. This idea of its being a parasite was the most obvious suggestion, when its origin was unknown; and as a parasite CUVIER described it, from a specimen furnished by LAURILLARD, who had detected five of them on the bodies of the Octopus at Nice: three in the funnel of one female, and one on the arm of a male; in the latter case it had almost destroyed and replaced the arm, so "that at first sight it might have been mistaken for the arm itself."[2] This was coming very near the discovery. As a parasite, however, it continued to be classed, until COSTA, a Neapolitan naturalist, made a bold but premature guess at its nature: he said it was simply the cephalopod's *spermatophore*.[3] Seven years later, DUJARDIN made a nearer approach to the truth. He confessed himself unable to decide upon its nature, but was quite positive that it was not a parasitic worm. "One might call it," he said,[4] "an arm torn from some other cephalopod." The presence of a long white thread suggested that this might be a bundle of spermatozoa; and that the Hectocotylus might be a portion of the cephalopod, detached from its body, and subservient in some way to fecundation.

Meanwhile KÖLLIKER investigated several specimens of Hectocotyli, and the result of his investigation was "that these supposed worms are nothing but the *stunted males* of the cephalopoda on which they are found."[5] These views were adopted, with slight modification, by VON SIEBOLD, in his work on Comparative Anatomy. But the peculiar marvel of the Hectocotylus was simultaneously discovered by

---

[1] DELLE CHIAJE: *Memorie sulla Storia e Notomia degli animali senza Vertebre del regno di Napoli*, 1823-9.

[2] CUVIER: *Annales des Sciences Naturelles*, 1829.

[3] COSTA: *Annales des Sciences Nat.*, 1841.

[4] DUJARDIN: *Histoire Naturelle des Helminthes*, 1848.

[5] KÖLLIKER: *Annals of Nat. History*, 1845; and *Bericht von der Königlichen Zootomischen Anstalt zu Würtzburg*, 1849.

H. MÜLLER, VERANY, and VOGT, who found that this animal was neither a worm, nor a parasite, neither a spermatophore, nor a stunted male, but simply the *modified arm* of the male cephalopod, an arm which developes within it the generative organs, and on detaching itself from the body, fastens itself by suckers to the body of the female, and impregnates her. Thus the Hectocotylus is not an independent animal, although capable of a brief independent existence; it is not an animal, in spite of its circulation, and its power of locomotion; it is a *detached organ*, an organophore!

§ 185. This discovery excited great astonishment; and before the thrill at such a surprising phenomenon had subsided, another thrill was given by Von SIEBOLD's announcement that Aristotle had anticipated it: "he appears to have been acquainted with the natural history and internal structure of the cephalopoda, to an extent which even now must be astonishing. From the following passages VERANY and MÜLLER will learn with amazement that Aristotle may fairly contest with them the priority of their discovery."[6] Von SIEBOLD then quotes, from SCHNEIDER's Latin version, the following passages, which I will translate from the original as strictly as possible:—

Hist. Animal. lib. iv. c. 1.—"The Polypus uses its arms as feet and as hands; for with the two which are above the mouth it introduces its food. The extreme arm, which is distinguished by its sharp and bifid end and the whiteness of its back, is used in sexual congress."

Ibid. lib. v. c. 5.—"*Some say* that the male has a kind of generative apparatus in the arm which carries the largest suckers; this extends as a tendinous substance into the middle of the arm, and is thrust into the nose (*i. e.* funnel) of the female."

---

[6] SIEBOLD und KÖLLIKER: *Zeitschrift für Wissenschaftliche Zoologie*, 1852. The papers of SIEBOLD, MÜLLER, VERANY, and VOGT were translated by HUXLEY in the *Scientific Memoirs*, 1853.

Ibid. c. 10.—" The male is distinguished from the female by a longer head, and the white body in his arm, *which the fishermen call* his genitals."

§ 186. Whoever remembers not only that so eminent an investigator as Von Siebold could see in these passages Aristotle's claim to a knowledge of the Hectocotylus, but that the claim has been admitted all over Europe without a murmur of doubt, must feel the necessity which exists of revising our first impressions. On reading Von Siebold's announcement I shared his enthusiasm, and was blinded by it. Instead of being on guard against the tendency of facile acquiescence in the glory of an ancient, I followed the lead, and *read into* these passages a meaning Aristotle never conceived. But when I came to prepare this chapter, and to scrutinize the evidence, it very soon became apparent that Aristotle knew absolutely nothing more than the idle conjecture of fishermen.

§ 187. Let us first hear all that he says in the passage of which Von Siebold only quotes a portion. " The Polypi, in congress, hang mouth to mouth, with their arms interlaced. One of the Polypi rests on the ground with that part which is called its head, and extends its arms ; the other then arrives, and entwines its arms with the arms of the former, so that they mutually fix each other by their suckers. *Some say* that the male has a kind of generative apparatus in the arm which carries the largest suckers ; this extends as a tendinous substance into the middle of the arm, and is thrust into the nose (*i. e.* funnel) of the female. The Sepia and Loligo, on the contrary, swim together mouth to mouth, and arms entwined."

To this let us add a passage from the work on Generation.[7] " The cephalopoda embrace each other in the region of the mouth by grasping and supporting each other with their arms. This mode of congress is caused by the fact that Nature

---

[7] *De Gen. An*., I., 15, 720.

has so bent the part whence the secretion issues, that it lies close to the mouth."

Whoever attentively considers these passages will see that Aristotle knew *nothing* of the Hectocotylus; not even of its existence; much less of its being the arm of the male, detached, and living parasitically in the mantle-cavity of the female. *This*, which is the peculiar marvel, was totally unsuspected by him. Had he gained even a glimpse of it, he would assuredly have mentioned it, especially in the work on "Generation," where all known peculiarities are so carefully registered. His account obviously repeats what he had heard from fishermen; it is true that by a lucky guess they assigned a generative function to the "tendinous substance" in the arm; but it was only a guess; and the loose ground on which it rested may easily be imagined.

§ 188. Although there is no evidence to warrant the idea that Aristotle did know anything of the Hectocotylus, there is nothing in the nature of the discovery which he might not have known, had his attention been rightly directed. It is otherwise with the second example on our list.

II.—*The Parthenogenesis of Bees.*

This could never have been known until certain delicate anatomical and physiological researches had furnished an assured basis; accordingly we must *à priori* reject the idea of Aristotle's having known it. In an interesting essay on the subject, AUBERT and WIMMER [8] have cited *in extenso* all the passages in which he explains his views; and these passages at first convey the impression that he really knew the chief phenomena; but on a closer scrutiny we find that it is we who read into them our own knowledge.

§ 189. Let us glance at the present state of opinion on

---

[8] In SIEBOLD und KÖLLIKER's *Zeitschrift für Wissenschaftliche Zoologie*, 1858.

this subject. The ultimate fact in the Generation of plants and of animals seemed attained when it was discovered that impregnation essentially consists in the union of a spermcell with a germcell. This splendid generalization still continues to be the true expression of the widest classes of phenomena. But it is not absolute. There are many indisputable facts pointing to an important variation in the law; a variation felicitously named Parthenogenesis,[9] and successfully traced as a frequent mode of reproduction in Polypes, Entomostraca, Bees, Moths, and Aphides. It has also been asserted, by distinguished botanists, as a mode of reproduction in plants; but the latest investigations throw such doubt on all the specified cases, that for the present we must hold a verdict of "not proven."[10] No such doubt is permissible respecting the fact in animal generation. In all those named above, we have the most rigorous evidence that *unfertilized ova* have produced perfect progeny, which in turn were fertile, either as virgins, or coupled with males. I speak with the more confidence because I have patiently investigated the question, tested the evidence, and added some contribution of new observations.[11] But the single observation about to be cited from BONNET, suffices to prove that such a phenomenon does occur.

§ 190. The Aphis, a winged insect familiar with our rose-trees and other plants, and vulgarly called the plant-louse, deposits its eggs at the close of summer, in the axils of the leaves of plants. These eggs are hatched in the following spring. The insect which issues is, however, wingless and sexless. Although sexless, and although isolated from every other individual of its kind, this insect brings forth other sexless insects; and brings them forth *alive*, not

---

[9] OWEN, in his work *On Parthenogenesis; or the successive production of procreating individuals from a single ovum*, 1849.

[10] CURREY: *Report on Vegetable Parthenogenesis*, in the *Natural History Review*, Oct., 1861.

[11] For fuller detail, see *Seaside Studies*, 2nd ed., 1860, pp. 296, seq.

simply as eggs. BONNET [12] separated one as soon as it was hatched, reared it in the strictest seclusion, watching it daily, almost hourly, with the patient tenacity of genius. He has recorded his anxieties, his tremulous agitation lest its death should frustrate all his hopes; and his joy, (after seeing his captive four times shed its skin and thus reach its normal development,) to observe that this absolute virginity did not in the least interfere with fertility. On the eleventh day this secluded Aphis produced a live Aphis, which was instantly secluded in like manner; another succeeded, then another. Every twenty-four hours the brood was increased by three, four, and even ten fresh comers; so that at the end of twenty-one days this virgin insect had given birth to ninety-five living insects! Nor does the marvel end here: each of these virgin products will in turn produce virgin progeny; and this goes on for several successive generations.

§ 191. This is enough to prove the fact; how can we explain it? Is it the decided contradiction to the general law of reproduction that it appears to be? On what does the law of the union between spermcell and germcell itself repose?

Some speculative biologists have likened this union to the union of an acid with a base which gives a new product differing from either. But the comparison is untenable. One striking result of modern Histology is that germcell and spermcell, ovum and spermatozoon, are *identical*, and in the earlier phases of their development they are indistinguishable. It is only in their subsequent stages that they differ.[13] If therefore Histology on the one hand proves the identity of germcell

---

[12] BONNET: *Traité d'Insectologie*, 1745, I., 26, seq.

[13] CHARLES ROBIN: *Comptes Rendus de l'Académie des Sciences*, 1848, p. 427. In this memoir it is shown that in the male organs, both of animals and plants, an ovule is formed identical with the ovule formed in females. Its vitellus spontaneously subdivides into the embryonal cells, each of which becomes a spermatozoon, or a pollen grain.

and spermcell; observation on the other proves that animals, normal in structure and functions, are sometimes developed from germcells alone: the unfertilized egg developes into an animal identical with that developed from the fertilized egg. The influence of fertilization—the union of spermcell with germcell—cannot therefore be like the union of an acid with a base, to form a salt. No alkali developes spontaneously into a salt; without the acid, the alkali is powerless to assume any of the saline forms. But the germcell does develope into an embryo, without the aid of a spermcell; and even in those cases where the union with a spermcell is indispensable for the full development of an embryo, the germcell alone spontaneously passes through the same early phases of development as it would pass through if fertilized.

§ 192. The germcell of a reptile, bird, or mammal, is unable to *continue* this development without the aid of a spermcell. But in Polypes, Entomostraca, Bees, Aphides, and Moths, the development may continue. One may accept therefore the general fact that every ovum has within itself a power of development, unaided by a spermatozoon. In the more complex organisms this unaided development falls very far short of an embryo; but it travels some distance on that road; and when, as in insects, the goal is not very distant, it may be reached alone. I have compared the spermatozoa to the extra pair of horses put to the carriage when a steep hill has to be crossed. Two horses bring the carriage to the foot of the hill, and by precisely the same route as four horses would have taken; but here, at the foot of the hill, other horses are indispensable.

Newport's investigations in the artificial impregnation of the ova of amphibia, led him to believe that although impregnation *commences* at the instant of contact between spermatozoon and ovum, yet a certain *duration* of contact is requisite for the completion of development; and although subsequent researches have modified this conclusion by proving that it is not contact alone, but the entrance of the spermatozoon into the ovum, which determines fecundation, the result is the same. An exceedingly minute quantity of spermatozoa suffices; but development takes place much more slowly than when the quantity is abundant; and below a certain minimum the impregnation is only partial, the yelk is imperfectly segmented.[14]

§ 193. So much on the general question. Let us now see how it stands with the Bees. The fact of Parthenogenesis in Bees has been placed beyond cavil by the researches of DZIERZON and Von SIEBOLD.[15] It is a fact which is guaranteed by anatomical data, no less than by careful observation, rigidly controlled and verified.

Anatomical investigation has discovered that the Queen-bee is a perfect female; the Worker an imperfect female; and the Drone a perfect male. In the first and last, the generative organs are complete; in the second they are present, but in so undeveloped a condition as to forbid congress. One of these organs in the female is curious: it is a spermatic receptacle (*receptaculum seminis*)[16] which is filled with spermatozoa during congress, and retains them during the greater part of the Queen's life; only those ova which are fertilized by the spermatozoa develope into Queens and Workers; the unfertilized ova become Drones.

It has further been ascertained that the Queen only becomes impregnated during her wedding flight. If her flight be prevented, by the removal of her wings, or any other means, she is forced to remain a virgin; nevertheless in this state she deposits eggs, and these eggs become bees, no less

---

[14] "Manifesta igitur est sententia proposita: marem formam solum tribuere: fœminam autem universam materiem, formam verò usque ad aliquid."—CÆSALPINUS: *Quæstionum Peripateticarum*, 1571, p. 102.

[15] VON SIEBOLD: *On true Parthenogenesis in Bees and Moths*, trans. by W. S. DALLAS, London, 1857.

[16] VON SIEBOLD has since discovered a similar organ in Tritons and Salamanders.—*Zeitschrift für Wissen. Zool.*, 1858. It is found also in snails, Trematoda, and many insects.

than if they had been fertilized. In like manner the virgin Workers lay eggs, when the Hive is deprived of its Queen. But there is this peculiarity common to the eggs under both these conditions: they only become Drones, never Workers, nor Queens.[17]

§ 194. The anatomical data which thus form the basis of the theory of Parthenogenesis in Bees were not, and could not have been, known to Aristotle; nor were the experimental proofs by which it is verified suggested to him. All he knew on the subject was derived from the loose observation of bee-keepers. If some of his sentences now read like a lucky anticipation of the truth, we have only to compare them with other sentences, to see that the agreement is delusive. He was wholly in the dark respecting the sexual differences. He thinks it improbable that the Queen should be a female, and the Drone a male, *because* the Queen has a sting, "and Nature never bestows a defensive weapon on females:" an argument as unfortunate in its teleology as it is inaccurate in its data. On the other hand he holds it to be improbable that the workers should be males, and the drones females; *because* the workers take care of the young, "and this the male never does." Again the data are wrong: some males take upon themselves the entire charge of the young; and the male pipefish (*syngnathus*) even hatches the eggs.

But the conclusive proof that he knew nothing of Parthenogenesis as an exceptional process, is that he insists on the fact of *no* impregnation ever taking place among bees—since, he says, it has never been witnessed, and must have been witnessed had it been in the order of nature. He thought that all generation in bees resulted from a mingling of the male and

---

[17] Let no sarcastic conclusion be precipitately drawn from this fact of the male bee proceeding from unfertilized eggs. In one kind of Moth (*Psyche*), it is the female which proceeds from the unfertilized egg. In the silkworm moth the virgin progeny are both male and female.

female principles. There was no act of congress. They were self-generated, by a sort of hermaphroditism such as was observed in fish.

§ 195. We are thus led to the third case on our list:—

III.—*Hermaphroditism in Fish.*

Here, again, we have a delicate anatomical problem, such as Aristotle had no means of solving.

Many plants are diœcious, and many of the lower animals (as snails) are double-sexed, *i. e.* capable either of self-impregnation, or of mutual impregnation. This Hermaphroditism is confined to the invertebrata, with the single known exception of certain species of Perch. Had the term diœcious been carried over from the vegetable to the animal kingdom, there might have been an avoidance of the confusion which now exists, because the term, Hermaphroditism, includes two widely different groups of phenomena: 1st, the *normal* organization of a complete generative apparatus of both sexes in the same individual; 2nd, the *abnormal* organization, in which arrest or excess of development in one or more parts of the generative apparatus presents some of the appearance, though not the reality, of two sexes.[18] I venture to propose the terms *dichogamism* for the bisexual class, and *hermaphroditism* for the abnormal class.

§ 196. It must be borne in mind that the organs of both sexes are formed on the same plan, and are, in their earlier stages, absolutely indistinguishable from one another. There is at first neither male nor female; but both these forms branch from a common root, and never even in their ultimate development lose the discoverable traces of their common type. It is not strictly accurate to say that at first all

---

[18] See this subject fully treated in MÜLLER: *Bildungsgeschichte der Genitalien*, 1830, p. 121. ISIDORE ST. HILAIRE: *Histoires des Anomalies de l'Organisation*, 1836, II., 30, 174. MECKEL: *Traité d'Anatomie comparée*, Paris, 1828, I., 298.

organisms are female, and then gradually develope into the male;[19] but it is true that the earlier stages of the male have a resemblance to the later stages of the female.[20]

Hermaphroditism is consequently wholly unlike the normal dichogamic type of structure. It arises from an arrest, or excess of development in one organ of the generative apparatus; and considering that the organs in male and female are both formed on the same plan, we can easily understand how an arrest, or excess, will produce in the male a resemblance to the female, in the female a resemblance to the male. But this resemblance only affects the *form*, it does not affect the *function*. The Hermaphrodite is always of one sex, and, in spite of deceptive appearances, we never find such an organism producing both spermatozoa and ova, but only one of these. When both sexes are united in one individual, we have dichogamism, properly so

---

[19] "Il n'y a primitivement ni mâle ni femelle; à un second temps en apparence il n'y a que des femelles; puis les organes d'apparence femelle se transforment en organes mâles. Toutes les femelles à une certaine époque de leur formation ont l'air d'être hermaphrodites."— SERRES : *Précis de l'Anatomie transcendante*, 1842, p. 104.

[20] " Embryo primus a formatione et inchoatæ vitæ momentis peculiari sexu donatus non est, sed genitalium utriusque sexus rudimentis instructus est, et a virium physicarum, quæ vitam et partium organicarum evolutionem moderantur, quantitate et directione dependet, an mas an vero fœmina prodeat."— ACKERMANN: *Infantis Androgyni historia*, quoted by MÜLLER: *Bildungsgeschichte der Genitalien*, where ample and accurate details on this delicate and important point may be found. See also RATHKE: *Abhandlungen zur Bildungs und Entwickelungsgeschichte der Menschen und Thiere*, 1832, I., 45-92; KÖLLIKER : *Entwickelungsgeschichte des Menschen*, 1861, p. 443; or LONGET: *Traité de Physiologie*, 1850, II., p. 208. Quite recently ROUGET has proved that the erectile apparatus of man, often, but erroneously, called erectile *tissue*, has its anatomical and functional analogue in the woman. *Mémoire sur les organes erectiles de la Femme*, in BROWN SEQUARD'S *Journal de Physiol.*, 1858, pp. 47, 320, 479. One of the most curious of the morphological identifications is that of the *vesicula prostatica* in the male with the uterus and vagina of the female. See LEUCKART: *Vesicula prostatica*, in the *Cyclopædia of Anat. and Physiol.* The disputes on this point may be settled, I think, by GEOFFROY ST. HILAIRE's luminous guide, the *principe des connexions*, which best determines homologies.

called,[21] *i. e.* the bisexual structure, as in diœcious plants, in which the characteristic developments of both sexes are found, and both spermcells and germcells are produced. The simplest form of this bisexual condition in animals I found to exist occasionally in Sea-anemones and some Polypes, namely, the normal production of germcells and spermcells in one and the same spot. The next step is in the differentiation of one special organ for the production of germcells, and of another organ for spermcells.

§ 197. Of the two kinds of Hermaphroditism, commonly confounded, but in the preceding paragraphs markedly distinguished, the first has been detected in all classes of animals ; as, indeed, may be anticipated from the fact of its being a defect of development. The second, common enough in Radiata and Mollusca, has never yet been detected in Insects, Arachnida, or—with the single exception of the Perch—in Vertebrata. That this single exception should have been known to Aristotle may well excite surprise. We are, however, prepared to receive the announcement with some scepticism, and are disposed to believe that he was merely repeating the hearsay of fishermen, or that he was advancing some crude hypotheses to explain an ill-observed fact. A brief history of the discovery will best display this.

§ 198. RONDELET, in 1654, after citing Aristotle's remark that the perch (*serranus*) is capable of self-reproduction, and that no males had been found, suggests that perhaps the perch is at once both male and female; but he does not throw much

---

[21] The generative apparatus has three pairs of organs: external, median, and internal. These three pairs are nourished by three pairs of arteries: the external iliac, the hypogastric, and the spermatic. Any one pair, or one of each pair, may be arrested or accelerated in development, and thus produce abnormal hermaphroditism. Cases have been known of *lateral* hermaphroditism, in which the organs of each side have been differently developed.—ISIDORE ST. HILAIRE, *Op. cit.*, vol. II. Comp. also MÜLLER: *Bildungsgeschichte*, p. 130.

emphasis on this suggestion, which was only a lucky guess.[22] CHARLETON, in 1667, mentions it as an exception to the whole class of fishes, that in this genus there is *no* distinction of sex. He does not suspect them to be bisexual, but asexual.[23] CAVOLINI described both the ovaries and testes present in the same individual;[24] but described them so imperfectly that RUDOLPHI declared he had mistaken the ovaries, in an imperfect state of development, for testes;[25] and MECKEL confirming this, adds that he himself never found any but females. VALENCIENNES espoused the opinion of Cavolini, which was also adopted at first by CUVIER, who afterwards in the second edition of his *Règne Animal*, came to doubt its accuracy. DUVERNOY pronounced decidedly against it.[26]

With such an array of authorities against the idea, it is difficult to suppose that Aristotle, if he happened to be right where they were wrong, could have had very solid grounds for his opinion. They knew of the opinion, examined its evidence, and rejected it. That they were wrong, has been satisfactorily settled by the researches of DUFOSSÉ;[27] but this result in no way vindicates Aristotle's opinion. Dufossé examined 368 specimens of *serranus scriba, s. cabrilla* and *s. hepatus;* and both by anatomical inspection, and direct observation, discovered them to be normally bisexual. He not only recognized spermatozoa and ova, but observed the fish depositing their ova, and at the same time casting their milt.

---

[22] RONDELETII: *De Piscis marinis*. Lib. IV., p. 185: "Verum de hâc re nihil statuo, sed liberum cuique judicium relinquo." Quoted by DUFOSSÉ in the *Mémoire* presently to be cited.

[23] CHARLETON: *Exercit. de Differentibus et Nominibus Animalium*, 1677. *Pisce*, p. 14.

[24] CAVOLINI: *Memoria sulla generazione dei pesci*, 1787, p. 91.

[25] MECKEL: *Traité d'Anat. comp*. Paris, 1828. I., 300.

[26] DUVERNOY ET CUVIER: *Leçons d'Anat. comp.*, 1846. I., p. 193. References 24 and 26 are from Dufossé's *Mémoire*.

[27] DUFOSSÉ: *Annales des Sciences Nat.*, 1856, p. 295, where the organs are described and figured in minute detail.

Instead of this anatomical evidence, which Aristotle could not have had, and this evidence of observation, which he might have had, but had not, it is clear that he was relying upon fishermen's report as to there being only females;[28] and this he makes the evidence for his assumption that they are self-impregnating, like the bees.

§ 199. This third example has thus turned out no more favourable to the idea of his having anticipated modern discoveries, than its two predecessors. Let us consider a fourth.

IV.—*Placental Fish.*

The three preceding examples might *à priori* have been dismissed as obvious cases of the facility with which modern opinions may be read into ancient texts. They all three depend upon minute and accurate anatomical knowledge, and could not possibly have been correctly known, so long as the anatomical basis was unknown. Were it true, therefore, that Aristotle had rightly guessed, we could not accept the guess as an anticipation, nor glorify his sagacity; since a guess in science has only value when it is founded on some positive facts which it endeavours to explain, or when it leads to some specific research. A guess is scientific when it is a genuine hypothesis—a finger-post on the laborious route of inquiry, not a phrase which is accepted for an explanation.

§ 200. In the cases now to be examined we shall find Aristotle at more advantage. He is recording simple facts of observation; and as these demand neither preliminary knowledge, nor difficult inquiry, we may readily admit that he has seen and noted what subsequent naturalists had no opportunity of seeing, or had overlooked.

§ 201. The first of these is the existence of placental fishes. To a modern biologist the announcement is startling;

---

[28] See § 473, where it appears that he did not even believe these statements.

and when he learns that the announcement is strictly true, and that Aristotle was perfectly aware of the fact, his surprise is apt to express itself in exaggerated admiration. But all readers who are imperfectly acquainted with embryology, will understand from their own experience the state of Aristotle's mind. They will see nothing startling in the announcement, because they will not have present to their minds the systematic knowledge which it seems to contradict. Surprise starts from a background of knowledge, or fixed belief. Nothing is surprising to ignorance, because the mind in that state has no preconceptions to be contradicted. To the ancients it could be but small matter of surprise when told that animals were generated spontaneously, or that mice became impregnated by licking salt. Before these things could be surprising, a certain amount of knowledge respecting the laws of generation must have been systematized. Had Aristotle really known the facts of Parthenogenesis and Metagenesis, which so much astonish us, they would probably have excited no wonderment in his mind, because they would have disturbed no deeply-rooted convictions. Before surprise at a phenomenon can be felt, we must have learned to rely on an uniformity which seems contradicted by it. A chemist would feel a painful difficulty in believing that an acid had become converted into a salt without the presence of a base. An ordinary man would feel no difficulty at all in it; he would believe it as easily as the reverse. In like manner, a biologist hears with surprise that in the same genus of fishes there are species which bring forth their young alive, like other viviparous fishes and reptiles, and also species which bring forth their young like mammalia, with a *placenta*—hears it with so much surprise as to demand rigorous proof of the fact; whereas Aristotle hears and records the fact without any surprise at all.

§ 201 *a*. The fact is of considerable interest, and, as no

mention of it occurs in the English text-books that have fallen in my way, we may pause a moment to examine it.

Animals are classed as oviparous and viviparous. The obvious differences implied in bringing forth young alive, or bringing forth eggs which develope into young, require corresponding differences in terms; but to the speculative biologist, oviparity and viviparity are identical processes; *identical*, observe, not the *same*. Since DE GRAAF [29] commenced, and VON BAER [30] completed the discovery of the mammalian egg, and since it has been known that this egg is developed into an embryo under conditions identical with those of all other animals, passing through precisely analogous phases of differentiation, the conclusion has been irresistible that *all* animals are oviparous; and, inasmuch as the eggs, when deposited, are all alive, it follows that all animals are viviparous.[31]

§ 202. We still speak of the metamorphoses of insects and batrachians, as if such changes were peculiar to insects and batrachians; whereas we know that all animals, man included, undergo successive metamorphoses quite as remarkable; but they undergo them while within the egg, or within the parent body. A striking illustration of this is seen in the two kinds of salamander. In one—the aquatic—the young is born a tadpole; in the other, the land salamander, (*Salamandra atra*), it is born a perfect animal. We observe the tadpole swimming in the pond, where it gradually loses

---

[29] DE GRAAF: *De Mulierum organis Generationum*, p. 80, 158. *Opera*, Lugd., 1678.

[30] VON BAER: *Epistola de ovi mammalium et hominis genesi*, 1827. I know this only through the translation published by BRESCHET: *Répertoire général d'Anat. et de Physiol. Pathologique*, Paris, 1829, to which is also added VON BAER's commentary of 1828.

[31] As indeed was clearly seen by HARVEY: " All animals are in some sort produced out of an egge; for the fœtus of viviparous creatures is produced after the same manner and order out of a pre-existent conception, as the chicken is formed and constituted out of an egge . . . For an egge is an exposed conception, from which a chicken is produced, but a conception is an egge which is retained within until the fœtus have attained its just bulk."—*Exercitations concerning the Generation of living Creatures*, 1653, p. 391.

its gills and acquires its four limbs by successive metamorphoses. But precisely these metamorphoses are undergone by the other salamander within the body of its mother. I have removed them from the mother's body when in this tadpole condition, placed them in water, and observed them swim about, indistinguishable from the ordinary aquatic tadpole. Again : the white ant passes through all its metamorphoses while in the egg; other insects pass through the stages of grub and pupa before reaching that stage of development reached by the white ant on emerging from the egg.

It is needless to insist on the differences observable between these two forms of reproduction, since underneath the differences which adapt the young of the one species to an aquatic, and the young of the other to a terrestrial existence, there persists the physiological identity. Whether all the stages of development be passed through within the parent or in the water, there is no difference whatever in the successive stages themselves, nor in their final issue—a consideration, by the way, which shows how untenable is the plausible generalization that the longer the period in which the embryo remains within its parent's body, the more complex will be its organization. The dog is as complex as the camel, yet the dog requires only nine weeks', and the camel twelve months' gestation. The aquatic salamander is as complex as the terrestrial, yet *all* its development, from the very moment of fertilization of the ova, takes place outside the parent's body; while that of the terrestrial salamander takes place inside the parent's body.

§ 203. There are several varieties in the conditions under which the impregnated egg will develope :—

1st. It may be left to the agency of oxygen, and the very slight amount of heat in the water.

2nd. It may be left to the agency of oxygen and greater amount of heat in the air. In each of these two cases an exchange of gases takes place, passing through the shell.

If the shell be varnished, or if the exchange of gases be hindered, no development takes place.[32]

3rd. It may be hatched under the protection of the parent's body; *outside*, as under the breast of the bird, or in the pouch of the male pipefish; *inside*, as in the viviparous infusoria, molluscs, fishes, reptiles, and mammals.[33]

§ 204. But under all these varieties the process is identical, the successive changes are uniform. The egg, once impregnated, is an independent living being; its connection with the parent is indirect, and (with the strange exception of the *Salpæ*) only approaches distinctness in the higher animals, called placental animals. In one sense the mother feeds the offspring in all animals: in some she simply furnishes the yelk of the egg, which will be used up in the development of the embryo; in others, as in molluscs and batrachians, the eggs are embedded in a mass of transparent mucus which serves the young as food;[34] in others the egg is nourished within the parent's body; but not by any more direct means. The egg is free and unattached in the oviduct, or uterus, and while there it receives nourishment in some unexplained way.[35]

---

[32] DARESTE: *Mémoire sur l'influence qu'exerce sur le developpement du poulet l'application partielle d'un vernis sur la coquille de l'œuf.—Annales des Sc. Nat.*, 1855, IV., 119.

[33] " Besides, as a chicken is hatched out of an egge by the fostering heat of the sitting hen, or some other adscititious hospitable patronage, so also the fœtus is produced out of the conception in the egge by the soft and most natural warmth of the parent."—HARVEY: *Exercit. concerning Generation*, p. 393.

[34] Physiologists little suspect the power possessed by the embryo of assimilating material, however minute may be the quantities present. For example, I placed three tadpoles immediately on their emerging from the egg into about two ounces of filtered water, with no visible substance, animal or vegetable. The water was never changed, nor was any food added; nevertheless, the tadpoles lived rather more than a month, lost their gills, and increased to about four times their original size !

[35] Unexplained, but indubitable. The embryo notoriously increases *in utero*. The chick, on emerging from the shell, weighs *less* than the original egg, deducting the shell. According to GEOFFROY ST. HILAIRE the loss is as much as one-sixth; see his *Mémoire*, cited by his son: *Vie, travaux et doctrine de Geoffroy St. Hilaire*, 1847, p. 457. This loss is explicable : during the whole period of incubation the chick has received nothing but heat (imponderable)

Owen has shown how in the kangaroo, and other *implacental* mammalia, the embryo is nourished. But as we arrive at the placental mammalia we seem to come upon a totally different arrangement, namely, a direct communication between the embryo and parent. This placenta (or "afterbirth") seems actually to unite the two; yet although there is, so to speak, physiological union, there is no anatomical union; and this physiological union only differs in degree from that which is seen in the implacental vivipara. In point of fact, the placenta [36] is a contrivance whereby the bloodvessels of the uterus lie *side by side* with the bloodvessels of the chorion; that is to say, one portion of the maternal bloodvessels is brought into contact with a portion of the embryo's bloodvessels; and at this point of contact the two vessels *exchange gases and liquids* by osmosis through their walls; so that the placenta forms an organ of nutrition and respiration for the embryo. It is by this channel that the mother may communicate diseases to her child. Indeed, whatever affects her blood, must affect its blood. Nevertheless, in spite of this seeming union, the embryo is truly independent; it is fed from the maternal blood, as a few months later it will be fed by the maternal milk. But embryo or infant, it is equally independent.

---

and oxygen; whereas it has given off a large amount of water by evaporation, and of lithic acid, &c., by secretion. Now compare this loss *in ovo* with the gain *in utero:* according to Dr. John Davy, the average weight of the torpedo's egg is 182 grains, the weight of the torpedo developed from it inside the parent is 479 grains. Davy: *Anatomical and Physiological Observations*, 1839, I., 65; yet there is no vascular connection between mother and offspring. Compare chap. XV., note 11.

[36] On certain delicate points in the structure of the placenta the student may consult Charles Robin: *Mémoire sur quelques points d'Anatomie et Physiologie de la muqueuse utérine*, in Brown Sequard's *Journal de la Physiologie*, 1858, I., 47. and Farre: *Uterus and its Appendages*, in the *Cyclopædia of Anatomy and Physiology*. Compare also Von Baer: *Untersuchungen über die Gefässbindung zwischen Mutter und Frucht in den Säugethieren*, 1828; and Sharpey in Baly's translation of Müller's *Physiology;* also the memoir cited in note 37.

§ 205. I have been somewhat more minute than was absolutely necessary to explain the particular point now in hand; but all these details will be needed in future pages, and therefore I have not hesitated to give them in this place as the most convenient.

The survey we have taken of the main differences in the animal kingdom respecting the connection of the embryo with the mother, showing as it does that except in the Salpa only in the highest organisms does the connection approach directness, and that in all other organisms there is no semblance of connection, will explain the surprise and interest felt in MÜLLER's rediscovery of the fact announced by Aristotle— that one of the cartilaginous fishes (*Mustelus*) resembled the mammalia in possessing a placenta, though not exactly of the mammalian structure;[37] the more so, since it was known that other viviparous species had no trace of it.

"Although STENON had seen something of the kind," says MÜLLER, "and CUVIER mentions a fact which must recall a passage to the memory of every student of Aristotle, yet the fish named by Aristotle has hitherto remained totally unknown, and none of the fishes hitherto examined presented the phenomenon noticed by him; so that this statement of the great philosopher, like so many other remarkable facts of natural history observed by him, has remained unexplained."

§ 206. Zoologists might learn from this a lesson. Although many of the statements to be found in Aristotle are notoriously inaccurate, yet in all those cases not proved to be wrong, it would be prudent to assume the possibility of their being right. They should by no means be accepted; but they might serve as finger-posts. Research should be made to verify or to refute them.

As an example let us cite his assertion that the cuttlefish

---

[37] See MÜLLER's elaborate memoir, *Ueber der glatten Hai des Aristoteles*, in the Berlin *Abhandlungen der Akademie der Wissenschaften*, 1840, p. 187.

embryo has its head united with the vitellus, which hangs from its mouth. This singular statement turns out to be nearly accurate, as was proved by the researches of KÖLLIKER.[38]

§ 207. Again he says that a fish called Physeis makes a nest like a bird; a statement which CUVIER tells us was always doubted until an Italian naturalist, Olivi, had occasion to verify it.[39]

§ 208. Respecting the vision of the Mole some confusion prevails. "Until our own days," says CUVIER,[40] (alluding of course to the researches of GEOFFROY ST. HILAIRE,[41]) "it was always denied that the mole had eyes, in spite of Aristotle's assertion; but quite recently his observation has been verified."

GEOFFROY ST. HILAIRE begins his memoir by asserting that Aristotle and all the Greek philosophers thought the mole was blind; for what purpose should it have eyes with which it could not see?

Both these illustrious men somewhat misrepresent the real position of Aristotle. GALEN, ALDOVRANDUS, and SCALIGER maintained that the mole had eyes and could see; but Aristotle's assertion is that the mole has eyes yet cannot see. "All the red-blooded viviparous animals," he says, "have all the senses, though in some cases one is imperfect, as in the mole, which cannot see, for externally it has no visible eyes. But if we remove the thick skin of the head, we find on the spot where the eye is wont to be, an eye, imperfect indeed, but nevertheless possessing all the essential

---

[38] VOGT: *Zoologische Briefe*, 1851, I., 381; GEGENBAUER: *Grundzüge der Vergleichenden Anatomie*, 1859.

[39] CUVIER: *Hist. des Sciences Nat.*, 1841, I., 157. The nest-building fishes, namely, the Stickleback, the Goramy, and the Hassar, have since been carefully studied.

[40] *Ibid.*, I., 159.

[41] GEOFFROY ST. HILAIRE: *Histoire Naturelle des Mammifères*, 1834, Leçon XVI., in which there is an extremely interesting account of the structure and habits of the mole.

parts of an eye. We detect the pupil and the cornea, only they are smaller than usual."[42]

Two questions are raised, Has the mole eyes? and Is the mole mentioned by Aristotle the *talpa* known to us? On the first point we may reply with Sir THOMAS BROWNE: "That the moles have eyes in their head is manifested unto any that want them not in their own; and are discoverable not only in the old ones, but, as we have observed, in young and naked conceptions taken out of the belly of the dam."[43] GEOFFROY ST. HILAIRE not only proved that the mole had perfect eyes, but proved also that it had perfect vision.

With regard to the second point, LAMARCK[44] mentions that a traveller had discovered in Syria a species of mole which perfectly corresponds with Aristotle's description, and hence he concludes that this was the species to which the Stagirite referred, and not our common European mole. CUVIER's editors also remark that in Greece there does exist a little subterraneous animal, called the *rat-mole*, which is totally incapable of vision.[45]

§ 209. CUVIER's desire to glorify Aristotle has led him into error, in attributing to him the discovery, "which has only been verified in our own day," that molluscs have a brain. This is trebly unfortunate. The word ($\mu a \lambda \acute{a} \kappa \iota a$), which is here translated molluscs, was not used by Aristotle to designate any wider group than the cephalopoda; he did not suppose the pinna, solen, oyster, cockle, mussel, &c., to possess a brain: he expressly states that *no* "bloodless"

---

[42] *Hist. An.*, IV., 8.
[43] BROWNE: *Vulgar Errors*, ed. WILKINS, 1852, I., 312.
[44] LAMARCK: *Philosophie Zoologique*, I., 241.
[45] According to an Italian naturalist, quoted by SONNENBURG (LAWI: *Memorie sopra le Talpa*, Pisa, 1822), the Italian mole has its eyes covered, as described by Aristotle, there being only a microscopic opening visible between the lids. To the same effect the old Neapolitan, IMPERATO, says of the mole: " Vive sotterra, senza occhi manifesti, ma oscuramente formati sotto la pelle.' —*Dell' Historia Naturale, Libri XXVII.*, Naples, 1599, p. 776.

animal has a brain. The "brain" of the cuttlefish and calamary is almost as obvious as that of a rabbit; so that no discovery was anticipated in naming the brain of these animals. Secondly, the discovery of the brain in the less highly-organized molluscs was *not* "one of our own day;" it is as old as SWAMMERDAMM.[46] Thirdly, the masses which Aristotle and Cuvier call the "brain" are by modern anatomists recognized as only cephalic ganglia, and cannot be considered as homologous with cerebrum and cerebellum.

§ 210. Although I have not exhausted the list of cases in which Aristotle is said to have anticipated moderns, but must leave the others to fall in as they occur in the analyses of the works, those already cited will suffice to give a more definite and accurate opinion respecting the claims so frequently urged by the too facile enthusiasm of his eulogists. That opinion may be thus briefly expressed:—Aristotle had certain facts brought under his notice which were not known to his successors; but in no single instance, and under no legitimate extension of the term, can he be said to have made a discovery.

§ 211. I have indicated the reasons why he could not have made a discovery, when it involved a precise appreciation of delicate or complex phenomena; but in cases where the phenomena are not too remote or too complex for the unassisted senses, where the intellect is chiefly tasked, he is no longer under the same disadvantage as when having to deal with data discoverable only through the arduous research of ages. Here the mighty intellect displays itself. Here the mind, which could not avoid falling into absurdities when theorizing about heat without the aid of a thermometer, and about Physics without knowledge of the laws of motion, rises into admirable eminence when treating of the higher generalities of Life and Mind.

---

[46] SWAMMERDAMM: *Bibel der Natur*, Tab. IV., fig. 6, Tab. VI., fig. 1. See also HALLER: *Elementa Physiologiæ*, Lausanne, 1762, IV., 2.

CHAPTER XII.

LIFE AND MIND: *DE ANIMA*.

§ 212. AMONG the various works of Aristotle, the treatise *De Animâ* holds eminent rank. The extreme interest of its problems and the profundity of its views, render it the most valuable and valued of ancient attempts to bring the facts of life and mind into scientific order. A really good edition is still much needed;[1] but it must come from a physiologist. I do not mean by this to intimate that the work is not a treatise on psychology; but *nemo psychologus nisi physiologus* (to quote JOHANNES MÜLLER), and the saying is peculiarly apposite respecting a treatise which is occupied with the Soul as the Vital Principle.

§ 213. The word ψυχή is untranslatable in modern lan-

---

[1] For scholars little is left to be desired by the valuable edition of TRENDELENBURG (Jena, 1833), with its voluminous commentary. But for men of science another kind of work is needed. (Since this note was written A. TORSTRIK has published a new recension of the text from newly discovered MS., Berlin, 1862. It is addressed solely to scholars. I have consulted it during the revision of this chapter.) Of translations there are several; one in English by Dr. CHARLES COLLIER (*Aristotle on the Vital Principle*, Cambridge, 1855), has been laid under contribution in these pages, though I have frequently departed from it when a more rigid accuracy seemed indispensable. M. BARTHÉLEMY ST. HILAIRE has given one in French, of which report speaks highly. There are two or three in German. There is also a curious Tuscan paraphrase by SEGNI: *Il trattato sopra i libri dell'Anima d'Aristotele*, Florence, 1583. Of the numerous commentaries on this treatise, published at the revival of Learning, I have consulted only the elaborate and tiresome work, NIPHI: *Expositio subtilissima necnon et collectanea commentariaque in tres libros Aristotelis de Anima*, Venice, 1559. This is one of the fourteen folios which Agostino Nifo published on Aristotle; and although valuable and curious as an index of the philosophy of that time, is fully entitled to the cobwebs which now cover it.

guages. It is commonly rendered by *Anima*, or its equivalents, *Ame*, *Seele*, *Soul*. This has caused a general misconception of the profounder meanings conveyed in Aristotle's treatise. Since the days of DESCARTES there has been a broad distinction between Life and Mind, for which two separate essences or principles were required; and this distinction having permeated every modern language, we are at a loss for a single word which will express the union of the two, as it was conceived by Aristotle and all the early thinkers. The word ψυχή represents Soul as both Life and Mind—*anima* and *animus*. Yet if we translate the title of Aristotle's treatise, "On the Soul," it will be as misleading in its suggestions as the translation, "On the Vital Principle." Both phrases are narrower in their meaning than the Greek; the one excludes the physiological, the other the psychological meaning. Sir ALEX. GRANT justly remarks that the word means more and less than our word soul; "more, as having on one side, at all events, a directly physical connection; less, as not in itself implying any religious association. We cannot translate ψυχή 'vital principle,' because, though it is this, it is a great deal besides; nor, 'mind,' because this would leave out as much at the one end as the former translation did at the other."[2] Yet on many accounts "Vital Principle" is better than "Soul," and represents more accurately the meaning of ψυχή (which literally means breath, "the breath of life," as *anima* also means breath, ἄνεμος),[3] more accu-

---

[2] GRANT: *The Ethics of Aristotle*, 1858, p. 236.

[3] "This *anima* meant originally blowing or breathing, like *spirit* from *spirare*, and was derived from a root, *an*, to blow, which gives us *anila*, wind, in Sanskrit, and *anemos* in Greek. Ghost, the German *geist*, is based on the same conception. It is connected with *gust*, with *yeast*, and even with the hissing and boiling *geysers* of Iceland."—MAX MÜLLER: *Lectures on the Science of Language*, 1862, p. 382. "Quod Græci veteres unico ψυχῆς nomine significarunt," says PATRIZIO, "id duplici Animi et Animæ expressere Latini. In etymis eorum, erravere utrique. Illi quod ψυχήν a verbo ψυχάζω, refrigere, deduxere. Contrario ab ejus opere significatu. Quoniam nullibi sit animus, ψυχή, quin ibi calor quoque existat. Isti quod a voce Græca ἄνεμος, qui ventus

rately, because Aristotle's view is *not* that of STAHL, and the celebrated Montpellier school of "animists," which conceives the Mind to be the animating principle, bestowing on the body all activity, determining all vital functions, and thus including under its supremacy all physical and physiological phenomena. Instead of conceiving Life as one of the manifestations of Mind, Aristotle taught the precise obverse, namely, that Mind is only the highest development of Life.[4] He always exhibits Life as the *general* form of organic activity; Mind as only one of the *special* forms, developed in later stages, but wholly absent from the earlier. "Plants," he says, "have no sensation. By this the animal is separated from that which is not animal. *Numerically*, therefore, it (the soul) is one and the same part; but in its *mode of being* it is many and different."[5]

---

est, parva admodum detorsione animum et animam derivavere. Contraria maxime a vera re sententia. Nihil enim minus, quam ventus, animus est et anima. Error hic uterque a respiratione venit. Nam ea quæ confesso animam habent, animantia sunt et animalia. Hæc vero respirant. Respiratio fit vento, ventus internum refrigerat calorem. A vento animus, a refrigeratione ψυχή sunt efformata."—FRANCISCI PATRITII : *Nova de universis philos., libri LV., comprehensa*, Venice, 1593: *Pampsychia*, I., p. 49. STAHL, in his dissertation, *De mechanismi et organismi diversitate* (*Theoria Medica Vera*, ed. CHOULANT, Leipzig, 1831, I., 45), tries to prove that ψυχή is a corruption of φυσέχη, *quasi* ἔχων τὸ φύειν. This is somewhat in the manner of Aristotle's derivation of αἰθήρ from ἀεί and θεῖ: *De cœlo*, I., 3, 271. PLATO also derives it from φυσεχὴ, as the driver and sustainer of nature: ἢ φύσιν ὀχεῖ καὶ ἔχει, φυσέχην ἐπονομάζειν· ἔξεστι δὲ καὶ ψυχὴν κομψευόμενον λέγειν. — *Cratylus*, ed. Bekk. Berlin, 1817, p. 38. But he had previously given the common derivation from respiration.

[4] To my knowledge no writer has seen this radical distinction between the two views, owing, doubtless, to their *verbal* similarity. The Montpellier editors of STAHL persist in asserting that Stahl and Aristotle teach precisely the same doctrine (*Œuvres de Stahl*, 1860, III., p. lxi. and cxxxix.) M. BLONDIN says, "Stahl n'a jamais dit que c'est l'âme pensante, c'est à dire en fonction d'intelligence, qui exécute les fonctions vitales et organiques," which is true; but that Stahl attributed all the vital and organic functions to the soul as soul, and taught that this immaterial principle was pre-eminently intelligent, seems to me clear from his treatises, *De mechanismi et organismi diversitate*, and *De differentiâ λόγου et λογισμοῦ*.

[5] *De juventute*, I., 467: ἀριθμῷ μὲν οὖν ἀναγκαῖον ἓν εἶναι καὶ τὸ αὐτὸ τοῦτο τὸ μόριον, τῷ δ'εἶναι πλείω καὶ ἕτερα.

§ 214. There are one or two passages which raise a doubt as to whether Aristotle had made this point clear to himself in the sense in which it is held by the most advanced psychologists; indeed, it is evident that he had but imperfectly appreciated the necessary correlation between an ascending complexity of organization and an ascending complexity in vital phenomena, since he had not clearly and steadily mastered the fundamental relation between organ and function. Nevertheless, if he sometimes stopped midway, if he wavered in his conception of the relation between organ and function, the majority of moderns, even physiologists, have not been less wavering, and he stands at the point of view now generally occupied by the most advanced thinkers.[6]

---

[6] " We have already pointed out the impossibility of drawing any exact limit between the vital and the spiritual facts of our nature. . . . We have first presented to us a being manifesting vital properties only ; next to this we see the nerve force appearing in the double phenomena of sensation and motion; and then, lastly, out of these we see consciousness and intelligence gradually evolved."—MORELL: *An Introduction to Mental Philosophy, on the Inductive Method,* 1861, p. 28. This return to the Aristotelian point of view is quite recent. Less than thirty years ago SCHROEDER VAN DER KOLK mentioned with pain that some new writers " were not ashamed " to announce that Soul and Vital Principle were words of equivalent meaning; and the object of his Dissertation *über den Unterscheid zwischen todten Naturkräften, Lebenskräften und Seele,* Bonn, 1836, is to disprove such an hypothesis. He maintains the existence of a specific nerve-force, which forms the bond of union between soul and body. It is a curious point in the history of speculation that the doctrine of Aristotle, which was regarded for many centuries as the orthodox Christian doctrine, and was declared such by the Œcumenical Councils, should, since DESCARTES, have been regarded as dangerous to religion, so that its modern revival has been generally stigmatized. Descartes limited the functions of the Soul to thought alone; and having thus limited the meaning of the word, another word was employed to indicate Life; See BOUILLER: *Du principe Vital et de l'âme pensante,* 1862; and BLONDIN: *Du vitalisme animique,* in the 3rd vol. of the *Œuvres de Stahl traduites et commentées,* 1860. A similar change in doctrine is noticeable in the views of the early Church respecting the soul. " Je pourrais multiplier à l'infini les citations," says GUIZOT, " toutes prouveraient que la matérialité de l'âme était dans les premiers siècles, une opinion, non seulement admise, mais dominante."—*Histoire de la Civilisation en France,* Leçon VI., Bruxelles, 1839, II., 199. See the collection of passages from the Fathers, asserting that only God is incorporeal, in ABELARD: *Sic et Non,* ed. HENKE et LINDENKOHL, Marburg, 1851, pp. 105 seq. At the end of the 4th century the doctrine of immaterialism began to assume

CHAP. XII.] LIFE AND MIND: *DE ANIMA.* 225

In the following analysis, the phrases "Vital Principle" and "Soul" will be used alternately, but always as designating Life, of which Mind is the highest manifestation.

§ 215. BOOK I., *Chap. I.*—The inquiry opens with a question as to the nature of the Vital Principle: whether it is a something—an essence—or simply quantity or quality, or some one of the other categories; also, whether it is in itself a *potentiality* (τῶν ἐν δυνάμει ὄντων) or a *reality* (ἐντελέχεια). The reader is probably familiar with the Aristotelian distinction, which subsequently played so great a part in Scholasticism, between potential existence and actual existence; at any rate, he must have heard often enough of the *entelechie* or *reality* (completeness) of a thing, to understand that it was no idle inquiry to ascertain at the outset whether the soul was, or was not, such an *entelechie.* "We have to consider also whether the Soul is divisible or without parts; and whether every Vital Principle is, or is not, the same in kind; and if not, whether the difference is generic or specific." He warns the inquirer against the dangers of studying man exclusively; and insists on the study of animals being included.

He settles that there is only one Vital Principle. "It is difficult to say whether we should study the parts before their functions, as the mind before thought, and sensibility before sensations. If expedient to commence with functions, it may be questioned whether it would not be better to study their opposites first, *i. e.* the object of perception before that which perceives, and thought before that which thinks. Now the

---

this view; CLAUDIAN MAMMERTUS (in the 5th century) exhausted all the capital arguments by which DESCARTES was thought to have established it irrefragably. In the analysis of his treatise, *De natura animæ*, given by the learned Benedictines of St. Maur, we read, " Il fait voir que l'âme n'est jamais sans penser, et que la pensée n'est point différente de l'âme; qu'elle est toute volonté et toute pensée; que penser, vouloir et aimer est sa substance. Qu'il n'y a point de corps sans longueur, largeur, et profondeur; que l'âme n'a point ces dimensions, et que par conséquent elle est incorporelle."—*Histoire littéraire de la France, V. Siècle,* II., 447, Paris, 1735.

15

knowledge of anything in itself seems to be useful towards a right conception of the causes of the *accidents* (attributes—συμβεβηκότα) in substances; but the knowledge of accidents contributes largely towards knowing what the thing essentially is; for whenever we are able, from the appearance of any substance, to recount the whole, or the greater number of its accidents, we are then best prepared to say what its essential existence is."[7] By essential existence, οὐσία, is not meant *noumenon*, in the modern sense, but the reality of a thing as known to us. (See § 95 for an explanation of οὐσία.) "The essential existence is the proper beginning for every demonstration, so that all those definitions which do not make known, or make it easy to conjecture what may be the accidents of any substances are to be regarded as profitless subtleties."

§ 216. Whether all the affections of the soul (τὰ πάθη τῆς ψυχῆς) are also affections of the body is not clear; if there is any exception to be made, it must be in favour of thought, that appearing to be most *peculiar* to the Vital Principle; "but whether thought be imagination of some kind, or never unaccompanied by imagination, still we must admit that it cannot exist without the body. If, therefore, there is any one affection, or function, which is *peculiar* to the Vital Principle, we should admit that it might be isolated from the body; but if no one belongs to it exclusively, then we say that it cannot be separate." Here, as elsewhere, he maintains that thought is separable from the body in our abstraction, but not in-fact; the separation is subjective not objective, similar to the separation of whiteness from white bodies.

§ 217. It is for the physiologist (φυσικός), he says, to

---

[7] To a similar effect GOETHE in the Preface to the *Farbenlehre* :—" Denn eigentlich unternehmen wir umsonst, das Wesen eines Dinges auszudrücken. Wirkungen werden wir gewahr, und eine vollständige Geschichte dieser Wirkungen umfasste wohl allenfalls das Wesen jenes Dinges."— *Werke*, 1840, XXXVII.

study the soul. The Dialectician and the Physiologist would differ in their explanations; the latter would explain " anger as an ebullition of blood, or excess of heat about the heart; the former would declare it to be a desire for retaliation, or some such motive." The reader will probably be of opinion that the dialectician seems here to have the best of it.

§ 218. *Chap. II.* is wholly devoted to a review of the opinions expressed by the early thinkers.

§ 219. *Chap. III.* examines the Principle of Motion, and whether the Soul be self-moved, or moved externally. If moved, it can only be moved by sensations. After glancing at some other opinions, he concludes thus :—" The same incongruity, which occurs in most of the theories about the Vital Principle, is met with here, namely, that the writers join this Principle to a body, and place it in a body without having first settled for what purpose the body is to receive it, or how it is fitted to this office. This, however, must be settled, since it is through such a connection that one acts and the other is acted on; and these are relations which cannot be attributed to chance. There are writers who content themselves with saying what the soul is, without determining anything about the body, its recipient, as if any kind of soul might clothe itself with any kind of body. But everything, on the contrary, seems to have its own particular species and form (εἶδος καὶ μορφήν). We might as well maintain that the architect could work with musical instruments; for, as each art must employ its own instrument, so each soul its own body."

§ 220. *Chaps. IV.* and *V.* are devoted to the examination of more theories. At the close occurs this important passage : " Since the faculties of knowing, feeling, thinking, desiring, willing, and the appetites in general, as also locomotion, growth, maturity, and decay, are properties of the soul, we may inquire whether each of these properties is given by the soul as a whole, or are different offices assigned to different parts? Is Life in one part, in more than one, or in all the parts? or is there some other cause of Life besides the soul? Some say the Vital Principle is divisible—one part thinking, another part desiring; but, if this be so, what holds the parts together? Not the body, certainly, for the Vital Principle appears to hold *it* together, since, from the moment of its departure, the body expires and decays.[8] If there be something which makes it one, that something is, in the strictest sense, the Vital Principle. . . . . With respect to the parts of this Principle, it is difficult to determine what is the office assigned to each in the body, for, if it is the whole which sustains the body, then we must conclude that each part sustains one part of the body. But this is very like an impossibility, for it is difficult even to conjecture what part the intellect could connect with other parts, and *how* it could do so.[9] Thus plants, when divided, are seen to live, and so are certain insects, as if still possessing the same Vital Principle, considered *specifically*, though not the same *numerically*.[10] Each of the divided parts has sensation and locomotion for a time; and there is no room for surprise at their not continuing to manifest these properties, seeing that the organs necessary for the preservation of nature are absent.[11] Nevertheless, in each divided part coexist all the parts of the Vital Principle." Here he contradicts what he has said elsewhere respecting the absence of the vital centre from the separated head (§ 89).

---

[8] Compare STAHL: *Theoria Medica vera de Vita et Sanitate*, p. 229. "Hæc ipsa conservatio rei tam corruptibilis, ne ipso actu corrumpatur, est propriè illud quod sub usitato *vitæ* vocabulo intelligi debet."

[9] ποῖον γὰρ μόριον, ἢ πῶς ὁ νοῦς συνέξει.

[10] τὴν αὐτὴν ἔχοντα ψυχὴν τῷ εἴδει, εἰ καὶ μὴ ἀριθμῷ.

[11] This acute remark solves many difficulties. Aristotle's view, both of life and mind, is adopted by MÜLLER: *Elements of Physiology*, 1843, II., 1334. For examples of "divided vitality," see *Physiology of Common Life*, II., 225, 421. The old writers puzzled themselves incessantly over this difficulty. See, for example, BASSO: *Philosophiæ Naturalis adversus Aristotelem*, Amsterdam, 1649, p. 260; or TAURELLUS: *Contra Cæsalpinum*, 1650, p. 850; neither of them comparable to Aristotle.

Probably he was thinking only of Plants, for he continues—"and those parts are specifically the same with each other and with the whole—with each other as being inseparable, and with the whole as being inseparable. The vitality of plants is due to a kind of Soul, common both to animals and plants; and this may be separated from—*i.e.* exist without—the sentient principle; but without it no sentient principle can exist."[12]

§ 221. BOOK II., *Chap. I.*—The preliminary arguments of the first book clear the way for a definition of Life. Numerous as have been the attempts to frame such a definition, that of Aristotle holds rank with the best. One great source of confusion has been the radical error of conceiving Life to be an Entity, apart from, and only *inhabiting* the organism (§ 72 *b*); just as the several Forces were for centuries conceived to be independent of matter, instead of being regarded as matter in dynamic conditions. To escape from such a confusion, and to have seen thus early the positive solution of the difficulty, implies immense intellectual force. A glance at some modern definitions will enable us the better to appreciate Aristotle's.

KANT defines Life "an internal principle of action;" and an organism, "that in which every part is at once means and end." Yet Fermentation, which no one calls Life, is such an internal principle.

TREVIRANUS defines it—"The constant uniformity of phenomena under diversity of external influences," which may

---

[12] In the preface to DESCARTES: *Traité de l'Homme*, Paris, 1729, written by SCHUYL, there is this remarkable passage, which contains samples of the metaphysical and scientific modes of viewing phenomena: " C'est par une imprudence presque semblable et par une prodigalité aussi inconsidérée, que, *contre l'intention du créateur*, le Peripatétisme attribue aux plantes une âme vivante ; qu'il ne fait pas simplement *consister dans la disposition et le mouvement de leurs parties, en quoi consiste toute la cause de la végétation;* mais que l'ignorance où il est de sa véritable cause, lui fait considérer, selon son caprice, comme un esprit ou une substance entièrement différente de la matière ou du corps de la plante."

be said with equal truth of a watch, since, if some external influences disturb the mechanism of a watch, external influences will not less disturb an organism.

BICHAT'S famous definition: "Life is the sum of the functions by which death is resisted," is only another form of the one already quoted from STAHL (Note 8), and is every way objectionable; for on the one hand it is a paraphrase of the truism that "life is the means by which we live;" and on the other hand it declares that there is a fatal *antagonism* in external agencies; whereas we know that such agencies are necessary *co-efficients*, Life being inconceivable without a medium.

DUGÈS defines Life "the special activity of organized beings."

BÉCLARD says: "Life is the sum of the phenomena proper to organized beings. It consists essentially in this, that organized beings are all during a certain time the centres to which foreign substances penetrate and are appropriated, and from which others issue."

DE BLAINVILLE's definition, adopted by COMTE and CHARLES ROBIN, runs thus:—"Life is the twofold internal movement of composition and decomposition at once general and continuous." But this only embraces the phenomena of vegetal life, and even there is too restricted.

HERBERT SPENCER says, "Life is the definite combination of heterogeneous changes, both simultaneous and successive, in correspondence with external co-existences and sequences."

In a former work, after citing these definitions, I proposed the following:—"Life is the dynamical condition of the organism." The advantage of such a formula is that it embraces every form of life, from that of the simple cell to that of the most complex mammal. It further expresses every variation in the intensity or the complexity of vital phenomena, according to the activity or complexity of the organism; and their dependence on external and internal agencies.¹³

§ 222. By conceiving Life simply as the function of the organism, we do not rob it of its solemn mystery. It is still the dark Dynamis which must ever remain impenetrable; but a similar mystery hangs over the course of the planets, the ebb and flow of the tides, the vehement impulses and repulsions of chemical elements; yet, as in these we have detected order, and gained some glimpse of law, so in the manifold phenomena of Life, we may likewise discern order and law if we study them aright.

That Aristotle conceived Life thus, may be read in the following sentences:—"Among natural bodies some have, and some have not, life; and by life we mean the faculties of self-nourishment, self-growth, and self-decay. Thus every natural body partaking of life may be regarded as an essential existence (οὐσία); but then it is an existence only in combination (ὡς συνθέτη). And since the organism is such a combination, being possessed of life, it cannot be the Vital Principle. Therefore it follows that the Vital Principle must be an essence, as being the *form* of a natural body holding life in *potentiality;* but essence is a *reality* (entelechie). The Vital Principle is the original reality of a natural body endowed with potential life; this, however, is to be understood only of a body which may be organized. Thus the parts even of plants are organs, but they are organs that are altogether simple, as the leaf which is the covering of the pericarp, the pericarp of the fruit. If then there be any general formula for every kind of Vital Principle, it is—the *primary reality of an organism.*" ¹⁴

---

¹³ KANT: *Kritik. der Urtheilskraft* (*Werke* IV., 260); TREVIRANUS: *Biologie;* BICHAT: *Recherches sur la Vie et la Mort;* DUGÈS: *Physiologie Comparée,* I., 3; BÉCLARD: *Anatomie Générale;* COMTE: *Cours de Philos. Positive,* III., 295; HERBERT SPENCER: *Principles of Psychology,* 1855, p. 354. Compare *Physiology of Common Life,* 1860, II., 426.

¹⁴ ἐντελέχεια ἡ πρώτη σώματος φυσικοῦ ὀργανικοῦ.

"It is, therefore," he adds, "as idle to ask whether the Vital Principle and body are one, as whether the wax and the impress on it are one; or whether the matter formative of any object, and the object formed, are one; for *one* and *being* have many significations, but they are correctly designated by the word reality (entelechie). Thus if an eye were an animal, vision would be its Vital Principle; for vision, abstractedly considered, is the essence of the eye; but the eye is the body of vision, and if vision be wanting, then, save in name, it is an eye no longer."

This admirable illustration, profoundly misconceived by TELESIO,[15] not only shows that Aristotle conceived Life as the *function* of the organism, but also points to the answer he would have made had the common objection been urged, that the organism remains entire even after the departure of the breath of life. It does *not* remain entire, he would have replied; the *conditions of its activity* are removed; it is an organism only in name.[16] He fell into none of the confusions of subsequent philosophers. The animal body, without its soul, was, he said, no longer an animal body; for an animal is body *and* soul, as an eye is pupil *and* vision.[17]

§ 223. *Chap. II.* carries this conception further, showing that not only has the whole organism its life—or sum of functions—but that each separate organ has its life, or function. One simple form of vitality suffices for simple organisms, as plants; more complex forms being demanded by more highly organized beings, such as animals.

"The term *living* has many significations, but if only one

---

[15] In his argument against the soul being the form of the body: TELESIUS: *De Natura Rerum*, 1586, V., 184. He might have been saved from this misconception had he attended to what NIPHUS had said on this point in his *Expositio subtilissma*, Venice, 1559, p. 245.

[16] μᾶλλον γὰρ ζῆλον ὅτι ὁ νεκρὸς ἄνθρωπος ὁμωνύμως.—*Meteor.*, IV., 12, 3, 38.

[17] "Ita enim ex hisce duabus partibus homo constat, ut neque animus sit homo, nec item corpus, sed tertium quiddam quod et animo constet et corpore."—PHILELPHUS: *Epist. familiarum libri XXXVII.*, Venet., 1502, p. 253, *verso*.

of its forms be manifested (*i. e.* mind, sensibility, locomotion, and rest, as well as nutrition, growth, and decay) we say the object is living. And, therefore, all plants are alike, for they have within them a principle by which they acquire growth, and undergo decay in opposite directions. It is possible for nutrition to exist independently of the other functions; but the others cannot exist in the absence of nutrition. This is manifest in plants, since no other form of life has been given them. Life is thus first manifested by this function. But animal life is characterized by sensibility; for we say that creatures endowed with sensibility are not simply living, but are animals, even though incapable of moving. *Touch* is the first form of sensibility manifested by animals; just as nutrition may be independent of all other functions, so may Touch exist independently of all other sensibilities. Life, or Soul, may therefore be defined as the principle of nutrition, sensation, intellection, and locomotion."

§ 224. In the next paragraph occurs one of those passages which render it difficult to come to a decision respecting his views on the immortality of the soul, or rather of the thinking principle; a question hotly debated in the 15th and 16th centuries, by friends and foes desirous of defending, or of incriminating his orthodoxy.[18] Having alluded to the fact that insects, when divided, manifest life and sensation—and "if sensation, then also imagination and desire"—in each divided half, he adds : "Respecting mind, and the theoretic faculty, nothing as yet is evident; but it seems to be another kind of soul, and is alone capable of separation, as the everlasting from the perishable."[19] Thus it is manifest from

---

[18] His views are briefly but lucidly stated by PHILELPHUS: *Op. cit.*, p. 48. Comp. NIPHUS: *Expositio subtilissima*, p. 642.

[19] περὶ δὲ τοῦ νοῦ καὶ τῆς θεωρητικῆς δυνάμεως οὐδέν πω φανερόν, ἀλλ' ἔοικε ψυχῆς γένος ἕτερον εἶναι, καὶ τοῦτο μόνον ἐνδέχεται χωρίζεσθαι καθάπερ τὸ ἀΐδιον τοῦ φθαρτοῦ. The mortality of all three souls was distinctly maintained by GALEN. In one of the brief treatises translated by DAREMBERG, he says, "Il y a trois espèces d'âmes; ces trois âmes habitent l'une dans le foie,

what has been said that the other parts of the soul are not *distinct* from the body, although, considered abstractedly, they are *different* from it: for the mode of being in a sentient creature must differ from that in a cogitative creature, since feeling differs from thinking. (*See* § 466.)

§ 225. *Chap III.* treats of the simpler manifestations of Life, especially Touch and Taste, the latter being a kind of Touch. It is to be observed that, in giving animals sensation, he also adds appetite, passion, and volition, remarking that it is uncertain whether those which have simply Touch have imagination also.

§ 226. *Chap. IV.* is on Life as a cause and origin of the living body. "Cause and origin have several significations, for the Vital Principle is equally a cause according to any one of the three defined modes of causation; 1, as that whence motion proceeds; 2, as that for which motion is produced; 3, as the essence of living bodies."

His grounds for considering it a final cause are these:— As the mind acts for an end, so does Nature, and that end is her aim; and such an aim has the Vital Principle by its nature in living bodies. Thus all plants and animals are its instruments, and are what they are for its purposes. The term final cause has two meanings: it implies that *for* which and that *by* which any result is obtained; and the Vital Principle is a final cause, being that from whence locomotion is derived, although this is a function that does not belong to all animals.

§ 227. Nutrition he defines "a contrary acted upon by a contrary; but this does not mean *any* kind of contrary; it refers only to such as can generate from, and give growth to, one another." He here perceives a difficulty, namely, the axiom that like is increased by like; he eludes it by saying

---

l'autre dans le cœur, la troisième dans l'encéphale. Si donc la partie rationelle de l'âme est une espèce d'âme, cette espèce sera mortelle, car elle est elle-même un certain tempérament de l'encéphale."—*Œuvres de Galien*, 1854, I., 52-5.

that food, inasmuch as it is undigested, is a contrary nourishing a contrary; but when it is digested it is a like increasing a like.

There are three things: something to be nourished, something by which it is nourished, and something which is nourishment. That *by* which it is nourished is the primal soul [20]—the first Vital Principle—which is capable of generating another like itself.

§ 228. *Chaps. V. and VI.* pass to the consideration of Sensibility. Having defined sensation "the result of a motion, and an impression," he starts this difficulty:—Why is there no sensation from the senses themselves? That is to say, why, in the absence of external objects, do not the senses give sensation, since fire and earth and the other elements are present in them, and it is from these that sensation is derived?

The answer runs thus:—Because the sensibility is not in a state of *actuality*, but only of *potentiality*;[21] and, therefore, it is with it as with a combustible body, which alone, without something on fire, does not burn; for, otherwise, it might set fire to itself, and could stand in need of no actual fire.

§ 229. He then indicates the distinction between primary and secondary qualities; each of the special senses perceives a special quality, as sight, colour, hearing, sound, &c.; but, besides these, there are qualities more generally perceived, belonging not to one sense alone, but to all in common—such are motion, form, number, magnitude.

§ 230. *Chaps. VII.-IX.* treat of Sight, Hearing, and Taste (topics which we shall have to consider more fully hereafter); but why these, which are subsequent in development, should be spoken of earlier than Touch, is by no means clear. A logical arrangement would have reversed this order.

---

[20] τὸ μὲν τρέφον ἐστὶν ἡ πρώτη ψυχή.

[21] It will not escape the reader that this answer is only a restatement of the difficulty in other words; but it has more the appearance of an answer than that given by HERMOLAUS BARBARUS: *Compendium Scient. Nat. ex Aristotele*, 1547, V., *de Animâ*, p. 51.

§ 231. *Chap. X.* is on Touch, the first and most important of the senses. "It is difficult to specify the organ percipient of tangible qualities, whether or not it is the flesh, and that which is analogous to flesh in other creatures; yet flesh is only a *medium*, and the essential organ, πρῶτον αἰσθητήριον, must be something different and internal. . . . Is, then, this sentient organ within the flesh, or is it the flesh itself which is immediately perceptive? No indication can be obtained from the fact of sensation being simultaneous with tangible impression, for were any one to extend a membrane over his flesh, the part would be equally sensible when touched, and sensible at the moment of contact; and yet, clearly, the sentient organ cannot be in that membrane. . . . When the sentient organ itself is touched, no sensation can there or then be produced, any more than a white object can be seen when placed immediately over the surface of the eye; and thus it is evident that the part perceptive of tangible impressions must be *internal*." Although not stated here, we know that by this *internal* part, which is perceptive, he means the heart, the central seat of all sensibility.

§ 232. *Chap. XII.* is on Perception. "It must be admitted that each sense is receptive of the *sensible forms* of things (ideas, images) without their *matter*, as wax takes the impress from a seal-ring without the iron or gold of which the ring is made."

Why, then, do plants not feel, seeing that they have a psychical organ (μόριον τι ψυχικὸν), and are impressible by tangible objects? The reason is that they want the *central* faculty (μεσότητα), which alone would admit of their being impressed by sensible forms without the matter. Constituted as they are (§ 177), they receive the matter along with the forms.

§ 233. Book III., *Chap. I.*, continues the discussion of Sensibility. We have, he says, but five senses. Touch makes us aware of whatever is tangible; all other qualities are perceived, not through touch, but through the media air and water. The sentient organs are constituted of these two simple bodies: the pupil is composed of water, the organ of hearing is composed of air, and the organ of smell is of one or the other. Fire forms no part of any organ; or rather it is an element common to all, since there is nothing sentient without heat.

We are furnished with several senses, instead of one, in order that the common properties of bodies—motion, magnitude, number—may the less readily escape notice. If vision were our only sense, then all other qualities except colour would escape notice, seeming to be identical with it. But as common properties are manifested by different bodies, it is evident that they must also be different.

§ 234. *Chap. II.*—" Vision must be by sight, or by some other sense; but if by some other sense, then *it* will be perceptive of sight and colour, the subject of sight, and thus there will be two senses for one office, or the sight itself will be the percipient. But if to perceive by sight is seeing, and if that which is seen is colour, or something having colour, then if any sense is to see, that which sees must first have colour.[22] It is thus manifest that perception by sight is not a single perception, for when we cannot see, it is still by sight that we judge both of darkness and light, although not in the same manner."

This, as may be imagined, has been an enticing passage to commentators, and is full of pitfalls both of equivoque and psychological subtlety. Much of the obscurity of psychological questions arises from the tendency, almost irresistible, to refer all perceptions to the organs of sense, instead of to that consciousness which is affected by the organs of sense in their action: *e. g.* perceptions are referred to the retina rather

---

[22] Wär nicht das Auge sonnenhaft,
 Wie könnten wir das Licht erblicken?
    GÖTHE.

than to the optic centre. Hence, also, the confusion of objective with subjective, as when we speak of a colour which is unseen, of a sound which is unheard.

§ 235. " If motion, production, and impression, are in the product, it follows that sound and hearing, in an active state, must pre-exist *potentially* in hearing; for the action of the motor exists naturally in that which is acted on. It is, therefore, not necessary that the motor itself should be in motion. The action of a sonorous body is sound, or sounding; that of the auditory sense is hearing; for hearing is double, as sound is double. The same applies to other senses and perceptions. Since production and impression are not in that which acts, but in that which is impressed, so the action of the object of perception, and the sensibility are in the sentient organ. But while for some senses the two states have been distinguished by separate names—such as sound and hearing—there are others for which one or the other state is without a name. Thus, the action of vision is called sight, but the action of colour is unnamed; the action of the gustatory sense is called taste, while that of savour is without a name. Since the action of the object and the sentient organ is one and the same, though different in mode of acting, it follows that hearing and sound in this sense must be lost together, or together preserved. But this does not hold of such relations in *potentiality*. The earlier writers expressed themselves ill, in saying there could be neither black nor white without sight, nor savours without taste. And yet they were partly right; for as senses and sentient impressions have a twofold acceptation, according to their potentiality or activity, so what was advanced by these writers may be true of one state, and not true of the other. But they reasoned about things considered as isolated which do not in truth admit of being isolated."

§ 236. " Each sense is perceptive of its own objects, is innate in its own organ, as an organ, to discriminate qualities —Sight judging of black and white, Taste of bitter and sweet. But how do we perceive that qualities differ? Evidently by some sense, because the impressions are sentient; and the flesh cannot be that final sentient, ἔσχατον αἰσθητήριον, since to judge of qualities it must of necessity first touch bodies."

His meaning here is by no means clear. He says emphatically that we have only five senses; that each sense can only discriminate its own objects; that that which perceives white to be different from sweet cannot be the sense of Taste nor the sense of Sight, yet it must be a sense, because the impression is sentient; finally he says that the sense cannot be Touch, because to judge of qualities, that sense must first touch bodies—by which he probably means that white and sweet not being tangible, cannot be perceived by Touch.

What, then, is this judicial sense? He has nowhere told us. He enters upon discussions as to whether the judging faculty is divisible or indivisible, and this numerically or locally; but *what* it is, or *where* it is, he has not explained in this treatise. Elsewhere we gather that he means the common sensorium, which is in the front centre (heart) of each animal.[23]

§ 237. *Chap. III.* " The soul being characterized generally by the faculties, locomotion and thought, judgment and sensibility, it would seem that thought and reflection are considered to be forms of sensation. All writers assume that thinking, like feeling, is corporeal, and that Like is comprehended by Like. But they should have noted the liability of the senses to produce error. It is manifest that feeling is not the same as reflection; the one belonging to all creatures, the other only to a few. Neither is the judging faculty, which discerns right from wrong, to be confounded with sensation; for sensation being derived from particulars is always true,

---

[23] ἕν τι κοινὸν αἰσθητήριον.—*De Juventute*, I., 467. Compare also *De Somno*, II., 454.

and belongs to all animals; but error lies in judgment, and none are liable to error save those which have reason."

§ 238. Imagination is then treated. He says it is neither sensation nor judgment, yet it is never called up without sensation. It is the faculty by which an image of some kind is called up within us, and is to be ranked with those faculties, such as sensation, opinion, and knowledge, by which we form judgments.

§ 239. *Chap. IV.* has peculiar interest, being devoted to the νοῦς, or intellect, "that part of the Soul by which it both knows and reflects."

"If thinking be similar to sensation," he says, "then may it be some kind of impression by the object of thought, or some other analogous agency. But that which thinks must then be passive, ἀπαθὲς, receptive of the Forms of objects, and identical with the objects in potentiality, though not so in actuality. In a word, the Intellect must be related to objects of thought, as sensibility is to objects of perception. Thus, the so-called Intellect of the Vital Principle (and by Intellect I mean that which judges and compares) has in actuality no existence prior to the act of intelligence.[24] It is very improbable, therefore, that the mind should have been commingled with the body; for if this were so, it would be a quality of some kind, as hot or cold; or *it would have some kind of organ such as there is for sensation;* but there is none such."

§ 240. "It is well said that the Soul is the *place of Forms* (τόπος εἰδῶν); but this is not to be understood of the whole soul, only of the cogitative part; and of Forms, not in actuality, but in potentiality."

---

[24] οὐθὲν ἐστιν ἐνεργείᾳ τῶν ὄντων πρὶν νοεῖν. This, if I understand it aright, means that the mind has no substantive existence, but exists only in act, as a function. The passage is very obscure. TRENDELENBURG, who has a long note on the parenthesis, which does not require one, is silent on the only real difficulty. TOHSTRIK says, "intellectus non est actu idea antequam cogitet (οὐκ ἐστιν αὐτοῦ φύσις οὐδεμία ἀλλ' ἢ αὕτη ὅτι δυνατόν=οὐθὲν ἐστιν ἐνεργείᾳ τῶν ὄντων πρὶν νοεῖν), ed. *De Animâ,* p. 198.

§ 241. He argues that the reflective faculty is not the sensitive faculty in a state of repose. "The mind judges of flesh and ideal flesh, either by some different faculty, or by being itself differently affected. It is by sensibility that we judge of hot and cold and other properties of flesh; but it is either by some distinct faculty—or as a curved line is to a straight line—that we judge of ideal flesh."

§ 242. *Chap. V.*—The soul is creative. It is essentially an energizing influence. Knowledge *in activity* is identical with the object; but in potentiality, it pre-exists in the individual. "Yet rigorously speaking that cannot be said to pre-exist which sometimes is, and sometimes is not, reflected on. But that alone, whatever it be, which is separate from everything else, is deathless and eternal. We have no memory of it because it is passionless (ἀπαθὲς); and the impressible mind is perishable, and without it there can be no reflection."

§ 243. *Chap. VI.* briefly reiterates the argument that the senses are free from error, which arises solely from the judgment.

§ 244. *Chap. VII.*—The opening sentence may be read as a vague anticipation of the modern hypothesis, that knowledge, or rather the aptitude for acquiring knowledge, becomes developed in the race, and is thus transmitted from parent to child, so that the offspring of European parents is capable of acquiring a higher degree of intellectual development than the offspring of Australian parents reared under similar conditions.

Hume's doctrine[25] that the mind is simply the succession of impressions is thus formularized at the close of the chapter: "The mind in the act of thinking is the things thought of."[26]

§ 245. *Chap. VIII.* is a repetition of former arguments.

---

[25] HUME: *Treatise on Human Nature*, Works, 1826, I., 269.
[26] ὅλως δὲ ὁ νοῦς ἐστὶν ὁ κατ' ἐνέργειαν τὰ πράγματα νοῶν.

§ 246. *Chaps. IX.* and *X.* are devoted to the locomotive powers considered as parts of the Vital Principle. The nutritive and generative functions which belong to all living beings originate the motions concerned in the processes of growth and decay. These are motions, but how does locomotion originate?

Not by the nutritive faculty, since animal progression has always some cause in imagination or appetite; and no being moves except when urged by desire or fear, unless there be some external impulse. Besides, if nutrition were the cause of locomotion, plants would move.

Not by the sentient faculty, since there are many sentient beings which are stationary throughout life.

Not by the rational faculty, or mind, as we call it; for the theoretic faculty never thinks upon what is to be done, or suggests what should be pursued and avoided; but progression is always an act of pursuit or of flight. Nor does the rational faculty even when reflecting on flight or pursuit at once bid the animal move, since it often dwells upon something terrible or agreeable without suggesting alarm, although the heart may be agitated. Moreover, although the mind may bid, and reason suggest, that something should be fled from or pursued, the animal does not necessarily move, but acts like an intemperate man, according to the dictates of passion.

Finally, it is not appetite that causes progression, since the temperate, even while desiring and yearning after something, do not act in order to secure it, but follow their understanding.

§ 247. Having thus excluded Nutrition, Sensation, Reason, and Appetite as incapable singly of causing locomotion, he proceeds to show that the motor principles are Appetite and Reason; an apparent contradiction, but when read by the light of a previous passage (§ 160), seen to mean that Reason and Appetite must act in combination to produce locomotion. "It is mind as a logical and practical power," he adds, "and which differs from the theoretic mind in its aim. Every appetite has an aim; the appetite which is the principle of the practical mind has always an object in view, and this object is the principle of action. Thus appetite and practical reason may be regarded as the two motors."

§ 248. *Chap. XI.* raises the question whether those inferior animals which have only the sense of Touch can have motion and imagination. They appear sentient of pleasure and pain, and hence must feel desire; but how can imagination be present? Even as their motions are indeterminate, so also may imagination exist in them indeterminately.[27] The sentient imagination belongs to other animals; the voluntary imagination only to such as are rational: for whether this, or that, shall be done is a matter of reasoning; and as the individual is to pursue the better of two courses, he must be guided by a rule of some kind which enables him out of many images to select one.

§ 249. *Chap. XII.* reiterates the statement of an ascending complexity of organisms. It is necessary that every living being should have the nutritive soul, but it is not necessary that every living being should be sentient. All animals must be sentient, if Nature does nothing in vain; since without sensibility a progressive animal would perish, being unable to select its nutriment. Creatures which are stationary obtain their nourishment on the spot. But it is impossible that a progressive animal which has been generated should possess a Vital Principle and a judging faculty, and not be sentient.

Touch and Taste are the primary and indispensable senses. The other senses are given only to the higher animals; for if these are to preserve their existence, they must not only be sensible of objects touching them, but also at a distance.

---

[27] This is analogous to the hypothesis of many zoologists, that nerve tissue may exist in a *diffused* state in all those animals which manifest sensibility, yet seem to be destitute of nerves. Both opinions arise from loose conceptions of Psychology and Anatomy. An imagination without images, and a nerve tissue without definite structure, are not more acceptable than liquid crystals.

§ 250. *Chap. XIII.*—This final chapter argues that the animal body cannot be homogeneous, *i. e.* made up of one element only. The sentient organs may be composed of all the elements except earth, for these organs all receive impressions through media (§ 233). But Touch is made sensible by contact with bodies, and hence its name. Other organs likewise perceive by contact, but it is through media—through something foreign to themselves—whereas Touch perceives directly. So that an animal body cannot be constituted of any of the other elements exclusively, nor can it be formed of earth alone; for Touch is the medium of tangible impressions, and its organ is perceptive not only of the distinctions which pertain to earth, but also of hot and cold, and all other tangible qualities. Hence it is that we have no sensation in bones, hair, and analogous parts, because they are formed of earth; and plants, for the same reason, being formed of earth, have no sensation.

§ 251. While Touch is necessary for continued existence, some animals have other senses, not simply for existence, but for enjoyment. They have Vision, in order that living in air or water, in a transparent medium, they may see. They have Taste, that by discerning what is grateful or nauseous in food they may desire and obtain, or avoid it. They have Hearing, that others may signify something to them; and a Tongue that they may signify something to others.

§ 252. If now we review the contents of the treatise just analysed, we shall note first how very slightly it touches on those faculties which are more prominently indicated by the modern word Soul, and how it enlarges on physiological, rather than psychological questions. Secondly, we shall note here, as in almost every one of his scientific works, the want of masterly and logical arrangement of subject, and the want of the elementary requisites of good composition. There is no progression, no culmination. One chapter might be transposed in the place of another, one paragraph might precede its predecessor without affecting the symmetry, or rather the asymmetry of the work. Were this not equally observable in other works, we might not unreasonably lay the blame at the door of the earlier editors and copyists; but such an argument is untenable in the presence of compositions so uniformly defective. Thirdly, we suspect, what detailed examination proves to be the fact,[68] that the work was the great text-book of Psychology until modern times, the additions made by Aristotle's successors up to the 17th century being unimportant. Fourthly, we shall note the profundity of many of its views, and their singular accordance with much that is taught in the best writings of our own times.

---

[29] FRIES: *Handbuch der psychischen Anthropologie*, 1820, I., 59.

CHAPTER XIII.

ON THE SENSES.

§ 253. ARISTOTLE has written much about the senses in several works. The treatise *De sensu*, in the *Parva Naturalia*, is perhaps the best source we can consult; and it may, therefore, be analysed briefly here.

§ 254. The early philosophers sought in the four elements, earth, air, fire, and water, for the several bodies constituting the senses. As there are five senses, and only four elements were generally recognized, a fifth element was imagined. What that element is, Aristotle does not say; elsewhere we learn it is the Ether.

I.—*Vision.*

§ 255. Every one, he says, believes Vision to be of fire; the reason is that men misconceive the phenomenon of sparks dancing before the eyes when rubbed, especially in the dark. But if we cannot deny that we feel and see that which we see, it necessarily follows that the eye sees itself. Now, why have we this sensation only when the eye is rubbed?

The explanation offered is that smooth bodies shine naturally in the dark, though without producing light; now the pupil of the eye is smooth; and when the eye is rubbed it seems as if that which was one became two. The rapid motion makes the eye which is seen and that which sees appear different. The phenomenon is not producible unless the eye be rubbed quickly, and in darkness (I suppose he means by darkness the eye being closed, otherwise the qualification is erroneous), smooth bodies shine no less than certain fish heads, and the ink of the cuttlefish. When the eye is rubbed slowly, the sensation is not such as to make us think that what sees and what is seen are one and the same, so that the eye may see itself as in a mirror.

§ 256. This, it must be confessed, is not a fortunate attempt at explanation. NEWTON, in one of his celebrated queries added to the *Optics*, first clearly stated that the sparks which arise when the eye is rubbed "arise from such motions excited in the bottom of the eye by the pressure and motion of the finger, as at other times are excited there by light for causing vision." But it was JOHANNES MÜLLER, stimulated by the *Farbenlehre* of GOETHE, who placed beyond a doubt the fact that each special nerve of sense responds only in one special manner, no matter how various may be the stimuli, so that whatever excites the optic nerve excites a luminous sensation; whatever excites the auditory or gustatory nerves, excites sonorous and sapid sensations; and the pressure on the skin-nerve which excites pain excites in the optic nerve not pain, but a luminous sensation.

§ 257. Aristotle, knowing nothing of the properties of the optic nerve, could not, of course, give an explanation of the phenomenon. But his explanation is better than that of EMPEDOCLES and PLATO, who held "the eye to be of fire." He asks, àpropos of this, "If vision is produced when light passes from the eye, as from a lantern, why can we not see in the darkness? To pretend that light is extinguished by the darkness, on quitting the eye, is absurd."

§ 258. He thinks DEMOCRITUS "right in asserting that the vision is 'of water,' but wrong in asserting it to be an image (appearance, ἔμφασις), for the image is produced because the eye is a smooth surface, and vision is not in it, but in the seeing faculty. The affection is a refraction, ἀνάκλασις γὰρ τὸ πάθος. But in those days the theory of images and refraction was not understood. Moreover, it is absurd not to have asked why the eye alone can see, and not other bodies."

§ 259. " It is correct to say that vision is of water; not because it is of water, but because it is diaphanous, and this quality is common to air. Water, however, retains and receives it better than air, and that is why the pupil and the eye are of water. The soul is assuredly not at the surface of the eye, but within; hence the eye must be translucent and capable of receiving light. Thus men in battle wounded near the temple, so that the optic channels (nerves, πόροι) are divided, have felt darkness come on as if a lamp had been extinguished; for indeed the diaphanous and the pupil form a sort of lamp."

§ 260. " Thus it is evident we must assign an element to each sense, and say that the part of the eye which sees is of water, that which hears is of air, and that which smells is of fire. Touch is earthy. Taste is a kind of Touch. The eye is a part of the brain; and the brain is the moistest and coldest part of the body. Touch and Taste are connected with the heart, which is the hottest part of the body."

§ 261. We have next an exposition of Colour. He defines Light " the colour of the diaphanous *per accidens;*" or, as he expresses it in the *De Animâ,* " colour is a movement of the diaphanous," which may be interpreted into an anticipation of the modern undulatory theory, the diaphanous standing for the elastic ether, and the movement being its undulations.

" When there is an igneous body (πυρῶδες τι) in the diaphanous, we have light; when none, we have darkness.[1] That which we call the diaphanous does not belong exclusively

---

[1] TELESIO held Light to be visible heat—lux caloris species est—which is *tinged* by the colours of the objects through which it passes.—*De Rerum Natura*, 1586, VII., 292-3. This is a much more superficial view than that of Aristotle; and the same may be said of most of his deviations from the doctrines of the Stagirite.

to water, air, and other bodies which are translucent. It is some common nature and force, which not existing separately exists in these bodies and in others, in some more and in some less."[2]

What that force was supposed to be I cannot discover from the writings now extant; he seems to have considered it sufficiently described by its name.

§ 262. "As all bodies have necessarily a limit, so also has the diaphanous, and this limit is colour, which is either the limit of bodies or *at* their limit; and hence the Pythagoreans call colour ' the surface.'"

"Colour being the limit of the diaphanous in a limited body, it is possible that that which produces light in the air will also be in the diaphanous in limited bodies, or will not be there; and thus, as in the air there may be light or darkness, so in bodies there may be white and black. The white and black may be placed side by side, so that both may be invisible separately, on account of their minuteness, yet, nevertheless, the result of the two will be visible. But this result can be neither black nor white; but as it must have some colour the colour will be a compound of the two. That is how different colours arise. Many colours are also produced by the combination of the parts: thus three may be arranged with two, or four, and other combinations. Those colours which depend on proportional numbers are harmonious, such as purple and scarlet."[3]

II.—*Taste and Smell.*

§ 263. "These have great similarity, though produced in different organs. The nature of flavours is more evident than

---

[2] ἀλλά τίς ἐστι κοινή φύσις καὶ δύναμις, ἣ χωριστὴ μὲν οὐκ ἔστιν, ἐν τούτοις δ' ἐστὶ καὶ τοῖς ἄλλοις σώμασιν ἐνυπάρχει, τοῖς μὲν μᾶλλον τοῖς δ' ἧττον.

[3] For an elaborate exposition of the views held by the ancients on the subject of colour, see PRANTL: *Aristoteles über die Farben, erläutert durch eine übersicht der Farbenlehre der Alten,* Munich, 1849. But perhaps the most intelligible account is that given by GOETHE: *Geschichte der Farbenlehre. Werke,* XXXIX.

that of odours, because our sense of smell is less keen than it is in other animals; on the other hand, we have Touch more sensitive than any other animal, and Taste is a kind of Touch.

§ 264. " Although water is insipid by nature, it is necessary that water should contain all flavours which escape our perception on account of their feebleness; or that it should contain a matter which is the germ of all flavours; or finally, that water having no difference of flavour in it, the cause is heat. Thus the flavour of fruit is developed by heat. All the flavours to be found in fruits are to be found also in the earth. At least the ancients thought that water varied with the soils through which it passed, which is evident from salt waters, as salt is also a kind of earth.[4] Thus water filtered through cinders contracts a bitter taste, and so of the rest. We may hence see why plants have their various flavours; for moisture, like everything else, is modified by its opposite, and dryness is the opposite of moisture. Thus moisture is modified by fire, for fire is by nature dry. Thus when something sapid is dissolved in water, the water becomes sapid; and in the same way nature acts upon the dry element, and the earthy element: it filters the moisture through the dry and earthy, setting it in motion by heat, and giving it all the necessary qualities. This modification of moisture is flavour."

§ 265. " As various colours arise from the combinations of black and white, so various flavours arise from the combinations of sweet and bitter; and these combinations may be proportional or indefinite. Those which are agreeable depend on numerical proportion. The kinds of flavour resemble those of colour: both are seven in number."

§ 266. " Odours are perceptible in air and water; they are transmitted by the diaphanous which is common both to air

---

[4] Who were these ancients? The commentators declare that METRODORUS and ANAXAGORAS are alluded to. Perhaps so; yet the opinion may be found very distinctly expressed by HIPPOCRATES: *De Aëre, Locis et Aquis.*

and water. That water alone suffices is proved by the fact that fish have the sense of smell. Odour is dry flavour conveyed by the moisture in air and water. All sapid bodies are odorous."

III.—*Hearing.*

§ 267. Either Aristotle forgot to include Hearing in this treatise, or else the chapter has been lost. But his views are expressed in the *De Animâ* (II., 8), from which we may borrow them in a compressed form.

§ 268. " Sound is both potential and actual; for we say that some bodies, such as sponge, wool, &c., are without sound, and others, as brass, wood, hard and smooth bodies, have sound, because able to make sound *actual* by the *action of the medium between the object and the ear.* Actual sound is the result of something in relation to something, and in something; for its cause is percussion. But with only one body there can be no percussion; so that the sonorous object sounds by its relation to another. Without movement there can be no percussion, and sound is not produced by the percussion of every substance; and hollow bodies create, by reflex, many percussions after the first, owing to the medium within them having been set in motion, and being unable to escape. Sound is audible in air, and less distinctly in water.[5] But neither air nor water can be the cause of sound, since there must be a percussion of solid bodies against each other and against the air."

§ 269. "A vacuum is justly called the lord of hearing (κύριον τοῦ ἀκούειν), for the air appears to be a vacuum, and when moving continuously creates hearing. But being very diffluent, it gives out no sound, unless when that which is

---

[5] An error which observation might have guarded against; since very simple experience shows water to be a better conductor of sound than air. The velocity with which sound traverses water has been calculated as four times its velocity through air.

percussed is smooth: in this case the air becomes *uniform* over its surface, for the surface of a smooth body is *one*. Every sonorous body sets in motion the air which is, by continuity, one with the organ of hearing; and sound being in the air, the air without the organ sets in motion the air within. An animal, therefore, does not hear in every part, for every part does not contain air. The air itself, owing to its diffluence, is without sound; but when confined, its motion produces sound. The air within the ear is so immured as to be incapable of escape;[6] and this, in order that the sense may perceive accurately all variations of its movement. And thus we are enabled to hear in water; for the water cannot gain access to the congenital air, or pass through the convolutions of the ear. The ear is constantly giving out sound, as a horn does; for the air within it is continually moving in some peculiar manner. Hence we speak of hearing by a vacuum and something resonant, because we hear by the part which contains the air confined within it."

IV.—*Sensation in general.*

§ 270. Having passed the Senses in review, he then touches on certain general questions relative to sensation. And first of its divisibility *ad infinitum.*

If bodies are infinitely divisible, are the impressions they make on us equally so? This question Aristotle answers with

---

[6] The translation in the text came spontaneously from my pen, because I was not aware that the language of Aristotle had puzzled the commentators. (See TRENDELENBURG, p. 386, for an example.) The sense is so plain that I cannot even now comprehend how it has been missed. Aristotle says the air in the ear is immoveable or unmoved, ἀκίνητος; *immobilis* is BUSSEMAKER'S translation, *immoveable* is COLLIER'S. Yet inasmuch as the movement of this air is mentioned immediately afterwards, the verbal contradiction is glaring; yet it is only verbal. If we suppose that ἀκίνητος has reference to the air which ἐν τοῖς ὠσὶν ἐγκατῳκοδόμηται (is immured within the ears), the meaning is obvious enough. A man is said to be immoveable from his studio or bureau without any imputation on his power of movement; but commentators, boggling at small contradictions, and passing by great ones without remark, would point out that a man cannot be immoveable if he move at all.

manifest superiority over Sir WILLIAM HAMILTON, who, probably from an unsuspected reminiscence, has used the very same illustrations to justify his own doctrine of "latent consciousness." That our consciousness may arise out of unconscious modifications is evident, according to HAMILTON, in the fact of a *minimum visible*, which is the smallest surface that can be seen: "It is plain that if we divide this *minimum visible* into two parts, neither half can by itself be an object of vision or visual consciousness. They are, severally and apart, to consciousness as zero. But it is evident that each part must have produced in us a certain modification, real though unperceived, for as the perceived whole is nothing but the union of unperceived halves, so the perception is only the sum of the two modifications, each of which severally eludes our consciousness." [7]

§ 271. The fallacy of this argument may be disclosed in a counter illustration: the stick which at a distance of three feet just touches us, and produces the sensation of contact, will no longer produce that sensation if broken in half, and held towards us at a distance of three feet: it will not affect our consciousness at all: the two halves thus pointed towards us do not produce modifications in our consciousness the sum of which is perceived when the whole touches us. HAMILTON'S mistake lies in the vague conception of a *minimum visible*, which being the extreme point of visual consciousness, anything beyond that extreme must necessarily pass altogether beyond the sphere of consciousness. It does not become *latent;* for consciousness it becomes nonexistent. The difference *in degree* has amounted to a difference *in kind*.

§ 272. Aristotle justly says that the sensible qualities are named such because they produce sensation. "All magnitude

---

[7] HAMILTON: *Lectures on Metaphysics*, 1859, I., 350. It is strange that neither the erudite Hamilton, nor his erudite editors, should have mentioned Aristotle in this place.

is necessarily sensible, otherwise it would not *be* magnitude. Were it otherwise there would be bodies which had no colour, no weight, nor any other quality, and which consequently would not be perceptible to us, since it is by such qualities that we have perception. But the sensible is composed of sensible qualities, and assuredly not of mathematical definitions.[8] How do we form any judgment of sensible things? By the intellect? But the ideas are only possible when based on sensations. The solution of these questions makes manifest why the kinds of colour, taste, &c., are limited, or finite. It is because in all things which have extremes there must also be intermediate points of limitation; now contraries are extremes, and in all sensible impressions there are contraries, as white and black in colour, sweet and bitter in taste. A body that is continuous therefore may be infinitely divided into *unequal* parts, but its divisibility into *equal* parts is finite. That which is not continuous as a whole has its parts (species) finitely divisible. Since we call the sensible qualities species, and they are always continuous, we must distinguish between the *actual* and *potential;* and hence we do not see the millionth *part* when we see the million, nor do we hear the quarter-tone when we hear the melody; the interval is imperceptible and is lost in other sounds. It is the same with the infinitely little in other sensibles : they are *potentially* visible, but not *actually* visible when isolated.[9] Thus the line of one foot is potentially in the line of two feet; but exists actually only when alone. The infinitely small qualities are lost in surrounding bodies, as drops of perfume poured into the sea. This infinitely little which transcends sensation is neither

---

[8] πᾶν εἶναι μέγεθος αἰσθητόν· ἀδύνατον γὰρ λευκὸν μὲν ὁρᾶν μὴ ποσὸν δέ· εἰ γὰρ μὴ οὕτως, ἐνδέχοιτ' ἂν εἶναί τι σῶμα μηδὲν ἔχον χρῶμα, μηδὲ βάρος, μηδ' ἄλλο τι τοιοῦτον πάθος· ὥστ' οὐδ' αἰσθητὸν ὅλως· ταῦτα γὰρ τὰ αἰσθητά. Τὸ ἄρ' αἰσθητὸν ἔσται συγκείμενον οὐκ ἐξ αἰσθητῶν. Ἀλλ' ἀναγκαῖον· οὐ γὰρ δὴ ἐκ γε τῶν μαθηματικῶν. VI., 445.

[9] δυνάμει γὰρ ὁρατά, ἐνεργείᾳ δ' οὔ, ὅταν χωρισθῇ.

sensible in itself nor by itself, for it is only sensible potentially in the larger quantity."

I have preserved the Aristotelian phraseology, but the reader will find little difficulty in disengaging the meaning, and will perceive how this distinction of the potentially and actually visible agrees with and yet rises superior to HAMILTON's idea of our being unconsciously modified by that which never reaches the consciousness, so that two zeros may make an unit.

§ 273. In the concluding chapter, he enters upon the question whether we can have two different sensations in the same instant of time; a question of some psychological interest. He answers it in the negative.

§ 274. In reviewing Aristotle's opinions on the Senses, it is requisite to bear in mind that he was wholly without the anatomical and physiological, no less than the physical and chemical knowledge, which could have given an assured basis to his speculations. It is a subject which, even in our own day after so much laborious inquiry, is only beginning to be understood; and the psychologist will have many years yet to wait, before science furnishes him with the data he requires.

CHAPTER XIV.

ON MEMORY, SLEEP, DREAMS, AND LONGEVITY.

§ 275. AMONG the *Parva Naturalia*, there are four treatises which must be briefly analysed here :—

I.—*Memory and Recollection.*

This treatise, which Sir W. HAMILTON in his Notes on REID has illustrated (obscured, some may think) with his usual prodigality of erudition, is held by admirers to be both exhaustive and profound. Let the reader judge.

§ 276. What is memory? what is recollection? To what part of the soul do they belong? They do not always accompany each other: sluggish minds have the best memories; the quickest minds, those which are readiest at learning, have the strongest recollection.

§ 277. Memory being always of things absent, the question arises: How can the mind perceive that which is absent? All that is actually present is the *affection*, πάθος, of the soul. This is the explanation: the original sensation left a *trace* behind it, an *impression*, such as the seal leaves upon wax; and it is the perception of this impression which constitutes memory. But as this is a description of perception itself, and as memory is something different, we must add thereto the idea of Time. The impressions, or we may say the pictures painted on the mind, and retained there to be presented again in memory, require a certain physical condition in the sensorium, suitable to the impression. If the sensation be too violent, or if the mind be in a state of agitation, no more impression is made than would be made on running water; and if the sensorium be too hard, as in old age, no impression is made. That is why the young and the old have no memory. Those also who are very vivacious, and those who are very slow, have little memory: the brains of the former are too moist, ὑγρότεροι; the latter too hard, σκληρότεροι; so that in the one case an image will not remain, in the other the image cannot be impressed.

§ 278. The problem is thus stated: How is it that, in memory, we think of the absent *object*, and do not think of the *image* which is really present? But the answer given is purely verbal. An animal painted in a picture, he says, is both an animal and a copy, and while being that one and the same, it is nevertheless two things at once. The animal and the copy are not identical, and we may think of the picture either as an animal or as a representation. This also is true of the image within us; and the idea which the mind contemplates is something in itself, although it is also the image of something else.

§ 279. He then passes to Recollection, which is a distinct faculty, according to him. It is in this place that he gives expression to the glimpse he had attained of the law of association of ideas, over which HAMILTON has blown such emphatic trumpets. My only remark is that here, as in so many other cases, modern knowledge supplies the telescope with its lenses. Had Aristotle really conceived the law *as a law*, he would have applied it to the explanation of psychological questions, in the way moderns have applied it. The fact that he did not attempt this, suffices to show how imperfect was his appreciation of the law.

II.—*Sleep.*

§ 280. This is a problem which even yet is so far from a solution, that the very conditions on which sleep depends are under dispute. The majority of physiologists assume that sleep is caused by a temporary congestion of the blood-vessels in the brain, the pressure of this congestion suspending the activity of the brain.[1] Were this fact established, we should still have to inquire into the cause of the congestion; but is it established? Although I have myself in a former work argued as if the fact were certain, I am forced now to confess that further inquiry has not only shown me that there is absolutely *no* good evidence for such an opinion; but has also shown me that all the phenomena may be even better explained on the assumption of an anæmic condition. A considerable withdrawal of the circulation from the brain would better account for the general inactivity of the brain during sleep; for the partial activity of dreams; and for the rapidity with which the whole activity is restored by a rush of blood, under any stimulus. Congestion implies relaxation of the vessels; the instantaneous recovery of mental energy when a sleeper is awakened by the alarm of fire, or the like, would scarcely be compatible with such a relaxed condition.

§ 281. Whichever view may be the correct one, we are at present condemned to conjecture, since we are without the means of verifying either hypothesis. Until some method shall be disclosed of accurately determining the condition of the cerebral circulation during sleep, we cannot know what are the conditions of the phenomenon.

§ 282. Aristotle, as may be supposed, had no suspicion of the brain being the important agent in sleep. He asserted simply that Sleep and Waking are two functions of the animal economy, and are recognized by similar signs: when a man

---

[1] In the very latest work on the subject this opinion is assumed as if it were beyond cavil. See MAURY: *Le Sommeil et les Rêves*, Paris, 1861.

manifests sensibility we say he is awake; when he manifests none, we say he is asleep. "Hence we conclude that it is the sentient principle which sleeps and wakes. Now sensibility belongs neither to the soul nor the body, but to the union of the two. Only animals sleep, because they only are sensitive; and there is no animal which always sleeps, none which always wakes. Since every organ becomes fatigued after a certain exercise, the fatigued eyes no longer see, the wearied hand no longer grasps."

§ 283. Although he maintains deductively that every animal must sleep, he does not pretend that observation in every case warrants the conclusion. "Sleep has been observed, he says, in all terrestrial and aquatic animals; in all fish and cephalopoda; and in all those which have eyes. Those which have hard eyes, like insects, sleep but little; and hence the doubt has arisen whether they sleep at all. The testacea have not been directly observed; but on this point we must be guided by probabilities."

§ 284. The modern naturalist will be tempted to ask what kind of observations suggest that fish, cephalopoda, and insects ever sleep? It is evident that they take repose; but repose is not the same as sleep. Are they shut out from all perception of external objects, as is the case in the sleep of higher animals? We are completely in the dark. (§ 345.)

§ 285. After a survey of sleep in the animal kingdom, Aristotle concludes the chapter with the assertion still unhesitatingly repeated in our text-books, that Nutrition is most active during Sleep; and that the waste of the day is then repaired. I have endeavoured to show [2] that this opinion is not only unsupported by any plausible evidence, but is in flagrant contradiction with known facts and the physiological inferences they suggest. Were it true, the longest sleepers should be the strongest animals, since their repair of waste

---

[2] *Physiology of Common Life*, II., 358.

would be the most effectual. Were it true, many dreadful cases of slow atrophy might be cured by opiates. Were it true, the sleepless maniacs, and men who sleep but little, would show a rapid destruction of their substance. To admit that muscular and nervous tissue require intervals of *repose*, is not equivalent to admitting that their *nutrition* is only, or even mainly, effected during Sleep.

§ 286. The cause of Sleep is thus expounded by Aristotle. There are four causes of everything (§ 95). The final cause of Sleep is the health of animals; but the aim which Nature has in view is not Sleep, it is Waking, since the aim of all animals is constituted by feeling and thinking, because these are the Best, and Nature always works for the Best.

§ 287. This subjective explanation will probably satisfy few readers. Let us, therefore, hear his physiological explanation.

When the food enters the organs allotted to its reception, an evaporation, ἀναθύμιασις, takes place into the veins; there it is transformed into blood, and carried to the heart. That which evaporates must ascend to a certain height, and then descend, turning back like the tides of Euripus. Now, the warmth in every animal is borne upwards; having reached the uppermost parts, it turns back again and descends. Hence Sleep chiefly comes on after a meal, for then there is much and thick moisture which ascends, and this standing still oppresses the head, and creates sleepiness; no sooner does it descend and in its descent drive away the warmth, than sleep arrives, and the animal drops off. This is proved by the effects of narcotics, for all these produce a heaviness of the head; and those who are sleeping are in a similar condition, unable to raise their eyelids or their heads. And it is especially after meals that such a condition supervenes, because of the great evaporation from the food.

§ 288. Moreover, Sleep follows fatigue, for fatigue is a dissolver, συντηκτικόν; and that which is dissolved acts like undigested food, if it be not cold. Certain diseases produce the same effect, especially those which arise from excess of warmth and moisture, as, for example, Fever and Lethargy.

§ 289. The reader will have noticed what a supreme disregard of everything like evidence, or even logical connection, is displayed in this explanation; yet Aristotle had no suspicion of its wanting either. He applies it to the elucidation of several phenomena, as if it were an established truth. Thus he says, "The reason why young children sleep much is because *all* their food is carried upwards," and, as this latter position may require some proof, he adds, "the proof is seen in the fact that in infancy the upper parts are larger compared with the lower parts, and because it is in the upper that the growth is most active."

§ 290. More is made of this excess in the upper parts. It is the cause why infants, until they are about five months old, are unable to turn their heads round; "it is with them as with drunken men—an immense quantity of moisture is carried upwards."

§ 291. Nay, this also serves to explain Epilepsy. "Sleep is said to be very like Epilepsy; hence this disease often begins in sleep, and its crises never occur in a waking state," a statement which will not receive the assent of pathologists. Epilepsy is produced "when a quantity of moisture has ascended, and in its descent swells the veins, which thus compress the windpipe," an explanation which will also be rejected by pathologists.[3]

§ 292. We further learn that those who have large heads and small veins are great sleepers; whereas those who have large veins sleep little; the former because the narrowness of their veins prevents the descending moisture from descending freely, and the greatness of their heads occasions a powerful

---

[3] It is almost unnecessary to inform any reader that Epilepsy is now known to be a disease of a nervous centre. Consult SCHRÖDER VAN DER KOLK: *Bau und Funotionen der Medulla Spinalis und Oblongata*, 1860, and the writings of BROWN SEQUARD.

evaporation; whereas in the latter, who have large veins, the descent is easy and rapid, unless there be some other cause of obstruction. Bilious people sleep little, because their interior is always cold, and consequently there is but small evaporation going on in them; and for a similar reason they are large eaters and have hard flesh, their body being ill adapted to absorb. The bile, being cold by nature, makes the nutritive and secretive organs also cold.

§ 293. My purpose will be greatly misunderstood if these absurdities are supposed to be dragged forward in triumphant hostility to the great name of Aristotle. Admirers have carefully ignored such things, and thereby deprived the general public of the lesson to be learned from seeing how an intellect so vast and so stored with various knowledge, could, nevertheless, allow itself to be the dupe of phrases, without ever raising one question as to the validity of the facts on which these phrases were formed. Seriously contemplated, there is something pathetic in the fatal facility with which the human mind at all periods has accepted a phrase as a revelation, never pausing to see whether the facts truly are what they are assumed to be, but satisfied if the phrase seems to explain the difficulty.

§ 294. Some difficulties, indeed, he attempted to remove. They are thus stated:—

"Sleep appears, from what has been said, to be an inward concentration of warmth, and a reaction, or counter action.[4] Hence in the sleeper there is much movement; hence, also, he becomes weaker and colder, and, on account of the cold, his eyelids droop. The upper and outward parts of the body are cold, the lower and inner parts are warm; for example, the feet and viscera. But, perhaps, some may be surprised that Sleep should follow meals, that wine should be a narcotic, and that other heating things should produce

---

[4] ὁ ὕπνος ἐστὶ σύνοδός τις τοῦ θερμοῦ εἴσω καὶ ἀντιπερίστασις φυσική.

Sleep. It seems incomprehensible that Sleep should be a growing cold, and yet warmth be the cause of Sleep. Shall we say that when the stomach is empty it is warm, and when full it is made cold by movement, in the same way that the passages of the head and other places are made cold when the evaporation is carried there? Or shall we say that, as those who drink suddenly a warm liquid are seized with shivering, so here also the heat ascending, the cold which arises from concentration makes the body cold, and drives away the natural warmth? The same effect may arise from a quantity of food being taken, which acts like wood thrown on fire. Thus Sleep comes on when the heavy evaporation is carried by warmth to the head, and, unable to ascend higher, is forced to descend. Hence also men lie down when the heat which kept them erect is withdrawn; for man alone, of all animals, has an erect position,[5] and the descent of the vapour on the heart takes away all sensibility, and afterwards imagination."[6]

§ 295. We now perceive the part assigned by Aristotle to the brain in the production of Sleep. Its part was that of a cooler of the evaporations from food. It is the coldest organ in the body (§ 164). "As the moisture, evaporated by the sun's heat, on reaching the upper air is chilled by the cold there, and falls back again in rain, so does the vapour of food, on reaching the cold brain, become condensed, and falls back again in mucus (hence the pituitary fluxion seems to come from the head), but that portion which is nutritive and not noxious descends and tempers the heat of the body.[7] Not only is the brain cold, but the smallness of its veins

---

[5] Compare § 391 a.

[6] ὕστερον δὲ φαντασίαν, which BUSSEMAKER renders " deinde vero imaginationes subgerit," an interpretation warranted by A.'s theory of dreams.

[7] This notion of fluxions from the brain plays an important part in the history of Medicine. See HIPPOCRATES: *De Aëre, Locis et Aquis*; and compare it with VAN HELMONT's amusing and energetic protest: *Catarrhi deliramenta*, in his *Opera Omnia*, 1055, p. 271.

prevents the vapour from easily penetrating; and thus, in spite of the great heat, it becomes cooled by the brain."

§ 296. "When the food is entirely cooked, and the heat being gathered into a small space, overcomes the cold, and when the thick blood has been separated from the thin, we awake. The blood which is in the head is thinnest, that which is in the lower parts is the thickest and most turbid; and it is because after meals the blood is the least separated that Sleep lasts until the thinner blood goes upwards and the thicker downward. No sooner is this effected, than the animal, freed from the weight of food, awakes."

§ 297. Large space has been given to this treatise on Sleep, because it illustrates the thoroughly vicious method Aristotle pursued. We may also perceive in it a great want of logical connection, even with its own premisses.

III.—*Dreams.*

§ 298. This little treatise stands in favourable contrast to its predecessors. Herein we see how the mere fact that the writer is no longer called upon to expound processes discoverable only by laborious investigation, leaves his mind disengaged from the trammels in which it moved so clumsily, and allows it full play. By this it is not meant that Dreams are not also dependent upon physiological laws; but that they are to be elucidated by psychological observation, and for this Aristotle was as well equipped as any modern, except that he had a smaller range of recorded facts to draw from. If, therefore, his treatise still seems remarkable, we must attribute it either to his sagacity, which thus early detected the real elements of the problem, or else to the circumstance that being ourselves without a true solution, we are unable to see wherein his errors lie.

§ 299. He begins by inquiring to what part of the soul dreams address themselves. It cannot be the sensible part, since Sleep consists in insensibility. Nor can it be the understanding. We hear and see in dreams, but not as when awake. A dream is a kind of image. Imagination has been defined (in the treatise *De Animá*) as the motion produced by our sensibility *in act*. Sensible things produce sensations, and the motions thus produced continue after the exciting cause has vanished. Thus on going into a dark place, we are at first unable to see because the motions produced by the sun have not yet subsided. If we look steadily at a coloured object the sensation remains when the eyes are carried to other objects. To this must be added the fact of hallucination. We are constantly liable to deceptions of the senses when in the tumult of passion. During fever the patient sees animals in the lines on the wall of his room.

§ 300. These motions, which in the tumult of sensations are unperceived, because overpowered by the stronger movements, as a small fire is by a large fire, are perceived in the calmness of sleep. The inactivity of each special sense brings all these motions, which during the day are unperceived, to the origin of sensation (*i. e.* the sensitive centre: ἐστὶ τὴν ἀρχὴν τῆς αἰσθήσεως), and in the calmness become sensible. Like the ripples and circles caused by eddies, the sensations have their after movements; sometimes these ripples and circles are repeated in the same forms; at others they are broken and distorted by the obstacles they encounter. Young children do not dream; nor do adults dream soon after meals,[a] because then the movement caused by the ascending heat is great, and an image can then no more be formed than in troubled water; or if an image be formed it will be distorted and unlike the object. But when the water is calm the images are clear.

§ 301. Thus, in Sleep, images are formed; the after-motions of sensations, when the disturbance is great, are

---

[a] KANT: *Anthropologie*, *Werke*, 1838, VII., 30, maintains that we never sleep without dreaming; for, he argues, to cease to dream would be to cease to live. Yet he would hardly have maintained that we dream during syncope.

either destroyed or distorted, and our dreams are terrible, monstrous. It is the same with men drunk or in a fever. But when the separation of the blood has taken place, the after-motions are perceived, and then we see and hear. It is owing to these after-motions that we often, when awake, seem to see and hear sights and sounds not really existing.

§ 302. Dreams are the images, or after-motions of sensation. But it is not every image presenting itself during sleep which is to be called a dream; for if, when asleep, we hear a noise, feel a touch, or perceive a light, there being actually present the objects which excite these sensations, we cannot consider these to be dreams.

§ 303. Such is the theory of Dreams propounded by Aristotle. If we disengage it from the peculiar physiology in which it is enveloped, it will appear not unworthy a place beside modern theories, of which there are so many. And we may further remark that the theory seems to have been entirely his own, since he does not allude to the opinions of any predecessor.

IV.—*Longevity.*

§ 304. The treatise *De Longitudine et Brevitate Vitæ* has several points of interest illustrative of his physiological views. After noticing the varieties in the longevity of animals he undertakes to explain the cause. We must assume, he says, that an animal is naturally moist and warm, and that Life depends on these conditions; whereas old age is dry and cold, and so is Death, since so it manifests itself. The material of the body being thus compounded of moisture and warmth, dryness and cold, it is obvious that in growing old we dry up. It is necessary, therefore, that the moisture should not easily dry up. Hence fat bodies are preserved from decay because they are of air, and air acts like fire in relation to other things.[9] Now fire does not become putrid.

The logic of this last sentence is strangely arbitrary. If

---

[9] ὁ δ' ἀὴρ πρὸς τἆλλα πῦρ·

fire does not become *putrid*, its power of drying moisture is too familiar to have been overlooked.

§ 305. Moreover the moisture must not be too small in quantity. Hence we see why the larger plants and animals live longer; they have more moisture. But this is not the sole reason. There are two causes operative: the quantity and the quality. The moisture must not only be considerable, it must also be warm; so that it may neither congeal nor dry up easily. This explains why man is longer lived than much larger animals. Those animals which have less moisture will be long-lived if the quality of their moisture makes up for its deficient quantity. There are some whose fat and warmth makes it difficult to become dry and cold.

§ 306. Here the reader makes acquaintance with that radical moisture which played so conspicuous a part in old medical theories, and to which Walter Scott humourously alludes. The modern may, if he please, read into it an anticipation of the importance of water to the organism, of which it constitutes more than two-thirds by weight; and in the accompanying warmth, he may also detect the agent of all organic activity. But the ancient ideas of moisture and warmth were founded on very different data from ours; and few things would have astonished Aristotle more than hearing that water formed an integral constituent of solid bone, nay, even of the hardest of organic substances, such as the enamel of the teeth; and that animal heat was mainly produced by the action of that very air which, he thought, cooled the body.

§ 307. Another cause of Longevity is moderation in secretion; for all secretion destroys the animal, either by causing disease, or by its own action. The action of a secretion is adverse and destructive both of the whole organism and its parts. This is the reason why salacious animals quickly grow old; why the mule lives longer than its parents; why females live longer than males; and why male sparrows are short-lived.

§ 308. Fatigue also shortens life. Why? "Because fatigue produces dryness, and old age is dry. Males ought by nature to be longer-lived than females, since they have more warmth.[10] Animals live longer in warm than in cold climates for the same reason that the larger live longer than the smaller; and it is those which are by nature cold which in warm countries grow to a great size: serpents and lizards in warm countries become enormous. Warmth and moisture are the causes of growth and life. But as the moisture in animals becomes more fluid in cold countries it more easily congeals. Hence in cold countries we find animals without blood, or with very little; or if we find any, they are very small and die young. Cold takes away their power of growth.

§ 309. "When plants and animals take no nourishment they perish: they then consume their own substance (συντήκει γὰρ αὐτὰ ἑαυτά). For as a flame destroys a smaller flame by consuming its food, so animal warmth which is the primary digester destroys the substance in which it is." Here again a willing admirer may read an anticipation of modern physiology, which has no better explanation to give.

§ 310. Plants are, the longest lived of all beings because they are less watery and less easily congealed; they are fat and viscid, and therefore, although dry and earthy, they do not easily lose their moisture.

§ 311. From the knowledge gained in the preceding chapters respecting Aristotle's physiological and psychological theories, we are now in a proper condition to examine the three great treatises on the "History of Animals," the "Parts of Animals," and "Generation and Development," which will conclude our survey.

---

[10] Modern investigations show that the average of life is slightly in favour of women; and that their temperature also is slightly superior to that of men.

CHAPTER XV.

"THE HISTORY OF ANIMALS."[1]

§ 312. "I cannot read this work," says Cuvier, "without being ravished with astonishment. Indeed it is impossible to conceive how a single man was able to collect and compare the multitude of particular facts implied in the numerous general rules and aphorisms contained in this work, and of which his predecessors never had any idea."[2]

By the time we have reached the end of the chapter it will probably be seen that this astonishment was very easily excited by the prestige of a great name, and that there is no

---

[1] The best edition of the *Historia Animalium* is by Schneider, 4 vols., Leipzig, 1811. That by J. C. Scaliger, Tolosæ, 1619, with the notes of Maussacus, is of interest to scholars only. There is a German translation by Strack, Frankfort, 1816, which is tolerably accurate; and a well-known French translation by Camus, Paris, 1783, with the text, and a volume of notes, which, although no longer representing the zoology of our day, has interesting matter. I can find no Italian or Spanish version. The Spanish work of Diego de Funes mentioned by Buhle (*Opera*, I., 269), is not a translation at all, but a compilation. (See note 13, chap. xvi.)

During the revision of these pages there have appeared, 1st, a proposal for a new translation into English; and 2nd, the execution of such a proposal. The first is by the Rev. Mr. Houghton, in the *Natural History Review*, April, 1862, with the first book as a specimen, and decisive proofs of the utter untrustworthiness of Taylor's version. The execution is by Mr. Cresswell: *Aristotle's History of Animals, in ten books*, 1862 (Bohn's Classical Library).

[2] Cuvier: *Histoire des Sciences Nat.*, 1841; I., 146. Inasmuch as the works of A.'s predecessors have all perished, it is rather perilous to assert their absolute deficiency in rules and aphorisms.

impossibility at all in conceiving how a single man achieved what Aristotle actually did achieve—which is, however, wholly different from what CUVIER supposes him to have achieved.

"The *History of Animals*," he continues, "is not properly a zoology, that is to say a series of descriptions of various animals; it is rather a sort of philosophic anatomy, in which the author treats of the generalities of organization presented by various animals, in which he explains their differences and resemblances, founded on a comparison of their organs, and in which he lays the bases of grand classifications irreproachable in accuracy."

§ 313. There is a difficulty, we know, in speaking of Aristotle without exaggeration; but the language of Cuvier passes all bounds permissible to sincere enthusiasm; the more so because of the authority attached to his own eminent name. Others speak with a like exaggeration, but not with a like authority. I am very far from any desire to understate the claims of Aristotle; but it is my purpose to control the reckless assertions of critics who would severely scrutinize the claims of contemporaries, while they lavishly exaggerate the merits of the ancients.[3]

---

[3] See BUFFON: *Histoire Naturelle*, I., p. 62. DE BLAINVILLE: *Histoire des Sciences de l'Organisation*, 1847, I. CARUS: *Traité d'Anatomie Comparée*, Paris, 1833, *Introd.* ISIDORE GEOFFROY ST. HILAIRE: *Histoire Générale des Règnes organiques*, 1854, I. BURMEISTER: *Manual of Entomology*, by SHUCKHARD, 1856, p. 597. SPIX: *Geschichte und Beurtheilung aller Systeme in der Zoologie*, 1811, p. 18. SWAINSON: *Discourse on the Study of Natural History*, p. 6 (quoted by HOUGHTON), says, "Had this extraordinary man left us no other memorial of his talents than his researches in Zoology, he would still be looked upon as one of the greatest philosophers of ancient Greece, even in its brightest and highest age." This may be accepted; but MACGILLIVRAY passes from Greece to modern times when he says that Aristotle was not only acquainted with numerous species, "he described them also according to a *comprehensive and luminous method, which perhaps none of his successors have approached!*"—*Lives of Eminent Zoologists*, 1834, p. 55. The simple fact being that he has not described a single species, nor even attempted it. Of the same accuracy is the assertion that he has treated comparative anatomy with genius, "and best deserves to be taken as a model. The principal divisions which are still adopted by naturalists in the animal kingdom are those of Aristotle, and he proposed some which have been resumed after

Looked at historically, that is to say with reference to the works which for centuries succeeded it, the "History of Animals" is a stupendous effort; but looked at absolutely, that is to say in relation to the Science of which it treats, it is an ill-digested, ill-compiled mass of details, mostly of small value, with an occasional gleam of something better. There is, strictly speaking, no *science* in it at all. There is not even a system which might look like science. There is not one good description. It is not an anatomical treatise; it is not a descriptive zoology; it is not a philosophy of zoology; it is a collection of remarks about animals, their structure, resemblances, differences, and habits. As a collection it is immense. But it is at the best only a collection of details, without a trace of organization; and the details themselves are rarely valuable, often inaccurate.

§ 314. Aware of the paradoxical aspect which such a judgment must present to the mind of every reader unprepared by a previous acquaintance with the "History of Animals," I shall bestow some pains to justify it in the following analysis.[4]

And first let me endeavour to correct the very misleading remark of CUVIER respecting the immense variety of particulars *implied* in its general aphorisms. Are they really generalized conclusions, drawn from an exhaustive survey of particulars? When Aristotle asserts that no terrestrial animal is fixed to the ground, that all winged insects which have their stings at the fore part of the body are two-winged, whereas those which have the sting at the posterior part of the body are four-winged—the generalizations may imply either extensive observation, or rashness in drawing conclu-

---

having been unjustly rejected." A similar strain of exaggeration may be read in SONNENBURG: *Zoologische-Kritische Bemerkungen zu Aristoteles Thier-Geschichte*, Bonn, 1857, p. 6. It is not thought enough to glorify Aristotle unless moderns are dwarfed beside him.

[4] The appearance of the English translation will enable every reader to control this analysis.

sions. CUVIER assumes the former. He says they "supposent un examen presque universel de toutes les espèces." Now, from my acquaintance with Aristotle's mode of procedure in general, and his facility in leaping to absolute conclusions on the slenderest warrant, I am extremely doubtful on the point of his having carefully examined many, much less *all* insects before he concluded as to the relation borne by the stings to the number of wings; not only is it unlike him to have pursued this laborious plan, but it is improbable from the very absoluteness with which he states the relation. If we reflect that the fact is wholly without illumination from physiology, and that no rational suggestion has yet been offered why the *diptera* should not carry their offensive weapon behind, we shall conclude it to have been simple rashness in Aristotle to have done more than notice it as a coincidence in all the insects observed by him.

§ 315. CUVIER has instanced four generalizations to prove the immense acquaintance Aristotle must have had with particulars. I will quote four others (forty might be found), all taken from the first book, which exemplify plainly enough how easily large and careful induction could be dispensed with.

1. The lion has no cervical vertebræ, but a single bone in its neck.

2. Long-lived persons have one or two lines which extend through the whole hand; short-lived persons have two lines, and these do not extend through the whole hand.

3. Man has, in proportion to his size, the largest and the moistest brain.[5]

4. The forehead is large in stupid men; small in lively

---

[5] Neither statement is correct. The *relative* size of the brain is much greater in birds, rodents, monkeys. The notion of a greater moisture in the human brain (several times repeated by him) may have arisen from one seen in a state of decomposition; or was perhaps purely a hypothetical assumption. Elsewhere, he speaks of the brain as one of the fluids (ὑγρῶν), adding that of fluids it is the driest or most consistent (αὐχμηρότατον).—*De Partibus*, II., 7.

men; broad in men predisposed to insanity (ἐκστατικοί); and round in high-spirited men.

§ 316. We are not justified, therefore, in assuming that Aristotle was acquainted with all, or most, of the particulars which may be implied in his generalizations; since we see that he is quite ready to frame generalizations in the absence of anything like an inductive warrant.

§ 317. Are we justified in interpreting some of his generalizations as profound attempts at classification? This is a more delicate inquiry. There are probably few who do not believe that among his claims to eminence as a biologist, must be named the first outline of a scientific Classification; and were this idea correct, his rank would indeed be very high, for Classification is one of the latest results of scientific research. I may say at once that it is only by bringing together certain general statements, and *disregarding the whole context*, that a plausible scheme can be drawn up from his works; and so far from his having laid "the eternal bases" upon which moderns have erected their classification, it does not appear that he had ever *attempted* a special arrangement of the various groups of animals.

The reader must not reproach me with inconsiderate antagonism. Polemical discussion is forced on me by the reckless and misleading assertions of respected historians and critics. Except DR. WHEWELL and AGASSIZ I know of no one who treats this topic of Classification with any apparent solicitude to state the simple truth. Rhetorical exaggeration is supported by an arbitrary selection of phrases, and an omission of all the passages which contradict or qualify them.

"Aristotle," says CUVIER,[6] "divides animals into two grand classes: those which have blood, and those which have

---

[6] To the same effect DELLE CHIAJE: *Istituzioni di Anatomia e fisologia comparata*, 1832, I., p. xxxv.; and indeed almost every writer who mentions the classification.

no blood; in other words, he divides, as we do, animals with red blood from animals with white blood." On turning to the original, do we find any such systematic division as this? By no means. We find the distinction noted, but it comes in quite casually at the close of a chapter, having no relation to what has gone before, none to what comes after it. True, it is frequently referred to in subsequent chapters; but only as to a general remark, a sort of popular distinction, useful for its brevity. It is nowhere used as a principle of classification, but simply as a generality. The succeeding chapter opens with a remark of equal generality, which is not less frequently referred to, namely, " some animals are viviparous, some oviparous, and others vermiparous. The viviparous include man, the horse, the seal, and all animals which have hair; also among aquatic animals the cetacea, such as the dolphin and cartilaginous fishes."

The next chapter opens with another remark of the same kind: "Animals have either feet or no feet; the former have either two feet—as man, and no other animal, except the bird; or four feet—as the lizard or dog; or many feet—as the centipede, or bee." From this he passes on to the fins of fish, and the feathers of birds.

§ 318. Occasional reference is made to each of these three distinctions; but no one distinction is used as a principle of classification. The reason why no attempt was made is to be read in the treatise on the "Parts of Animals." He there argues at length *against* the idea of forming a classification upon a "principle of negation;" and not only does he argue thus, but specially mentions this very case of bloodless animals as being of all others "the most difficult, nay impossible."[7]

---

[7] πάντων δὲ καλεπώτατον ἢ ἀδύνατον εἰς τὰ ἄναιμα. I., 3, 9. TITZE reads ἀντικείμενα, "contraries," instead of εἰς τὰ ἄναιμα. But this lection, which has no other authority, really makes very little difference in the meaning, since under the general term of contraries must be included the special distinction of animals with and without blood.

§ 319. Even were not his views thus explicitly stated, we might gather from his practice that he never thought the division of animals, according to their blood or no blood, was a principle of classification; rather should we seek one, if at all, in the division of viviparous, oviparous, and vermiparous; for he did not know the extent to which Nature overleaps such boundaries, presenting us with viviparous amphibia, viviparous snails, viviparous insects, viviparous worms, and viviparous infusoria.[8] But it is evident that he had no idea of making generative distinctions the grounds of a classification.

§ 320. Returning to the distinction of animals into sanguineous and exsanguineous, we may observe that it does not quite represent the "animaux à sang rouge, et à sang blanc," for by exsanguineous Aristotle meant without blood, and not blood of a different colour. He held that the lower animals, *i. e.*, reptiles and our invertebrata, had a fluid which was not blood, but analogous to it.[9]

---

[8] Although he knew that *some* of the cartilaginous fishes are viviparous, he too precipitately generalized the fact. The genera *Raia* and *Scyllium* are oviparous: LACEPÈDE: *Histoire naturelle des Poissons* 1798. Aristotle excepted the *Lophius piscatorius;* but he erred in supposing it to be a cartilaginous fish. The viviparous osseous fishes, *Blennius* and *Anableps,* he could not have known; the former being found only in the German Ocean, and the latter in the waters of Surinam. See RATHKE: *Abhandlungen zur Bildungs und Entwickelungsgeschichte des Menschen und der Thiere.* 1853, II., *Erste Abhand.*

[9] *De Partibus,* I., 5, 15. Compare also KÖHLER: *Aristoteles de Molluscis cephalopodibus,* Rigæ, 1820, p. 2. DELLE CHIAJE makes it a reproach that Aristotle "reputò senza sangue que' viventi che ne sono a dovizia proveduti, ed in taluni di essi è questo rosso, di che lo stesso gran Linneo non si avvide." *Istituzioni di Anat. e fisiologia comparata,* 1832, I., xxxvii. SWAMMERDAMM first pointed out that many of the earth worms had red blood; and he adds that the blood of the snail is a viscid reddish fluid.—*Bibel der Natur,* Leipzig, 1752, p. 54. CUVIER himself was forced to admit the "vers à sang rouge." Since then the blood of several annelids has been found to be green, pale yellow, and red; while that of some Tunicata and the *Sipuncula* is red, orange yellow, yellow, violet, blue. See *Seaside Studies,* 1st ed., 1858, p. 66; 2nd ed., 1860, p. 70; and compare ROUGET: *Comptes rendus de la Société de Biologie,* 1859, p. 172; also in BROWN SÉQUARD: *Journal de la Physiologie,* 1859, II., 660.

§ 321. Another distinction he names is that of winged and wingless: the winged animals have feathers, like birds, or membraneous wings, like insects, or wings of skin, like bats. The first and last have blood; the second are bloodless.

§ 322. The principal classes which have blood enumerated by him are birds (not reptiles: these he held to be bloodless), fish, and cetacea. "There is also another class, covered with a shell, vulgarly called shellfish; and an anonymous class, the soft-shelled (malacostraca), which comprises crabs, carcini, astaci; and another of mollusca (cephalopoda); and another of insects. The common character of the four last-named classes is to have no blood, and to have more than four feet when they have feet at all. There are no large classes besides these, for there are many forms which are not included under any common form; but either stand alone, without difference between them, as Man; or, if there are any different species they have not been named."

"All wingless quadrupeds have blood. Of these some are viviparous, some oviparous. Most of the oviparous have hair; the oviparous have scales. . . . Not all animals which are viviparous have hair, since some fish bring forth their young alive; but all hairy animals are viviparous. In the class of viviparous quadrupeds there are many genera (εἴδη), but anonymous; hence we are forced to name them severally, as man, lion, stag, horse, dog. On the other hand, there is a class which is made out of animals having manes—such as the horse, the ass, the *oreus* (Mule), the *ginnus* (Hinny), the *innus* (also a Mule), and the so-called *hemionus* (Half ass) of Syria, which is called a mule from its resemblance only, for it is really a distinct genus, which breeds with its own kind."

§ 323. He expressly tells us that this sketch is only an outline, or foretaste; but there is no intimation that he regarded it as inaccurate; nor is there an intimation that he attempted to make any other classification than what naturally presented itself in the obvious differences of structure, habits, and habitat. All men had spontaneously grouped animals as fourfooted, winged, aquatic, terrestrial, oviparous, &c.; nor has Aristotle attempted any more systematic grouping. Indeed, it is to mistake the whole course of scientific development to suppose that Classification can precede the labours which it can only succeed: its principles must be eliminated from the extensive research of comparative anatomy. From the days of Aristotle to those of LINNÆUS there was no important step taken towards such an elimination, and this was mainly owing to the backward state of comparative anatomy. For what is the aim of a classification? It is to group animals in such a manner that each class and genus shall indicate the degree of complexity attained by the organism, and thus the external form betray the internal structure.

§ 324. No such scheme ever entered the head of Aristotle. He only wished to mark out the obviously distinctive characters by which the common eye could recognize each class or genus. Historians have drawn up a scheme from his remarks, and presented it as his classification. But, naturally enough, they cannot agree among themselves as to the details. MEYER,[10] after mentioning the various schemes which have been drawn up, from PLINY to EHRENBERG, points out the violent contradictions visible in these attempts, and that these writers are not agreed as to Aristotle's method, main divisions, and subdivisions. Nay, more: not only do these doctors differ respecting the nature of the disease, but there are some who doubt whether there is any disease at all: they are not unanimous as to whether Aristotle had or had not a system. FURLANUS is angry at such a doubt, and cannot conceive how any one should fail to detect the system. ARTEDI and REAUMUR are equally puzzled to detect one. BUFFON and CUVIER see the system plainly enough. AGASSIZ declares that "Aristotle cannot be said to have proposed any regular

---

[10] MEYER: *Aristoteles Thierkunde*, Berlin, 1855, p. 64.

classification. He speaks constantly of more or less extensive groups under a common appellation, evidently considering them as natural divisions; but he nowhere expresses a conviction that these groups may be arranged methodically so as to exhibit the natural affinities of animals."[11]

The fact of such dissidences, on a point which ought not to admit of two opinions, is decisive. There can be no classification where students mistake both the leading principles and particular applications. Zoologists may read a classification in Aristotle's pages; but they do violence to the plain meaning of the text; they disregard context, and piece together from far and wide detached observations never meant to be connected with each other. WHEWELL aptly remarks that the construction of a classification "consists in the selection of certain parts as those which shall peculiarly determine the place of each species in our arrangement. It is clear, therefore, that such an enumeration of differences as we have described, supposing it complete, contains the materials of all possible classifications. But we can with no more propriety say that the author of such an enumeration of differences is the author of any classification which can be made by means of them, than we can say that a man who writes down the whole alphabet writes down the solution of a given riddle or the answer to a particular question."[12] We may add that ALBERTUS MAGNUS, GESNER, and the other followers of Aristotle, saw no system in their master's work; and why should we?

§ 325. Having cleared away some of the obstructing mists of prejudice, we may now look at "The History of Animals" with more impartiality.

---

[11] AGASSIZ: *Essay on Classification*, London, 1859, p. 302. Compare also J. C. SCALIGER in his commentary on the *Hist. Animal.*, 1619, *Lib.* I., c. vii., p. 53, from which it is evident that *he* found no system of classification in the work.

[12] WHEWELL: *History of the Inductive Sciences*, 1857, III., 289.

The abruptness with which it opens is so contrary to the practice of Aristotle, that there can be no reasonable doubt of the original introduction having been lost or transposed. PATRIZIO thought that the whole treatise was a continuation of the *De Partibus*;[13] but this idea will not withstand close scrutiny; the *De Partibus* manifestly succeeds the " History of Animals" (§ 357).

The ingenious suggestion of TITZE[14] seems at first sight to remove the difficulty. He thinks the first book of the *De Partibus* has been transposed from the " History of Animals," to which indeed it forms a very good introduction. To this FRANZIUS, in his edition of the *De Partibus*, has given his assent. Yet on a due consideration, it seems to me that the difficulty is only shifted; the one work gains an introduction which the other loses. A commencement of the *De Partibus* at the second book will be not less abrupt than the present commencement of the " History of Animals;" moreover, there is a passage distinctly referring to the " History of Animals " in this first book (§ 357).[15]

§ 326. BOOK I. opens, without a word of preamble, by a division of the organism into similar and dissimilar parts, which may be regarded as the first dawn of a conception of philosophic anatomy, such as FALLOPIA more distinctly conceived, and BICHAT made the foundation of modern histology. Since BICHAT, the organism has always been understood as composed of elementary *tissues*, which combine to form *organs*, and these organs combine to form *systems*. It is, therefore,

---

[13] PATRITII ; *Discussionum Peripateticarum tomi quatuor*, Bâle, 1581, I., c. ix., p. 118.

[14] TITZE : Ἀριστοτέλους λόγος ὁ περὶ φύσεως τῆς ζωϊκῆς μάλιστα μεθοδικός, Prag., 1819.

[15] Neither RITTER nor BRANDIS makes any mention of TITZE's proposal; whence we may conclude that they thought little of it. It is, however, adopted by SUNDERALL: *Die Thierarten des Aristoteles*, Stockholm, 1863 ; a valuable and candid exposition of the subject, which came into my hands too late for more than this passing recommendation.

difficult without equivoque to use Aristotle's language; but if by similar parts, *partes similares*,[16] we understand those which are general, and by dissimilar parts, those which are individual, his meaning will be plain.

§ 327. "The parts of animal bodies," is the opening sentence, "are either simple, that is, admit of being divided into similar parts—as, for example, muscle into muscles;[17] or they are composed of dissimilar parts—such as the hand, which can no more be divided into several hands than the face into several faces. Some of these parts are also called limbs, those namely which, while they form wholes, are composed of many parts, such as the head, the foot, the hand, the arm, and the thorax. All these compound parts are formed of simple parts—as the hand from flesh, sinews, and bones."

§ 328. In some animals all the parts are the same, in others they differ. In those which are of the same class, the parts only differ in excess or defect. But some animals do not agree thus. They have parts which from their resemblance may be called analogous. "Thus a bone is the analogue of a fish bone, a nail of a claw, a hand of a crab's nipper, a feather of a fish's scale, for it is plain that what the feather is to the bird, that is the scale to the fish."

Here we see another germ of modern science, the *théorie des analogues*, which, especially since GOETHE, and GEOFFROY ST. HILAIRE, has given so much precision to transcendental ·anatomy, when coupled with the theory of homologies.

§ 329. After dividing the simple parts into those which are moist, and those which are dry, he proceeds to enumerate

---

[16] Aristotle was the first to use the term ὁμοιομερῆ. Compare PHILIPPSON: ὕλη ἀνθρωπίνη, p. 4.

[17] οἶον σάρκες εἰς σάρκας. He did not know muscle as we understand it; yet I cannot otherwise intelligibly render the phrase. STRACK says, "Fleisch und Fleisch *fasern*;" but this conveys the erroneous impression that A. knew the fibrous structure of muscles. (CRESSWELL is boldly literal, "flesh, into pieces of flesh.")

the various grounds of distinction among animals. This is done rapidly and in outline, details being left for future occasions. He then proceeds to examine the constituent parts of animals; and first of man, because of all animals man is the best known. By this he means the external parts of man are the most familiar; and after a very dry and somewhat trivial enumeration of these familiar parts, he says that the internal parts being unknown, we must compare them with the parts of animals most resembling man.[18]

§ 330. He commences his exposition of the internal organs with meagre and inaccurate notices of the brain, lungs, heart, kidneys, liver, &c. Even CUVIER is forced to admit that on these topics "his ideas have not the same exactitude;" but tries to save his character by adding,— "One sees that on certain points of detail he is a better observer than the majority of his successors." Now this is certainly untrue of GALEN, whose knowledge of anatomy was incomparably more accurate than Aristotle's; nor, with the single exception of the questionable mention of the Eustachian tube, is there one point upon which Aristotle can be said to have observed what his successors overlooked.

§ 331. BOOK II.—Having in the first book described the external and internal parts of man, he now proceeds to describe those of animals. Here, as throughout, we have to note the singular prodigality of detail which is displayed: almost every line contains a fact, and often a generality embracing a wide range of facts. There may be, and indeed there is, considerable inaccuracy in his statements, but we see the mighty energies of dawning Science in this gathering together of facts which Philosophy was but too prone to ignore. Had he only been half as solicitous about the quality,

---

[18] So carelessly is Aristotle spoken of even by historians of science that we find SPIX declaring "A. makes man the standard both for internal and external structure, and executes his descriptions in a masterly style."—*Geschichte und Beurtheilung aller Systeme in der Zoologie*, p. 18.

as he showed himself about the quantity of his facts, the work would perhaps have delighted his contemporaries less, but it would have been an instructor for all time. To cite a third of the examples of careless observation and rash generalization would be to inflict a needless weariness on the reader; yet as the accuracy of Aristotle's observation is not unfrequently vaunted, a specimen or two, taken at random, must be given.

§ 332. I. "The male has more teeth than the female in man,[19] sheep, goats, and swine. In other animals the observation is imperfect."

II. "Fish have no external organs of Sense, not even the passages of hearing and smelling."

III. "The heart of the ox is peculiar; for there is a kind of ox, though not every kind, which has a bone in its heart; and in the heart of the horse there is also a bone." (§ 389.)

IV. "Some animals have a gall-bladder attached to the liver, others none. The Achaïnian deer seems to have one on its tail; that which is called the gall-bladder in this animal resembles it in colour, but is not liquid, and is more like the spleen in structure."

§ 333. Naturalists have been interested to find the mention of a ruminating fish in this book. Here is the passage: "Fish have one simple stomach, but it differs in form; in some it is like an intestine, as in the *scarus*, and this is the only fish which seems to ruminate."

The statement is repeated twice.[20] We note that the fact is unaccompanied by any expression of surprise (compare § 201), and also unaccompanied by anything like evidence. If true, the fact must be one difficult of observation, since

---

[19] It may be supposed that a fact so easily verified as the normal number of teeth in woman could hardly have been misstated unless on the warrant of some superficial evidence; and as some women never cut their wisdom teeth—a fact also noticed in certain men—an example of this kind may have furnished Aristotle with his conclusion.

[20] In Book VIII., c. xiv., p. 675, and in *De Part.* III., 14.

fish will not exhibit their ruminating propensities out of the water; and *in* the water, it could hardly have been watched. Is it true?[21]

§ 334. Book III. continues the enumeration of the internal organs. It casually reveals the fact that there were illustrated books in those days; since references are made to a diagram in which the letters *a, b, c, d,* indicate the parts spoken of in the text, just as in a modern work.

The descriptions of veins, sinews, muscles, hair and flesh need not be cited here; but the chapter on the blood is too interesting to be passed over. First be it noted that the blood is said to be, in common with the brain and spinal marrow, *without sensation*. What does this mean? Probably he wishes to guard against the false conclusion that blood may be sensitive, because flesh is the medium of sensation, and blood is transformed into fat, marrow, and flesh. Or it may be that he is simply protesting against PLATO, who held that opinion.

§ 335. "The taste of blood in a healthy condition is sweet, and its colour red; but when of inferior quality, or damaged by sickness, it is black." The sweetness of the blood is probably a metaphorical expression. The blackness was observed in blood drawn from the veins, and, as it was only drawn in cases of sickness, the coincidence stood for cause.

§ 336. "Inside the body blood has a certain warmth and fluidity: but outside it coagulates, except in deer and animals resembling them. The blood of other animals coagulates, unless the fibres are removed: ἐὰν μὴ ἐξαιρέθωσιν αἱ ἶνες."

---

[21] MILNE EDWARDS states it without misgiving in his *Leçons sur la Physiologie et l'Anat., comparée,* 1861, VI., 290, referring to OWEN's *Lectures on the Vertebrata,* as his authority. In a private note Prof. OWEN informs me that the *Scarus* named by Aristotle has not been identified, but that "the carp by a rotatory motion of the gullet brings the vegetable food-contents of the stomach successively within the sphere of the action of the strong pharyngeal grinding teeth, whence the pulp is returned to the stomach fitted for passing the pylorus."

This is a remarkable passage. Although the blood of deer is really no less coagulable than that of other quadrupeds, there is some probability in a genuine observation having originated the error; since modern physiologists affirm that in the blood of a hunted animal the fibrine disappears, or is so much lessened, as to prevent coagulation. Now, it is possible that Aristotle's observation was made on the blood of a hunted deer.

Even more noteworthy is the mention of fibrine or fibres, αἱ ἶνες, as the cause of coagulation. One might, without an over-anxiety to read modern discoveries into ancient texts, regard this as an anticipation of MALPIGHI's discovery of fibrine being the coagulable material;[22] an anticipation also of the further discovery by BORELLI that this fibrine is liquid while in the blood-vessels, and only coagulates on exposure to the air;[23] since it might be argued that Aristotle knew the fibrine to be liquid in the blood; otherwise, when specifying the fluidity of the blood, he would have excepted its fibres. Yet such an argument would be very questionable. He was only repeating the notion shared by PLATO respecting the existence of fibres in the blood; and we have but to open the *Timæus* to see how far that notion was from the truth. Plato thought the fibres actually existed *as* fibres in the blood, and that by their aid its motions were effected!

§ 337. Aristotle seems to have made, or collected, some observations on the comparative rapidity of coagulation, for he states that the blood of oxen coagulates more rapidly than that of any other animal. I am not aware whether this is exact; but experiment has proved that the blood of oxen sheep and dogs coagulates faster than that of man.

§ 338. "Fat animals have purer blood, but in small quantity. Man has the purest and thinnest; oxen and asses

---

[22] MALPIGHI: *De Polyp.*, p. 125, in *Opera Omnia*, Lond., 1686.
[23] BORELLI: *De Motu Animalium*, Rome, 1681, II., prop. cxxxii., p. 265.

the thickest and blackest." These imaginary facts are succeeded by the following *à priori* statement, deduced from the axiom that the upper must be the nobler part:—" In the lower parts of the body the blood becomes thicker and blacker than in the upper parts." Of equal value is the assertion that the blood of woman is thicker and blacker than that of man.

§ 339. The book concludes with remarks on milk and its coagulation, from which may be cited the mention of the occasional appearance of milk in the male. He speaks of a male goat at Lemnos which yielded enough milk for cheeses to be made from it, and whose male descendants inherited the peculiarity. Nor is this the fable it was long held to be. BURDACH [24] cites several well-attested cases of males yielding milk. HUMBOLDT saw a man in America who suckled his child for five months, during the illness of his wife; and ISIDORE GEOFFROY ST. HILAIRE had for some years, in the Jardin des Plantes, a male goat with largely developed udders yielding milk.

§ 340. BOOK IV.—The first seven chapters of this book are devoted to the anatomy of invertebrata, and are not only rich in details, but approach more nearly to the demands of a systematic treatise than any other portion of the work. The cephalopoda are first described, and with a minuteness which could only come from familiarity with their forms. That he gathered much of his information from fishermen is obvious: yet it will be remarked how singularly free his statements are from the absurdities which commonly distort the narratives of fishermen. Not only does he withhold credence from their marvellous stories, which is in itself remarkable, when we consider how credulous were his contemporaries and successors, and how uncritical he himself often is respecting facts and explanations; but in another place he distinctly intimates the reason of fishermen's ignorance,—" that these

---

[24] BURDACH: *Traité de Physiologie*, Paris, 1839, IV., 382.

people never make direct observations for the sake of knowledge."[25]

§ 341. Every naturalist recognizes at once, by unmistakeable though indefinable indications, the portions of a work which are compiled without direct knowledge; and will see in Aristotle's treatment of the cephalopoda traces of that personal knowledge which he, perhaps, first gained in the pleasant idleness of boyhood.[26] Yet although he was doubtless familiar with them from his early years, as with many other forms of marine life in his book, there are no traces of the naturalist's enjoyment. It has no out-of-doorness. We never feel the sea-breeze blowing; we never hear the delicious ripple of the waves against the advancing keel; we never hear the creaking whirr of the net being hawled on board. From anything to be gathered from this book, we might conclude that the author had only toiled amidst the dust of libraries and museums, like the veriest professor of an inland university.[27]

§ 342. He next describes the Crustacea, and then the Testacea; in both displaying more anatomical knowledge than is shown in the descriptions of the vertebrata. A brief

---

[25] οὐθεὶς γὰρ αὐτῶν οὐθὲν τηρεῖ τοιαῦτον τοῦ γνῶναι χάριν.—*De Gen. Animal.*, III., 5, 756. His rejection of the fables reported by writers such as CTESIAS shows even more discrimination; for as PLINY truly says, though his own excessive credulity renders the phrase rather ludicrous in his mouth, "mirum est quo procedat Græca credulitas! Nullum tam impudens mendacium est, ut teste careat." VIII., 22. Compared with this writer, or with Pliny, Aristotle is a model of sober sagacity; compared with the naturalists of this century, he is somewhat easy in credulity.

[26] KÖHLER: *Aristoteles de Molluscis cephalopodibus*, Riga, 1820, has collected all the passages in which A. speaks of the cephalopoda in his three principal treatises. See a still more exhaustive notice in the essay by AUBERT: *Die Cephalopoden des Aristoteles* in the *Zeitschrift für Wissenschaftliche Zoologie*, 1862, XII., 372.

[27] Yet a genuine naturalist could say of it: "It is less intended as a summary of his general views respecting their organization and habits, than as a popular exordium calculated to engage the attention of the reader and excite him to the study of Nature."—MACGILLIVRAY: *Lives of the Zoologists*, 1834, p. 62; and SONNENBURG has the courage to assert that its "natural and simple style" gives it a charm which is wanting to most modern works.—*Zoologische-kritische Bemerkungen*, p. 6.

description of the structure of Insects completes his survey. No classes are proposed for worms, polypes, medusæ, &c., the reason for which he has given elsewhere. "No groups have been made because there is no one form which embraces many forms."

§ 343. *Chap. VIII.* passes to the enumeration of the organs of Sense, in invertebrata. I will only pause to notice one detail. "With regard to sight and hearing in the Testacea," he says, "nothing is very clear. The *solen* seems to fly when any noise is made, and on feeling the approach of the iron rod which is used to capture it; and the *pecten*, when a finger approaches, opens and shuts as if it saw." He here contents himself with recording the observed facts, which seem to imply the existence of senses. He did not know that the *pecten* has eyes, studding its mantle like jewels; but, whatever vision the *pecten* may possess, it does not open and shut at the approach of a finger.

§ 344. *Chap. IX.* is devoted to the voices of animals, distinguishing between Voice and Sound, and Speech, which is different from both. Voice is only produced by the pharynx; therefore, no animal without lungs has a voice. The rigorous exactness of this distinction is seen when he comes to treat of the so-called voice of fishes. "Fish are mute, for they have no lungs, no windpipe, no pharynx. Some of them emit sounds and squeaks, which are hence said to have a voice. But some of these produce the sound by the friction of their gills which are spinous; others produce the sound internally, near the stomach. And all have an organ of breathing (air-bladder?) which causes a sound when pressed and moved. Some cartilaginous fishes also seem to whistle, but they cannot properly be said to have a voice, only to utter a sound." [28]

---

[28] JOHANNES MÜLLER in his *Archiv für Anat. und Physiologie*, 1857, p. 249, has given an elaborate survey of existing knowledge on the voices of the fish with valuable additions of his own. DUFOSSÉ has also treated the subject in a Mémoire addressed to the *Académie des Sciences*, Feb., 1858.

§ 345. *Chap. X.* treats of Sleep. In a former paragraph (§ 284) we drew attention to the distinction between Sleep and Repose; and the remark must be repeated àpropos of this chapter, in which the various indications of animal sleep are brought together. Aristotle thinks it by no means clear that oviparous animals dream, but is certain that they sleep.

§ 346. *Chap. XI.* enumerates the distinctions of sex; but this subject is more fully treated elsewhere.

§ 347. Book V. commences the enumeration of the chief particulars concerning Generation. Chapters I. to XIV. specify the various modes of congress, the breeding periods, and periods of puberty. Out of the mass of details here collected, true, false, and trivial, we shall only cite one; and this not as a specimen of the rest, but as an example of the unreasoning credulity which propagates vulgar errors, and from which, as we have seen, even Aristotle was by no means free. The hen-partridge, he says, is impregnated if the wind blows from the male; nay, at certain periods, it is frequently enough for them only to hear his voice as he flies over them and they become impregnated by his breath.

§ 348. *Chap. XIV.* suddenly quits the subject of Generation and without any transition passes to a description of the structure and habits of Sponges; a defect in composition which might justify a suspicion of this being an interpolation, did not the whole work exhibit extreme laxity in the arrangement of its materials.

§ 349. *Chap. XV.* to the end of the book continues the subject of Generation.

§ 350. Book VI. is a continuation of the same subject, the first nine chapters being devoted to Birds; the next eight chapters to Fish; and the remainder to viviparous animals with feet. As we shall hereafter have to consider his views on generation more in detail, we need not pause over these chapters, except to notice the spontaneous generation of eels from mud.

"Eels are not reproduced from sexual congress, nor are they oviparous. Dissection reveals neither sperm nor eggs, nor the generative organs. And this is the only animal possessing blood which does not arise from congress or from eggs. That this is so, however, is evident, since after rain they appear in ponds which have been dried up. But they are never produced in dry places, nor in ponds always full: they are nourished by rain-water. They originate in the bowels of the earth."

§ 351. BOOK VII. is only a fragment, and is devoted to a continuation of the subject of the two former books, but restricted to man. For the reason already mentioned (§ 350), we pass it over with the simple remark that in it may be found many of the notions current in medical literature up to the eighteenth century.

§ 352. BOOK VIII. opens with a description, already quoted (§ 175-179), of the ascending complexity in the scale of organic life, and then passes on to a variety of details respecting animals. First of the different localities they inhabit; then of their food; then of their migrations; then of their hybernation and their various relations to temperature. It next treats of the diseases to which they are subject. Here, as may be expected, there are many absurd notions, some so contradicted by ordinary experience that it is difficult to understand how a man of his amazing sagacity could have given them credence. For example, mentioning the madness of dogs, he says that all animals bitten by rabid dogs become rabid, *except man*. Again, "horses ranging the meadows suffer from no disease except gout, which destroys their hoofs; one sign of this disease is the appearance of a hollow wrinkle beneath the nose." Domesticated horses suffer from various diseases. The Elephant is only troubled with two diseases, flatulence and diarrhœa.[29] Mice die if they drink during summer.

---

[29] Repeated by PLINY, *Hist. Nat.*, VIII., 10.

§ 353. Book IX. is on the habits and instincts of animals. The details are frequently very interesting, and on the whole tolerably accurate; but they are merely collected as details, without any attempt at systematic arrangement, so that the book is a quarry rather than a composition. It shows Aristotle's love of facts for their own sake; but it shows little of the philosophic power with which naturalists have so gratuitously credited him. Like most boys, and many men who call themselves naturalists, he was eager enough in collecting facts and anecdotes; but there is no more illumination of such facts by biological principles, no more attempt so to co-ordinate them as to evolve general principles, than in the labour of species-mongers who pass their lives in registering the spots on a butterfly's wing, the curves of a shell, or the markings of Diatomaceæ. Spix has had the courage to avow this: "Aristotle was so far from giving a form to his wealth of details that he was content to publish a chaos of observations and opinions as materials for some future architect. His 'History of Animals' thus resembles a great market where each one may choose what he wants."[30] Only he must not want accuracy.

§ 354. From the foregoing analysis the reader will be able to judge how far Cuvier's opinion is acceptable, and with what justification this work can be pronounced "one of the greatest monuments which the genius of man has raised to Natural Science."[31] That it is a marvellous work, considering the period at which it was produced, and the multiform productions of its author, every one must admit. But this is not admitting its claim to be regarded as a great monument of Science. It is no more a monument than a brick-kiln is an architectural achievement. There are plenty of facts, some valuable, some trivial, many false. There is no colliga-

---

[30] Spix: *Geschichte und Beurtheilung aller Systeme in der Zoologie*, 1811, p. 22.

[31] Cuvier: *Op. cit.*, I., 166.

tion of these facts—none of the general principles which could bind them into a serviceable system, and form a work of science. In his day it was a great thing for an eminent thinker to bestow so much care upon the collection of facts; but this could only be a preparation for future science;[32] and one luminous principle is worth a thousand unconnected facts, for it contains within it the seeds of a thousand discoveries.

§ 355. There is not a single principle established by Aristotle in this work which would lead the student to new discoveries, or enable him to illuminate the old. He could not, knowing this work by heart, class a single new animal, even provisionally, nor explain a single biological phenomenon. And the best answer to its eulogists is History, which teaches that no zoological science was even begun until many centuries afterwards. Had Aristotle really laid the "eternal bases," had he placed in the hands of men a new instrument of research, Zoology would have advanced as Astronomy advanced from HIPPARCHUS to PTOLEMY.

§ 356. Once more let me remind the reader that these objections are not directed against Aristotle, but against his careless panegyrists. They would be preposterous if urged against the great thinker in the early days of science. One might as well insult Greek civilization by a triumphant enumeration of its deficiencies, and point to its want of a post-office or a free press. But the language of panegyrists is as sweeping as it is exaggerated. The real historical greatness of Aristotle does not suffice them; they insist on our accepting him as an authority.

---

[32] "In so complex a science as that which relates to living beings," says HUXLEY, "accurate and diligent empirical observation, though the best of things as far as it goes, will not take us very far; and the mere accumulation of facts without generalization and classification is as great an error intellectually, as hygienically would be the attempt to strengthen by accumulating nourishment without due attention to the *primæ viæ*; the result in each case being chiefly giddiness and confusion in the head."—*On the Cell-Theory* in the *British and Foreign Medical Review*, Oct., 1853, p. 291.

CHAPTER XVI.

"ON THE PARTS OF ANIMALS."[1]

§ 357. The position of this treatise immediately after the one just analyzed is clearly indicated in Aristotle's programme of study. " First, we must understand the phenomena of animals; then assign their causes; and finally, speak of their generation." The " History of Animals " undertakes the first; the *De Partibus* undertakes the second; and the treatise to be analyzed in the next chapter undertakes the third.

The work now before us has been comparatively little studied. Editors have neglected it; translators have avoided it; students generally have found it uninteresting. And indeed it wants the abundance of detail, and the more attractive subject of the " History of Animals ;" it is, moreover, very difficult to understand. Yet as an attempt to explain the causes of biological phenomena, it deserves close attention.

§ 358. Book I., *Chap. I.*, opens with the question whether " it is necessary to treat of each individual separately, or to treat of that which is common to them all. For there are many things alike in different animals, such as sleep, respiration, growth, decay, and death. Of these we can say

---

[1] The best edition of the *De Partibus* is that by Franzius, with a translation and excellent notes, Leipzig, 1853. I cannot find any English, Italian, Spanish or French versions.

nothing clear or certain as yet. But it is evident that by separate treatment the same things must frequently be repeated. . . . It is otherwise with those things which are included under one name, but which have nevertheless differences of kind, such as Locomotion, which may be flying, creeping, swimming, or walking. Hence we must first settle whether our inquiry is to begin with that which is common to the whole class, and then proceed to the particulars, or at once commence with each animal by itself."

There being several causes, for example, the moving cause and the final cause, we must settle which of these naturally comes first. The final cause must evidently be treated first, for it is the reason, λόγος, and reason is the beginning of every product of art and nature.

§ 359. Here follow metaphysical distinctions respecting necessity, form, and cause, from which the following is all that need here be quoted: " We must say since man *is to be*, therefore he has such and such parts, for without these he cannot be. Since he is such a being, he must of necessity have such an origin, and in such a manner: therefore this part and then that part is originated."

§ 360. In his teleology will be noticed an opinion directly the reverse of the one now generally current. In modern science, final causes, long since almost banished from astronomy and physics, find refuge mainly in biology; whereas Aristotle thought that the order and regularity of astronomical phenomena more decidedly implied the action of a final cause than the irregular and capricious phenomena of the organic world.

§ 361. Without very explicitly stating his views, Aristotle gives us to understand that he held a similar opinion to that of moderns respecting Species, as real existences, or Types. " It is evident," he says, " that there must be something which we call nature, ὅ δὴ καὶ καλοῦμεν φύσιν." The word φύσις, however, had to the Greek mind different suggestions from that which the word Nature has to us, and resembled rather the *natura naturans* of SPINOZA. The passage just given is thus elucidated: " For it is not *any* thing that issues from a seed, but a particular body from each particular seed, and every seed from its own particular body. The seed is therefore the *beginning* and the plastic material of that which is formed out of it. But prior to it is the Being, of which it is the seed; for the seed is the genesis, and the final cause is the existence."[2]

§ 362. *Chaps. II.* and *III.* treat of classification, or of such rude attempts as were then in vogue. His criticism of dichotomy is obviously directed against PLATO. As before noticed (§ 318), he considers the attempt to classify by dividing genera according to two characters, partly difficult and partly impossible. Dichotomy, he says, would scatter allied animals —some birds, for example, would be placed in one division, and others in another. The strongest objection, however, is that the dichotomist must erect Negation into a principle: " but there can be no distinctions under a negation; for it is impossible that there should be species of nothing; there can be no species of wingless or footless as of winged and footed animals." It is difficult to draw such distinctions even in animals which present species, as, for example, in the division of winged and wingless, since one and the same animal may be both, as in the case of the ant, the glow-worm, and some others.

There can be little doubt that Aristotle has here pointed out the scientific error of all classifications founded on negatives; and that his criticism reaches even the familiar division established by LAMARCK, and now universally accepted, of vertebrata and invertebrata. The vertebrata form a natural division, characterized by an obvious peculiarity; but to lump together all other animals, no matter how manifestly different, merely on the negative character of their having no vertebral

---

[2] γένεσις μὲν γὰρ τὸ σπέρμα, οὐσία δὲ τὸ τέλος.

column, is—except as a provisional expedient—eminently unphilosophic.[3]

§ 363. But although dissatisfied with the systematic attempts of predecessors, Aristotle does not offer one of his own. He follows the common method of grouping together all animals which have several obvious characters, rather than grouping them by any single character. "This is the way the vulgar have grouped birds and fishes."

"No part of an animal arises without matter (ὕλη); nor can it exist as matter alone; since there is no animal, nor part of an animal which is simply body (σῶμα.) Moreover, it is necessary to distinguish between what is essential, and what is accidental. . . . . Also, we must classify according to opposites; for opposites imply differences, as black and white, straight and crooked."

§ 364. *Chap.* IV.—He here says that some surprise may be felt at men not having classed aquatic and winged animals together, since they have several characters in common. But there is a good reason for it. All kinds which differ only in degree have been united under one genus; those which only resemble each other by analysis have been separated. Birds, for example, are distinguished among each other by some preponderance, one having the wings shorter, another longer; but fish are distinguished from birds, because their resemblance is only one of analogy: the one having scales, the

---

[3] On the principles of classification compare LEUCKART: *Über die Morphologie und die Verwandtschaftsverhältnisse der wirbellosen Thiere*, 1848, p. 7. MECKEL: *Traité d'Anat. Comp.*, Paris, 1828, I., p. 90. VICTOR CARUS: *Systeme du thierischen Morphologie*, 1853. VAN DER HOOVEN: *Handbook of Zoology*, trans. by CLARK, 1856. DE BLAINVILLE: *De l'Organisation des Animaux*, 1832, I. BRONN: *Die Klassen und Ordnungen des Thierreichs*, 1859, I. AGASSIZ: *Essay on Classification*, London, 1859. VON BAER: *über Entwickelungsgeschichte der Thiere. Erste Theil*, 1828, p. 89, 90, and the whole of the 5th *scholion*; also his essay in the *Nova Acta Physico-Medica*, 1826, translated by HUXLEY in the *Scientific Memoirs*, Lond., 1853, I., p. 176. ISIDORE GEOFFROY ST. HILAIRE: *Hist. Nat. des Règnes Organiques*, 1854, I. It is unnecessary to name works which will spontaneously present themselves to the reader's mind.

other feathers. But to carry this out through all animals is not easy; for many animals have the same analogies."

We see here a dim perception of the Natural Method; but, as SCHLEIDEN[4] justly remarks, it is only such a perception as lies in the common knowledge of all peoples, and which necessarily precedes the Artificial Method. To credit Aristotle with any profound insight into the superiority of the Natural over the Artificial Method, is to misconceive the whole course of historical development. He had no tolerable example of the Artificial Method before him. He had not even arrived at the conception of Class, Order, Family, Genus, and Species. His groups were all roughly marked out by certain obvious characters.

§ 365. *Chap. V.* contains an earnest defence of the study of Biology: a defence not wholly superfluous even in our own days, when protests against a "trivial curiosity respecting flies and tadpoles" may occasionally be heard issuing from grave men too facile in contempt of what they do not understand. "Even in objects unattractive to the vulgar eye, Nature offers inexpressible delights to the philosophic mind capable of studying her causes. For it would indeed be strange and foolish if we, who take delight in such objects when we see them represented in art, should not be even more attracted by Nature herself. Nor must we indulge in childish repulsions; for in all natural objects there lies marvellousness; and if any one despises the contemplation of inferior animals, he must despise himself."

§ 366. BOOK II., *Chap. I.*—He now proceeds to explain what is known of the parts of animals. Referring to the *History of Animals*, in which has been explained "out of what, and of how many parts they are composed," he has now to inquire into the causes why each part is what it is. Our threefold study of structure, chemical, histological, and ana-

---

[4] SCHLEIDEN: *Grundzüge der wissenschaftlichen Botanik*, 1861, p. 7.

tomical, may be found indicated in the opening of this book. There are three kinds of composition, he says; the first is that of the elements—fire, earth, air, and water; the second is that of similar parts—bones, flesh, &c.; the third is that of dissimilar parts—face, hands, &c. This, although the order of our study, is not the order of nature, which indeed is the reverse. For that which is last formed in the animal, is the first in its essence or being; just as a house does not exist for the sake of the bricks and mortar, but prior to them. In respect of Time, substance and its formation are prior to the formed animal; but in respect of Reason (*i.e.* according to our conceptions) the essence and the form are prior. It is evident that the conception of house-building includes the conception of a house; but the conception of a house does not include that of house-building. Thus we see that the elements are for the sake of the similar parts; and the similar parts are for the sake of the dissimilar.

§ 367. Some parts of the animal are *functional*, and others are *sensitive*. The functional parts are all composed of the dissimilar parts: the sensitive of the similar.

The reason he alleges is characteristic. Sensation must arise in the similar parts because every sensation is of one kind. No philosopher has ventured to assert that the hand, face, or any other dissimilar part was fire, earth, air, or water; but they have assigned the various sensations to air and fire.

§ 368. "Although sensation has its seat in the similar parts, yet it is natural that Touch should be in a simple, though not altogether simple, part; for it has several kinds, such as Warmth and Cold, Dryness and Moisture; and the part which is sensitive to these—the flesh and its analogue in animals without flesh—is the most corporeal of sensitive structures.[5] . . . As it is impossible for an animal to

---

[5] σωματωδέστατόν ἐστι τῶν αἰσθητηρίων. A statement repeated in chap. VIII., p. 654.

exist without sensation, it necessarily follows that all animals must have some simple parts, because it is in these that they have sensation; and their functions are performed by dissimilar parts."

§ 369. *Chap. II.* is on the *partes similares.* They are of two classes—1. moist and fluid, such as flesh, fat, suet (στέαρ), marrow, lymph, blood, bile, milk; 2. hard and solid, as vessels, sinews, bones, and cartilage.[6]

§ 370. Distinctions arise according to the relative goodness of these parts; blood, for example, being sometimes warmer, sometimes colder, sometimes thicker, sometimes thinner, not only in different animals, but also in different parts of the same animal. The blood in the upper parts is distinguished from that in the lower, on the *à priori* ground of the upper being the nobler part. "Thick and warm blood is better adapted for plastic purposes; thin and cold blood better for sensation and thought.[7] Hence bees and other animals are more intelligent, φρονιμώτερα, than many animals with red blood; and of the red-blooded those are the most intelligent which have the thinnest and the coldest blood. The best of all are those which have warm, pure, and thin blood; they are distinguished by fortitude, ἀνδρεία, and intelligence. Hence the upper and lower parts, the right and left sides, the male and female, manifest their differences."

§ 371. In those days philosophers were fond of discussing relative heat and cold. He notices their discussions respecting the temperature of animals, some asserting the aquatic animals to be warmest, because they have to compensate, ἐπανισοῦν, by their own heat, the cold of the medium in

---

[6] ἄκανθα must obviously be here rendered by cartilage, though elsewhere it means fishbone and porcupine quills. Of course his ideas on the nature of bone wanted the precision now attained.

[7] Whatever the modern reader may think of this hypothesis, he should know that it was applauded by HARVEY: *Exercitations on Generation,* 1653, p. 282, Exer. LII.

which they live; an opinion very near the truth, though founded on insufficient data. Aristotle remarks that these disputes are due to the fact that warmth is a phrase used to express very different meanings; and it is necessary to settle first in what sense a thing can properly be called hot or cold. I quote his argument to show the inevitable weakness which arose from the absence of an objective standard, such as a thermometer, whereby heat could be measured with an accuracy impossible to any measurement by sensation.

§ 372. He first asks whether heat is simple or multiple. "It is necessary to ascertain how the heat manifests itself, for in one sense that body will be called warmest which most warms another body touching it; in another sense, that which creates the most sensation when touched, especially if accompanied with pain. This, however, often seems erroneous, for sometimes individual disposition is the cause of the pain. Further, that body is hottest which is most capable of melting the fusible, and burning the combustible. Again, when there are two sizes of the same substance, the larger is the warmer. We also say that the body which cools slowly, and warms quickly, is hotter by nature than that which is slowly warmed. . . . . Boiling water heats more than flame, but flame burns the combustible, and melts the fusible, which water cannot do. Moreover, boiling water is warmer than a small fire, but water cools more, and more quickly than fire; for fire never becomes cold; water always does. Again, water, in relation to feeling, is warmer, indeed, than oil, but it cools and becomes solid more speedily. Blood is warmer to the touch than water and oil, but becomes solid more rapidly. Further, stones and iron, and such like, are slower in warming than water, but they burn more when warmed. Besides, some warm bodies have warmth of their own added to what they get from others; but there is a great difference whether a body is warm in one way or the other, for the one may be accidental, as if we were to say a musician is warmer than another man, because one in a fever happened to be a musician. But of two bodies, one warm by nature, the other warm by accident, the former will cool more slowly, but the latter will often seem hotter to the feeling; the former will burn better; for example, flame burns more than boiling water, but boiling water is hotter to the touch, although its heat is accidental. Hence it is clear that we cannot easily decide which of two bodies is the warmer, one being warmer in this sense, the other in that."

§ 373. He has repeated these statements elsewhere.[8] They curiously illustrate the nature of ancient science. They show the hopelessness of attempting to measure physical forces by subjective standards. That this is the source of their weakness, and not deficient sagacity, may be seen in the following passage from BACON, who was equally without an instrument to measure heat: "Fire burneth wood, making it first luminous, then black and brittle, and lastly, broken and incinerate; scalding water doth none of these. The cause is—for that by fire the spirit of the body is first refined, and then emitted: whereof the refining or attenuation causeth light; and the emission, first, the fragility, and after, the dissolution into ashes. Neither doth any other body enter; but in water, the spirit of the body is not refined so much; and besides, water entereth, which doth increase the spirit, and in a degree extinguish it; therefore, we see that hot water will quench fire."[9]

§ 374. Had the ancients possessed an instrument capable of measuring temperature, they would have learned, as easily as we learn, the immense difference between that of boiling water and flame, and the various degrees of heat which various flames contain. Before science had explained the phenomenon, the fact that a finger can be passed through

---

[8] *Problemata XXIII.*
[9] BACON: *Sylvia Sylvarum*, VII. Works by SPEDDING and ELLIS, 1857, II., 552.

flame and scarcely feel the heat, whereas through boiling water it cannot pass without pain, naturally suggested that boiling water must be hotter than flame. The paradox disappears when we learn that before the skin of the finger can be attacked by the flame, its moisture must first be evaporated; this moisture, which serves as a temporary shield, while the finger passes rapidly through the flame, cannot, of course, protect the skin in water.

§ 375. The invention of the thermometer, or objective standard of heat, rendered a science of Thermotics possible; but great as is its superiority over any subjective standard, the superiority of quantitative over qualitative knowledge being thereby attained, it is itself too gross for the needs of modern science; and the more delicate susceptibility of the thermo-electric pile has revealed facts of the highest importance which would have been as far beyond the reach of the thermometer as the facts revealed by the thermometer were beyond the reach of any appreciation by sensation.

§ 376. *Chap. III.*—Aristotle having explained his views on heat, applies them to Digestion, which he held to be, as the Greek word implies, a kind of cooking. Heat, and heat alone, is the agent by which food is made fluid and metamorphosed into assimilable material.[10] Plants take up, by their roots, the food prepared for them by the earth; the earth is their stomach, and its warmth cooks their food.[11] Blood is perfected food. The conclusion drawn from this is not, however, easy to follow. He says, that because it is perfect food, blood gives no sensation when touched; in this resembling every other secretion and excretion. Nor is blood the same as flesh; for flesh when touched gives sensation. Nor is blood directly connected with flesh; nor does it form an integral part of it; but is contained in the heart and veins, as in a vessel.

---

[10] καὶ τούτων ἡ πέψις γίνεται καὶ ἡ μεταβολὴ διὰ τῆς τοῦ θερμοῦ δυνάμεως.
[11] τῇ γὰρ γῇ καὶ τῇ ἐν αὐτῇ θερμότητι χρῆται ὥσπερ κοιλίᾳ.

§ 377. *Chap. IV.* is also devoted to the blood, repeating what is said in the *History of Animals* respecting its fibrine coagulation and the dependence of intelligence on its thinness and purity. He adds that those animals which have watery blood are the most timorous, " for fear makes cold." This is rather confused reasoning. A man under terror feels cold; the action of the heart being checked, the blood quits the surface. But how does terror affect the blood? By congealing its water, says Aristotle. Granting the accuracy of this assertion, it will only explain how terror *might* make an animal cold; it will not explain why watery blood should predispose the animal to terror. Out of such hypothetical assumptions Logic might deduce the cause of the coldness which follows terror; but Logic will at any rate protest against putting the effect for the cause, as Aristotle does in this case.

§ 378. Besides becoming cold, animals in terror are motionless, discharge excretions, and some of them change colour. It is noticeable that this is said only of the bloodless animals, and from a subsequent passage of this work (IV., 5,) it is evident that he refers to the discharge of ink and the change of colour in the cephalopoda. We are not, however, to suppose that by this he had overlooked the obvious facts exhibited by animals with blood; but that he called attention to the less familiar facts exhibited by the cuttlefish and its fellows.[12]

§ 379. In contrast to the watery-blooded animals he places

---

[12] In attributing the change of colour in the cuttlefish to a mental emotion, Aristotle is more excusable than many modern naturalists who have fallen into the same error; *e. g.*, D'Orbigny : *Mollusques vivants et fossiles*, 1855, p. 113. In *Seaside Studies*, 2nd ed., 1860, p. 100, I showed that the phenomenon was not directly dependent on the mental condition of the animal, but was manifested by a strip of skin from the body of a dead animal; which also disproves the suggestion of Delle Chiaje, that it may be connected with respiration. *Descrizione e notomia degli animali invertebrati della Sicilia Citeriore*, Naples, 1841, I., 15.

those whose blood contains more fibrine, and is consequently more earthy. These are of a more earthy character, more passionate, more easily angered.[13] "For anger makes warm, and that which is solid when warmed becomes hotter than that which is fluid; and as fibrine is solid and earthy, so anger occasions fomentations in the blood. Hence bulls and boars are so wrathful and easily driven wild with rage, their blood being exceedingly rich in fibrine." If this is somewhat wildly hypothetical, it is far less so than VAN HELMONT's explanation of the poisonous quality of bull-beef.[14]

§ 380. *Chap. V.* is on Fat and Suet. Both are made of the blood, which has not been devoted to the formation of flesh. "This is evident from their shining; for the shining of a fluid is the product of fire and air.[15] Hence no bloodless animal has fat nor suet." We must not be surprised at his not knowing that the bloodless animals produced fat; the means of detecting it were then too imperfect.

§ 381. Fat in certain proportion, he says, is useful, but in excess injurious. Why? "If the whole body were of fat or suet, it would perish, because an animal is that which has sensation. Now flesh and its analogue are sensitive;

---

[13] In the words of the Spanish compiler, DIEGO DE FUNES Y MENDOÇA: "Los animales que tienen la sangre fibrosa y llena de cosas gruessas, estos tienen naturaleza mas terrena, son mas animosos, y ayrados, y ansi mismo furibundos."--*Historia General de Aves y Animales de Aristoteles traduzida de Latin en Romance*. Valentia, 1551, p. 280. It is the title of this work which misled BUHLE into the supposition that Mendoça was one of Aristotle's translators. The book is a compilation of absurdities from all ancient sources ready to hand; and is interesting as a specimen of Natural History in the 16th century.

[14] "Do you desire to be informed why the blood of a Bull is poisonous, but that of an Oxe, though brother to the Bull, is safe and harmlesse? The reason thus: the Bull at the time of slaughter is full of secret reluctancy and vindictive murmurs, and firmly impresseth upon his own blood a character and potent signature of revenge. A Bull dyes with a higher flame of revenge above him than any other animal."—*Ternary of Paradoxes*, translated by CHARLETON, 1650, p. 67.

[15] δηλοῖ δὲ τὸ λιπαρὸν αὐτῶν· τῶν γὰρ ὑγρῶν τὸ λιπαρὸν κοινὸν ἀέρος καί πυρός ἐστιν.

but, as I said before, blood is not; consequently fat and suet are not sensitive." He further notices why excess of fat causes sterility in females: the blood which would have formed progeny being used up for fat.

§ 382. *Chap. VI.* is on Marrow, also a product of Blood, and not as some think (alluding to PLATO), a product of the spermatic fluid. In some animals marrow is fatty, in others suety. The important ganglionic mass forming the Spinal Chord, is considered by him, as it is by the vulgar of our day, to be the Spinal Marrow, bearing the same relation to the vertebræ that marrow bears to the hollow bones; but he distinguishes it from every other marrow as being less fatty or suety.

In this chapter there is nothing more to be noticed, unless it be one more example of rash generalization from imperfect observation, namely, the statement that some animals—among them the lion—have no marrow.

§ 383. *Chap. VII.* treats of the Brain, by many then held to be also marrow and the origin of the spinal marrow; but this appears absurd to Aristotle, "for the Brain is the coldest part of the body, the Marrow is by nature warm, as is *evident* by its shining and its fat." This contrast of cold and warmth, is the reason why brain and spinal marrow are in connection, Nature being careful to compensate for excess in one direction by excess in another; and the cold brain is therefore fitly placed in juxtaposition with the warm marrow.

§ 384. "That the spinal marrow is warm is evident in many ways." He has already mentioned its shining, which implies the presence of fire. "The coldness of the brain appears when we touch it; it is also the most bloodless of moist parts." (§ 164.)

§ 385. Modern readers, accustomed from boyhood to hear the brain spoken of as the seat of sensation, will feel some surprise on meeting with a passage directly contravening that opinion, as the following :—"It is evident from simple inspection that the brain is in no direct connection with the sensitive parts ; still more evident in the fact that when touched it yields no sensation." The first clause is a deduction from the theory of flesh being the medium of sensation. The second clause indicates an important fact—the insensibility of the cerebrum—which in our own day has caused surprise, and some absurd speculation.[16] The difficulty admits of easy explanation. When observation proves that the brain is insensible to direct stimulus—that it may be pinched, cut, torn, or galvanized without producing any evidence of sensasation in the animal operated on—the conclusion is that the brain is not a *transmitter* of stimuli, as a nerve is; the brain is sensitive, and only when the *stimulated nerve* acts upon it is its sensibility excited. To imagine that Sensibility could be excited in the brain by the same means as Neurility is excited in the nerve (*i.e.* by simple external stimulus) is to overlook the important distinction between nerve-action and ganglionic action—or, as I have proposed to name them, Neurility and Sensibility.[17]

In the days of Aristotle there was no suspicion of any such distinction as that of excitor and excited ; and finding the brain *insensible*, when touched, he was justified in denying it to be the seat of sensibility.

§ 386. But although the psychical office of the brain is thus denied by Aristotle, he gives it, as we have seen (§ 164)

---

[16] HARLES: *Versuch einer Gesch. der Hirn und Nervenlehre im Alterthume*, 1801, p. 80, apparently unaware of this fact, thinks that Aristotle invented it to suit his theory. Compare CÆSALPINUS: *Peripateticarum Quæst.*, 1571, lib. V., quæst. 3 and 6 ; and his antagonist TAURELLUS: *Alpes Cæsæ*, 1650, p. 926. The insensibility of the cerebrum is discussed by HALLER: *Elementa Physiologiæ*, Lausanne, 1762, IV., 312 seq., where numerous observations and experiments are recorded. All the best modern works contain ample evidence on the point.

[17] *Reports of the British Association for the Advancement of Science*, 1859, and *Physiology of Common Life*, 1860, II., 14-24.

a physiological office—that of moderating the excessive heat of the blood.

"Man has the largest brain in relation to his body, and larger than woman; for he has the warmest thorax, which is most abundantly supplied with blood. Hence, also, man alone has an erect position, because heat in gaining strength works an increase from the centre, according to the direction of its path."[18]

§ 387. He also treats, in this chapter, of the sutures of the skull; and in doing so, illustrates the fanciful deduction and careless observation which characterize ancient science. "Their office, he says, is to permit the escape of vapours from the brain." I know not how long this explanation found credit, but it was still flourishing in the time of GALEN.[19]

"The number of sutures, he says, is greatest in man; greater in man than in woman." The observation is in every way unfortunate. Among mammalia, the number is precisely the same; in fish and amphibia it is much greater than in man; and if the skulls of old women, from their more rapid ossification, do occasionally present fewer apparent sutures, a very little circumspection would suffice to discover that there is really no difference in the number possessed by each sex.

§ 388. *Chap. VIII.* treats of Flesh, the most important of the *partes similares*. It is the seat of sensibility; the mark of animality, "since we define an animal, that which has sensation." This is a much higher attribute than that

---

[18] ἡ γὰρ τοῦ θερμοῦ φύσις ἰσχύουσα ποιεῖ τὴν αὔξησιν ἀπὸ τοῦ μέσου κατὰ τὴν αὑτῆς φοράν. This obscure passage is thus rendered by BUSSEMAKER: "Caloris enim natura invalescens incrementum de medio agit secundum sui itineris directionem." It may be thus paraphrased: "The direction of heat is upwards, and it will, therefore, determine growth upwards, thereby giving man his erect position." Though why animals do not more gradually approach this erect position is not stated, unless it be implied in the fact that they have too little warmth to be compared with man.

[19] GALEN: *De usu Partium*, IX., I., 688.

assigned by PLATO, who said flesh was made in order that it might be a preservative against the cold of winter, and the heat of summer; besides being a shield against blows.

§ 388 a. "The primary sensibility is that of Touch, and its organs are the respective parts. Other sensibilities were not necessary; they might have been left uncreated; but Touch was necessary, for it is, if not the *only* corporeal sensation, at least the most corporeal, σωματῶδες." (§ 368.)

§ 389. All other parts, such as bones, sinews, skin, vessels, hair, and nails, are present only as servitors to sensation, *e. g.* bones being for the protection of the soft parts.

§ 390. *Chap. X.* developes this idea of the subordination of parts to the Flesh; or as moderns would say, the subordination of parts to the animal organism. Aristotle distinguishes bone from fish-bone and cartilage. He holds cartilage to be a *mixture* of the earthy substance of bone with soft marrow; whereas in bones the two are separate, the marrow lying inside. He could not know that cartilage contains fat. But he might have avoided the error of asserting that bone and cartilage are alike in not being regenerated when broken or cut. Bone happens to be one of the most easily regenerated of tissues; and hence the observed rapidity with which even large broken bones are mended, or removed pieces replaced. Cartilage, on the contrary, *never* regenerates, but is replaced by another structure. "When fractured, as sometimes happens with the rib cartilages, there is no reunion by cartilaginous matter, but the broken surfaces become connected by fibrous tissue." [20]

---

[20] SHARPEY: in *Quain's Anatomy*, 1856, I., c. vii. The physiological reason of this difference I take to be this: bones grow, and consequently are regenerated from the *periosteum*, or enveloping membrane; and hence by transplanting a portion of this membrane to another body, or another part, new bone will grow from it (see note 21 to Chap. X.) But cartilages do not grow from a *perichondrium*.

§ 391. *Chap.* X.—" All animals have two indispensable parts : those which take in food, and those which get rid of the waste. Plants have no excretory organs, for they take their food ready digested from the earth, and give in return seed and fruit. . . . Plants, inasmuch as they are fixed to the ground, do not need much variety in their organs. But those creatures which have sensation as well as life possess a more varied structure, and some more varied than others, when Nature thinks not only of life but of good life. Such is the case with man. For he is the only living creature known to us who has a portion of the divine in him; or, at any rate, he has more of it than any other creature. On this account, and because his external forms are best known, we must speak of him first: for his parts are disposed according to Nature; since his upper part is directed upwards to the supreme of all." [21]

§ 391 *a*. It is curious to find men in all ages laying so much stress on a very unimportant peculiarity, and making man's supremacy to consist in a power of gazing upwards, which is shared by every goose that waddles across his path.

> L'homme élève un front noble et regarde les cieux,

says Louis Racine, in imitation of Ovid's well-known lines:

> Pronaque cum spectent animalia cætera terram,
> Os homini sublime dedit, cœlumque tueri
> Jussit.

Galen justly ridicules this notion; it is, he says, refuted by the fact that there are fish which always have their eyes directed towards the heavens, and that man can only direct his eyes upwards by bending back his head.[22] As to the erect position, no one till Isidore Geoffroy St. Hilaire thought of the familiar fact that many birds, such as the penguins,

---

[21] εὐθὺς γὰρ καὶ τὰ φύσει μόρια κατὰ φύσιν ἔχει τούτῳ μόνῳ, καὶ τὸ τούτου ἄνω πρὸς τὸ τοῦ ὅλου ἔχει ἄνω.

[22] Galen: *De usu Partium*, III., 3.

have the vertical attitude, and some mammals—such as the gerboa and kangaroo—approach it very closely.[23] If the attitude of man is more perfectly erect, this is but a question of degree, not worth making a cardinal distinction.[24] Better than all such trifling marks of superiority is the grand characteristic expressed in LAMARTINE's verse—

L'homme est un dieu tombé qui se souvient des cieux.

§ 392. The remaining chapters of this book are not, as might be expected from the passage previously quoted, devoted to the various organs of Nutrition and Excretion, but to an enumeration of the various parts of the head. The style is rambling, one remark suggesting another without any attempt at order. I will specify but one: " Man is of all animals the one having the greatest abundance of hair on the head; this is necessary, because of the humidity of the brain and the sutures of the skull; for growth must be greatest where there is most warmth and humidity."[25] One cannot but remark the want of logic in this facile physiology, which, after assuming that warmth and moisture determine excess, makes

---

[23] ST. HILAIRE: *Histoire des Règnes Organiques*, 1856, II., 191.

[24] Lord MONBODDO maintained that the erect position is *acquired*, like speech, and acquired with difficulty. *Origin and Progress of Language*, 2nd edit., I., 186. In his *Ancient Metaphysics*, 1779, III., 74, he adds this corroborative story, which he professes to have received from a Swedish gentleman, a pupil of Linnæus, who told the story in his class: " There was a human creature caught in the woods of Saxony, in the time of Frederick Augustus of Poland. He was running wild upon all fours with the bears, and like them fed chiefly upon honey. The greatest difficulty in taming him was to make him walk upright; for which they hung weights to his shoulders to counteract that propensity which he had to fall prone. After he was civilized, had learned to speak, and had lived several years with men, he still retained his bearish love for honey, and inclination to rob the bees." MONBODDO adds that he " holds it to be a vulgar error that walking upright is an essential quality of human nature ;" and this opinion is also maintained by MOSCATI: *Delle corporee differenze essenziali che passono fra la struttura de' bruti e la umana*, Milan, 1770, cited by ISIDORE ST. HILAIRE.

[25] Compare GALEN: *De usu Partium*, XI., 14. This old notion of the brain nourishing the hair is not yet quite extinct among the vulgar. I was told of a country haircutter, whose theory was that " The brain, sir, percolates through the skull, and nourishes the roots of the 'airs ; that's what it's for, sir."

no attempt to show why the excess should be that of hair rather than anything else.

§ 393. BOOK III., *Chaps. I., II.*, and *III.*, continue the enumeration of the parts of the head and neck, namely, teeth, mouth, horns, œsophagus, and trachea. The larynx is confounded with the pharynx; the trachea he calls ἀρτηρία, windpipe, and is described as going to the lungs and the heart.

§ 394. *Chap. IV.* describes the viscera, σπλάγχνα, which were parts tolerably familiar through the practice of augury. The bloodless animals are said to have none; but this is no doubt to be understood in the same sense as when they are said to have no blood. At any rate, he describes the analogues of heart and liver in the Cephalopoda. He objects to the statement of DEMOCRITUS, that the viscera are present but invisible on account of their smallness; for, he justly adds, the viscera are quite visible in the embryo of the vertebrate animals. He says the heart of the chick is visible on the third day, as a mere point; which indicates an amount of embryological investigation such as few moderns would anticipate. In the little treatise *De Juventute* (III., 468), he also mentions that the heart is the first organ developed: " This is certain from the facts observed by ourselves in the development of animals."[26] Modern research has discovered that the heart is not the first organ to make its appearance: the priority is claimed by the nervous axis. The heart appears later even than many bloodvessels.[27]

§ 395. The viscera are formed out of the blood, and there-

---

[26] Compare also *De Gen. Animal.*, II., 1, 734.

[27] MALPIGHI: *De formatione pulli in ovo*, p. 5 (*Opera*, 1686), doubts which is the first to appear, heart or vessels. C. F. WOLFF, in his masterly *Theorie der Generation*, 1764, p. 168, first rightly observed the order of genesis. See KÖLLIKER: *Entwickelungsgeschichte des Menschen und der höheren Thiere*, 1861, pp. 83, 87, 88, 90, for the latest views. The heart is first a solid string of cells; then a cylinder ; then this becomes twisted into the form of an S; and then the cavities are formed.

fore are only found in sanguineous animals, which necessarily have a heart; for it is clear that, having blood, which is a fluid, they must have a vessel to contain it, and hence also Nature has created veins; and for these veins the origin must necessarily be one, since one, whenever possible, is better than many. The heart is the origin of the veins: this is seen in the fact that they spring from it, and do not go through it; also they resemble it in structure. The heart has the chief position, namely, that of the centre, but more upwards than downwards, and rather in front than behind: for Nature is accustomed to seat the noblest in the noblest place, unless any stronger reason prevails : οὗ μή τι κωλύει μεῖζον."

§ 395 a. He says, "those who assert that the origin of the veins is in the head do not rightly consider the case." Why? Because Anatomy says otherwise? No such objection occurs to him. He prefers the logical objection that "they thus make the origin manifold and separate, and moreover in a cold place, whereas the heart region is warm." Thus could even so earnest an advocate of the inductive method allow himself to arrange the facts of nature deductively.

§ 396. "It is manifest that the emotions of pleasure and pain, and all other feelings, have their origin in the heart and return to it. And there is logical ground for this : for the origin must be one, when possible. And of all places the centre is that which is most natural (εὐφυέστατος), for the centre is one, and is related to all in an equal or nearly equal manner. Further, it is clear that neither the blood nor the bloodless parts can have feeling, therefore that which first has blood, as in a vessel, must necessarily be the origin. This," he characteristically adds, "not only appears evident, according to our ideas, but also according to sense; for in the embryo the heart appears in motion before all other parts, as if it were a living animal, and as if it were the beginning of all animals which have blood."

Here he strangely couples together metaphysics and embryology. Although it is not quite correct to make the heart the origin or starting-point of animal development—although the early stages of development are not dependent on the blood, which, indeed, is somewhat late in making its appearance—although the heart begins to pulsate even before the blood appears—still the notion of the heart as the *punctum saliens* is strictly scientific, warranted by what was then good evidence. It is, however, a notion awkwardly yoked with that of the heart being the origin of sensation because it is *one*, because it is the origin of the animal, and because the animal is animal only in virtue of sensation.

§ 397. "The Liver is also found in all sanguineous animals, yet no one can suppose it to be the origin of the body, or of the blood." The reason is noticeable. "For its position is by no means one worthy of an origin." [28] And as if this were not enough, he adds: "It has also an equipoise in the spleen in all the most perfect animals."

§ 398. The heart lies in the centre, and in front, not only because these are the noblest positions, but also because the breast is least protected by flesh against cold, and the warmth of the heart keeps it warm. In other animals the heart occupies the exact centre; but in man it leans a little towards the left side to compensate the greater coolness of that side: "for of all living creatures man has the coldest left side." This amazing statement, obviously one of his teleological fancies to account for the inclination of the heart, illustrates the deductive method of dealing with facts; he never could have instituted the most casual inquiry into the comparative temperature of the left side, but assumed the fact needed by his theory. A little further on he says, that the right cavity of the heart has warmer blood than the left cavity; this is correct; [29] but he is right by accident: he had no better reason

---

[28] κεῖται γὰρ οὐδαμῶς πρὸς ἀρχοειδῆ θέσιν.

[29] See CLAUDE BERNARD: *Leçons sur les propriétés Physiol. des Liquides de l'Organisme*, 1859, I., 56. DAVY thought that he had proved the left

for the statement than his metaphysical notion of the right side being nobler, therefore warmer, than the left.

§ 399. Another example of rash theorizing from very imperfect observation meets us here. It is a fact that normally in turtles, and exceptionally in elephants, horses, and oxen, there is an ossification of the septum of the heart. Aristotle saw, or heard of, one of these "bones" in the hearts of a horse and an ox, and forthwith generalized the observation thus: "The heart is destitute of bones except in horses and in a species of ox; these, however, in consequence of their size, have something bony as *a support*, just as we find throughout the whole body." His Spanish follower FUNES Y MENDOÇA improves on this by saying that the bone acts like a stick to support the weight of the heart, which is very great.[30]

§ 399 *a*. "The difference in size and consistence of the heart determines differences in character. The unfeeling have hard hearts; the sympathetic have soft hearts. Animals with large hearts are timorous; with small hearts courageous."

"Of all parts the heart least withstands disease." The reason alleged is that if the heart, which is the origin of the body, be diseased, there is no other part from which help can

---

ventricle to be warmer than the right: *Researches Physiol. and Anatomical*, 1839, I., 149. But there was a source of fallacy in his experiments which he completely overlooked, namely, that the left ventricle having much thicker walls than the right, cools less rapidly when the chest is opened to admit the thermometer.

[30] "Tiene muy gran coraçon, tanto que dice Aristoteles que tiene un huesso en el, que le serve como de baculo para sustentarle por la grandezza que tiene."—DIEGO FUNES Y MENDOCA: *Historia general de Aves y Animales de Aristoteles traduzida de Latin en Romance*, Valentia, 1521, p. 330. GALEN states the normal existence of the bone as a fact, and agrees with Aristotle as to the cause, though he adds, "it is more correct to say that Nature has everywhere attached the ends of ligaments to a cartilage or to a cartilaginous bone; and she could not, therefore, neglect the ligaments of the heart nor the tissue of the arteries."—*De usu Partium*, VI., 20. PLINY, of course, repeats the statement without misgiving. I believe VESALIUS first accurately explained the exceptional fact, as owing simply to an induration of the septa, and not to the presence of a true bone.—*Opera Omnia*, ed. BOERHAAVE and ALBINUS, 1725, p. 512.

come. By way of guarantee for this *à priori* view, he notices that in animals which had been sacrificed no diseased hearts had been observed, whereas all other viscera had been found diseased.

§ 399 *b. Chap. V.* passes to the veins and arteries, which are, of course, not properly discriminated. The course of the bloodvessels through the body is aptly compared with the irrigation of a garden. " Since every part of the body is made from the blood, it is necessary that blood should be conveyed to every part " (which, however, is *not* the case). " The veins pass from larger to smaller, till they become too small for the passage of the blood; through these therefore the blood can find no egress, but only the excretion of moisture which we call sweat, ἰδρῶτα; and this especially when the body is warmed and the veins open wider." (See § 155.)

§ 399 *c. Chap. VI.* treats of the Lungs, which are given to all terrestrial animals to cool their bodies. It is necessary these bodies should be cooled, because they are warm, and warmth demands an equipoise. Animals with blood require that this cooling process should be effected from without, because they are so warm; whereas animals without blood are enabled to cool themselves by their natural breath or spirit, τῷ συμφύτῳ πνεύματι,—whatever that may be.

It is an error, he says, to suppose the lungs cause the beating of the heart; "for man, alone, presents this phenomenon of heart-beating, because he, alone, is moved by hope and expectation of what is coming." One would fancy, from this passage, that Aristotle had never held a bird in his hand. "Moreover," he adds, " it is in man the farthest removed from, and lies higher than the lungs, so that they can in no way cause the beating."

§ 399 *d. Chap. VII.* is on the single and double organs. BICHAT tried to establish a generalization which has been much admired, namely, that all the organs of Animal life are double and symmetrical, while all the organs of Vegetal life are single and asymmetrical.[31] Unhappily the facts do not fit. In the commencement almost *every* organ is double and symmetrical; and only in the later stages of development do the differences appear.[32] Even in the matured organism we find many striking exceptions to BICHAT'S generalization. Thus the parotid, sublingual, and mammary glands, the lungs, the kidneys, ovaries and testes, are all vegetal organs, and all generally double.[33] And if the heart and uterus are classed as single organs, then must the brain and spinal cord be classed thus. While in birds the liver is double and symmetrical.

§ 399 *c*. BICHAT'S generalization is in the spirit of Aristotle, yet Aristotle avoided it. He merely noticed that some of the viscera are single, others double. Among the single organs he names the heart and the lungs, though it is far from clear how he came to consider the lungs single, since the reason of any organ being double is because the body has two halves, each requiring its own organ, and hence the brain has

---

[31] BICHAT: *Recherches sur la Vie et la Mort.*

[32] " Le fait primitif de tous les organismes est leur dualité. Tous sans exception (?) sont doubles à leur apparition, tous sont pairs : on trouve à droite du jeune embryon la répétition exactement de ce qui est à gauche ; les organismes impairs qui vient plus tard sur la ligne médiane formé des arcs boutants ou des clefs de la voûte, ne deviennent tels que par la fusion de la dualité primitive qui les constituait dès leur début."—SERRES: *Précis d'Anat. transcendante*, 1842, p. 238. This statement is somewhat too absolute. The intestine is at no period double, and the heart is single from the first. See Note 27.

[33] Not always, nor in all animals. The lung is single in many serpents, and the ovary is single in almost all birds. Both ovaries are present, it is true, in the embryo bird, but very soon after its exit from the egg the right ovary finally disappears. The date varies. MÜLLER says that on the ninth day of hatching the diminution begins in all but birds of prey; in these latter the diminution is not visible until about the end of the hatching.—*Bildungsgeschichte der Genitalien*, 1830, p. 30. Yet I once found the right ovary not quite disappeared in a chick just ready to escape from the shell. In the viviparous Blenny RATHKE says there is but one ovary. The same is true of the Perch; and I believe of some other fishes. On the imperfect symmetry in animal organs, see MECKEL: *über die seitliche Asymmetrie im thierischen Körper* in his *Anat. Physiologische Beobachtungen*, Halle, 1822. Compare also his *Traité d'Anat. Comparée*, Paris, 1828, I., 20.

a tendency (βούλεται) to become double; and the heart has its two chambers. The Liver and Spleen puzzle him, but he is disposed to regard them as balancing each other.

§ 399 *f.* *Chaps. VIII.* and *IX.* treat of the gall-bladder and kidneys. As in the other chapters, there is abundance of detail, true, false, and fanciful; but nothing needful to be extracted here.

§ 399 *g.* *Chap. X.* is on the diaphragm. It divides the heart and lungs from the stomach in order that the heat of the sensitive soul may be protected, and not easily endangered by the exhalations from the food, and by adventitious warmth. Nature has thus separated the Upper from the Under, for the Upper is the *end* and the *best;* the Under is created for it. That the diaphragm acts as a protection against the warmth is evident, for when it attracts the warm secretions, thought and feeling are immediately confused; and hence it is called *phrenes,* as if it participated in thinking. But it has really no part in thinking, yet, being near the organs which are active in thinking, it certainly operates a change in consciousness.

§ 399 *h.* Although Aristotle here departs from the idea of the *phren* as the seat of the mind,[34] he makes the diaphragm play its part in consciousness: "and when warmed it quickly makes itself felt, as we see in laughter, for those who are tickled laugh quickly because the movement quickly reaches this place." Man is the only animal that is ticklish, because of the fineness of his skin, and because he is the only animal that laughs, "and tickling is laughter from a motion of this kind of the parts about the armpit "[35]—a physiological explanation rather puzzling to understand.

The remainder of this Book is occupied with notices of

---

[34] The various opinions formerly held respecting the diaphragm are cited by HALLER: *Opuscula Anatomica,* 1751, p. 19.

[35] ὁ δὲ γὰρ γαλισμὸς γέλως ἐστὶ διὰ κινήσεως τοιαύτης τοῦ μορίου τοῦ περὶ τὴν μασχάλην.

different forms of viscera, and a minute account of the intestines.

§ 399 *i*. BOOK IV., *Chap. I.*, opens with remarks on the viscera of the Apoda. When he says that none of these, except the tortoise, possess a bladder, he is wrong anatomically; but he is wrong Aristotelically when he assigns the reason, namely that these animals drinking little because they are without blood, their moisure is converted into scales, as that of birds is into feathers.

§ 399 *k*. He separates the vipers from other serpents on the ground of their being viviparous, "or rather," he says, "they are at first ovo-viviparous, ᾠοτοκήσαντα." Had he known that all the viviparous snakes are poisonous, and the oviparous harmless, it is probable that he would have suggested some strange metaphysical cause for it.

§ 400. *Chap. II.* treats of bile and the gall-bladder. As we see in our word "choleric," the bile was thought formerly to be intimately connected with anger and other emotions. Brutus tells Cassius that he must "digest the choler of his spleen," as if *that* were the final clearance of bad tempers. Aristotle will not admit that the bile has anything whatever to do with feeling, for he remarks some animals have no gall-bladder—such are the horse, the ass, the mule, the deer, the camel, and the seal. Because the word used by him, $\chi o \lambda \acute{\eta}$ means both bile and gall-bladder, it is difficult to correctly seize his meaning; however, except the seal, all the animals named by him are without a gall-bladder, though not, of course, without bile. He adds this strange assertion:—"In the same species some appear to have the gall-bladder, and others not to have it, as the mice. To this class also belongs man. Some men have manifestly a gall-bladder attached to the liver, others not." Does not this look very like the sort of information he might have derived from the embalmers? It is difficult to suppose that any anatomist could have been so careless.

§ 401. After disputing the opinion expressed by ANAXA-GORAS, that bile is the cause of acute diseases, he adds that the bile is an excretion, and serves no end. "It is true that nature sometimes uses excretions to some good end, but we must not on that account seek a final cause in all things, but, inasmuch as certain things have certain properties, there will necessarily follow from these many effects." [36] This important passage should be a set-off against the many formal declarations of teleology to be met with in his writings. It shows that he had a glimmering of the philosophic conception, and that, like the modern advocates of teleology, he was only disposed to employ final causes where proximate causes were hidden from him.

§ 402. *Chaps. III., IV.,* and *V.*—After describing the omentum and mesentery he passes on to the viscera of molluscs and insects, or to such analogues as may be found in them, for these animals not having blood cannot have the viscera which are formed from blood. They have no vessels, no bladder, no breathing organs. But it is necessary that they should have the analogue of a heart, "for the sensitive part of the soul, and the cause of life, has in all animals a definite seat." This seat must be the centre.

Among the noticeable details of this chapter is the classification of sea-anemones and ascidians as intermediate between plants and animals.

§ 403. *Chaps. VI.* and *VII.*—He then treats of the external forms of molluscs and insects; and says that the former are inactive, which is the reason why they have not many limbs. It is doubtful whether he really meant to put the effect for the cause in this way, since the continuation of the passage, though confused, seems to indicate the contrary. "The more limbs an animal has, the more active it must be,

---

[36] οὐ μὴν διὰ τοῦτο δεῖ ζητεῖν πάντα ἕνεκα τίνος ἀλλὰ τινῶν ὄντων τοιούτων ἕτερα ἐξ ἀνάγκης συμβαίνει δια ταῦτα πολλά.

because of their functions; for more organs are required by those which have more functions."

§ 404. In the many discussions raised respecting the uniformity of composition in the animal organization, much stress has been laid on the fact that in the invertebrata the relative position of the nervous system is the reverse of that in the vertebrata. The dorsal surface of the one corresponds with the ventral surface of the other. CUVIER and his followers point to this as a proof that the plan is not uniform. GEOFFROY ST. HILAIRE and his followers declare that it only proves the mollusc to be a vertebrate animal reversed. Aristotle sees in it only an adaptation to modes of life; all testaceous animals have the head downwards, like plants. "The reason is because they take the food from below,.as plants do with their roots. They have, therefore, the peculiarity that with them the Upper is Under."

§ 405. *Chap. X.*—After describing the organs of the Crustacea (in *Chap. VIII.*), and of the Cephalopoda (in *Chap. IX.*), he returns to the viviparous sanguineous animals.

Man is discriminated from all other mammals by the possession of hands and arms. Not that monkeys are here overlooked; they are always spoken of by Aristotle and GALEN as quadrupeds, or, as they have been termed since TYSON and BUFFON, *quadrumana*.[37]

---

[37] " L'homme est le seul qui soit *bimane* et bipède. . . le Lamantin n'est que *bimane* . . le singe est *quadrumane.*"— BUFFON : *Nomenclature des Singes,* cited by ISIDORE ST. HILAIRE. But as HUXLEY : *Man's Place in Nature,* 1863, p. 90, points out, the word quadrumanous was first employed by TYSON in 1699 : moreover, as Huxley elsewhere remarks, " Before we accept the diagnosis that man has two hands and two feet, while apes have four hands, we must ask to have the difference between hands and feet clearly defined; and this is by no means so easy as it appears." I am not aware that any one has defined it. If the name follow the *function*, then it is certain that apes *grasp* even more than they *walk*, and so far seem to be fourhanded ; but the grasping function of the human foot has only fallen into disuse, and when uncramped by the use of shoes, as in savages and sailors, the toes are " very moveable, very flexible, and capable of prehension by opposition not only of

§ 406. "Man alone of all living beings is erect, because of his godlike nature and his godlike essence. The function of a godlike nature is knowing and thinking; but this would be difficult if the upper part of the body were large, for weight makes thought and common sensibility slow."

This explanation, which is teleological, may be compared with the physical explanation formerly given (§ 386).

§ 407. "Animals are four-footed because their souls are not powerful enough to carry the weight of their bodies in an erect position. Therefore all animals in relation to man are dwarfs, for dwarfs are those which have the upper parts large and the organs of progression small." By the upper parts he means the trunk of the body, or thorax, as he calls it. "In man there is a proper proportion between the trunk and the limbs; but when newly-born, the trunk is large and the limbs small. Hence infants crawl and cannot walk; at first they cannot even crawl, nor move alone, for all infants are dwarfs. On the contrary, among quadrupeds the under part is at first the larger; but as they develope, the upper part becomes the larger. Hence colts are little—if at all—shorter than horses, and when they are young they can touch their heads with their hind feet, which they cannot do as adults." Birds and fishes are likewise dwarfs. "Hence all animals are less intelligent, ἀφρονέστερα, than man. And among men, children and dwarfs are less intelligent than the adult and the well-grown. The reason is, as before

---

the toes to the sole, but of the great toe to the second," as witness the boatmen of China, the weavers of Senegal, and the Brazilian horsemen, who put their feet to the same purposes as those for which we employ our hands; not to mention Miss Biffin and the painter Ducornet. If, on the contrary, the name follows the anatomical *structure*, then it is clear that "the arrangement of the bones and muscles of the terminal segment of the hind limb in every ape whatsoever is, in all essential respects, similar to that which obtains in the foot of man and other mammals, and is totally different from the hand of man and terminal segment of the forelimb of other mammals. In fact, there is no four-handed mammal in existence."—*Natural History Review*, January, 1862, p. 6. On the counter side compare VICQ D'AZYR: *Œuvres*, 1805, IV., p. 149-50.

stated, because the physical principle is very difficult to move, and is corporeal.[38]

§ 408. Another deduction from man's erect position is, that he cannot use his anterior limbs as legs and feet, but only as arms and hands. GALEN thinks this is because man has no need of the velocity to be attained by four legs; but was meant by nature to tame horses, aided by his intelligence and his hands.[39] Elsewhere,[40] GALEN highly applauds Aristotle for having, in this very place, refuted the opinion of ANAXAGORAS, who preceded HELVETIUS, in deriving the intellectual superiority of man from the possession of hands. Aristotle thinks it far more logical to say that man possesses hands because he is the most intelligent of animals. "The hand is an instrument. Nature, like a rational being, always bestows instruments on those who can use them. For it is better to give a flute to a flute-player, than to make a flute-player of one who possesses a flute; since the inferior ought to be given to the greater and nobler, and not the nobler and greater to the inferior. If, therefore, it is better so, and as Nature always acts for the best, when possible, evidently man has hands because he is the most intelligent; and is not the most intelligent because he has hands." The reader will not fail to appreciate how entirely the solution of a deeply interesting problem is frustrated by this seeming explanation.

§ 409. A little further on we meet with this amusing explanation of the statement (which is erroneous), that the lioness has only two teats. "The reason is, not because the lioness brings forth few young, for she often brings forth more than two, but because she has little milk; and she has little milk, because her food is converted into her own substance; and she does not eat much because she is carnivorous."[41]

---

[38] πολλῷ δὴ δυσκίνητός ἐστι, καὶ σωματώδης.
[39] GALEN: *De usu Partium*, III., 1. [40] *Ibid.*, I., 3.
[41] This is improved on by DIEGO FUNES Y MENDOCA, who says, "No tiene la Leone mas que dos tetas, con que cria sus hijos, y tan poca leche en ellos, que siempre los trae muertos de hambre."—*Historia General de Aves y Animales*,

§ 410. Nor is the reason alleged for the position of the elephant's teats between the forelegs less amusing. "The reason why she has but two, is because she only brings forth a single young one; and she has them between the forelegs because she has cloven feet, and no animal with cloven feet has the teats under the groin; finally, she has them between the forelegs because it is there that most milk is found."[42]

He further observes that man has nipples, but that some male animals have them, and others are without them. Not content with this carelessness as to facts, he adds that those males which have nipples resemble their mothers.

§ 411. The anatomist will read with surprise that man is the only animal which has flesh on its legs; but the cause will, perhaps, surprise him more. "There is but one cause, and that is the erect position. In order that the Upper part should be light and easily carried, Nature has taken away the substantial from the Upper, and placed it in the Lower: hence she has made the buttocks, thighs, and calves fleshy. At the same time she made the buttocks for repose (sitting); since quadrupeds can stand without fatigue, man needs a seat."

Man has no tail, like other quadrupeds, because the formation of his buttocks uses up all the available material. Nor does the existence of tailless apes disturb this argument. The ape has neither tail nor buttocks, because he is intermediate between man and quadruped: he has no tail, because he is biped; no buttocks, because he is quadruped.

§ 412. The treatise we are now considering is devoted to an exposition of causes, and represents the physiology of Aristotle. On this account I have selected typical examples,

---

1521, p. 256; and gravely he copies from PLINY the following: "Conoce si la leone le ha hecho adulterio con solo el olor; aunque ella se suele huyr, ò lavarse en algun rio, si le ha cometido." The idea of a lioness, ashamed of her adultery, bathing herself in the stream to escape detection, is very droll.

[42] Compare GALEN: *De usu Partium*, VII., 21.

both of insight and error, which might convey a just idea of his method and its results. Perhaps some readers may have felt that this has been done too minutely; but although fewer examples would have displayed the method, I believe that a less exhaustive analysis would have failed to rectify the false and exaggerated estimate of Aristotle's scientific eminence. Throughout these pages I have had to contend against the very natural prejudice in favour of a mighty fame. Half a dozen examples, no matter how absurd, would not have shaken the prejudice, because the reader would have supposed that, in spite of these, the works contained enough to justify their reputation.

In conclusion, we may observe that, far as this treatise "On the Parts of Animals" may be from the modern standard, it is of great interest in the History of Science, not only for the material it furnishes, but also as one of the earliest attempts to found Biology on Comparative Anatomy. Although for centuries animals were studied rather as curiosities than as furnishing scientific data, and, until quite recently, Zootomy formed no recognized branch of biological research, Aristotle, we see, had early comprehended its true position, and sought for the laws of life in all organic beings. He would recognize the moderns as his inheritors, and would hear with satisfaction that "to Zootomy we owe almost all the important discoveries in Anatomy and Physiology."[43] Those grave physicians who sneered at JOHN HUNTER's "wasting his time over flies and frogs," might have known that it was in the study of animal organization that HARVEY discovered the circulation; and that ASELLI, PECQUET, RUDBECK, and BARTHOLINUS enlarged this discovery by detecting the lymphatics, and their transport of the chyle into the veins; and that

---

[43] TIEDEMANN: *Physiologie de l'homme*, Paris, 1831, I., 41. Compare also SYLVIUS (Leboë): *Opera Omnia*, 1679, p. 875. HALLER: *Elementa Physiologiæ*, Lausanne, 1757, I., 3. DELLE CHIAJE: *Istituzioni di Anatomia e Fisiologia comparata*, 1832, I., p. xiii.

Malpighi and Leeuwenhoek *completed* the great discovery by that of the capillaries. It was thus that Hoffmann, Wirsung, Stenon, and Wharton, discovered the excretory ducts of the pancreas and salivary glands. It was thus De Graaf discovered the function of the ovaries. It was thus Harvey, Malpighi, and Wolff, laid the foundations of Embryology. It was thus that almost all our knowledge of the nervous system was attained. It was thus that almost all we know of the chemical changes going on during respiration and digestion was gained. To Aristotle such information would have seemed like the realization of his dreams; and that he should thus early have perceived the importance of comparative anatomy, is one more of the many evidences of his prodigious scientific insight.

But, and the remark is important in its bearing on Method, although Aristotle fully saw how wide and fertile was the field of investigation, and how completely it was identified with the study of human life, he failed to discover a single physiological process or a single anatomical fact, not patent to the vulgar eye.

(325)

CHAPTER XVII.

ON GENERATION AND DEVELOPMENT.

§ 413. The treatise "On the Generation of Animals,"[1] is the last we shall have to analyze. It is an extraordinary production. No ancient, and few modern works, equal it in comprehensiveness of detail and profound speculative insight. We there find some of the obscurest problems of Biology treated with a mastery which, when we consider the condition of science at that day, is truly astounding. That there are many errors, many deficiences, and not a little carelessness in the admission of facts, may be readily imagined; nevertheless, at times the work is frequently on a level with, and occasionally even rises above, the speculations of many advanced embryologists. At least so it appears to me; and the reader knows how little I am disposed to discover in ancient texts the fuller meanings of modern science, and how anxiously I strive to represent what Aristotle actually thought. It is difficult to disengage ancient texts from the suggestions of modern thought; but I should not be candid were I to conceal the impression which the study of this work left on my mind, that the labours of the last two centuries from Harvey to Kölliker have furnished the anatomical data to confirm many of the views of this prescient genius. Indeed, I know no

---

[1] A valuable edition, with a German version and notes, has recently been published by Aubert and Wimmer, Leipzig, 1860. I can find no other version except the imperfect one of Gaza.

better eulogy to pass on Aristotle than to compare his work with the "Exercitations concerning Generation" of our immortal HARVEY. The founder of modern physiology was a man of keen insight, of patient research, of eminently scientific mind. His work is superior to that of Aristotle in some few anatomical details; but it is so inferior to it in philosophy, that at the present day it is much more antiquated, much less accordant with our views.

But in expressing my admiration of Aristotle's treatise, I am naturally solicitous not to exaggerate, nor to convey a wrong impression of the kind of excellence discoverable in it. In this chapter, therefore, as in its predecessors, the errors and deficiences will be carefully indicated. That the errors are not more numerous is marvellous, when we reflect on the enormous difficulty of embryological research, and the deficiency, in Aristotle's day, of those means of observation which have assisted moderns.

§ 414. As an introduction it may be useful to give a brief summary of the various forms of Generation and Development recognized by modern embryologists. The more so, because we have no philosophical treatise which rigorously sets them forth; and some confusion is noticeable in the common subdivisions of the subject, especially as regards three very distinct groups of phenomena relating to the origination, the development, and the gestation of the embryo. These groups not being well defined, the student is frequently perplexed, because questions of *origin* are confounded with questions of *history*. It is clear, for example, that the conditions which determine the origin of a new being—the union of a germcell with a spermcell—are of another order from the conditions which determine the subsequent development of that being; and these, again, are different from the conditions of gestation and incubation, whether the development goes on within the parent organism, or outside it. Let us severally examine these three groups.

I.—Origination.

§ 415. This is genesis. If we exclude the form of Spontaneous Generation, as not properly coming within the circle of established truths,[2] all the phenomena of genesis range under two rubrics, which may be entitled Monogenesis, when the origin is from one cell, or one parent; and Digenesis,[3] when the origin is from two cells, or two parents.

§ 416. *Monogenesis* may occur under three forms :—1. by spontaneous fission; 2. by external gemmation—budding; 3. by internal gemmation—parthenogenesis.

1st. Spontaneous fission—also, but inaccurately, by a confusion of the ideas of *origin* and *birth*, called *fissiparity*—is a well-known phenomenon in the vegetal and animal kingdoms. A single cell divides into two cells; these two again divide into four, and so on indefinitely. The cells may either cohere and form a filament, or they may separate into many independent individuals. Not only will the single cell spontaneously divide, but, among the lower animals, a similar division of the whole organism is observed. Thus a *Vorticella* becomes, by longitudinal division, two distinct animals on one stem.

2nd. External gemmation—also, but inaccurately, called *gemmiparity*—is well known as the production of buds in plants, and is also observed in certain animals, such, for example, as the Polype. In the origination of the young *Hydra* from the substance of the parent body without *any sexual agency whatever*,[4] there is nothing distinguishable from ordinary processes of growth, except that, instead of forming an increase of the parental substance, it forms a new Hydra, which finally separates from the parent. The young Hydra is a bud like a plant-bud.

---

[2] On this point see *Blackwood's Magazine*, February, 1861.

[3] BURDACH: *Traité de Physiologie*, Paris, 1837, I., 47, 83. VAN BENEDEN: *Mémoire sur les Vers Intestinaux*, Paris, 1858, p. 296.

[4] Repeated examination has assured me of the accuracy of what HUXLEY has stated on this point in his important memoir *On the Agamic Reproduction and Morphology of the Aphis*, in the *Linnæan Transactions*, XXII., 217.

3rd. Internal Gemmation, or Parthenogenesis, has been already explained (§ 189–190), and need not, therefore, be further dwelt on here.

§ 417. *Digenesis* may occur under two forms :—1. *Conjugation;* and 2. *Fertilization*.

1st. Conjugation is a phenomenon well known to botanists; two cells, apparently similar in all respects, having, perhaps, become two by spontaneous fission, *unite* their contents, and originate a new cell.

2nd. Fertilization is the union of two *dissimilar* cells, called spermcell and germcell, or spermatozoon and ovum. This is the normal mode of genesis in the majority of plants and animals; the exclusive mode in all the animals of a complex organization (see § 191–2.) It is a matter of indifference where these dissimilar cells are produced, whether in the same organ, or in organs morphologically different; whether they are produced in one and the same plant or animal, or in plants and animals of different sexes; the cardinal fact is simply the union of the two dissimilar cells, the fertilization of the germcell by the spermcell. This is fundamental; everything else is accessory.

II.—*Development*.

§ 418. Here begins the *history* of the new being. The *genesis* having been effected, *histogenesis* (or formation of tissues) commences. In the case of the vegetal seed, a long period may elapse before this development begins. The seed may lie, as in Egyptian tombs for thousands of years, fertilized, yet undeveloped, because the necessary conditions of histogenesis are absent. In animals also there is often a lapse of time. In the deer for example, the impregnated ovum lies four months and a half in the uterus before development commences.[5]

---

[5] I am indebted for this curious fact to Professor BISCHOFF, the embryologist.

The various laws of histogenesis may be ranged under these two heads:—

1st. *Differentiation*, in which the primitive homogeneous germinal membrane becomes more and more heterogeneous, through successive differentiations, both of composition and form, giving rise to *tissues*, the tissues forming *organs*, and the organs grouping themselves into *systems*.

2nd. *Assimilation and Disintegration*, a continuous process, coincident with differentiation, by which the several elementary structures are nourished.

III.—*Incubation*.

§ 419. Our third group relates entirely to the *habitat* of the impregnated ovum. It has obviously nothing to do with the genesis of the new being, and is only an accessory condition of its early history. There are two forms of Incubation :—

1st. *Oviparity*. The female having produced an egg, this is developed either *entirely* outside her organism,—or *mainly* outside, and partly inside,—or almost *entirely inside*. It is developed entirely outside in the majority of fishes and batrachians.[6] It is developed mainly outside, but partly inside, in some infusoria, polypes, some fishes, and all birds. It is developed almost entirely inside in what are called the ovo-viviparous and viviparous animals, and thus insensibly passes into—

2nd. *Viviparity*, in which the chief metamorphoses have

---

[6] The Ephemeron (dayfly) must be ranked with these, according to SWAMMERDAMM. He describes the deposit of the eggs in the water, and their subsequent fertilization by the male.—*Die Bibel der Natur*, 1725, p. 100. So accurate an observer is not lightly to be contradicted, and the fact, as he states it, may be true for one species. RÉAUMUR, however, feels great hesitation, and says that his own observations do not confirm Swammerdamm:—*Mémoires pour servir à l'histoire des Insectes*, Paris, 1762, VI., 500. BURMEISTER: *Manual of Entomology*, London, 1836, takes no notice of it. Be the fact as it may, even if congress does occur, the impregnated egg can only remain a few minutes before it is deposited.

taken place while the embryo is within the parent's body, so that, at the time of birth, it is said to be capable of independent existence.

We have seen already (§ 201 *a.*, 202-3-4) that, strictly speaking, no distinction exists between oviparity and viviparity as regards organic processes, though the terms are convenient for ordinary purposes; and to what is there said, may be added the illustrative parallel between the development of the viviparous Blenny and the oviparous Fowl, which, as RATHKE has shown,[7] presents only this difference: that after the changes have advanced to a certain stage in the hen's egg, a shell is formed and the egg is extruded, to be hatched externally, whereas the Blenny's egg is hatched internally.

§ 420. If now we turn to Aristotle, and ask how much he knew of the forms of Reproduction just sketched, we shall find that, except Spontaneous Fission, they were all more or less familiar to him. The evidence upon which he believed in Monogenesis was indeed very imperfect; still we find him positively recognizing it; and we shall see in the course of our analysis how lucky were many of his anticipations on other points.

§ 421. BOOK I., *Chap. I.*—The work opens with the declaration that it is a sequel to the treatise on the "Parts of Animals," and will concern itself with the parts devoted to Generation, also, with the causes of Generation.

"In all animals having distinct sexes, offspring issue from the union of the sexes. But this distinction of sex is not universal, though few exceptions occur among the sanguineous animals (by the exceptions, he means certain fishes). Of ex-sanguineous animals, some have distinct sexes, which reproduce their kind; others reproduce, but *not* their kind : such are those which do not issue from parents, but from putrefaction and excrement." He reckons in this class insects

---

[7] RATHKE : *Abhandlungen zur Bildungs-und-Entwickelungsgeschichte des Menschen und der Thiere*, Leipzig, 1833, II., p. 9.

and all those animals which, like the oyster and mussel, remain fixed to one spot. These have no more distinction of sex than the plants they resemble. Plants are partly developed from seeds, and partly from putrefaction, by spontaneous generation.

§ 422. *Chap. II.*—Of plants he promises to speak in a separate work (no longer extant), and, therefore, only speaks of animals here. And first he desires us to understand the masculine and feminine *principles:* the masculine principle being the origin of all motion and generation; the feminine principle being the origin of the material generated.[8] The proof is furnished by observation as to the origin of the sperm. It is because these principles are secreted *from* the male, and *in* the female, that they are masculine and feminine, "for we name masculine that which engenders in another; and feminine, that which engenders in itself. On this account we regard the earth as a mother, and the heaven, or sun, as the genitor and father."

After more of such not very luciferous metaphysics, he briefly touches on the sexual differences in male and female, and notices the great disturbance in the organism occasioned by any modification of the sexual organs, which he regards as a proof that the Masculine and Feminine are veritable *principles*—*i.e.* vital causes.

§ 423. *Chap. III.* briefly describes these organs. As may be expected, his anatomical knowledge was very imperfect. He entirely misses the correct analogy of the uterus, which he makes the analogue of the testes. Yet inasmuch as he never discriminates between the uterus and the ovaries, but always employs the same word to designate both, a defence might be set up for him, were he not on other points so vague and inaccurate. It is only in Mammalia that a true uterus is present, and modern research has discovered that the uterus

---

[8] τὸ μὲν ἄρρεν ὡς τῆς κινήσεως καὶ τῆς γενέσεως ἔχον τὴν ἀρχὴν, τὸ δὲ θῆλυ ὡς ὕλης.

is a modification of the oviduct. The serial development is as follows:

In the simplest animals there is no permanent organ answering to the ovary; but the ova are developed in a temporary organ, a mere fold of membrane.[9]

Higher in the scale, we find a permanent organ,—ovary,—but no oviduct. The ripe ova burst through the membrane, and fall into the general cavity of the body, where they are fertilized; or else they pass out into the external medium.[10]

Still higher, we meet with an oviduct into which the ripe ova pass, and are thence extruded, or are sometimes developed there as in an uterus.[11]

In mammals, the development of the ova begins in the fallopian tube, which is the upper part of the oviduct, and finishes in the uterus, which is the lower part.

§ 424. That Aristotle should not have discriminated between the uterus and ovaries, is little remarkable, for the function of the ovaries was never rightly understood until STENON[12] recognized them as the analogues of the organs which in the ovipara produced eggs, and, therefore, he *named* them ovaries. The name was adopted by REGNIER DE GRAAF in 1672, in his chapter *de testibus mulieribus sive ovariis*.[13]

---

[9] In Sea Anemones; or any part of the body except the arms in Freshwater Polypes.

[10] This may be seen in certain fishes without oviducts. VOGT et PAPPENHEIM: *Recherches sur l'anat. comp. des organes de la génération chez les animaux vertébrés*, in the *Annales des Sciences Naturelles*, 1859, p. 357.

[11] In the viviparous Blenny the ovary itself is the organ wherein the embryo is developed.—RATHKE: *Op. cit.*, p. 8. The fluid Rathke found in the ovary of the impregnated Blenny doubtless serves to feed the embryo. Compare Chap. ix., note 34. FABRICIUS ab ACQUAPENDENTE: *De formatione pulli*, and HARVEY speak of the hen's ovary as an uterus.

[12] STENON: *Element. Myologice specimen*, 1669, p. 145.

[13] DE GRAAF: *De Mulierum Organis*, Chap. xii.; towards the close he remarks, "Hinc potius mulierum ovaria quam testes appellanda veniunt: siquidem nullam similitudinem tum formâ tum contento cum virilibus testibus propric dictis obtinent." The early anatomists held with HIPPOCRATES that the female, as well as the male, furnished sperm; they considered the ovaries to be testes. It is as testes that the ovaries are described by VESALIUS: *Opera Omnia*, ed. 1725, p. 459; by FALLOPPIUS: *Observationes Anatomicæ* (printed

§ 425. *Chap IV.*—Aristotle's anatomical knowledge was imperfect; this imperfection stimulated his readiness to explain phenomena by final causes. In noticing certain differences in the male organs, he undertakes to explain the *purpose* of the testes. "Everything in nature occurs either from necessity, or for the best. Now it is manifest that testes are not necessary, since there are animals (fish and serpents) which have none. They have only canals—*vasa deferentia*.[14] What, then, is the end attained by the testes? The chief object of the organism in most animals, as in plants, is that of producing seed and fruit. And just as animals with straight intestines are the most voracious, so animals which have no testes, but only canals, are the most procreant. But those animals which are more moderate in desire, have long winding

---

in the ed. of Vesalius, p. 750), and by all anatomists till STENON. In an epitome of VESALIUS by FONTANUS (Amsterdam, 1642), they are rudely figured and named as testes; and the question "generatne fœmina semen?" is answered "Generat; sed modicum," p. 32. Aristotle always denies the existence of sperm in the female; and is thus superior to his predecessors and successors. TAURELLUS, in his attack on CÆSALPINUS, controverts this, asserting that anatomy proves women to have testes, and observation detects their sperm: *Alpes Cæsæ*, 1650, p. 819. FALLOPPIUS says: "Omnes anatomici uno ore asserunt in testibus fœminarum semen fieri, et quod semine referri reperiantur, *quod ego nunquam videre potui*, quamvis non levem operam, ut hoc cognoscerem, adhibuerim. Vidi quidem in ipsis quasdam veluti vesicas aqua, vel humore aqueo, alias luteo, alias vero limpido turgentes. Sed nunquam semen vidi, nisi in vasis ipsis spermaticis, vel delatoriis vocatis," p. 750. See the reply of VESALIUS, p. 820. The "vesicles" mentioned by Falloppius were by DE GRAAF thought to be ova (*Epistola ad Lucam Schacht*, p. 72, and *De Mulierum Organis*, pp. 80, 158); and although VON BAER proved that these vesicles contained the ova, and were not the ova themselves, still we must see in this observation a firm basis of fact. DOMINIC de MARCHETTIS: *Anatomia*, 1656, p. 70, describes the ovaries as testes, without misgiving. To the same effect WESSLING, in his *Syntagma Anatomicum*, chap. vii., ed. BLASIUS, Amst., 1666, p. 98, and their product as "semen analogicè." EVERARDUS: *Novus exortus hominis et animalium*, Medioburgi, 1662, p. 26, thinks that they secrete a sperm, but one not perfectly cooked. HARVEY denies that the ovaries are testes, and denies that the female has any "preparing, leading, and ejaculatory vessels," or that she produces any sperm.—*Exercitations concerning Generation*, 1653, p. 399, Exerc. LXV. He regards the function of the ovaries as "intended to secure the divarications of the veins, and retain a moisture in them whereby to keep the parts glib" (p. 406). Thus did these illustrious men grope in the dark.

[14] This error was refuted by DE GRAAF: *Op. cit.*, p. 23.

intestines, and spermatic canals, in order that the nutritive and procreative instincts should not be too rapidly gratified. It is for this the testes are given : they retard the movement of the sperm."[15]

§ 426. *Chaps. V., VI.,* and *VII.,* continue the subject of the male organs, with some remarks on the modes of congress. *Chap. VIII.* is on the uterus (including the ovaries), which is variously constituted in different classes. "Thus in Man and the Quadrupeds it is situated in the groin; the viviparous cartilaginous fishes, on the contrary, have it under the diaphragm. The other viviparous animals have it below; birds and oviparous quadrupeds above. All these variations have their reasons. Some, as the fish, lay imperfect eggs, which are perfected and developed outside the organism; the reason being that fish are very fertile, and if they had to develope perfect eggs, it could only be in small numbers. But they produce so many, that one-half of the ovary of the smaller fish seems to be nothing but one egg. Birds and oviparous quadrupeds, however, lay perfect eggs, which must have a hard shell for protection; but they are soft-shelled during their growth. This hard shell is produced by warmth, which evaporates the moisture from the earthy matter; and the place where this occurs must, therefore, be warm. Hence they are developed in the region of the diaphragm where the food is cooked."

§ 427. *Chap. IX.*—There are also differences among the vivipara. Some produce their young within themselves, as man, horse, dog, and all hairy animals; and among the aquatic animals the dolphin, the whale, and other cetaceæ.

§ 428. *Chap. X.*—Cartilaginous fish and vipers not only produce living young, but first produce eggs, and indeed perfect eggs, from which the embryos are developed. For from

---

[15] This idea is not even original with him ; it is borrowed from PLATO'S *Timæus,* and, though I cannot now recover the passage, I believe it is repeated in GALEN.

perfect eggs embryos are developed, not from the imperfect. The reason why these animals do not deposit their eggs is because they are by nature cold, and not, as some assert, warm.

§ 429. *Chap. XI.*—They produce soft-shelled eggs, because they have so little warmth that the external surface of the egg cannot be dried; and because they produce soft eggs they never deposit them, lest the eggs should perish. No sooner is the embryo developed than it descends to the region of the groin.

Having shown the reasons for the variations in position, he adds, " It is impossible for the young embryo to be produced under the diaphragm, since it must have weight and movement, and this could not be tolerated so near the centre of life." Why it could not be tolerated he does not explain. " Moreover, birth would be rendered difficult, on account of the length of the route ; as we see in women, who have difficult parturition if they yawn during the time, or if by any movement they draw the womb upwards."

§ 430. The modern reader will be puzzled, perhaps, by this mention of the womb moving upwards, especially during the act of yawning. It is an ancient notion, which was made to explain the choking sensation felt during the hysterical attack—*globus hystericus.* " Even the empty womb," says Aristotle, " produces strangulation when it moves upwards." PLATO, as usual, is even more audaciously fanciful. He says the womb is an animal fervently desirous of producing children, and when this desire is thwarted beyond a certain time, the womb, growing indignant, wanders about the body,[16] stopping the breathing passages, throwing women into the greatest trouble, and causing many diseases.

§ 431. Having thus accounted for the observed differences Aristotle proceeds, *Chaps. XIII.* and *XIV.*, to inquire why the

---

[16] PLATO: *Timæus,* ed. *Dek.*, p. 140. πλανώμενον πάντῃ κατὰ τὸ σῶμα.

uterus lies inside, and the testes sometimes outside, sometimes inside; with other questions of a similar nature. In *Chap. XV.* he touches on the congress of the cephalopoda; the passage has already been quoted (§ 187). There is also this remarkable sentence: " The female has an organ which must be regarded as an ovary, for it contains that which at first is an *undifferentiated* egg,' and which becomes by differentiation many eggs."[17]

§ 432. *Chap. XVI.*—Some insects have congress, and reproduce insects of the same kind and name as themselves, such as the grasshopper, cricket, spider, wasp, and ant; others, again, have congress, but produce worms, and their origin is to be sought in putrefying liquids and substances: such are flies and fleas. Others, again, have no parents, nor do they have congress; such as the ephemera, tipula, and the like. Among insects which have congress the females are generally larger than the males; because the larger body can better contain the weight of the impregnated eggs.[18]

§ 433. *Chap. XVII.*—After a lengthy, yet not minute, description of the organs, he now proceeds to consider the sperm. " Inasmuch as some animals indubitably have it, but with regard to others—insects and cephalopoda—it is uncertain whether they have it or not, the first inquiry must be why the exception exists, if it exist; and then whether females have or have not sperm, or something analogous?" This is an important inquiry. Before expounding his views, it may not be superfluous briefly to sum up the results of modern research, in order that we may appreciate the absolute, no less than the historical interest of his remarks.

§ 434. In the lower animals the spermcells and germ-

---

[17] ᾠὸν γὰρ ἴσχει τὸ μὲν πρῶτον ἀδιόριστον, ἔπειτα διακρινόμενον γίνεται πολλά.

[18] This is correct. The termite ant begins to swell immediately after congress, so that by the time she is ready to lay her eggs her abdomen has grown to 1,500 times the size of her body.

cells, out of which the embryo is originated, are developed in precisely the *same* parts of the organism. Somewhat higher in the scale, these cells are developed in *similar*, but not the *same*, organs. Still higher in the scale they are developed in organs so very dissimilar in structure, aspect, position, that it is only by the minute morphological studies of recent times that the conviction of their identity has been confirmed. In this last stage the organs are named testes and ovaries.

§ 435. The identity of structure carries with it identity of function. If the testis is the male ovary, it will comport itself in all essential respects as an ovary. This has not been sufficiently borne in mind; otherwise we should have seen physiologists recognizing *Semination* as a distinct function, corresponding with that of *Ovulation;* instead of vaguely classing it under the head of secretion. Thus the function of the testis is the production of spermcells—Semination. The function of the ovary is identical, it is the production of germcells—Ovulation. These functions belong to the organs, and are prior to, and independent of, any act of congress. Spermcells and germcells are developed, not only prior to any act of congress, but even in animals which from their birth have been kept isolated from all sexual stimulus. Nay, in the ovary of an embryo may be seen the germcells which would become ova at a later period.[19] The spermatozoa cannot indeed be thus early recognized in the male; but the spermcells which will hereafter become spermatozoa are present.

Ovulation is a spontaneous process. Every one knows, what indeed was known to the ancients, that the hen lays eggs spontaneously, without congress. These eggs do not, it is

---

[19] This may be easily seen under the microscope in a thin section from the ovary of a new-born kitten, previously hardened in alcohol. The ova are densely crowded at the periphery. Indeed, the ovary itself, at first, seems nothing but a mass of the original germinal cells. In the virgin *Aphis* an embryo may be found, and in this embryo there are ova ! See HUXLEY *On the Agamic reproduction of the Aphis.*

true, develope into chicks; but the eggs of virgin-bees and virgin-moths develope into insects capable of reproducing their kind (§§ 189—193). In mammals, during the rutting period, and in women, during the catamenial period, eggs are matured, and made ready for impregnation. These eggs are spontaneously developed, and if not impregnated by congress, they are either extruded from the ovary by the bursting of the Graafian vesicle, or they wither and are reabsorbed. There is considerable uncertainty among embryologists respecting these alternatives, although both seem to me consonant with known facts. One school maintains *l'ovulation spontanée*, as it is termed by M. POUCHET; declaring it to be an invariable law that ova are spontaneously developed and discharged quite irrespective of congress. The other school maintains *l'ovulation excitée*, as it may be termed; asserting that the stimulus of congress is necessary to secure the perfect maturation and discharge of ova, which would otherwise be reabsorbed.[20] I believe that the true case is this: *Ovulation,* or formation of ova, is always spontaneous, being the simple function of the healthy ovary; but the *ovipont,* or discharge of ova, though generally spontaneous, especially in mammals, sometimes requires the stimulus of congress, to prevent the ova from being reabsorbed. BLUMENBACH compares the bursting of the Graafian vesicle, in which the ovum is contained, to the spontaneous bursting of an abscess. Guided by this analogy, we may suppose that when the vesicle does not burst, it is reabsorbed like an abscess which disappears without rupture. The excitement may be a very efficient agent in the rupture.

§ 436. Let us compare Ovulation with Semination, and we shall see the probability of what has just been said. Semination is indubitably spontaneous; but the discharge,

---

[20] The evidence on both sides is well summed up in Dr. ARTHUR FARRE'S admirable monograph, *The Uterus and its Appendages,* p. 568, in the Supplement to the *Cyclopædia of Anat. and Physiology.*

although it may, and does, occur spontaneously, usually requires the stimulus of congress. When there is no stimulus, the spermatozoa, though formed, are not discharged, but are reabsorbed. We seem justified in asserting, therefore, that Ovulation and Semination are both spontaneous—the simple functions of the ovaries and testes; but that the *Ovipont* and *Seminipont* depend on other causes; and require a stimulus, which is sometimes effected by mere periodic congestion, at other times requires the more energetic excitation of congress.

§ 487. Having thus made clear to ourselves that both male and female spontaneously prepare the spermcells and germcells, the union of which forms the origin of an embryo, let us return to Aristotle. He knew nothing of the important fact that the mammalian female produced germs, although the eggs of insects, fish, reptiles, and birds ought, we are apt to suppose, to have suggested the idea. It is, however, a modern idea, and we must not look for it in his work.

In examining the origin of sperm, he asks whether it is derived from the whole body, or only from a part. There are four grounds upon which it may be argued that it is derived from the whole body. 1st. The force of the voluptuous sensation; for the sensation is stronger in proportion to its fulness, and will be fuller if it arise from all parts than if only from one. 2nd. Maimed children issue from maimed parents; and if sperm is derived from all parts that part which is wanting in the parents, will necessarily be wanting in the offspring. 3rd. The resemblance of offspring to their parents in the whole body, and in the particular organs; which shows that each part furnishes its quota. 4th. It is logical to conclude that if the whole arises from a First Principle, each part must have its First Principle; and hence if there is a sperm for the whole, there must likewise be a particular sperm for each part. Children are observed to resemble their parents not only in congenital peculiarities, but also in those which are subsequently acquired. They inherit even the *scars* of their parents.

§ 438. *Chap. XVIII.*—He now proceeds to refute these reasons: If closely examined they will prove the very opposite conclusion. Resemblance can be no proof that the sperm comes from the whole body, for resemblance extends to voice, nails, hair, and movements, from all which nothing can be derived.[21]

His next objection is more plausible, though erroneous in its assumption. "Children also resemble their ancestors from whom they can derive nothing. The resemblance is propagated through many generations; as may be noted in the case of the woman in Elis who had a daughter by an Ethiopian, and this daughter although not black produced a black son.[22] The same is seen in plants. It is evident that seed does not arise from all the parts of a plant, since many parts are absent, others can be cut off, and others grow subsequently. Nor can seed come from the pericarp, yet this always has the same form."

§ 439. "We must ask those who hold this opinion: Does the sperm come from the *partes similares*—*c. g.*, flesh, bone, and sinew; or from the *partes dissimilares*—*c. g.*, face and hands? If from the former, we observe nevertheless that the resemblance is in the latter. And if the resemblance in these parts does not arise from the sperm being derived from all parts, there is no reason against the supposition that the resemblance in the dissimilar parts arises from some other cause. If we suppose it only arises from the dissimilar parts, we thereby admit that it does not arise from all. It would be more correct to suppose that the similar parts being the first,

---

[21] πρῶτον μὲν οὖν ὅτι οὐθὲν σημεῖον ἡ ὁμοιότης τοῦ ἀπιέναι αὐτὸ παντός, ὅτι καὶ φωνὴν καὶ ὄνυχας καὶ τρίχας ὅμοιοι γίγνονται καὶ τὴν κίνησιν, ἀφ' ὧν οὐθὲν ἀπέρχεται.

[22] "Cette histoire est une fable prise au sérieux par Aristote."—Coste, cited by Aubert and Wimmer, who justly remark that analogous well-authenticated examples exist.

and those from which the dissimilar parts are formed, it is from them the sperm comes, and that the resemblance in face and hands must have been preceded by resemblance in flesh and nails. If we suppose the sperm to come from both similar and dissimilar parts, what will be the mode of generation? For the dissimilar are formed out of the similar, and if the sperm came from the former, it would be the same as if it came from the latter and their union. It is as with names. If anything is derived from the whole name, it must be derived from every syllable, and if from every syllable then from the letters and their union. If therefore flesh and bone are composed of fire, and the like, we must go back to the elements. For how is it possible that sperm should arise from union? and yet without it there could be no resemblance. But if some subsequent cause produces this union, it will be the cause of the resemblance, and not anything derived from the whole."

§ 440. This argument is an illustration of the helplessness of the mind when trying to force a pathway through the marsh of metaphysics. Whatever may be the fallacy of the reasons he refutes, they bear at least some direct relation to the facts, as then understood; whereas his own argument is logical quibbling, withdrawing attention altogether away from the phenomena. In continuing his objections he advances an argument which was much used in after times when the great battle of Epigenesis (§ 457) was fought. "If," he says, "the parts pre-exist in the sperm, how can they live separate? if *united*, then they already form a miniature animal. And how about the generative organs? since those organs which come from the male are unlike those which come from the female. Moreover, if the sperm is derived from all parts of both parents, the issue will be two animals, since it will have each part of each parent. And wherefore should not the female generate from herself alone, if the sperm is derived from all parts, and she has the proper receptacle?"

Growth presents another difficulty. He agrees with ANAXAGORAS that "flesh becomes added to flesh by means of food; but those who maintain that sperm comes from the whole body have to explain how increase of size can be effected by that which is different if the addition itself remain unchanged? And if the addition has the power of change, why not at once assume that the sperm has this power, and can become flesh and blood without being originally alike? For growth is not to be explained by mixture. For on this idea the sperm would contain each separate part in its purest state, but we see that it becomes subsequently flesh and blood and every other part. And the idea of one portion of the sperm being sinew and another portion bone is beyond our conception."

"Another difficulty is this: many animals are not produced by animals of the same kind, nor even by animals of different kind—*e.g.*, flies and fleas; from these worms are produced. It is clear that in these cases the offspring cannot arise from sperm derived from all parts; for they ought to resemble their parents if resemblance is a proof that the sperm comes from the whole body."

§ 441. He then considers the other arguments. The reason why maimed parents produce maimed children is the same as that which in other respects causes the resemblance; and he adds that many perfectly-formed children are born to maimed parents; also that many children are unlike their parents. Finally, the female has no sperm; this is proof that sperm does not come from the whole body.

§ 442. After thus viewing this question from so many sides he proceeds to define sperm thus: "Sperm is in its nature an origin, or Principle, out of which arise all things which are naturally formed."[23] There are many ways in which

---

[23] βούλεται δὲ τοιοῦτον τὴν φύσιν εἶναι τὸ σπέρμα ἐξ οὗ τὰ κατὰ φύσιν συνιστάμενα γίνεται πρῶτον, οὐ τῷ ἐξ ἐκείνου τι εἶναι τὸ ποιοῦν; which

one thing may arise from another, as one after the other—*e.g.*, day from night, the man from the boy. Another example is when a statue is produced from brass, a bed from wood, and wherever a whole is formed from pre-existing material. A third is when from a contrary a contrary is developed—*e.g.*, a cultivated from an uncultivated man, a sickly from a healthy man. A fourth is that which EPICHARMUS calls 'by climax'—*e.g.*, when from calumny and abuse a quarrel arises. From all these the principle of action has an *origin*, ἀρχή. This principle lies *within*, as when calumny is a part of the whole disturbance; or *without*, as the arts of the artists, or the light of a house on fire. It is clear that the sperm must belong to one of these categories: either it is the material or the principle of action." Is the reader enlightened?

§ 443. The sperm is a Principle of motion; the cause of organic development in the material furnished by the female. Aristotle cannot always be clearly understood, because just as moderns call both the impregnated and unimpregnated egg an *ovum*, he has a similar ambiguity in speaking of the sperm sometimes as synonymous with the fertilized seed, and at others as the fertilizing agent. He here defines the γονὴ, or seminal fluid, as that which in animals of different sexes contains the principle of generation; σπέρμα, sperm, as that which contains the principles of *both* parents (*i. e.*, the impregnated ovum).

§ 444. Sperm is shown to be a secretion. "All secretions must be either from available or unavailable nutritive elements. It is clear that sperm is not useless, but is a portion of the material available for nutrition." This important position enables him to indicate that relation between growth and reproduction already noticed (§ 172). "Instead of saying that sperm comes *from* all parts of the body, we should say

---

BUSSEMAKER renders: Talc autem sua natura semen esse requirit, ut ex eo (tanquam) primo oriantur ea quæ secundum naturam constituuntur, non ita ut exstet aliqua res quæ ex eo aliquid facit.

that it goes *to* them. It is not the nutrient fluid, but that which is *left over*, secreted; like the colour on a painter's palette which has not been employed in the picture. Hence the larger animals have fewer young than the smaller animals, for by them the consumption of nutrient material will be larger, and the secretion less. Another point to be noticed is, that the nutrient fluid is universally distributed through the body, but each secretion has its separate organ." This is a very remarkable passage. "Sperm," he continues, "is absent during infancy, old age, and severe illness. In illness, on account of weakness; in old age, because the food can no longer be sufficiently cooked; in infancy, because the rapidity of growth uses up all available material. For in man, the body seems in its fifth year to have reached half the size it will subsequently attain."

"There are great differences in the quantity of sperm produced by various animals. Some, indeed, produce none at all, and this not from weakness, but the very opposite, since that which should become sperm is devoted to the whole body; thus in men who are unusually developed, with much flesh and fat, the secretion of sperm is trifling, and they are less salacious; so, also, vines, which from excess of food are over-luxuriant in growth, run to leaf rather than to fruit, just as over-fed goats are feeble in generation. Hence the object of pruning the vines; the unpruned vines are named *goat* vines." [24]

In these passages are indicated with great clearness the relation between growth and reproduction, which still remains the limit of our knowledge.

§ 445. *Chap. XIX.* Begins the inquiry whether the female also furnishes sperm, or something else. It was for centuries a vexed question.[25] Aristotle was correct in denying

---

[24] The play of words on τράγος, *goat*, and τραγᾶν, *luxuriance*, is untranslateable.

[25] See *Note* 13.

the existence of sperm; and as it was impossible, without a microscope, to have recognized the mammalian egg, the view he adopted was the most philosophical one open to him. The peculiarity of the catamenia in women and the rut in animals, and their obviously intimate connection with reproduction, suggested that the analogue of the sperm was to be found in the catamenia. In one place he actually speaks of it as the spermatic material of females.[26]

§ 446. What is the true relation between the catamenia and the spermatic fluid, according to moderns ? Not that the catamenia furnishes the plastic material out of which the embryo is formed by the spermatic agency, as Aristotle conceived, and as his successors have for centuries repeated; but that it is simply a phenomenon which *accompanies* spontaneous ovulation. Rigorously speaking, the two processes are independent. Ovulation and the ovipont may occur without any of the catamenial phenomena. They always occur thus in the majority of animals, and *sometimes* even in women. On the other hand, the uterine discharge not unfrequently occurs in women without any ovulation; under circumstances, indeed, which seem to exclude the possibility of ovulation, as in the cases of young children and very old women.[27]

That, normally, the phenomena are in the female intimately allied is indubitable. The relation is as follows : the egg ripens in the ovary. This ripening process acts as a stimulus to the organ and its surrounding tissues, which stimulus is irradiated even to the uterus, on account of the energetic sympathy established between ovary and uterus by their vascular and nervous connections; hence an increased turgescence of the blood-vessels which form what ROUGET calls the *corpora cavernosa* of the uterus;[28] and hence the sanguineous discharge.

---

[26] ἐν τῷ θήλει τὴν ὕλην τὴν σπερματικήν, III., 1, 750.

[27] See GUBLER: *Des Epistaxis Utérines simulant les règles*, in *Mémoires de la Société de Biologie*, 1863, IV., 149.

[28] ROUGET: *Sur les Organes Erectiles de la Femme*, in BROWN SEQUARD's *Journal de la Physiol.*, 1858, I., 749; and GUBLER: *Op. cit.*, p. 160.

§ 447. Aristotle could not have known this. He, therefore, concluded from the observed phenomena that the catamenia was the analogue of the spermatic fluid, γονή. "And it is thus intelligible why children resemble their parents, since that which makes all the parts of the body, resembles that which is left over as secretion: thus the hand, or the face, or the whole animal pre-exists in the sperm though in an *undifferentiated* state, ἀδιορίστως; and what each of these is *in actuality*, ἐνεργείᾳ, such is the sperm *in potentiality*, δυνάμει; either according to its substance, or according to some power which it has within it.[29] For it is not yet evident whether the substance of the sperm is the cause of generation, or has within it a motor and generative principle."

Especial attention is requested to this passage, which, with several others, shows how profound a glance he had directed into the obscure question, afterwards so hotly debated between the advocates of Epigenesis and Pre-existence (§ 457).

§ 448. He held, and not without considerable superficial evidence, that the formation of fat is at the expense of sperm in males, and its analogue in females; and he explained the great fertility of the invertebrata on the ground of their forming no fat—which, though wrong, is ingenious.

That the female had no sperm is proved, he thinks, by the fact of conception in the absence of sensation, and *vice versâ*, in sensation without conception.[30]

§ 449. *Chap. XX.* Having proved that the material-of the embryo is furnished by the female, and this material is

---

[29] Thus I render the ambiguous passage: ἢ κατὰ τὸν ὄγκον τὸν ἑαυτοῦ, ἢ ἔχει τινὰ δύναμιν ἐν ἑαυτῷ. AUBERT and WIMMER propose to read ἴχον for ἔχει; but this does not remove the difficulty which lies in the word ὄγκον. We can hardly suppose that Aristotle maintained that the sperm had within it the *bulk* of the embryo.

[30] Compare EVERARDUS: *Novus exortus hominis et animalium*, 1662, p. 31; DE GRAAF: *De virorum organis*, p. 27; BARCHUSEN: *De Medicinæ origine et progressu*, 1723, p. 44.

a secretion contained in the catamenial fluid, he refutes the notion that the fluid secreted by the female is seminal. He holds the uncomplimentary opinion that woman is an undeveloped man. " She is female by her weakness, since the coldness of her nature will not suffer her food to be cooked into sperm." [31]

§ 450. "In those living beings which are without the distinctions of sex, the sperm is a kind of conception (κύημα, a fertilized seed). I call the first mixture of the masculine and feminine principles, a conception. Hence from one sperm, one body is generated; as one stalk of wheat from one seed, and one animal from one egg: twins are from two eggs. But in those beings which have distinct sexes, many can be generated from one sperm." The mistake here arises from his not being aware of the immense multitude of spermatozoa contained in the sperm, and from his considering the sperm as one.

§ 451. He believes that the males give the form and principle of motion to the embryo; the female giving nothing but the plastic material.[32] As in the coagulation of milk, the milk is the *substance*, but the rennet is that which contains the *cause*, so that which is furnished by the female is divided, differentiated (μεριζόμενον), by that which comes from the male.[33] The chapter closes with this reflection:

---

[31] On this REGNIER DE GRAAF: *De virorum organis*, p. 2, remarks, " Nec minori contumelia Aristoteles fœminam marem imperfectum appellat: vel ut loquuntur barbari Philosophi *animal occasionatum*." TAURELLUS calls the idea blasphemous.—*Alpes Cæsæ*, 1650, p. 814. Comp. also SCALIGER *contra Cardanum*, p. 188, *verso*. But it was long maintained by very grave philosophers.

[32] The argument of CÆSALPINUS is that if the male and female both furnished material the one would interfere with the other, or there would be two offspring in lieu of one.—*Quæstiones Peripateticæ*, lib. V., p. 97 D. But why should they not be *blended?* He never thinks of this alternative. TAURELLUS laughs at him, but advances no solid argument.

[33] An idea frequently reproduced. See REGNIER DE GRAAF: *De virorum organis*, p. 57; and HALLER: *Elementa Physiologiæ*, Bern., 1761, VIII., 154. In modern times it has assumed this modified and not less absurd form: " La génération tient à ce que la liqueur femelle est oxidée par le sperme et réduite

"That the female furnishes no seminal fluid, but that she nevertheless furnishes something, and this something is derived from the catamenial fluid in vertebrata, and from its analogue in invertebrata, is evident from what has already been said. It is also clear from abstract considerations. Since, of necessity, that which generates, and that out of which it generates, must pre-exist; and if these are united in one, they must be different in kind; and when separated, the substance and the nature of the efficient and recipient must be diverse. If, therefore, the masculine is that which moves and forms, and the feminine is that which is moved and formed, it is clear that the female will not add seminal fluid, but simply material; which is indeed the fact, for the nature of the catamenia is that of a primary material."

§ 452. *Chap. XXI.* It has already been noted that the accurate data upon which modern embryology bases the conclusion that both parents furnish material *and* form, were not accessible to Aristotle. His view best accords with the facts then known, and far surpasses that of the majority of his successors. He held the male influence to be qualitative, not quantitative; [34] and he adduces this ingenious argument: "When a hen is heavy with 'wind-eggs,' if she be treaded before the eggs have so far developed as that the yolk has received its white, she will lay perfect eggs, and not 'wind-eggs.' And if she be treaded by another cock while the egg is still yellow, the whole brood of chicks will resemble this cock. Hence, those who wish to rear fine broods bring the hen to be treaded by two different birds, for they do not suppose the sperm mixes with the eggs, nor that it comes from all parts of the body, otherwise the chicks would be double. But the sperm gives a specific force to the egg;

---

en un caillot."—ACKERMANN, as quoted by BURDACH. Still more recently the great embryologist BISCHOFF has reproduced it under the form of a catalytic action similar to that observable in fermentation.

[34] οὐκ εἰς τὸ πόσον συμβαλλόμενον τοῖς ζῴοις τοῦ ἄρρενος ἀλλ' εἰς τὸ ποῖον.

and this is increased by the new sperm, which is warmed and cooked, for the egg receives nourishment as long as it' is growing. It is the same with fish. No sooner has the female laid her eggs, than the male casts his milt on them, and those eggs which are reached by the milt are fertilized, the others not."

There is nothing in the two remaining chapters which requires special mention here.

§ 453. BOOK II. *Chap. I.*—The individual is mortal because individual. The species is eternal, because it reproduces the individual. And the Masculine and Feminine exist only for this reproduction. But inasmuch as the first moving cause which determines species is higher and better than the substance determined, so it is better that the higher should be separated from the lower; on this account, when possible, the masculine is kept distinct from the feminine, for the masculine is the principle of motion, and is higher and more god-like, whereas the feminine represents only the substance.

§ 454. After this teleological argument he surveys the various forms of reproduction. One division of animals, he says, brings forth young alive, and resembling their parents; another division brings forth young without limbs, and differing from their parents. Of this latter division the sanguineous bring forth eggs; the exsanguineous, worms.

In rendering σκώληξ by *worm*, I follow the translators and commentators; and the vague notions which then prevailed, respecting worms, may justify the interpretation; but it is by no means certain that Aristotle meant what would now be understood by that term; and perhaps the word scolex would be less misleading. He thus explains himself: "Egg and scolex are in this distinguished: in an egg the embryo arises from one part, all the rest serving it as food; in the scolex, on the contrary, the embryo is developed from the whole."

§ 455. "Of viviparous animals some generate their young

immediately within themselves—as man, horse, dolphin. Others are ovo-viviparous, first generating eggs, which develope into embryos within the parent—as the cartilaginous fishes." Although this distinction has been destroyed by the discovery that the embryo of the vivipara is at first an egg, the nomenclature has been retained by many writers even to our own day. "Among the ovipara, some lay perfect eggs, which never increase after they are laid—such as birds and reptiles; others, as fishes, crustacea, and cephalopoda, lay imperfect eggs, which increase after they are laid." The increase here alluded to is supposed by AUBERT and WIMMER to be the swelling from imbibition of water; there is no other increase; the eggs of fish and crustacea are as perfect as those of birds and reptiles.

After noticing several other points of distinction, he touches on the protections of eggs: "fish, which have scales, and crustacea, which are earthy, lay eggs with hard shells; but the cephalopoda, which have slimy bodies, lay eggs imbedded in slimy matter."

§ 456. "Insects all bring forth scolices (worms); for they are all exsanguineous, and hence scoliparous." It is strange that he should not have known the eggs of insects. "Nature has admirably arranged generation in a series. The most perfect and the warmest animals bring forth their young perfectly formed, not indeed in *size*, for all grow after birth; and they generate directly within themselves. The less perfect do not generate their young directly within themselves, for they first produce eggs; but the young are born alive. Others, again, do not produce perfect young, but perfect eggs. Those, again, which are of a colder nature produce imperfect eggs. Finally, the coldest of all do not produce eggs, but scolices, which in time become similar to eggs; for the so-called chrysalis of the insect has the power ($\delta \acute{v} \nu a \mu \iota \nu$) of an egg, from which in the third metamorphosis an animal is produced."

§ 457. He now proceeds to sketch rapidly, yet firmly, his

doctrine of Epigenesis, which he has variously illustrated. Every one acquainted with the history of science is familiar with the long and fierce disputes which have surrounded the question, Does the embryo pre-exist in the germ? but as even men otherwise well-informed are quite unacquainted with Aristotle's views on this point, and suppose the doctrine of Epigenesis to date from HARVEY and CASPAR FRIEDRICH WOLFF, it may be useful here to set down the hypotheses advocated by the various schools, before expounding Aristotle's.

BLUMENBACH states that DRELINCOURT "collected no less than two hundred and sixty-two groundless hypotheses concerning generation advanced by his predecessors; and nothing is more certain than that Drelincourt's own theory formed the two hundred and sixty-third." [35] All these theories may be ranged under two classes:—

A. Those which relate to the action of the parents. This class may be further subdivided into:

1. The *Spermatist* theory—which makes the male parent the sole progenitor.

2. The *Ovist* theory—which makes the female parent the sole progenitor.

3. The *Syngenetic* theory—which makes both parents equally progenitors.

B. Those which relate to the changes in the egg. This second class may be further subdivided into:

4. The theory of *Evolution*, which makes the embryo pre-existent in the germ, and only rendered visible by the unfolding and expansion of its organs.

5. The theory of *Epigenesis*, which makes the embryo arise by a series of successive differentiations from a simple homogeneous mass into a complex heterogeneous organism.

§ 458. The spermatist theory is of immense antiquity. In the Hindoo code Man is considered as the *seed*, and

---

[35] Quoted by ALLEN THOMPSON: Art. *Generation*, in the *Cyclopædia of Anat. and Physiol.*

Woman as the *soil*; by their co-operation the new being is produced.[36] In the *Eumenides* of ÆSCHYLUS there is the same idea. Apollo declares that the mother is not a genitrix, but merely the rearer of the young germ. Life is generated by the father.

> οὐκ ἔστι μήτηρ ἡ κεκλημένου τέκνου
> τοκεύς, τροφὸς δὲ κύματος νεοσπόρου·
> τίκτει δ' ὁ θρώσκων. v. 615.

Most of the ancient philosophers held this view; and no sooner had LEEUWENHOEK discovered the spermatozoa [37] than it seemed as if a positive basis had been gained for this hypothesis. The spermatozoon is a microscopic, transparent, oval particle, with a long and delicate thread-like tail. It wriggles forward with amazing vivacity, and is in no respect distinguishable from an animalcule. What wonder, then, that the oval part was pronounced to be a head, and the thread a tail? Imagination *saw*, and an occasional draughtsman actually *figured*, the lineaments of a man in this microscopic particle.[38] And as these spermatozoa are only found in reproductive males, and always in them, the hypothesis of the spermatists seemed to have acquired a demonstration.

§ 459. The *ovists*, however, were not without their rival

---

[36] *Manava-Dharmasastra*, lib. IX., st. 33, quoted by LUCAS: *Traité philos. de l'hérédité*, Paris, 1850, II., 67.

[37] On the claims of HARTSOEKER to priority, see the note in BOSTOCK's erudite *System of Physiology*, 3rd ed., 1836, p. 642. Compare also VALLISNERI: *Historie von der Erzeugung der Menschen und Thiere, aus dem Italiänischen von* C. P. BERGER, 1739, p. 7.

[38] "L'imagination avait alors un vaste champ ouvert devant elle. Les uns crurent voir dans les animalcules spermatiques des embryons corporalisés, qui n'avaient plus besoin que de croître. Gautier les figura ayant des figures d'hommes. Suivant Andry, chacun d'eux va trouver l'ovaire, se glisse dans un œuf, ferme la porte derrière lui avec sa queue, et se développe ; si plusieurs veulent entrer à la fois dans un même œuf, ils se fâchent, se battent ensemble, et se brisent ou se luxent les membres, ce qui donnent lieu aux monstruosités."
—BURDACH: *Traité de Physiologie*, Paris, 1838, II., 287. In the German version of VALLISNERI: *Erzeugung der Menschen und Thiere*, the figures drawn by ANDRY are reproduced. Nothing more preposterous in the way of malobservation (if it were not a pure invention) can be named.

discovery. STENON and DE GRAAF had detected the mammalian ovum, or rather the Graafian vesicle, which they mistook for the ovum, but which VON BAER proved to contain it. This important discovery seemed to the ovists to prove that the female furnished the germ, and the male furnished only the exciting influence. MALPIGHI, VALLISNERI, HALLER, SPALLANZANI, RÉAUMUR, and BONNET lent this hypothesis their powerful support.[39] They held that the embryo *pre-existed* in the germ, and that its evolution was excited by the influence of the sperm.

§ 460. The theory of *Syngenesis*, which considers the embryo to be the product of both male and female, is as old as EMPEDOCLES, though it had no better basis than the observed resemblance between the offspring and both parents. Modern research has furnished a scientific basis, by showing that, while in the higher animals both ova and spermatozoa are equally indispensable, they are themselves only modifications of one and the same anatomical element (§ 191).

§ 461. Let us now glance at the theories of the second class. The first of these, or the theory of Evolution, assumes that the embryo *pre-exists* in the germ, and is only called into *visible* existence by the agencies of generation and development. Not only so, but the germs themselves were all contained in the original germ; the first generation *contained* all successive generations. This is the emboîtement theory of SWAMMERDAMM, MALEBRANCHE, VALLISNERI, RÉAUMUR, and BONNET, which was accepted by the great HALLER, and was not rejected even by CUVIER. Some one wittily observes that "l'hypothèse de l'emboîtement rend nécessaire l'emboîtement d'un infini d'hypothèses;" and it has the vice of being *meta-physiological*; yet of course it has many plausible arguments

---

[39] LUCAS: *Op. cit.*, declares that DE BLAINVILLE also adopted it in his *Cours de Physiologie;* but no exact reference is given, and I can find nothing in the Lecture to bear out Lucas's statement.

in its favour, otherwise it would never have been maintained by the judicious HALLER.[40]

§ 462. In the present day no one believes in the pre-existence of germs, or the evolution of the embryo. The doctrine of Epigenesis triumphs along the whole line. Since WOLFF showed how the primitive amorphous germ *became* an organism through successive modifications, each modification being the cause of others—part being added to part, not simply in the way of addition, but each being the product of some predecessor, and the cause of some successor[41]—the researches of hundreds of patient embryologists have made Epigenesis the only acceptable hypothesis. The argument of the evolutionists, that all the organs are formed *at once*, and not successively,[42] seems admissible when supported by the assertion that the extreme smallness and transparency of these organs prevent their being visible; but both assertions fall before microscopic investigation, which shows that the impregnated germ passes through several successive visible stages wholly irreconcileable with this notion of a pre-existent invisible organism. The germinal membrane, composed of three layers, is seen to form itself into two cylinders, the two outer layers curving upwards, the innermost layer curving downwards, and from each of these cylinders issue the rudimentary forms of the several organs.

§ 463. It will probably surprise the reader to hear that Aristotle very distinctly announced the doctrine of Epigenesis,

---

[40] HALLER: *Elementa Physiologiæ, VIII.,* 143-51. Compare also VALLISNERI: *Von der Erzeugung,* 1739, pp. 140, 442, 461; or RÉAUMUR: *Mémoires pour servir à l'histoire des Insectes,* 1734, I., 343, seq.

[41] There are few works of deeper insight or more patient research than C. F. WOLFF's *Theorie von der Generation, in zwo Abhandlungen erklärt und bewiesen,* Berlin, 1764, and I shall not easily forget the excitement with which I hurried through the Berlin streets in a storm to secure a copy at an old secondhand bookshop. In it may be found the origin of GOETHE's Metamorphoses of Plants, as well as the leading ideas since expounded with such mastery by VON BAER and his followers.

[42] HALLER, p. 148.

a doctrine commonly attributed to HARVEY. WOLFF is wrong in stating that Aristotle "affirmed, but did not defend, Epigenesis, simply because no one had thought of denying it." [43] It *had* been denied, and a counter theory proposed, which Aristotle refuted. "Either," he says, "the parts arise together and at once, or one after the other. That they do not arise at once is evident to sense; for we see that some parts are present, and others absent; and it is certain that these latter are not invisible simply because of their smallness, for although the lungs are larger than the heart, yet in development they are later. Since one part is earlier, and another later, it becomes a question whether the one *forms* the other, the latter being dependent on the former, or the one simply *arises* after the other. The heart does not form the liver, and this again the other parts; but the one part arises after the other, as the man comes after the boy, but not from the boy. The reason is this: In everything produced by Nature or by Art, the *actual* arises from the *potential;* and so must here the *species* and *form* exist in the earlier—for example, the liver must exist in the heart.[44] And this view is otherwise deceptive. For it is impossible that from the first a part of the plant, or animal, should exist ready formed in the sperm—whether capable or incapable of forming other parts—if all arise from the spermatic fluid. For if such a part be in the sperm, it must have been made by that which made the sperm. Now sperm must be the first; and this is the work of generation. Hence it is impossible that a part should pre-exist. Therefore the plastic power (τὸ ποιοῦν) has no organ within it, nor without it. Yet one or the other is necessary. Let us try to reconcile this contradiction."

---

[43] WOLFF, p. 60.

[44] ὅτι ὑπὸ τοῦ ἐντελεχείᾳ ὄντος τὸ δυνάμει ὂν γίνεται ἐν τοῖς φύσει ἢ τέχνῃ γινομένοις, ὥστε δέοι ἂν τὸ εἶδος καὶ τὴν μορφὴν ἐν ἐκείνῳ εἶναι οἷον ἐν τῇ καρδίᾳ τὸ τοῦ ἥπατος: The reader must bear in mind the distinctions of entelechie and dynamis, and of species and form.

To reconcile these views he adduces the comparison of the movements of an automaton in which one wheel, on being set in action, determines the movement in other parts. The sperm is this primary motor; and has the power of communicating movement long after its original impulse has ceased. No organ is the cause of development. The cause is that which first originated the movement. Hence one organ arises after another, and not all at once.

§ 464. As the analysis proceeds, we shall still further learn how firmly the doctrine of Epigenesis was grasped by him; for the present it is enough to have indicated his view.

Chap. II. is devoted to the physical nature of sperm, which is described as a kind of foam, or mixture of water and air. "The ancients seem to have known this, to judge from the name of the goddess Aphrodite."[45] The air ($\pi\nu\epsilon\bar{\upsilon}\mu\alpha$) here referred to, can hardly be understood as atmospheric air. It plays a considerable part in the speculations of the ancient and the Renaissance writers; but I have never been able to make out what was precisely meant by it. In theories of generation, it is the *aura* rising from the sperm, which, until the discovery of Spermatozoa,[46] was almost universally held to be the agent in fertilization.

§ 465. *Chap. III.* touches on other points connected with sperm. Especially worthy of note is the statement that sperm and seed are as the living animal and plant which will issue from them. "It is clear that they have the Vegetal Soul (nutritive principle), and in their further development they must acquire the Sensitive Soul, which constitutes them animals."

---

[45] ἀφρός in Greek means "foam."

[46] And even for many years afterwards. Thus, HALLER: *Elementa Phys. VIII.*, 154; and still later SCHNEEGASS maintained that "il se dégage du mélange de sperme et de mucus utérin une *aura seminalis*, qui monte le long des oviductes, et qui d'après KUHLEMANN pénètre à travers les membranes de l'ovaire."—BURDACH: *Traité de Phys.*, II., 195.

Not only is Aristotle an upholder of the doctrine of Epigenesis, but he is also to be ranked among the most philosophical teachers who have held the doctrine so luminously expounded by VON BAER, that the general and specific characters of the embryo are successively acquired, so that the mammalian embryo is first an animal, then a vertebrate, then a mammal, and finally, a particular kind of mammal. This doctrine is thus aphoristically expressed by Aristotle: "Not at once is the animal a man or horse; for the end is last attained; and the specific form is the end of each development. Hence it is an important question when, how, and whence comes the Intellect in those animals which possess it. We must evidently assume that the sperm and the unseparated conception (ovum) must possess the Vegetal Soul (τὴν θρεπτικὴν ψυχὴν) at least *potentially*; though not in *reality*, until the separated conception (fœtus) takes up nourishment, and thus fulfils the work of such a soul. At first it seems as if the embryo lived the life of a plant; it is only at a subsequent period that we can speak of a sensitive and intelligent soul. These, however, must necessarily pre-exist potentially before they exist in reality. Now either they must not have been actually present, and must have come in all together; or they were all present; or else some were present, and others not; and they must have come in with the germ, and not with the sperm; or reached the germ from the sperm. If in the sperm, they must have entered at once from without, or none did so; unless some did, and others did not. But it is impossible that they should have been actually present, since all the corporeal functions naturally require the presence of their respective organs,[47] *e. g.* there can be no walking without legs. For the same reason they cannot come from without.

---

[47] I depart here somewhat from the literal rendering, in order to make this remarkable passage intelligible. The illustration of walking sufficiently justifies my interpretation: ὅσων γάρ ἐστιν ἀρχῶν ἡ ἐνέργεια σωματική, δῆλον ὅτι ταύτας ἄνευ σώματος ἀδύνατον ὑπάρχειν.

Nor can they enter alone—being inseparable from their organs; nor in a body, for the sperm is a secretion from the metamorphosed food. Only the Intellect enters from without. It alone is godlike. Its actuality has nothing in common with corporeal actuality."

§ 466. This is the most decisive passage I have been able to find respecting the immortality of the soul (§ 224). It is the more explicit because it is made to express the distinction between the Intellect as a godlike and incorporeal principle, and the Nutritive and Sensitive principles which are obviously dependent on matter.[48]

§ 467. " The vital principles seem to belong to another body, which is of a more honourable nature than the so-called elements. And just as these principles differ in rank amongst each other, so also are they different in the nature of their common body. In all sperm there is the so-called heat, which effects generation. This heat, however, is not fire, but a breath ($\pi\nu\epsilon\tilde{\upsilon}\mu\alpha$) contained in the foamy nature of the sperm; and in this *pneuma* there is a nature analogous to that of the elements of the stars. Hence fire generates no living thing. But the warmth of the sun, on the contrary, has this power."

§ 468. Woman is undeveloped man. She furnishes the analogue of the sperm *minus* its vital principles. The proof of this is seen in the " wind-eggs " of the hen, which have the plastic substance, but which, wanting the formative principle of the sperm, never become living beings. In the Third Book (c. 7, p. 757) he explains this more clearly. The windeggs, he says, never become perfect chicks, because they want the sensitive soul; they have the nutritive soul, since *that* belongs to all females, and all living beings. And a windegg may therefore be regarded as a perfect vegetal seed, but as

---

[48] It was thus ROGER BACON understood it. " Intellectus agens est pars animæ, sed est substantia intellectiva alia et separata per essentiam ab intellectu possibili."—*Opus Majus*, Venet., 1750, p. 20.

CHAP. XVII.] AND DEVELOPMENT. 359

an imperfect animal seed. The influence of the male is necessary for a perfect animal.

§ 469. *Chap. IV.* is devoted to the catamenia. The intimate dependence of Lactation on this process is noticed; also the formation of the fœtal membranes from the corporeal elements of the fluid, after the evaporation of its moisture.

"No sooner is the conception (τὸ κύημα) formed, than it grows like the seed of plants in the earth. For even in the seed there is a self-contained principle of development, and from it arise stem and roots, through which it takes up nourishment. In the same way all the parts of an animal are potentially contained in the conception, and a principle of development. The heart is the first differentiated reality. For there must be an origin out of which all the rest will arise."

§ 470. He then passes to another problem. A conception is potentially an animal, although an imperfect animal. It must have food; but whence is the food derived? As the plant derives food from the earth, the fœtus derives food from the uterus. "Hence Nature has from the first sent two veins from the heart which, dividing into several smaller vessels, forms the umbilical cord (ὁ ὀμφαλὸς), and this goes to the uterus. This cord is a vein, in some animals several veins, enveloped in a membrane for its protection. These veins ramify like roots over the uterus, and through them the fœtus receives nourishment. It is on this account that the fœtus remains in the uterus, and not, as DEMOCRITUS thinks, in order that each part may be formed like the mother. This is evident in oviparous animals which develope their parts in the egg, away from the mother."

Although inaccurate in its details, this passage expresses in a general way the true relation of the fœtus to the mother. He then considers this question: "If blood be nourishment, and the heart first arises in order to contain it, and if food comes from without, whence the first nourishment? Or is it not correct to say that all nourishment comes from without, but that just as in the seed of plants there is a milky fluid, so in the fœtus there is a surplus of material from which it will receive nourishment?"

§ 471. "The differentiation of organs does not, as some think, take place by the attraction of like for like; but the child resembles its mother because her secretion is potentially of the same nature as her whole body, and hence contains the possibility, though not the reality, of all her organs."

This is further explained by the fact of the mother furnishing not only the plastic material but the nutritive principle, or vegetal soul. In plants there is no separation of sexes; but in those animals which have separated sexes the female cannot of herself produce offspring.

§ 472. *Chap. V.*—"Yet it may be asked: If the female possesses a soul, and if her secretion furnishes the material, why is the male influence indispensable? The reason this: The animal has a Sensitive Soul, and this is wanting to the plant."

Aristotle admits the power of vegetal reproduction in females, but denies them that of animal reproduction. It is true that unfertilized ova live, but what is their life? Not the life of animals, otherwise they would become animals; yet a life higher than that of inorganic substances, as we see by their decay. They possess only the lowest form of life—that which is common to plants and animals, *i. e.* the nutritive soul. This cannot form an animal organ.

§ 473. "If there is, indeed, a class of animals which, although feminine have no males, it is possible that such may produce young by themselves. But this is not yet credibly ascertained: even in fishes it is dubious. Of the so-called Erythrinnes no male has yet been found, but many females full of conceptions. But on this point we have no decisive experience. There are, however, fishes which are neither male nor female, such as the eel, and a species of *kestris* (supposed to be the mullet)."

Aristotle thought that eels were generated spontaneously in the mud. In those days spontaneous generation was received without difficulty by all minds.[49] But how the sexes of mullets came to be overlooked is not clear.

"Whenever the male exists the female is incompetent to generate alone; otherwise the male would be useless, and nature does nothing in vain. Hence in animals the male perfects generation, giving the sensitive soul."

§ 474. Since the organs are already *potentially* existing in the germ it is only necessary for the sperm to give the first impulse, and straightway all the organs begin to range themselves in due succession.[50] The heart is the first to appear. It is the origin and centre of development. That it is so is seen not only by direct inspection, but also in the fact that it is the last to die; since it is a law that that which appears last disappears first.

Modern research, as I have already stated, discredits the idea of the heart as *primum saliens*. The heart is not the first organ which appears, nor is it the last which dies, *ultimum moriens*. That it lives and beats for some time after the death of the animal, in amphibia for some hours, is quite true; but other organs also survive the organism. Hair grows, glands secrete, and the stomach will digest many hours after the heart has ceased to beat.[51]

§ 475. *Chap. VI.* sketches the phenomena of develop-

---

[49] Even so late as the 17th century we find JULIUS CÆSAR SCALIGER maintaining that mice were generated from corruption.—*Exercitationes contra Cardanum*, Paris, 1657, p. 31.

[50] " Solum semen masculum dormientem embryonis vitam excitat."— HALLER: *Elementa Phys.*, *VIII.*, p. 154. The whole of this 31st section might be taken as a translation of Aristotle, with the understanding that what the Greek regards as *potential* pre-existence, the Swiss regards as *actual* pre-existence.

[51] Twenty-four hours, in certain fishes, according to CHARLES ROBIN: *Comptes Rendus de la Société de Biologie*, 1853, V., 134. I found the hinder extremities of a Triton living, and capable of motion, three hours after the heart had ceased to beat. But the phenomenon is very variable, and sometimes the heart survives the extremities.

ment. Although in many points inaccurate, and in some purely fanciful, it shows that Aristotle had studied development, not indeed with the patience and caution necessary in an inquiry so delicate, but with quite as much as he thought fit to bestow on any other inquiry. He notices that the upper half of the body is first developed, the lower half being smaller and less distinct. The fact is so;[52] but the reason assigned is erroneous. The heart, he considers, as the origin of all development, the lower part being only for the sake of the upper.

§ 476. "The genesis of the *partes similares* takes place through cooling and warmth; the coagulation and solidification of some being determined by cold, and of others by warmth. The nutritive fluid filters through the veins and the canals of each part, like water in unglazed earthen vessels (ὠμοῖς κεραμίοις), and becomes flesh, or its analogue, coagulating in cooling; and hence it becomes dissolved by fire."

Although we should greatly err if we interpreted this language into an expression of the modern idea of the plastic elements oozing through the walls of the bloodvessels (§ 156), we cannot but remark how much nearer the truth Aristotle was than other physiologists, until the discovery of the capillaries by MALPIGHI made it impossible to accept the notion of the blood being poured on the tissues.

"That portion of the filtered fluid which is earthy, and has little warmth and moisture, becomes, during the cooling process, which evaporates the moisture, hard and earthy: such as nails, hair, hoofs, &c. Hence these become softened by fire, but not melted; others by liquids: for example, the shells of eggs. But under the influence of internal warmth, which dries up their moisture, sinews and bones arise; and hence they are not soluble by fire, for they are baked as in an oven by the genetic warmth." This warmth is contained

---

[52] Compare KÖLLIKER: *Entwickelungsgeschichte*, 1861, p. 50.

in the sperm, and possesses the motor and creative power necessary for each part. Whenever this is in excess or deficiency, it occasions a deformity in the embryo.

§ 477. "The skin is formed by the drying of the flesh, as we see a skin formed on the surface of cooked meat. But it is not the fact of its being the surface which causes this; the reason is because the viscid material (τὸ γλίσχρον) cannot evaporate, and remains at the top. In other cases this viscid material is dry, and thus forms the hard and soft shells of bloodless animals; whereas, in sanguineous animals, it has a more fatty nature, and hence we see only those which are not very earthy have fat under their skin—a proof that the skin arises from a similar material."

§ 478. The order of differentiation is noticed. In the course of this the parts are at first sketched in outline, and subsequently assume their colour, softness, hardness, &c., "just as the painter first draws an animal in outline, and then fills up the picture with colour."

§ 479. *Chap. VII.* begins with a description of the placenta, and then passes to the question why Hybrids are usually not fertile. In *Chap. VIII.*, after examining the opinions of his predecessors on this point, and even suggesting an *à priori* argument in their favour, he makes this remarkable observation: "But such a proof is far too abstract and empty. For reasons not drawn from the inherent principle of things are empty and only *seem* to explain them. Just as those only are geometrical proofs which are deduced from geometrical principles, so also in all other sciences. The empty argument seems potent, but is powerless."

He clenches his refutation of all the abstract arguments against the possible fertility of Hybrids by this pithy statement: "The fact is that many Hybrids *are* fertile." Yet his own explanation of the common infertility is not a whit more acceptable than the explanations he rejects.

§ 480. BOOK III.—The first seven chapters of this book

are devoted to an enumeration of the differences in the formation and development of eggs. Full of repetitions and destitute of any attempt at systematic arrangement, these chapters, like so many others in his scientific writings, resemble the unorganized contents of a note-book rather than parts of a treatise. One or two passages of interest have already been previously quoted in these pages.

§ 481. *Chap. VIII.*—Having mentioned that the cephalopoda are of distinct sexes, he refers to the opinion that all fishes are females, adding : " It is, however, too much to believe that cephalopoda are of distinct sexes, and fishes not; and the opinion is only an evidence of insufficient observation." At the close of the chapter he almost anticipates the modern discovery that the embryo of the cuttlefish, instead of having the yolk on its under surface, has it attached to the head ; in fact, the embryo seems to swallow the yolk.

§ 482. *Chap. IX.* is on the generation of insects, which he describes as being partly sexual, partly spontaneous. *Chap. X.* is on the generation of bees, already noticed (§ 194). *Chap. XI.* treats of molluscs, and gives a fuller exposition of his views on Spontaneous Generation than can be found elsewhere. To the mind of almost every biologist of our day, the idea of Spontaneous Generation appears excessively improbable, and certainly not proven, even with respect to the simplest plants and animalcules ; and with respect to worms, insects, or molluscs, it is universally rejected.[53] At present the massive weight of evidence is against the hypothesis. The chief argument in its favour rests on the difficulty of always proving the presence of germs ; and this is enforced by the facility with which some minds believe that whatever is *conceivable* must be true.

---

[53] The doctrine of spontaneous generation has been revived by POUCHET: *Hétérogénie ; ou traité de la Génération spontanée basé sur des nouvelles expériences*, Paris, 1859. See the Comptes Rendus of the Academy for the years 1859-63.

In Aristotle's day there was no difficulty whatever in believing that insects, molluscs, and eels were spontaneously originated in putrefying matters. Animals suddenly appeared in places where there had previously been no trace of their parents. To the ancients this was sufficient proof of spontaneous generation. Aristotle said that all plants and animals which arise spontaneously, do so in putrefying substances to which water has been added. "It is not from putrefaction, as such, but from *coction*, that the new being arises : the putrid substance is only a secretion from that which is cooked. Animals and plants arise in the earth, and in moisture, because water is present in earth, and in water there is air (*pneuma*), and in all air there is animal heat; so that in a certain sense all things have life (soul, ψυχή). Hence bodies are quickly formed when enclosed in a small space, and they are so enclosed *when by means of heat the fluid substance is formed into a kind of foam-vesicle*.[54] The differences of nobler and ignobler species depend on that vital principle which is enclosed ; and hence we must seek the cause both in what is enclosed, and where it is enclosed. In sea-water there is much earthy matter, and hence from the sea, testaceous animals are produced ; the earthy matter being hardened on their surface, for it is not to be melted by heat ; and internally the living body is enclosed. Only a few species have been observed in congress ; and it is uncertain whether generation was the result or not in these cases. We must inquire what here represents the material principle of other animals. Among females, it is a secretion which receives from the male its moving principle, and potentially

---

[54] ἐμπεριλαμβάνεται δὲ καὶ γίνεται θερμαινομένων τῶν σωματικῶν ὑγρῶν οἷον ἀφρώδης πομφόλυξ. AUBERT and WIMMER read in this curious passage a prefiguration of the modern cell-theory; but the resemblance is slight and purely verbal. A much closer resemblance is noticeable in OKEN's notion that the transition from the inorganic to the organic is the change into a vesicle.— *Programm über das Universum;* cited by LEYDIG: *Lehrbuch der Histologie,* 1857, p. 5.

contains the whole animal. But what is there to represent this here, and what represents the masculine principle? We must consider that, even in animals which generate, the heat prepares the secretion from the cooked food, and this is the origin of the germ. So also in plants, except that with them, as with some animals, the aid of the masculine principle is not needed, because it is contained, mingled in their substance; whereas in the majority, the secretion needs this aid. The food of some is water and earth; of others, substances prepared from these. That which is prepared from food by animal heat, is by the summer heat prepared from sea-water and earth, and is mixed and cooked. And that part of the vital principle which is contained in the air (pneuma), or is separated from it, forms the fœtus, and gives it movement."

If much cannot be said for this hypothesis, it at least satisfied Aristole and his successors. Eels were originated, he thought, out of the *casts* of the earth-worms. That testacea originate spontaneously, is proved he thinks by the fact of their sudden appearance on the keels of ships and other places. Nor is the spontaneous origin of mankind altogether incredible to him. "If this ever took place," he adds, "as many affirm, we must assume that it was either from a scolex, or from an egg. Since of necessity the original germ must have contained within it the requisite food (and such a germ is the scolex), or it must have procured the food elsewhere, and this either from a parent, or from a part of the germ. If, therefore, it is impossible that food should flow from the earth, as it does from the uterus to the fœtus, then must the food have come from a portion of the germ; and such we call an egg." And as eggs are produced only by parents, it is clear that the origin of our race, on this hypothesis, must have been a scolex.

§ 483. BOOK IV. *Chap. I.*—It is an old question, Why one child is masculine, and another feminine? and as the desire for male offspring is often intense, people have naturally lent a greedy ear to any philosopher who pretended to inform them how males could be obtained. ANAXAGORAS taught that the distinction is original, and exists in the sperm itself; the masculine coming from the right, the feminine from the left. EMPEDOCLES thought that the distinction was due to the coldness or warmth of the womb. DEMOCRITUS, who is generally nearer the mark than any other old philosopher, thought that the distinction arose entirely from the preponderance of one of the two secretions, the offspring being a male when the sperm predominated, and a female when the germ predominated. Aristotle refutes Empedocles and Anaxagoras by reference to facts. The existence of twins of different sexes in the same uterus disproves the idea of the relative temperature of the uterus being the determining cause; and the existence of both sexes, after the removal of one testis, disproves the idea of the right and left sides having their special sexes.[55] As these absurd hypotheses were reproduced many centuries later,[56] it is interesting to observe how thoroughly Aristotle recognized their absurdity. His comment is in the spirit of BACON: "Prophesying from their opinions what will be the fact, and anticipating, in lieu of observing, what the fact is."[57] But having dismissed these hypotheses, he admits that "there is *some* ground for the belief that sex is determined by the warmth of the respective sides,[58] since the

---

[55] It is by reference to similar facts that DE GRAAF refutes this notion. See his *De Virorum Organis*, p. 6, in *Opera Omnia*, 1678.

[56] See HALLER: *Elementa Physiologiæ*, VIII., 79. BAUHIN, in his work *De Hermaphroditorum Monstrorumque Natura*, Oppenheimii, 1614, not only advocates this view, but says with great gravity, as if he *had* opened pregnant dogs and sows, "Si prægnantem canem vel suem aperueris, in dextro latere mares, in sinistro vero fœminas reperies; ideo qui masculam prolem expetunt mulieres in latus dextrum cubare jubent," p. 60.

[57] μαντευόμενοι τὸ συμβησόμενον ἐκ τῶν εἰκότων, καὶ προλαμβάνοντες ὡς οὕτως ἔχον πρὶν γινόμενον οὕτως ἰδεῖν.

[58] This was long a very popular opinion. It is admitted by CARDAN among the three modes of procuring male offspring, though he reverses the sides, ordering the mother to lie on her left side, because it is the stronger, and males are formed in the stronger. He declares that he has prescribed this method to patients with great success.—*De subtilitate rerum*, lib. XII., Lugduni, 1554, p. 441. SCALIGER has nothing to object here, so we must presume he accepts the argument as valid.

right side is indeed warmer than the left (which it is *not*); but, such hypotheses do not touch the real difficulty; for that we must look into first causes."

§ 484. His own hypothesis is this: " The masculine and feminine are distinguished by a certain power, and a certain impotence. That is masculine which has the power of cooking, condensing, and secreting sperm containing the formative principle; and I do not call that a principle which becomes an individual from the material, but that which is the first moving cause, either in itself, or in another; the feminine, on the other hand, is that which receives, but is incapable of condensing and secreting sperm. If the cooking depends on heat, the male must necessarily be warmer than the female." After enlarging on this notion of heat, he adds, " Male and female are *contraries*, and have different generative organs, which have different functions. Moreover, according to our views, everything arises from contraries; and when there is loss or failure (ἡ φθορὰ) in the one contrary, that which cannot properly be fashioned naturally turns into the opposite. On these grounds it is easy to explain the sexes. Whenever the formative principle fails to gain the upper hand, and, from deficient warmth, fails properly to cook the material, and so fashion it into its own shape, then will this material necessarily pass over into the contrary; and the contrary of the masculine is the feminine. And since their difference consists in their functions, and these in their organs, the first change will be in the organs. Now when one important and *dominant* organ (ἑνὸς μορίου ἐπικαίρου) is changed, then *there is a change in the whole form of the organism*."

The reader will observe how luminously the idea of Epigenesis is expressed in the last sentence; and lest there should be any doubt as to his meaning, he adds, " This is manifest in castrated animals, which, being deprived of a single organ, lose their sexual appearance, so as in many respects to resemble the female. The cause is that certain organs are origins of development, and if one of these be altered, much that is connected with it must likewise change. When, therefore, the masculine is defined to be a kind of principle and cause, and is only masculine in as far as it possesses these which are wanting to the feminine—and when such power and such impotence are determined by the capability and incapability of cooking the final nourishment, called blood in the sanguineous, and its analogue in the ex-sanguineous; and when the origin of the blood is in the central organ, the source of animal heat, then it is necessary that a heart, or its analogue, should be formed, and that the embryo should be male or female."

§ 485. Whatever may be thought of this hypothesis, which becomes somewhat confused towards the close of the exposition, when we remember that he did not, and could not know that every embryo was at first *asexual*, passing from this indeterminate condition into determinate organs by successive morphological changes, we shall acknowledge that his answer is quite as good as that of any of his successors, and better than most. *What* determines the special changes remains to this day a profound mystery; all we know is that sex is not primitive, pre-existent, but—as was shown in KNIGHT's experiments on Plants—is determined by unknown conditions of temperature and nutrition.[59]

§ 486. *Chap. II.*—Connecting his hypothesis with the statistics of birth, as known to him, he finds further proof in the fact that more females are born during the youth and old age of the parents than during their prime: in the young the animal heat has not acquired maturity, in the old it is beginning to disappear. He also thinks that fruitful animals produce more females than males. That more males are generated

---

[59] See an interesting essay by PLOSS: *Über die Geschlechtsverhältnisse der Kinderbedingenden Ursachen*, Berlin, 1858, and compare PAGENSTECHER: *Über das Gesetz der Erzeugung der Geschlecter.* Aus dem Französischen von M. THURY. Leipzig, 1864.

during the prevalence of the north winds, may be explained on the ground of the secretions being then smaller in quantity, and more easily cooked; a similar cause operates in the appearance of the catamenia, chiefly at the last quarter of the moon, for this part of the month is *colder* and *moister*, owing to the disappearance of the moon. He quotes, without disapproval, the saying of shepherds, that males or females are produced according as the sheep have congress during a north or south wind; not only so, but it is an important condition whether the animals in congress look towards the north or the south, "so trifling a circumstance being influential in generation by determining heat or cold."

The chapter contains other passages which raise a smile. Variations of sex are attributed to the nature of the soil and the water, which with the atmosphere, influence the food. "Hence hard and cold waters occasion the sterility of women, and partly determine the generation of females." To this day the Egyptians attribute the fecundity of their women to the waters of the Nile; and HIPPOCRATES,[60] who thought that water issuing from hard rocks must necessarily be hard, mentions hard and cold waters among the causes of sterility.

§ 487. *Chap. III.* treats of the hereditary transmission of qualities from parent to offspring.[61] It has long been a question whether all the qualities, physical and moral, are transmitted, and whether one parent transmits one group, and the other another, or both transmit all. Even HALLER and BONNET, who thought the embryo pre-existed in the germ, could not deny that Hybrids partook of the characteristics of both parents. Holding the sperm to be merely the nutriment

---

[60] HIPPOCRATES: *De Aëre, Locis, et Aquis*, XX., 19. Compare BAUHIN: *De Hermaphroditorum Natura*, 1614, p. 59.

[61] The literature of this important subject will be found in BURDACH: *Traité de Physiologie*, II.; and LUCAS: *Traité de l'Hérédité naturelle*, 1847; see also GIROU DE BUZAREINGUES: *Traité de la Génération*, 1828; ORTON: *Lectures on Breeding*, 1859.

and excitor of the germ, they thought that the form of the embryo would vary with the quality and quantity of the sperm. It was thus they explained the fact of the mule having the ears and voice of the ass. The germ from which the mule proceeds is the germ of a horse; but the sperm of the ass containing more particles destined for the nutrition of the ears and vocal membranes, the mule resembles in these the ass.

§ 488. Those who held the doctrine of Epigenisis varied in their interpretations of parental influence. Some thought that the male gave the animal organs, the female only the vegetal organs. The superficial resemblance of the spermatozoon to the early form of the cerebro-spinal axis,[62] and the fact of the spermatozoon being endowed with movement, naturally suggested the idea of the nervous and muscular systems being due to the male, whence it was further inferred that the digestive and glandular systems came from the female. This idea has been favourably received by physiologists and cattle-breeders. I have elsewhere endeavoured to show how irreconcileable it is with the facts,[63] and may here briefly state an *à priori* argument which entirely disproves it. That the whole sum of the contribution to the formation of the embryo is limited on the part of the male to the spermatozoa, and on the part of the female to the ovum, is decisively proved in the generation of amphibia and fish, since in that generation, which takes place in the water, *outside* the parent, there is nothing but these two elements present. Now, we have already seen that spermatozoa and ova are identical (§ 191); and when to this it is added that in some animals ova *alone* suffice to form a perfect offspring (§ 192), there can remain no doubt that the contribution of the mother is *not* limited to any one system or group of organs, but embraces the whole organism. Unless, there-

---

[62] " Si le zoosperme n'est pas un système cérébro-spinal, et le vitellus un système digestif, ils possèdent en eux les élémens nécessaires au développement ultérieur de ces bases essentielles de l'animalité."—LALLEMAND: *Annales des Sciences Naturelles*, 1841, p. 281.
[63] *Physiology of Common Life*, II., 392.

fore, we return to the old hypothesis of the ovists, and regard the contribution of the male simply in the light of a stimulus to the germ (an hypothesis abundantly refuted by the facts of cross-breeding, in which the obvious characteristics of the male are transmitted), we have no alternative but to declare that both parents furnish their quota to every part of the offspring.

§ 489. Having thus glanced at modern hypotheses, let us consider the view taken by Aristotle. In the generation of man he says the progenitor is not simply a man, but a special individual such as Socrates or Koriskos. The individual and special have always predominance. Koriskos is man, as well as animal, but his speciality is as man rather than as animal. The individual predominates in generation because individuality constitutes the essence. But, inasmuch as when the formative principle fails to fashion the material, the *contrary* must be produced, so when Koriskos is a parent, if his influence *qua* man be feeble, his child will be a female, resembling him, his influence *qua* man having passed into its contrary; and if this influence is still feebler, the child will be a female resembling its mother. If the influence *qua* individual be feeble, the child will resemble its grandfather. But, whatever variation take place, the child always exhibits *human* characteristics.

The cause of all these variations is the check received by the Motor impulse from the Material moved. Action produces reaction. The edge of a tool is blunted by the material which it cuts; the heating body is cooled by that which it warms; "and sometimes the reaction is greater than the action; the warming body becomes cold, and the cold body warm, and hence the effect is lost or weakened."

§ 490. In extreme cases, the formative principle is so far checked that the child ceases to resemble human beings, and resembles an animal—in which case it is called a monster. Here the material is not fashioned into special forms, but the *general* remains (μένει τὸ καθόλου), and this is *animal*. " Thus, it is said that children are born with the heads of sheep or calves, and other parts resembling those of animals; for example, a calf with a child's head, or a sheep with the head of an ox. All such phenomena are due to the cause before-named; but we must not understand such statements literally; none of these monstrosities really *are* animals, but only resemble them. The same sort of resemblance may be seen in perfectly-formed healthy men. A Physiognomist once showed how all faces could be reduced to two or three animal types. But how impossible it is for one animal to have the parts of another is evident from the differences in the periods of gestation of men, sheep, dogs, and oxen. Each can only be formed in its own definite period."

This passage displays remarkable sagacity, and might have enlightened many of his successors. The belief in a race of men having the heads of dogs was easy to Lord MONBODDO, who confesses that such men have not been seen by any modern traveller, but they are spoken of by so many ancient authors, that he can hardly doubt of their having once existed.[64] Aristotle not only marks what is true from what is false in the popular belief, but refers to distinct physiological grounds, namely, that the child requires nine months, and the dog only nine weeks for its development. Whence he probably concluded that so great a difference in the development of the two would prevent any such organic union, as vulgar superstition accepted.

§ 491. He does not mention "mothers' marks," as we are reminded by HALLER.[65] We cannot say whether this omission was intentional; but he is hardly to be credited with having seen through the popular fallacy which attributes the marks

---

[64] MONBODDO: *Ancient Metaphysics*, 1779, III., 263. He also believed in the existence of a nation of one-legged men; and although he owns that STRABO rejects this as a fable, he reminds us that " a spirit of incredulity was begun as early as the days of Strabo," p. 251. He would have found support in his credulity in BAUHIN: *De Hermaphroditorum Natura*.

[65] HALLER: *Elementa Phys.*, VIII., 142.

on the child to the imagination of the mother, an absurdity that has found energetic defenders even in our own day.

§ 492. He treats of monsters *par excès*, in which six fingers, six toes, two heads, &c., are formed; and acutely remarks that although these phenomena are contrary to the ordinary course of nature they are not unnatural. Modern science has established on irrefragable grounds that deformities and monstrosities follow precisely the same laws of development as are followed in perfect embryos.[66]

§ 493. *Chap. V.* is on superfœtation.

§ 494. *Chap. VI.* treats of the condition in which the young of various animals are born, whether blind or not, and how far capable of maintaining independent existence; with several other matters not specially calling for notice here.

§ 495. *Chap. VII.* is on extra uterine gestation, and on the so-called *mola*. But it is too exclusively technical for this place. *Chaps. VIII., IX.,* and *X.,* are devoted to milk, and to the periods of gestation. He supposes that the period of gestation is in relation to longevity.

§ 496. The Final Book is occupied with discussions as to the cause of the variation in the colour of eyes and hair, the abundance of hair, the sleep of the embryo, sight and hearing, voice and the teeth. But interesting as some of these are, there is nothing which induces us to expand this chapter already too long.

§ 497. We close our analysis of this work with the re-

---

[66] GEOFFROY ST. HILAIRE: *Philosophie Anatomique*, 1830, vol. II.; SERRES: *Recherches d'anatomie transcendante et pathologique*, 1832; ISIDORE ST. HILAIRE: *Histoire des Anomalies de l'Organisation*, 1832. In the last-named work the literature of this extensive subject is copiously given. The treatise by BAUHIN: *De Hermaphroditorum Monstrorumque partuum Natura, libri duo*, Oppenheimii, 1614, is an exhaustive and very amusing collection of the ancient and mediæval opinions and fancies on this subject. I have already cited it more than once, but the following is too characteristic of what our credulous forefathers accepted as evidence to be passed over:—" Triginta sex filios vivos uno partu peperit Margarita Comitis Virboslai uxor, Cracoviensi agro. An. 1270, 20 Jan. Cromero et Guagninio testibus."—P. 74.

iteration of our conviction that it is his masterpiece in science. To those who open it prepared only by knowledge derived from modern writers it will necessarily appear at times jejune and not a little absurd; but to those who are familiar with the writers of the sixteenth, seventeenth, and eighteenth centuries, it will appear in its true greatness; and those who have familiarized themselves with the results and speculations of the most advanced embryologists will, I think, be surprised and delighted to find how often Aristotle seems at the highest level of speculation.

CHAPTER XVIII.

CONCLUSION.

ON reviewing the general impression of Aristotle's aims and achievements which the foregoing pages have endeavoured to convey, we first note the contradiction they present to the popular conception of his claims as a great observer, and a great legislator, in science. The uncritical enthusiasm of eulogists has been challenged; the unreflecting iteration of hyperbolical praises has been confronted with analyses of his works; and yet, in spite of the rigour of our scrutiny, there has been no stint of admiration where admiration seemed deserved. The inquiry has resulted in a verdict which considerably modifies, yet scarcely lessens, our idea of his greatness.

We have seen that the title of a great observer cannot fairly be awarded to him. Far from meriting this rank, he is not entitled to any place, great or small, among men specially distinguished as *observers*, in the scientific sense of the term: since not only did he fail to enrich Science with the valuable and accurate details which serve as the solid supports of speculation, he failed also to appreciate the primary conditions of successful observation. He collected many facts, he never scrutinized them.

So long as we consider him in his historical position, no serious blame can fairly be attributed to him for failing to appreciate the importance of Verification, and the means by which it may be sought; for in his day these were appreciated by no one; they could only gain adequate recognition during the slow evolution of scientific experience.

If, however, it would be unjust to blame him for an imperfection which was universal in his day, it would be eminently unphilosophical in an historian to overlook the imperfection. To overlook it would be to miss the great lesson of History, which teaches us that even the power of Observation is a late development in the mental evolution of our race, and not, as it may at first sight appear, the easy and spontaneous exercise of human faculties. There is as wide a distinction between the untutored observation practised by the early pioneers of science, and the cultivated caution of modern observers, as between the rude polity of savage tribes and the complex civilization of advanced nations. The ancient rarely attempted to analyze complex phenomena into their several elements, rarely suspected even that they *were* complex; and such analysis as was attempted was always executed without the aid of instruments of precision, consequently was inevitably imperfect and approximative. Unaided by instruments, and unaware of their indispensable value, the ancient philosopher was thrown upon his sagacity in guessing; and it is no wonder that he constantly duped himself and his hearers by mistaking mental distinctions and verbal analogies, for Nature's differences and resemblances. The modern, on the contrary, trained in the discipline of severer methods, and taught by those very methods to distrust whatever has not been rigorously demonstrated, is for ever seeking greater accuracy in his analyses, and greater delicacy of precision in the instruments by which analyses are to be made. Instead of relying on a supine credulity, he is tormented by a vigilant scepticism. Far from trusting to the uncontrolled observation of facts such as sufficed in early times, he has learned to distrust the accuracy of his senses, and to question closely the accuracy of his instruments. He has even learned the necessity of establishing what is called the *personal equation*, by which the delicate variations of sensitive organisms may be reduced to an average. Thus although the beats of a pendulum may seem accurate standards for the observation of a phenomenon in time, they admit of an inaccuracy which it is important to correct, since it has been found that no two persons agree precisely as to the moment of observation—one being always a trifle in advance of the other. Bessel found himself in the habit of noting phenomena in advance of his assistant, Argelander, by as much as $1''\cdot 22$; and Mr. Sheepshanks found himself 45-hundredths of a second behind M. Quetelet, and 35-hundredths before Mr. Henry. In astronomy such variations would lead to enormous inaccuracies; consequently, as a preliminary to observation, a personal equation has always to be established between the observers.

The Art of Observation is a late development. Science depends greatly on this Art for its progress; and yet the Art itself is only to be evolved during the slow advances of Science: the two go hand in hand: they act and react. In the early stages of scientific growth even an intellect so great as Aristotle's could not place itself at the point of view which is now taken by the humblest investigators. If his successors have become more cautious it is because they have been trained in a severer discipline—a discipline which it is his immortal glory to have inspired, by that scientific impulse which, as we have seen, he impressed on philosophy.

Another popular exaggeration has been treated in the foregoing pages: his claim to the anticipation of modern discoveries has been refuted. Where intellectual force alone was involved, there Aristotle appeared a giant. But no single mind can do the work of Humanity; no one man can anticipate the labours of ages. NEWTON, in Alexandria, could not have done the work of KEPLER; nor, in Syracuse, would GALILEO have surpassed ARCHIMEDES. How idle to expect that Aristotle in the fourth century before Christ should have made discoveries which were only possible nineteen centuries after Christ; only then possible because until then science was without the requisite data, and without the requisite instruments by which the data could be ascertained.

It is, therefore, unphilosophic exaggeration destructive of the whole significance of History to say that Aristotle "laid the bases" of any physical science. He laid no bases at all. He was not a legislator. Neither by his conceptions, nor by his methods, were any sciences finally rescued from Common Knowledge, and *constituted*, as Astronomy was constituted by HIPPARCHUS, or Statics by ARCHIMEDES, or Dynamics by GALILEO. The coincidences of some of his conceptions with those of modern philosophers have been exhibited in various parts of this volume, coincidences sometimes due to a profound sagacity, oftener due to our tendency to read into ancient texts the thoughts of modern thinkers. Instead of regarding him as a legislator, we must confess that, great as his indirect influence has been, his direct influence on the physical sciences is inappreciable. Could we eliminate the indirect influence exercised by his mind over the minds of succeeding generations, we might begin the history of every science without once naming him.

But, fortunately, we cannot estimate that influence. It has been immense, and his fame is justifiably colossal. None can pretend to appreciate the extent of that influence, mingled as it is with so many concurrent streams; but no one with a knowledge of History, and a sense of historical significance, will deny that the influence has been potent. In many passages of this volume criticism wears somewhat the appearance of polemics; an attitude to be regretted, but not to be avoided. I entered upon my task full of enthusiasm for the greatness of Aristotle, though with the determination to express in all sincerity whatever convictions might grow out of careful study. The critical attitude, proper to an historian who refuses to become a partisan, may, in my case, have been made somewhat rigid by the reckless eulogies of many writers whom I had to consult during my labours, and perhaps also by the inevitable swing of reaction in my own mind on discovering that I had been misled by excessive and misplaced praises; but in concluding my work I should be guilty of an injustice on the other side, if I did not endeavour to express my sense of Aristotle's intellectual supremacy.

After every deduction has been made, the instinctive and popular appreciation of his greatness will be ratified by a large philosophy. Among the great heroes of Humanity, his position must ever remain conspicuous. He claims precedence over hundreds who, under more fortunate conditions, have enriched science with priceless details. He rises superior to most of those who have illuminated science with great conceptions. And this superiority is claimed not only in virtue of his many achievements, but also in virtue of his native force. His comprehensive glance embraced the whole field of research; and if some other philosophers, ancient and modern, have taken as wide a survey, none have like him first opened the pathways they surveyed. But he might have had even greater comprehensiveness, and yet not have justified the glory which for centuries has surrounded his name. He had a greatness above this versatility. He had that kind of intellectual Force not easily defined, and mainly to be estimated through its vast results—the Force which creates epochs in the evolution of human progress. This power, which founds Religions and Philosophies, by changing the whole order of men's conceptions, is not to be measured by any of the standards we apply to discoveries developed from previous discoveries. It is to be measured rather by its results, immediate and remote. The creation of a Method is incomparably greater than the most brilliant application of that Method. And it is not because Aristotle himself made great discoveries, but because he deeply and extensively influenced the minds of discoverers, that his name is illustrious.

CONCLUSION.

We, who have grown up under the influence of the revolution which he began, are in no condition adequately to appreciate his work. Just as we cannot thoroughly understand why he was so careless with respect to accuracy in observation, just as we cannot appreciate the obstacles which in his day opposed the employment of vigilant scepticism and constant verification, so also are we at a loss to estimate what was the supreme difficulty of initiating the Scientific Method. To us it may seem little that he should steadily have renounced theological interpretations of natural phenomena, and that he should have attached primary significance to Fact as the basis of speculation. It may seem as if no alternative had been open to him. Thus we may be insensible to the value of his conception of Method, and of his gigantic efforts to apply it in all directions; and this insensibility will make us aware only of his deficiencies.

Instructed by History, we learn that in the resolute withdrawal of all explanations from theological interpretations, in the predominance assigned to Fact, and in the insistance on graduated Induction, there were the fruitful germs of as great a revolution as any which has hitherto modified the development of mankind.

The force of Aristotle's intellect, acting through the germinating power of his Method, gave him despotic power over succeeding generations, and sharpened in the hands of his antagonists the very weapons with which they assailed him. The despotism was in many respects disastrous, as all despotisms must be. His defects became more influential than other men's excellences. His guesses were more attended to than his sober precepts. And yet it was surely not altogether his fault that his Organon became an instrument of repression rather than of research, and that his practice was more readily followed than his precepts? However he may have been impelled to systematize on imperfect bases and to reason where he should have observed, it is not too much to say that had he reappeared among later generations he would have been the first to repudiate the servility of his followers, the first to point out the inanity of Scholasticism. His mighty and eminently *inquiring* intellect would have been the first to welcome and to extend the new discoveries. He would have sided with GALILEO and BACON against the Aristotelians.

(383)

INDEX.

ABELARD, his *Sic et Non* cited, p. 224
Absolute (the), idea of Hegel's disciples on, 80
Abstractions, tendency towards the impersonation of, 86; Whewell on the employment of, 88
Ackermann, on male and female organisms, 208; on female sperm, 347
Acoustics, their origin due to the Greeks, 39
Æschylus, the *Eumenides* cited, 352
After-birth. See Placenta
Agassiz, on Aristotle's classification, 277. Cited, 295
Albertus Magnus, cited, 190, 278
Alexander the Great, a pupil of Aristotle, 13 ; his reverence for his teacher, *ib.*; becomes Regent, 14; his magnificent patronage of Aristotle, *ib.*; Pliny's account of, 15; effect of his death in Athens, 16
Alexandria, human dissection practised in under the Ptolemies, 163
Ammonius, his Life of Aristotle discredited by Buhle, 5
Anatomy, its origin due to the Greeks, 39; failure of the Greeks in, 56; Aristotle's anatomy valueless, 157; whence he derived his knowledge of, 157, 158; Emil Braun's reference to the anatomical figures in the Vatican, 161; whence the Asclepiads derived their knowledge of, *ib.*; Boyle on the usefulness of, 162; absurdities of the Galenists, 163; A.'s confession as to the internal anatomy of man, 164; proofs of A.'s never having dissected the human body, 164, 165, 167; comparative anatomy an arrested embryology, 189; want of classification owing to the backward state of anatomy, 277; first dawn of philosophic anatomy, 279; account of the anatomy of the invertebrata, 285
Anatomists (ancient), their error respecting the Uterus, 332
Anaxagoras, his influence on Plato, 102; his opinion that bile is the cause of acute diseases, 318; his reason for the intellectual superiority of man, 321; on the origin of the sexes, 342, 367
Ancients, failure of their efforts in science, 47, 49, 60, 63; Playfair's verdict on their failure, 49, 51 ; their large collection of scientific facts, 52; their mental activity, 53; Dr. Whewell's conclusions as to their failure, *ib.*; their inferiority to the moderns, 57; their opinion as to the velocity of a falling body, *ib.*; their impatience in the investigation of science, 58; quotation from Bacon, *ib.*; source of their errors, 60; their chief mistake, 70; employed a Method on which all problems were insoluble, 71; their ignorance of anatomy, 161
Andry, his figures of the spermatazoon, 352
Animal Movements, Aristotle's explanation of, 177, 178. See Motion
Animals, identified with plants, 184 ; their resemblance in the embryonic stage, 189 ; their development the third step in natural gradation, 193; hermaphroditism of, 207; conclusion that all animals are oviparous, 213 ; their metamorphoses instanced in the salamander, *ib.*; alleged existence of the Nerve tissue in inferior animals, 243; Aristotle's division of, 273, 274, 275; Delle Chiaje on A.'s classification, 275; sanguineous and exsanguineous, 276; A.'s want of systematic grouping, 277; design of A.'s

classification, *ib.*; Agassiz cited, *ib.*; Sunderall's work on A.'s knowledge of animals, 279; analysis of A.'s *Hist. Animal.*, *ib.*; A.'s "partes similares," 279, 280, 298; analogy of parts in animals, 280; A.'s standard of animal structure, 281; account of the intestines of animals, 281, 282, 283; of the blood, 283, 284; mention of the appearance of milk in the male, 285; on the voice of animals, 287; their habits and instincts, 290; object of the *De Partibus*, 292; A. on their composition, 297; on animal temperature, 298, 299; cause of animal terror, 302; on watery-blooded animals, *ib.*; earthy-blooded animals, 303; Aristotle on animal fat, *ib.*; the direction of heat, 306; use of the flesh, 307; Man not the only animal with the erect attitude, 309; but he is the only one that is ticklish, 316; the quadrumanous animals of Tyson and Buffon, 319; Man a quadrumanous animal, 320; why he is the most intelligent, *ib.*; why the lioness has only two teats, 321; Funes de Mendoça's improvement on this last theory of A.'s, *ib.*; the generation of oviparous animals, 350

"Animists," the Montpellier school of, 223

Anna Manzolina. *See* Manzolina

Antigone (the), chiefly relates to the sacredness of the dead, 160

Aphis, its parthenogenesis, 202, 203

Aquapendente. *See* Fabricius.

Archimedes, an example of true scientific inquiry, 59; the founder of Statics, 147, 379

Aristotle, life of, p. 1; his intellect and attainments, *ib.*; insignificant result of his labours, *ib.*; revolt against his authority, 2, 21; attacked by the scientific reformers, 2; inferiority of his adversaries, 3; his biographies collected by Buhle, 4, 5; their contradictions, *ib.*; scant and untrustworthy materials for a life of, 4; his birth, 4, 6; his father, 7; called the "reader" by Plato, 8; attracted to Athens, *ib.*; his occupations there, *ib.*; Bacon's sarcasm, 9; he wins for himself a position at Athens, 10; his foppery in costume, 11; his alleged ingratitude to Plato, *ib.*; taught by Plato for seventeen years, *ib.*; his person and character, 11, 12; instance of his humour, 12; opens a school of philosophy, 12, 15; his work *De Divinatione* cited, 12; alleged object of his visit to Hermias, *ib.*; marries Pythias, adopted daughter of Hermias, *ib.*; story of his practising medicine at Athens, *ib.*; goes to Macedon, 13; fiction of his accompanying Alexander to Asia, 14; his return to Athens, 15; opens the Lyceum as a school. *ib.*; regarded with suspicion in Athens, 16; accused of irreligion, 17; quits Athens, *ib.*; authenticity of his writings, *ib.*; their encyclopædic character, 17, 18; his modern eulogists, 18, 23; contrasted with Plato, 19; without rank as an artist and writer, 20; his commentators, *ib.*; his errors pointed out by Gassendi, 21; his works declared heretical by Parliament of Paris, *ib.*; his legitimate position assigned by Fülleborn, Buhle, and Tennemann, 22; considered the profoundest of thinkers, *ib.*; various editions of his works, *ib.*; his true place in science, 23; his remarks on scepticism in science, 40; he illustrates the excellence and defects of the Greeks, 41; his explanation of the mysteries of nature, *ib.*; compared with the writer of *Ecclesiastes*, 42; his confidence in science, *ib.*; his study of nature for the sake of knowledge, *ib.*; alleged to have anticipated modern discoveries, 46; his failure in Biology, how far referable to the neglect of Ideas, 54; Dr. Whewell on the cause of his failure in Mechanical Science, *ib.*; his carelessness in scientific investigation, 59; his *Physics* compared with Newton's *Principia*, 67, 68; his formulas want the guarantee of Observation, 68; on the demonstration of things beyond the senses, 69; A. recognized the Ideal Test, *ib.*; his claim to the first outline of classification, 84; his deference to other men's opinions, 89; he defined words in order to expound facts, *ib.*; his defective conception of Method, 108; the father of Inductive Philosophy, *ib.*; his contrast to Plato, *ib.*; cause of his failure in scientific research, *ib.*; his reliance on sensuous perception, 109; his method compared with Plato's, *ib.*; on Experience and Induction, *ib.*; on the impossibility of thought without sensation, *ib.*; his Empiricism urged as a reproach, *ib.*; on the parthenogenesis of bees, 110; on hybridity, *ib.*; on Experience as the true guide in science, 110, 111; his anticipation of modern Psychology, 111; on the necessity of Observation, 110, 111, 112; A. points out the danger of the Platonic Method, 111; his perception of the value of experiment, 112, 113; anticipates the cardinal principles of Bacon's philosophy, 113; his neglect of his own method, *ib.*; places the Ideal above the Real Test, 117; his efforts wasted in pursuit of causes, *ib.*; his four causes unverifiable, 119; practically a metaphysician, *ib.*; his chief claim to our veneration, 120; his followers fascinated by his defects, *ib.*; Roger Bacon's desire to burn A.'s works, 121; his Physics, Meteorology and Mechanics, 122; his obstruction of Astronomical Science noticed by Herschel, 125; ignorant of the laws and nature of Motion, 126; compared with Newton, 127; his extant writings on physics, *ib.*; his definition of Nature, 129; his celebrated definition of Motion, 131; his theory of projectiles, 132, 133; fallacy respecting continuous motion, 133; his analysis of Motion, 134, 135; his work on the Heavens, 136; on the relations of space and gravitation, 136, 137; his idea of the form of the Heavens, 138; on the substance of the Stars, 138, 139; his theory of Heat and Light, 139; definition of an Element, 140; his protests against the *à priori* Method, *ib.*; ether as an Element, 141; on Gravity and Levity, *ib.*; on Ether as the substance of the Heavens, *ib.*; his work on Meteorology, 143; his explanation of the Milky Way, 145; on the chemistry of the Elements, 146; his *Problems*, 147; made no advance in Mathematical Science, 149; on Pressure and Percussion, 150; his disregard of the law of Inertia, 152; deficient in the transcendental postulates of Science, *ib.*; his efforts not in vain, 153; but the neglect of his physical speculations justified, *ib.*; his Anatomy, 154; Cuvier's exaggerated eulogy of Aristotle, *ib.*; his servile eulogists, 154, 155; De Blainville's admiration for, *ib.*; amazing extent of his biological survey, 156; Lauth's eulogy of his anatomical labours, *ib.*; A.'s anatomy valueless, 157; whence he derived his knowledge of Anatomy, *ib.*; assigns the Heart as the origin of the Blood-vessels, 158; his ignorance of the Muscles, *ib.*; his ignorance of the Nervous-system, *ib.*; and of the three most important parts of the organism, *ib.*; A. did not dissect the human body, 159; on the parts of the human body, 163, 164; his description of the Lungs, *ib.*; of the Uterus, *ib.*; his error regarding the position of the Heart, 165; in reference to the spleen, *ib.*; Blazius' anxiety to defend A., 166; Buonfede on A.'s ignorance of the Human Brain, *ib.*; Galen on A.'s ignorance of Human Anatomy, *ib.*; A.'s erroneous description of the Brain, *ib.*; alleged to have first discovered the nerves, 167; Scaliger's palliation of Aristotle, *ib.*; credited with discovery of Cerebral nerves, 168; his alleged discovery of the nerves discussed, 168, 169; knew nothing of the nervous system, 170; his Physiology, 171; he was ignorant of the phenomena of digestion, 172, 173; his ideas on respiration, 174, 175, 176; on the respiration of fish, 175, 176; his explanations of animal movements baseless, 177, 178; places the seat of sensation in the Heart, 179; on the senses of Touch and Taste, *ib.*; fallacy of his having laid the 'eternal bases' of Biology, 180, 181; his alleged anticipation of modern discoveries, 183, 187; recognizes the identity of Plant and Animal, 184; credited with the discovery of the Vertebral Theory, 186; his discovery that plants are nourished at expense of their seed, 187; his idea of an ascending complexity in Vital phenomena, 189; on Natural gradation, 190; his Organic and Inorganic kingdoms, *ib.*; on the Heart as the centre of sensation and thought, 191; on the different developments of plants and animals, 192; classes the Testaceous animals as plants, *ib.*; his reason for classing Sponges as animals, 193; his views of Plants and Animals stated by Hermolaus Barbarus, 194; makes Man the head of Animal creation, 195; anticipates Linnæus, *ib.*; the Hectocotylus instanced, 199, 200; ignorant of the parthenogenesis of bees, 206; his remark on the Perch, 209; Aristotle proved by Dufossé to be right where moderns are wrong, 210; his reliance on hearsay, 211; aware of the existence of Placental fishes, 212; his assertion respecting the Cuttlefish verified by Kölliker, 218; his statement regarding the nest-building fish verified by Olivi, *ib.*; on the vision of

25

the Mole, 218; made no discovery in Science, 220; his treatise *De Anima*, 221; ψυχή untranslateable, 221, 222; on Life and Mind, 223; his doctrine on the Soul declared orthodox, 224; on Sensation as the characteristic of the Soul, *ib.*; on the nature of the Vital Principle, 225, 226; his conception of the mystery of Life, 231; his views on the immortality of the Soul, 233; on sensibility, sight, hearing, &c., 235, 238; on Imagination, 240; his chapter on Intellect, *ib.*; on the Reflective faculty, 241; hypothesis of the development of knowledge, *ib.*; his views of Locomotion, 242, 243; denies that the animal body is homogeneous, 244; on the sense of Touch, *ib.*; his analysis of the Senses, 246 to 255; his definition of Light, 248; of Taste and Smell, 249; his explanation of Colour, *ib.*; on the divisibility of Sensation, 253, 254; his explanation of Memory, 256; his treatises on Memory, Sleep, Dreams and Longevity, *ib.*; his absurd theories on sleep, 258, 260, 261, 262, 263, 264; his treatise on Dreams, 264; his History of Animals, 269; Cuvier's description of the *Hist. Animal.*, 270; erroneous conclusions, 271, 272; Cuvier on A.'s classification of animals, 273, 274; Aristotle distinguishes Animals into sanguineous and exsanguineous, 275; on bloodless animals, 276; his sketch of those which have blood, *ib.*; disputes as to his system of classification, 277; doubts as to whether he had a system, *ib.*; no classification in the *Hist. Animal.*, 278; Sunderall's work on A.'s classification of Animals, 279; analysis of *Hist. Animal.*, *ib.*; his division of the organism into similar and dissimilar parts, 279, 280; on the parts of animal bodies and their analogy, 280; A.'s knowledge of Anatomy less accurate than Galen's, 281; instances of A.'s carelessness and rash generalization, 282; on the blood of animals, 283; his account of the anatomy of the Invertebrata, 285; his mention of the appearance of milk in Males, *ib.*; on the Crustacea, 286; on sight and hearing in the Testacea, 287; his assertion in reference to Hydrophobia, 289; on gout in Horses, *ib.*; his defence of the study of Biology, 296; on the composition of animals, 297; on animal fat, 303; on the composition of the brain, 304; on the composition of animal Marrow, *ib.*; cause of his belief in the insensibility of the Brain, 305; on the organs of Men and Plants, 308; his account of the Heart and Liver, 311, 312—examples of his rash theorizing, 311, 312, 313; his remarks on single and double organs, 315; his description of the Diaphragm, 316; his reason for the position of the Elephant's teats, 322; why man has flesh on his legs, *ib.*; asserts that man is tailless, *ib.*; work on generation and development, 325; compared with Harvey's work on Generation, 326; on sexual differences, 331; denies the existence of sperm in females, 333, 345; on the testes, 333, 334; his opinion that woman is but undeveloped man, 347; his doctrine of Epigenesis, 351, 355, 368, 369; on development of the Embryo, 357, 358, 359; on the power of reproduction in females, 360; his opinion that eels are generated spontaneously, 361; on the phenomena of development, 362; on the fertility of Hybrids, 363; supposed prefiguration of the Cell Theory, 365; origin of the sexes, 367, 368, 369; on hereditary transmission of qualities, 370, 371; his omission of "mother's marks," 374; his true rank in Science, 376; his claim to have anticipated modern discoveries, 378, 379; his immense influence, 379, 380, 381; one of the great heroes of Humanity, 380; he would have been an anti-Aristotelian, 382.

Arnold, Dr., his eulogy of Aristotle's Politics, 18
Artedi, cited, 277
Art, Greek, defects of, 41
Asclepiads (the), imperfectly acquainted with Anatomy, 7; whence their anatomical knowledge derived, 161
Association of Ideas, A.'s glimpse of the law of, 257
Assyrians, exaggerated antiquity of their records, 37
Astronomers (ancient), their belief in the uniformity of celestial revolutions, 33; Biot's remark thereon, 34
Astronomy (Egyptian), Martianus Capella on the antiquity of 37; slight acquaintance of the Chaldæans with, 66; Plato's depreciation of, 104; Aristotle's ideas of, 139
Athens, Aristotle attracted to, 8; his occupations at, *ib.*; declining glories of, 9, 10
Atoms, hypothesis of, beyond proof, 92

Attraction, stigmatized by the Cartesians as an occult quality, 84; the law of denuded of Metaphysics, *ib.*; again restored to science, *ib.*; Newton on, 93; its cause unknowable, 94; science concerned only with the law of Attraction, *ib.*
Auguries, the Druids' method of, 32
Averrhoes, on the infallibility of the Stagirite, 155
Avicenna, cited, 169; quoted by Roger Bacon on the seat of the Soul, 179

BACON, Lord, his sarcasm respecting Aristotle's quotations, 9; on the want of scientific instruments among the ancients, 58; on the psychological cause of error in science, 62; on the inequality of mind as a mirror of things submitted to it, 103; cause of his own failure in scientific research, 108, 113; his *Novum Organon*, cited, 109; not opposed to Aristotle, but to A.'s followers, 113; the cardinal principles of his philosophy anticipated by Aristotle, *ib.*; his *Sylvia Sylvarum* cited, 300; on the action of fire, *ib.* Cited, 41, 367
Bacon, Roger, cited, 21, 115, 169, 172; on Verification, 82; Jebb's preface to the *Opus Majus* cited, 121; his desire to burn Aristotle's works, *ib.*; on the optic nerve, 170; on the seat of the Soul, 179; his alleged discovery of the telescope, 186; on the Intellect, 358
Baer. *See* Von Baer
Bailly, his letters on the origin of the sciences, cited 46
Barbarus, Hermolaus. *See* Hermolaus
Barchusen, asserts that Aristotle dissected the Human Body, 159, 165; his opinion adopted by Haller and Harles, 159. Cited, 160, 346
Baronio, his successful grafting of parts of animals, 191
Barthélemy St. Hilaire. *See* St. Hilaire
Barthez, on Verification, 33
Basso, his attack upon Aristotle, 2; an admirer of Patrizio, 9. Cited, 228
Bauhin, on the origin of the sexes, 367. Cited, 370, 373, 374
Béclard, his definition of Life, 230. Cited 231
Bees, Aristotle on the Parthenogenesis of, 110, 206. *See* Parthenogenesis
Benedictines of St. Maur, their *Literary History of France* cited, 32; on the soothsaying of the Druids, *ib.* Cited, 225
Bernard, Claude, cited, 312

Bernouilli, J., his metaphysical trifling, 132
Bichat, on the "law of economy," 183; his famous definition of Life, 230; made Aristotle's division of the organism the foundation of modern histology, 279; on the distinction between animal and vegetable organs, 314, 315. Cited 190, 231
Biese, his analysis of Aristotle's scientific logic, 116. Cited, 140, 192
Bile, Aristotle's account of, 317, 318
Biology, Aristotle's failure in, how far referable to neglect of Ideas, 54; its two grand divisions, 156; amazing extent of A.'s survey, *ib.*; fallacy of Aristotle's having laid the eternal basis of, 180, 181; general principles of, 182; instance of A.'s alleged anticipation of modern speculations, 183; Aristotle's defence of the study of, 296; its obscurest problems treated in the *De Generatione*, 325
Biot, his work on *Indian and Chinese Astronomy* quoted, 34, 38
Bischoff, Professor, cited, 328, 348
Blakesley, his suggestion that Aristotle was a pupil of Xenocrates, 5. Cited, 6
Blazius, on the quantity of blood going to the brain, 166
Blondin, his *Vitalisme Animique* cited, 224
Blood (the), Aristotle's account of, 283, 284; the fibrine of, discovered by Borelli, *ib.*; the distinctions of, 298; A. on the influence of different kinds of, 302
Bloodvessels, Aristotle's account of, 314
Blumenbach, cited, 338, 351
Bodies, their passive and static condition, 123; Aristotle's ideas on their weight and lightness, 141, 142, 143
Bone, reason for the growth of, 307
Bonnet, his scheme of the origin of species, 187; proves the parthenogenesis of the aphis, 203. Cited, 353 371
Books, illustrated, in the time of Aristotle, 283
Borelli, his discovery in reference to the fibrine of blood, 284
Bossuet, an anatomist, 162
Bostock, his System of Physiology cited, 352
Bouiller, cited, 224
Boyle, on the usefulness of anatomy, 162
Brain, quantity of blood going to, 166; Blazius cited, *ib.*; Buonfede on Aristotle's ignorance of, *ib.*; A.'s erroneous description of, *ib.*; the seat of sensation, 179; functions ascribed to it by

Aristotle, 180; A.'s notion of the brain criticised by Galen, *ib.*; Davy's attempts to estimate its temperature, *ib.*; Cuvier's error on the brain of Molluscs, 219, 220; part assigned to it in production of sleep, 263; Aristotle's erroneous conclusion on the size and moisture of man's brain, 272, 306; its origin and composition, 304; A.'s belief that it is devoid of sensation, 305, and moderates the heat of the blood, 306
Brain-ducts. *See* Nerves
Brandis, cited, 6, 279
Braun, Emil, his reference to the anatomical figures in the Vatican, 161
Bronn, cited, 193, 295
Brown Sequard cited, 191, 208, 216, 261, 275, 345
Browne, Sir Thos., on the vision of the Mole, 219
Bruno, Giordano, cited, 2; his contempt for Patrizio, 9
Buffon, on the living universe as one family, 188. Cited, 270, 277, 319
Buhle, collects the ancient biographies of Aristotle, 4; discredits that by Ammonius, 5; his error regarding Funes y Mendoça, 303. Cited, 6, 21, 22
Bunsen, in reference to spectrum analysis, cited, 70
Buonfede cites Burnet's list of Aristotle's puerilities, 155; on A.'s ignorance of the brain, 166
Burdach, on milk in males, 285; on the spermatozoon, 352. Cited, 327, 348, 356, 371
Burmeister, cited, 184; his *Manual of Entomology* cited, 270, 329
Burnet, his list of Aristotle's puerilities cited by Buonfede, 155
Bussemaker, edits Aristotle's works, 22; his rendering of an obscure passage in Aristotle, 306. Cited, 263, 343
Buzareingues, Girou de, cited, 371

CÆSALPINUS, his erroneous defence of Aristotle, 168; on the brain as the seat of sensation, 179; on generation, 205, 347. Cited, 305
Camus, his French translation of the *Hist. Animal.*, 269
Cardan, on the respiration of fish, 176; on the generation of male offspring, 367
Cartesians, stigmatize Attraction as an occult quality, 84
Cartilage, reason why it never regenerates, 307
Carus, Victor, cited, 270, 295

Casaubon, his edition of Aristotle's works, 21
Castelli, declares Plato and Aristotle perfect anatomists, 159
Catamenia, modern ideas on, 345; Aristotle on, *ib.*
Caterpillar, its 4,041 muscles, 158
Causation, law of, transcends experience, 66; how demonstrable, 84; in itself unknowable, 91, 92, 93
Cause, desire to banish it from Inductive Philosophy, 90; its meaning in science, *ib.*; life regarded by Aristotle as a final cause, 234
Causes, no following of effects from, 91; causes and effects are simultaneous, *ib.*; Aristotle's efforts wasted in pursuit of, 117; the four kinds of causes, 117, 118; A.'s discussion on final causes, 129, 130
Cavolini, cited, 210
Cell Theory, Aristotle's alleged prefiguration of, 365
Cephalopoda, Von Siebold on Aristotle's acquaintance with, 199
Chabanon, his *Mémoires de l'Académie des Inscriptions* cited, 147
Chaldæans, exaggerated antiquity of their astronomical observations, 37; their slight knowledge of astronomy, 66
Charles' *Life of Roger Bacon* cited, 121
Charleton, cited, 195, 210, 303
Chemistry of the Elements, Aristotle on, 146
Children, their resemblance to their parents, 372, 373
Circulation of the Blood, important results of the discovery, 176
Classification, Aristotle's claim to first outline of, 273; one of the latest results of scientific research, *ib.*; Cuvier on Aristotle's classification, 273, 274; Meyer on the various schemes of, 277; general ignorance of A.'s attempts at, *ib.*; its mode of elimination and aim, *ib.*; Whewell on the construction of a classification, 278; Agassiz on Aristotle's grouping, *ib.*; Aristotle on, 294; but offers no classification of his own, 295; his dim perception of the natural method, 296
Claude Bernard, cited, 312
Claudian Mammertus, on the immaterialism of the Soul, 225
Cocchi, Antonio, denies that Aristotle dissected the Human Body, 159
Collier, Dr. Charles, his translation of the *De Animâ*, 221
Colour, Prantl cited, 249; Goethe

cited, 249; Aristotle's explanation of, *ib.*
Comparative Anatomy, the want of classification owing to the backward state of, 277
Comte, Auguste, on metaphysical conception of phenomena, 30; on mathematical precision, 39; on our limited physical knowledge of the planets, 70; his commentary on Laplace's theory of Motion, 98; led too far by his antagonism to Metaphysics, 99; on the necessity of Method and Education, 100; on the extension of gravitation beyond the solar system, 125; his proposition to fill up missing links in nature, 189. Cited, 34
Congreve, his edition of Aristotle's Politics cited, 16
Conringius, denies that Aristotle dissected Man, 159, 160
Contraries, principle of, 128
Copernicus, on hypotheses, 92
Corniani, his work on Italian Literature cited, 119
Cosmology, Plato's, 105
Costa, guesses at the nature of the Hectocotylus, 198
Coste, on Aristotle's story of the woman of Elis, 340
Cresswell, his translation of the *Hist. Animal.*, 269. Cited, 280
Crustacea. *See* Invertebrata
Currey, his *Report on Vegetable Parthenogenesis* cited, 202
Cuttlefish, Aristotle's assertion regarding, 218; cause of its change of colour, 302
Cuvier, on the existence of the "nervous fluid," 98; his eulogy of Aristotle, 154; describes the Hectocotylus, 198; his error regarding the brain of Molluscs, 219; his statement about Aristotle's predecessors, 269; his enthusiasm for Aristotle's *Hist. Animal.*, 269, 270, 271, 272; on A.'s classification, 273, 274; his admission of the "vers à sang rouge," 275; on A.'s knowledge of anatomy, 281. Cited, 23, 154, 210, 218, 290, 319, 353

D'ALEMBERT, on the truth in ancient ideas, 184
Daremberg, on Galen's ignorance of the anatomy of the human body, 163
Dareste, cited, 215
Darwin, cited, 188
Davies and Vaughan's translation of Plato's *Republic* cited, 103
Davy, Dr. J., his *Physiological and Anatomical Researches* cited, 180, 216; his fallacious experiments on the Liver, 313
D'Azyr, Vicq. *See* Vicq D'Azyr
Dead, feeling of the Greeks respecting the, 160
De Anima (the), Trendelenberg's edition cited, 118; its great eminence, 221; editions of, *ib.*; translations, *ib.*; Max Müller on the meaning and equivalents of *anima*, 222; analysis of, 225; enlarges more on physical than psychological questions, 244; its want of logical arrangement, *ib.*; profundity of many of its views, 245; its value as a scientific work, 290, 291. Cited, 265
De Animal. Motione (the), cited, 112
De Blainville, his eulogy of Aristotle, 154; his definition of Life adopted by Comte and Charles Robin, 230. Cited, 23, 154, 270, 295, 353
De Cœlo (the), cited, 110; analysis of, 136; Prantl's edition of, *ib.*
Deduction, one of the modes of scientific investigation, 57
De Generatione (the), cited, 110, 112, 310; its vast scope, 325; Aubert and Wimmer's edition of, *ib.*; analysis of, 330 to 376; pronounced the masterpiece of ancient science, 375
De Graaf, commenced the discovery of the Mammalian ovum, 213; on the Uterus, 332; on Aristotle's opinion that woman is undeveloped man, 347. Cited, 332, 333, 346, 347, 353, 367
De Juventute, Aristotle's, cited, 239
Delambre, *Hist. of Astronomy* cited, 38
Delle Chiaje, cited, 198, 273, 323; on Aristotle's division of animals, 275; on the change of colour in the cuttlefish, 302
Democritus, on Vision, 247; on the origin of the sexes, 367. Cited, 145, 359
De Partibus (the), cited, 110, 163, 274, 282; a continuation of the *Hist. Animal.*, 279; analysis of, 292; its object, *ib.*; its distinction of *partes similares*, 298; represents Aristotle's physiology, 322; its great interest in the history of science, 323
Descartes, his reliance on the Possible, 69; recognizes the Ideal Test, *ib.*; on the rule of Truth, 79; his errors, 81, 83; on the habitat of the Soul, 83; his neglect of the Real Test, *ib.*; his *Principia* cited, 92, 133; his hypothesis that brutes are mere machines, 196; on the functions of the Soul, 224
De Sensu (the), analysis of, 246. *See* Senses

De Somno, Aristotle's, cited, 239
Development, Aristotle on the phenomena of, 362. See Generation, Parthenogenesis, Organism, Embryology
Diaphragm, Aristotle's description of, 316; its part in consciousness, *ib.*
Dichogamism. See Generation, Parthenogenesis, Hermaphroditism
Dichotomy, Aristotle's criticism of, 294
Diego de Funes y Mendoça. See Funes y Mendoça
Differentiation of plants and animals, stated, 194
Digenesis, forms of, 328. See Generation
Digestion, Aristotle ignorant of the phenomena of, 172, 173; A. on the influence of heat in, 301
Diodorus, on the antiquity of Chaldæan astronomical observations, 37
Diogenes Laertius, the biographer of Aristotle, 4, 17
Diogenes, on the respiration of Fish, 176.
Dionysius of Halicarnassus, a biographer of Aristotle, 5
Dissection, evidences against Aristotle having dissected the human body, 159; Greek popular feeling against, 160; struggles of Science for, *ib.*; the disgust and fascination for, 161, 162; illustrious anatomists, *ib.*; Boyle on the usefulness of, 162; practised in Alexandria under the Ptolemies, 163; absurdities of the Galenists, *ib.*; proofs of A.'s never having dissected the human body, 164, 165, 166, 167
Dominic de Marchettis, on the ovaries of females, 333
D'Orbigny, cited, 302
Dreams, analysis of Aristotle's treatise on, 264, 265, 266; the images, or after-motions, of sensation, 266
Drelincourt, cited, 351
Druids, their method of predicting events, 32
Dufossé, proves Aristotle to be right where Moderns are wrong, 210. Cited, 287
Dugès, his definition of Life, 230. Cited, 231
Duhamel, on the growth of bone, 191; his éloge by Vicq d'Azyr, quoted, *ib.*
Dujardin, his *Natural History of Infusoria* cited, 193; on the Hectocotylus, 198
Dutens, his *Origin of Discoveries assigned to the Moderns* cited, 46
Du Val, his edition of Aristotle's works, 21
Duvernoy, cited, 210

Dynamics, their origin to be sought among the Greeks, 38; founded by Galileo, 147
Dzierzon, his researches on the parthenogenesis of bees, 205

ECCLESIASTICUS, comparison of, with Aristotle, 42
Eels, Aristotle's opinion that they are generated spontaneously, 361
Egyptians, their scientific claims discredited, 37; their observations and annals, *ib.*; without the rudiments of science, 38; their idea of female fecundity, 370
Ehrenberg, on the structure of the nerves, 168
Elements (the Four), Plato on the cohesion of, 105; Aristotle's definition of an Element, 140; the fifth element, *ib.*; A. on the chemistry of, 146
Elephant assigned only two diseases by Aristotle and Pliny, 289
Elis, story of the woman of, 340
Ellis and Spedding, their edition of Bacon's works cited, 115
Embryo, the "missing links" to be sought in the life of, 188; its assimilating power, 215; increases *in utero*, *ib.*
Embryology, how far equivalent to comparative anatomy, 189; identity of the spermcell and germcell, 203; identity of the male and female organisms, 208; summary of the modern science of, 327; *origination, ib.*; *development,* 328; *incubation,* 329; its modern forms known to Aristotle, 330; A. on the origin of the sperm, 339, 340; on the growth of the embryo, 342; his diagnosis of the sperm, 342, 343, 344; the form and principle of the embryo derived from the male, 347; hypotheses concerning, 351; A. on the development of the embryo, 357, 358 359. *See* Generation, Organism
Emil Braun. See Braun
Empedocles, held "the eye to be of fire," 247; on the origin of male and female, 367
Empiricism, Hegel on, 80; urged as the reproach of Aristotle, 109
Epicharmus, cited, 343
Epicurus, cited, 137
Epigenesis, theory of, 351; its triumph, 354; idea of grasped by Aristotle, 369. See Generation
Epilepsy, compared by Aristotle to sleep, 261; disease of a nervous centre, *ib.*

Equilibrium, the action of equal opposing forces, 126
Erasmus, his opinion of Hermolaus Barbarus, 118
Eratosthenes, an instance of the neglect of Verification among the Greeks, 59
Ether a fifth element, 140
Ethics (A.'s), quotation from, 11
Eulogists, Aristotle's, 18, 23, 154, 155
Eumenides of Æschylus cited, 352
Everardus, on female sperm, 333. Cited, 346
Evolution. *See* Generation
Experiment, what it is, 49; distinguished from Observation, 50; instances of Aristotle's perception of, 112, 113. *See* Empiricism

FABRICIUS AB AQUAPENDENTE, cited, 169, 170, 176, 177, 332
Fact (Scientific), definition of, 71; its implied antithesis to Idea or Theory, 71, 74, 75; the real distinction, 75, 76, 77, 78; its indissoluble connection with Idea, 72; its verification, *ib.*; real meaning to be assigned to, 73; tendency to use it as a final truth, 74
Falloppia cited, 279, 332; on the existence of sperm in females, 333
Farre, Dr. A., his article on the *Uterus and its Appendages* cited, 216, 338
Fetichism, cause of, 86
Final cause, tendency to invoke, a characteristic of Metaphysics, 86
Fischer, Karl, cited, 46
Fish, Cardan on the respiration of, 176; why they die out of water, *ib.*; the perch said to be self-reproductive, 209, 210; Aristotle's ruminating fish, 282; Milne Edwards and Professor Owen on the ruminating fish, 283
Flesh, Aristotle on the properties of, 307; subordination of its parts, *ib.*; cartilage, *ib.*
Flourens, his explanation of the respiration of fish disproved, 176
Force, advantage of the true conception of, 95; its existence as an entity, 96; methods of its investigation, *ib.*; the conception of its indestructibility modern, 123; the conditions under which it is apprehended, *ib.*; correlation of forces, *ib.*
Four Elements, Plato on the cohesion of, 105; Aristotle's definition of an element, 140; the fifth element, *ib.*; A. on the chemistry of the elements, 146
Frantzius, cited on Aristotle's *Hist.*

Animal., 279; his edition of the *De Partibus*, 292
Fraunhofer, cited, 70
Fries, his work on Anthropology cited, 245
Funes y Mendoça, cited, 269; on fibrous-blooded animals, 303; on the ossification of the heart, 313; follows Aristotle's opinion that the lioness has but two teats, 321
Furlanus cited, 277

GALEN, affirms that the Asclepiads were taught dissection, 7; his anatomical knowledge said to rest upon careful dissection, 158; he did not dissect the human body, 163; Daremberg, his editor and translator cited, *ib.*; on A.'s ignorance of human anatomy, 166; his conception of the Heart, *ib.*; his confusion regarding the nervous system, 167, 168; on the respiration of fish, 176; his *De Usu Partium* cited, 177; criticizes Aristotle's theory of the brain, 180; alleged to have discovered the incandescent gases, 185, 186; maintained the mortality of the Soul, 233, 234; on the three species of souls, 233; his knowledge of anatomy more accurate than Aristotle's, 281; on the sutures of the skull, 306; mentions fish having the *os sublime* of Ovid, 308; on the existence of bone in the heart, 313. Cited, 176, 321, 322, 334
Galenists, their absurdities, 163
Galileo, ridiculed by the Aristotelians, 57; his experiments on the velocity of falling bodies, *ib.*; his *à priori* idea as to the velocity of a falling body, 68; hesitates to identify celestial and terrestrial mechanics, 125; his refutation of Aristotle's theory of projectiles, 132; the founder of Dynamics, 147; finds the principle of "virtual velocities" in Aristotle, 148; his *Dialoghi* cited, 151; his story about the origin of the nerves, 168. Cited, 2, 143
Gassendi, an adversary of Aristotle, 3; on the errors of A., 21
Gautier, his figures of the spermatozoa, 352
Gaza, his imperfect version of the *De Generatione*, 325
Gegenbauer, cited, 194
Gellius, cited, 8
Generation, *normal* and *abnormal*, 207; male and female organisms, 207, 208;

INDEX.

hermaphroditism, 208 ; conditions of development of the impregnated ovum, 214, 215; loss of weight of the egg during development, 215, 216; A. on various modes of generation, 288, 289; summary of modern knowledge of, 327; *origination, ib.*; *development*, 328; *incubation*, 329 ; Aristotle on the origin of the sperm, 339, 340; and on the growth of the embryo, 342 ; various hypotheses concerning generation, 351 ; Hindoo theory of, 352; discovery of the mammalian ovum, 353 ; theory of syngenesis, *ib.*; of evolution, *ib.*; on the physical nature of sperm, 356; the *aura seminalis, ib.*; A. on the development of the embryo, 357, 358, 359; on the generation of fish, insects, and bees, 364 ; improbability of spontaneous generation, 364, 365; origin of male and female, 367; influence of each of the parents, 372. *See* Embryology, Organism

Genesis, Plato's idea of, as expressed in the *Timæus*, 104

Geoffroy St. Hilaire. *See* St. Hilaire, Geoffroy

Germcell, production of, 337

Gesner, cited, 278

Giordano Bruno. *See* Bruno

Girou de Buzareingues, cited, 371

Gland, pineal, the seat of the Soul, 83

Goethe, an anatomist, 162; his work on Morphology cited, 183 ; his *Farbenlehre* cited, 247. Cited, 226, 237, 249, 280

Graafian Vesicle, cause of its bursting, 338; Blumenbach, cited, *ib.*; mistaken for the ovum, 353

Grafting, animal, successfully practised, 191

Grant, Sir Alex., on the meaning of ψυχή, 222

Grant's Lectures on Comparative Anatomy cited, 155

Gravitation, law of, discovered by Newton, 29 ; Comte on its extension beyond the solar system, 125

Gravity, an abstraction, 95; its explanatory use, *ib.*; Aristotle's idea of, 141, 142, 143

Greeks, the inventors of astronomical instruments, 38; their scientific discoveries, 39; their adoption of scientific scepticism, 39, 40 ; Aristotle an illustration of their excellence and defects, 41; their desire of knowledge for its own sake, 43; the originators of science, 44; their slow progress in discovery, 45; Whewell on the cause of their failure in philosophy, 52, 88 ; their want of ideas examined, 55 ; neglect of facts, not of ideas, the cause of their scientific failure, *ib.*; their imperfect appreciation of the nature of evidence, 56; their recognition of the Inductive Method, *ib.* ; deficient both in facts and ideas, 58 ; their want of method and instruments, *ib.*; quotation from Bacon, *ib.*; their impatience in investigation, *ib.*; Whewell on their failure in science, 88 ; their superstitions respecting unburied bodies, 160; their stringent laws as to burial, *ib.*; their horror of dissection, *ib.*; Pliny on their mendacity, 286.

Greek art, defects of, 41

Gruner's *Analecta ad Antiquitates Medicas* cited, 160

Gubler, cited, 345

Guizot, on the materiality of the soul, 224

HALLER, cited, 159, 220, 323, 347, 353, 354, 356, 361, 367, 371, 374; his patient labours in Verification, 60; on the want of patient investigation in his contemporaries, *ib.* ; an instance of his great labours, *ib.*; his definition of Physiology, 156 ; maintained that Hippocrates dissected the Human Body, 160; on man's natural repugnance to dissection, 162 ; his estimate of the quantity of blood going to the brain, 166; on the insensibility of the Cerebrum, 305; his *Opuscula Anatomica* cited, 316

Hamilton, Sir W., his eulogy on Aristotle, 18, 22; on "divisible sensation," 253; his notes on A.'s treatise on Memory and Recollection, 256. Cited, 257

Harles, cited, 159, 167, 170

Harless, on the Asclepiads, cited, 7.

Harris, his *Philosophical Arrangements*, cited, 22

Hartsocker, his claim to priority in the discovery of the Spermatozoa, 352

Harvey, on the pulsation of the Heart, 174; asserts that all animals are oviparous, 213; on generation, 215 ; studies which led him to the discovery of the circulation of the blood, 323; compared with Aristotle, 326; denies the existence of female sperm, 333. Cited, 298, 305, 332, 355

Heart, assumed by Aristotle to be the seat of the Soul, 120; Aristotle's error in reference to the position of, 165 ;

Galen's conception of, 166; regarded as the great source of Motion, 174; assumed by A. to be the origin of the tendons, *ib.*; dependence of Aristotle's theories on, *ib.*; Harvey on the pulsation of, *ib.*; the seat of sensation, 179; A.'s opinion that it is the first organ developed, 310; genesis of, *ib.*; the origin of the veins and of emotion, 311; Aristotle on the ossification of the septum, 313; the heart the origin of character, *ib.*; its inability to withstand disease, 313, 314; the origin of development, 361

Heat, Aristotle's theory of, 139; his inquiries respecting animal heat, 299; the direction of animal heat, 306

Heaven, analysis of Aristotle's work *De Cœlo*, 136; the form of, 138

Hectocotylus of the Argonaut, 197, 198; described by Cuvier, 198; its peculiar wonder, 198, 199; the discovery supposed to be anticipated by Aristotle, *ib.*; A.'s passages on, 199, 200; his ignorance of the Hectocotylus, 200, 201; Von Siebold's error, 201

Heeren, his account of Classic Literature in the Middle Ages, cited, 8, 118

Hegel, his admiration for Aristotle, 18, 22; his disciples' idea of the Absolute, 80; his Introduction to Logic, cited, *ib.*; on the meaning of Truth, *ib.*; on Empiricism, *ib.*; his elucidation of Matter and Spirit, 81; his errors, *ib.*; denies the charge of Empiricism against Aristotle, 109. Cited, 21

Helvetius, his reason for the intellectual superiority of Man, 321

Herder, adopts Buffon's idea of the living universe as one family, 188

Hereditary transmission of qualities, 370, 371

Hermaphroditism, in fish, 207; explanation of, 208; hermaphrodites always of one sex, *ib.*; Serres cited on, *ib.*

Hermias, King of Atarneus, a disciple of Aristotle, 12; invites A. to his court, *ib.*; A. raises a statue to, 13

Hermolaus Barbarus, on the "final cause," 118; Erasmus' opinion of him, *ib.*; Scaliger's opinion of him, 119; on Locomotion, 134; on Aristotle's views of Plants and Animals, 194. Cited, 190, 235

Herpyllis, Aristotle's concubine, 17

Herschel, cited on causes and effects, 91; notices the obstruction of Aristotle to astronomical science, 125

Hesychius, a biographer of Aristotle, 5

Hindoo theory of generation, 352

Hipparchus, on the records of the Assyrians, 37; an example of scientific inquiry, 59

Hippocrates, an example of scientific inquiry, 40; never dissected the Human Body, 160, 163. Cited, 179, 250, 263, 332, 370

Histogenesis, laws of, 329

Histology, Modern, foundation of, 279

Historians of Science, their carelessness, 281

History of Animals (Aristotle's), various editions of, 21, 269; proposal and specimen of a new translation, 269; new translation by Mr. Cresswell, *ib.*; Cuvier's enthusiasm for, 269, 270; analysis of, 271, 279; criticisms on Cuvier's remarks concerning its generalizations, 271; no system of classification contained in, 278; Titze's ingenious suggestion concerning, 279; supposed to be a continuation of the *De Partibus*, *ib.*; its abrupt commencement, *ib.*; the introduction supposed to be lost, *ib.*; examples of its careless generalization, 282

Höfer, on Galen's extraction of the incandescent gases, 185, 186

Homologies of the skeleton, Aristotle's idea of, 157

Houghton, his proposal of a new translation of the *Hist. Animal.*, 269

Humboldt, cited, 140; mentions the case of a man suckling a child, 285

Hume, his treatise on Human Nature, cited, 241; his doctrine on the Mind, *ib.*

Hunter, his animal grafting, 191.

Huxley, on the value of scientific generalization and classification, 291; on the difference between Hands and Feet in Man, 319. Cited, 327, 337

Hybridity, Aristotle on, 110

Hybrids, Aristotle on the fertility of, 363

Hydrophobia, A.'s assertion in respect to, 289

Hypothesis, scientific importance of, 114

IDEA, *à priori*, of Galileo, powerless to stand the Ideal Test, 68; the indissoluble connection of Idea (Theory) with Fact, 72, 74, 75; the real distinction, 75, 76, 77, 78

Ideas, their reference to natural phenomena, 54; Aristotle's neglect of Ideas the cause of his scientific failure, *ib.*; the Platonic conception of, 83; the tendency to accept them as representations of things, 88; science careful

of their relative truth, 93; Plato's world of permanent existences, 103
Ideal Test of Inertia, conformable with Real Test, 67
Ideal Test, when subjectively true, 68; recognized by Aristotle and Descartes, 69; must be supplemented by the Real Test, 80; placed above the Real Test by Aristotle, 117.
Ideler, on *Greek and Roman Meteorology*, cited, 46
Imagination, Aristotle on its existence in inferior Animals, 243; definition of, 265
Immortality of the Soul, Aristotle on, 358
Imperato (the old Italian Naturalist), his description of Sponges, 193; on the vision of the Mole, 219
Impregnation, the union of a spermcell with a germcell, 202; Newport cited on artificial impregnation, 204
Incubation, the two forms of, 329; oviparity and viviparity, *ib.*
Induction, one of the modes of scientific investigation, 57
Inductive Method, accurately proclaimed by Aristotle, 47; Aristotle the father of Inductive philosophy, 108
Inductive Syllogism, the basis of science, 115
Inertia, law of, an abstraction, 67; Ideal Test of, *ib.*; law of, how demonstrable, 84; absolute Iner. a figment, 124; instance of Aristotle's disregard of the law of, 152
Inorganic: the gradation from the inorganic to the organic kingdom, 190; plants, the first step in the scale, *ib.*
Insects, metamorphoses of, 214; Aristotle on their external form, 318, 319; on their mode of generation, 336. See Parthenogenesis
Instruments, scientific, Greek want of, 58
Intellect, Aristotle's chapter on, 240
Intestines, Plato's description of, 106
Invertebrata, Aristotle's account of the anatomy of, 285, 286; their organs of sense, 287
Isidore St. Hilaire. See St. Hilaire

JEBB, his Preface to Roger Bacon's *Opus Majus* cited, 121
Johnson, his *Life of Linacre* cited, 119
Jourdain, his work on the ancient interpretations of Aristotle, cited, 21; his explanation of Roger Bacon's desire to burn Aristotle's works, 121

KANT, cited, 69, 231; on scientific speculation, 83; his proposal to form an introductory science to Physics, 84; on Plato's Method, 107; on the relativity of Motion and Rest, 124; his definition of Life and Organism, 229; on dreamless sleep, 265
Kepler, his doubts as to his own discovery respecting the orbit of Mars, 34; hesitates to identify celestial and terrestrial mechanics, 125
Kidneys (the), Serres' observation regarding, 165
Kirchoff cited on spectrum analysis, 70
Köhler, on the confusion of nerves and tendons, 167. Cited, 275, 286
Kolk, Schröder van der, cited, 224, 261
Kölliker, his investigation of the Hectocotylus, 198; his views adopted by Von Siebold, *ib.*; on Aristotle's assertion regarding the Cuttlefish, 218. Cited, 208, 310, 362
Kuhlemann cited by Schneegass, 356

LACEPEDE, his *Histoire Naturelle des Poissons* cited, 275
Lallemand, on self-contained elements of development in Spermatozoon, 371
Lamarck, cited as an instance of the metaphysical tendency, 97; on the sensibility of the Polype, *ib.*; on the causes of the variety of organisms, *ib.*; his retort against Cuvier regarding the nervous fluid, 98; on the degrees of the animal scale, 188; on the relations of organic life, *ib.*; denies the "chain of creation," *ib.*; on the organic and inorganic kingdoms, 193; his *Philosophie Zoologique* cited, 219; his division of animals into vertebrata and invertebrata, 294
Lamartine, his noble description of man, 309
Language, its influence in philosophy, 88, 89; its theory little understood, 89; moderns own no servility to, 89; Whewell on Aristotle's subservience to language, *ib.*
Laplace, on the law of Motion, 98, 124
Laurillard, furnishes a specimen of Hectocotylus described by Cuvier, 198
Lauth, his eulogy of Aristotle's anatomical labours, 156; his inconstency, *ib.*; cited, 158; on A.'s error regarding the Heart, 165; on A.'s claim to the discovery of the vertebral theory, 186
Lawi, his *Memorie sopra le Talpa* cited, 219
Lereboullet, his work on comparative Embryology cited, 189
Lessing, on Aristotle's Poetics, 21
Leuckart, thinks Sponges intermediate

INDEX.   395

between the vegetal and animal kingdoms, 188. Cited, 208, 295
Leuwenhoek, first described the tubular structure of the nerves, 168. Cited, 352
Levity, Aristotle's idea of, 141, 142, 143. *See* Bodies
Lewis, Historical survey of Astronomy of the Ancients cited, 37
Leydig, cited, 365
Libri, on the successful scientific studies of the Italians, 38; his *History of Mathematics* cited, 148
Life, various definitions of, 229; the impenetrable dynamis, 231; potential and real, *ib*.; regarded by Aristotle as a final cause, 234; causes of prolonged life, 266, 267, 268
Light, Aristotle's theory of, 139; his definition of, 248
Linnæus, his views regarding man anticipated by Aristotle, 195
Liver, Plato's description of, 106; Aristotle on the properties of, 149, 150, 312; Davy's fallacious experiments on, 313
Locomotion, A.'s views of, 242, 243
Logic, its danger, 81; Aristotle's scientific, 115, 116, 117
Longet, cited, 208
Longevity, Aristotle's treatise on, 266; his explanation of the causes of, 266, 267, 268
Lucas, cited, 352, 353
Lucretius, on the tendency of bodies in space, 137
Ludovicus Vives, on the comparison between the moderns and the ancients, 4
Lungs, Aristotle's description and theory of, 164, 314
Lyceum, opened as a school by Aristotle, 15; description of, *ib*.
Lyonet, his anatomical work cited, 158; his patient observation, *ib*.

MABILLON, refers to the figure of the telescope in ancient MS., 186
Macgillivray, his amusing eulogy of Aristotle, 155; his exaggerated estimate of A., 270; on Aristotle as a naturalist, 286
Magnetic Fluid, Lamarck's retort against Cuvier respecting, 98
Majendie, his *Journal de Physiologie* cited, 177
Malebranche, cited, 353
Malpighi, his estimate of the quantity of blood going to the brain, 166; alleged anticipation of his discovery respecting the fibrine of the blood,

284; discovers the capillaries, 362. Cited, 310, 353, 362
Mammals, varieties of vertebræ in, 85
Mammertus, Claudian. *See* Claudian
Man, compared by Plato to the universe, 106; Aristotle's confession as to man's internal anatomy, 164; derivation of the word *man*, 195; modern attempts to separate him from the animal kingdom, *ib*.; the stress laid on his erect posture, 308, 309; Lord Monboddo's man, who preferred going on all fours, 309; Lamartine's noble description of man, *ib*.; the only animal that is ticklish, 316; A.'s diagnosis of man, 319; a quadrumanous animal, 319, 320; A.'s inferences from man's erect attitude, 320, 321; A.'s reasons why he of all animals has flesh on his legs, 322; asserts that man is tailless, *ib*.; his spontaneous origin not incredible to Aristotle, 366
Manava-Dharmasastra cited, 352
Manzolina, Anna, her wax preparations the pride of Bologna, 162
Mars, Kepler's doubts respecting the orbit of, 34
Martianus Capella, on the antiquity of Egyptian astronomy, 37
Martin, Henri, cited, 14
Martins, his *Mémoires de l'Acad. de Monpellier* cited, 158; on the identity of the Humerus with the Femur, *ib*.
Mathematics, their Greek origin, 39; the most rigorous type of the true method, *ib*.
Matter, his *History of the Alexandrian School* cited, 16
Matter, Newton on the formation of, 97
Matter and Spirit, Hegel's elucidation of, 81
Maurice, his felicitous contrast of Plato and Aristotle, 19
Maury, his *Le Sommeil et les Rêves* cited, 258
Max Müller. *See* Müller
Mazzuchelli, his *Italian Writers* cited, 119
McDonnell, cited, 177
Mechanics, Rational compared with Practical, 82; Aristotle's work on, 122; A.'s distinction between celestial and terrestrial mechanics, 125; Kepler and Galileo's hesitancy, *ib*.
Meckel, on the gradation of organisms, 188; his views adopted in the *Vestiges of Creation*, 188. Cited, 207, 210, 295, 315
Medici, his work on the Anatomical School of Bologna cited, 163

Memory, Aristotle's explanation of, 256; analysis of A.'s work on Memory and Recollection, *ib.*; Sir W. Hamilton's notes on Reid, *ib.*

Metamorphoses of Animals, instanced in the Salamander, 213; whence Goethe deduced his theory of the metamorphoses of Plants, 354

Metaphysical conception of Nature, Mind impeded by, 31

Metaphysicians, overlook the Real Test, 82

Metaphysics, its efforts not without fruit, 66; its vanity lies in Method, *ib.*; as distinguished from Science, 84, 93; basis of, 87, 88; demands only the test of logical dependence, 90; its tendency active in the early stages of culture, 96; Aristotle a metaphysician, 119

Meteorology, Aristotle's work on, 122—147; its design and scope, 143, 144, 145; its failure for want of instruments, *ib.*; analysis of, 145

Method, the Subjective and Objective compared, 35; origin of the Subjective, 36; systematic adoption of Method due to the Greeks, 38; Mathematics the most rigorous type of the true Method, 39; the true Method impossible without scepticism, *ib.*; the Inductive accurately proclaimed by Aristotle, 47; the ancient Method powerless to lead to satisfactory results, *ib.*; Greek want of Method, 58; preference for the Subjective explained, 63; its gradual relinquishment, *ib.*; the scientific failure of the ancients referable to false Method, 64; account of the Subjective and Objective Methods, 65; error of the Subjective tested, 81; Method the distinction between Science and Metaphysics, 84; Plato's Method examined, 101; his frank avowal of the Subjective, 103; Kant's happy illustration of Plato's Method, 107; Aristotle's defective conception of, 108; impossibility of applying true Method in A.'s time, 113; Aristotle's scientific Logic, 115, 116, 117; A. protests against the *à priori* Method, 140

Meyer, cited, 140; on the error of Fabricius, 177; on the various schemes of classification, 277

Milky Way, Aristotle's explanation of, 145; theory of Democritus, *ib.*

Milman, his *Hist. of Latin Christianity*, cited, 121

Milne Edwards, on Aristotle's ruminating fish, 283

Mind, Plato refers the causes of all things to, 102; only the highest development of Life, 223

Moderns, supposed anticipation of their discoveries by the ancients, 46, 197; their superiority to the ancients in the investigation of facts, 57; psychological cause of their errors, 61; own no servility to current meanings of words, 89; some of their speculative views anticipated by Aristotle, 183; their uncritical attitude toward ancient authors, 185, 186

Moisture, assigned by Aristotle as a cause of longevity, 267; ancient ideas of, *ib.*

Mole (the), Aristotle on the vision of, 218; fierce debate of naturalists, 218, 219; an Italian Mole corresponding with Aristotle's description, 219; proved to have perfect vision by Geoffroy St. Hilaire, *ib.*; the Syrian Mole mentioned by Lamarck, *ib.*

Molluscs, Aristotle on their external form, 318, 319

Monboddo, Lord, cited, 22; mentions a man who preferred going on all fours, 309; maintains Man's *os sublime* to be merely artificial, *ib.*; his belief in monsters and one-legged men, 373, 374

Monogenesis, various forms of, 327

Monsters, Aristotle's and Monboddo's opinions on, 373, 374

Montucla, his *History of Mathematics*, cited, 38; his contempt for Aristotle's mathematical insight, 148; on A.'s mechanical Problems, 149

Morell, on the Vital and Spiritual Forces of our Nature, 224

Morley's *Life of Cardan*, cited, 176

Moscati, cited, 309

Mothers' marks, Aristotle's omission of, 374

Motion, its laws transcend experience, 66; formula of, 66, 99; our experience of, *ib.*; Laplace on the law of, 98; Comte on Laplace's theory, *ib.*; analysis of Motion, 124, 133, 134, 135, 136; Aristotle ignorant of the laws and nature of, 126; the ancient conception of, *ib.*; Mussenbrock and Rohault's conception of Motion and Rest, 126, 127; Aristotle's celebrated definition of, 131; fallacy respecting continuous Motion, 133; its three divisions, 133, 134; Hermolaus Barbarus on the "motion of place," 134; A. on accelerated motion, 151; the Heart regarded as the source of, 174;

INDEX. 397

theory of animal movements, 178; origin of all motion, *ib.*; Aristotle on the principle of, 227; Motion considered as part of the Vital Principle, 242

Müller, Johannes, his patient labours in Verification, 60; his discovery of Nervous System in Holothuriæ, 167; on Aristotle's announcement of a Placental fish, 217; adopts A.'s view of Life and Mind, 228; on the action of special nerves of sense, 247; on the voices of fish, 287. Cited, 23, 207, 208, 221, 315

Müller, Max, on the origin of the word *man*, 195; on the meaning and equivalents of *anima*, 222

Muratori, his *Dissertation on Italian Antiquities*, cited, 8; on a drawing of the telescope in an ancient MS., 186

Muscles, Aristotle's ignorance of the, 158

Muscular contractility, theories of, 177, 178

Mussenbroek, his Experimental Physics cited, 38; his conception of Motion and Rest, 126; on the idea of Space, 131; proposes a fourth kingdom, 190

Mythology (Ancient), its alleged embodiment of a lost Science, 46

NATURE, idea of uniformity not conceived by Aristotle, 125; A.'s definition of, 129; the principle of Motion and Rest, *ib.*; her ascending steps from non-living to living beings, 190

Natural gradation: the first step Plants, 190; the second step Plant-animals, 192; the third step animals, 193

Natural History. *See* Anatomy, Biology

Nerves, Aristotle said to have discovered them, 157, 168; his slight acquaintance with, 158; what are their Greek equivalents, 168; their tubular structure first described by Leuwenhoek, *ib.*; made familiar to Europe by Ehrenberg, *ib.*; Galileo's story on their origin, *ib.*; defenders of Aristotle's theory of the nerves, *ib.*; A.'s alleged discovery discussed, 168, 169; A. also credited with discovery of the cerebral nerves, 169; the optic nerves believed by Aricenna and Roger Bacon to be tubes or ducts, 169, 170

Nerve-tissue, its alleged existence in inferior animals, 243

Nervous system, Aristotle's ignorance of, 158; Galen's confusion respecting, 167, 168

Νεῦρον, meaning attached by Aristotle to, 167, 168

Newport, on artificial impregnation, 204

Newton, Sir I., discovers the law of gravitation, 29; his *Principia* compared with Aristotle's *Physics*, 67, 68; on Attraction, 93; N.'s metaphysical tendency, 97; on the formation of Matter, *ib.*; his hesitation in identifying celestial and terrestrial Mechanics, 125

Nicanor, Aristotle's adopted son, 17

Nicomachus, the father of Aristotle, 7; physician to Amyntas II., *ib.*; his death, *ib.*

Nicomachus, Aristotle's son, 17

Nifo's work on Aristotle cited, 221; his *Expositio Subtilissima* cited, 233

Nile, the cause of female fecundity, 370

Nizolius, his indignation against the blind worship of the Greeks, 2; compares Aristotle to the cuttle-fish, *ib.*

Novum Organum, its defective conception of Method, 108

Nutrition, the first stage of the Soul's activity, 190; Aristotle's definition of, 234; alleged by A. to be most active during sleep, 259

OBJECTIVE METHOD, replaces the Subjective in science, 26; contrasted with the Subjective, 35; arises from positive knowledge, 36; its origin, a late event in the history of man, *ib.*; due chiefly to the Italian Greeks, *ib.*; no evidence of it in the East, 37; its use impossible without instruments, *ib.*; its teaching on the "final cause," 119; its use in Physics, 123. *See* Subjective Method, Ideal and Real Test

Observation, compared with Experiment, 50; one of the modes of scientific investigation, 57; Aristotle on the necessity of, 110, 111, 112; use of the personal equation, 378; late development of the art of, *ib.*

Oken, cited, 184, 365

Olivi, verifies Aristotle's statement regarding the nest-building fish, 218

Ollier, M., his successful grafting of pieces of bone, 191

Optics, their origin due to the Greeks, 39

Organic, the gradation between the organic and inorganic kingdoms, 190

Organism, Lamarck on the causes of the varieties of, 97; its three most important parts unknown to Aristotle, 158; the differentiation of plants and animals stated, 194; male and female organisms, 207, 208; Kant's definition of an organism, 229; theory of ascending complexity, 243; Aristotle's division into similar and dissimilar parts, 279, 280; Bichat on the distinction between animal and vegetable organs, 314, 315; single and double organs, 315; A. on the sexual organs, 332; various authorities cited as to the ovaries, 332, 333; A. on the testes, 333, 334; the uterus, 334; A. on the origin of the sperm, 339, 340. *See* Generation, Embryology

Origin of Species, Robinet's wild scheme of, 187; Bonnet's scheme, *ib.*

Orton, his *Lectures on Breeding*, cited, 371

Ovaries, opinions of various physiologists on, 332, 333; their functions, 338

Ovid, his description of man's sublime gaze applicable to certain fishes, 308

Oviparity. *See* Incubation

Oviparous Animals, Aristotle on, 350

Ovulation, processes of, 337, 338; spontaneous ovulation, 338; compared with semination, 339

Owen, Professor, cited, 157; his work on Parthenogenesis, cited, 202; on the nourishment of the embryo, 216; on Aristotle's ruminating fish, 283

"Oxidation of tissues," a phrase used to cloak ignorance, 98

PAGENSTECHER, cited, 369

Parallelogram of forces, Aristotle's exposition of, 148; superior to that of Kant, *ib.*

Parents, their mutual influence upon their children, 371, 372

Paris, Parliament of, declares Aristotle's works heretical, 21; edict as to the doctrine of the ancients, *ib.*

Parthenogenesis, Aristotle on that of bees, 110; one of his anticipations of modern science, 201; present state of opinion on, 202; of the Aphis, 202, 203; the means of, discussed, 204; fact of that of bees placed beyond doubt, 205; researches of Dzierzon and Von Siebold, *ib.*; guaranteed by anatomical investigation, *ib.*; the anatomical data unknown to Aristotle, 206

"Parts of Animals." See *De Partibus*

Patrizio, his enmity to Aristotle echoed by Bacon, 9; contents of his Peripatetic Discussions, *ib.*; Giordano Bruno's contempt for him, *ib.*; he denied all distinction between Rational and Irrational, 195, 196; on the Greek and Latin equivalents for Soul, 222, 223. Cited, 279

Perch, Aristotle's remarks on the, 209; said by Rondelet to be both male and female, *ib.*; an exception to the whole class of fishes, 210; dispute as to its self-reproduction, *ib.*; the Perch bisexual, *ib.* *See* Fish

Peripatetics, origin of the name, 16

Personal equation, value of, 378

Phaedo, Plato's, cited, 102

Phenomena, three modes of conceiving, 26, 27, 30; invariability of, 28; Comte on the metaphysical conception of, 30; Vicq d'Azyr, on the Objective interpretation of, 31; Greek and Modern interpretation of, *ib.*; conceived to be dependent on a mutable will, 32; criteria of their three modes of interpretation, *ib.*; contrast between the metaphysical and scientific guarantee of, 33; modes of interpreting, 34; Aristotle's idea of an ascending complexity of Vital Phenomena, 189. *See* METHOD

Philelphus, on the connection of Mind and Body, 232. Cited, 233

Philip of Macedon entrusts Aristotle with tutorship of Alexander, 13; builds a gymnasium, *ib.*

Philippson, cited, 169, 170, 280

Philosophic Anatomy, first dawn of, 279

Philosophy, Greek, Whewell on the cause of its failure, 52, 88; Aristotle, the father of Inductive, 108; Prantl's reproach against ancient philosophy, 140

Physics, Kant's proposal to form an introductory science to, 84; Aristotle's failure to establish a transcendental idea of, 122; use of Objective Method in, 123; his extant writings on, 127; analysis of A.'s treatise on, 128; Barthélemy St. Hilaire's version of A.'s Physics, *ib.*

Physiology, Aristotle's anatomical knowledge insufficient for, 170, 171; A.'s neglect of Verification, 171, 172; A.'s physiology entirely one of conjecture, 180; studies which led to the great discoveries in, 323, 324, 325

Pineal Gland, the seat of the Soul, 83

Placenta, its use, 216

Placental Fish, Aristotle aware of their existence, 212; Müller on Aristotle's announcement of, 217

Planets, Comte on our limited physical and chemical knowledge of, 70

INDEX.   399

Plants, Aristotle's identification of, with animals, 184; his perception of an important morphological law, 187; Treviranus makes a separate kingdom of the Cryptogamic plants and Zoophytes, 188; they have life, 190, 191; their designation, 191; grafting no mark of distinction, *ib.*; plant-animals the second step in natural gradation, 192; Schuyl on Vegetable Life, 229; vitality of plants due to a Soul, *ib.*
Plato, Aristotle's alleged ingratitude to, 11; A.'s teacher for 17 years, *ib.*; contrasted with A., 19; P.'s pernicious influence, *ib.*; his noble faculties, 101; his Method, how far scientific and how far philosophic, *ib.*; his philosophy in reference to science, 102; his studies, *ib.*; he refers the causes of all things to Mind, *ib.*; the influence of Anaxagoras on him, *ib.* the method of eliminating scientific truth, 102, 103; his intensely Subjective method, 102, 103, 104; on genesis, *ib.*; his idea of Science, 103; his frank avowal of the Subjective method, *ib.*; causes of the scientific extravagances in the *Timæus*, *ib.*; his depreciation of Astronomy, 104; on the cohesion of the Four Elements, 105; his use of the five solids, *ib.*; his anatomical and physiological conclusions, 106; his description of the Liver, *ib.*; of the Intestines, *ib.*; his own reason for his conclusions, *ib.*; Kant's happy illustration of his Method, 107; his whole teaching vitiated, *ib.*; contrast to Aristotle, 108; his method compared with A.'s, 109; taught that all knowledge was reminiscence, 111; his evidence of the true scientific method, 115; his derivation of ἄνθρωπος, 195; on the derivation of ψυχή, 223; held "the eye to be of fire," 247; on the use of the Flesh, 307; on the Uterus, 335
Platonic Method, Kant on the, 107; danger of, pointed out by Aristotle, 111
Playfair, on the Physical science of the ancients, 49; inaccurate as to their scientific failure, 51
Pliny, on Alexander's assistance to Aristotle, 15; on the phenomena of scarlet fever, 172; on Greek mendacity, 286; repeats A.'s statement respecting the induration of the Heart, 313. Cited, 289
Ploss, cited, 370
Polypes, Lamarck denies the sensibility of, 97; held by Aristotle to be plants,

192; doubt as to whether A. confounded them with Sponges, 193; their bisexual structure, 209
Polytheism, remnants of, in the Christian Church, 29
Πόροι, what Aristotle meant by, 169
Portal denies that Aristotle dissected the Human Body, 159; on A.'s anatomical carelessness, 167
Poselger, his exposition of Aristotle's *Problems*, 147. Cited, 148
Pouchet, cited, 338, 364
Prantl, his edition of Aristotle's *Physics*, cited, 128; of the *De Cælo*, 136; on the priority of fire to earth, 138; his reproach against ancient philosophers, 140. Cited, 249
Precision, instance of Aristotle's scientific, 112
Primal Soul, see Vital Principle
Problems, Aristotle's work on, 147; expounded by Chabanon and Poselger, *ib.*; Montucla's comment on, 149; examples from, 150, 151, 152. Cited, 300
Projectiles, Aristotle's theory on, 132, 133; on the cessation of motion, 152
Psychology, modern, Aristotle's anticipation of, 111; reason for much of its obscurity, 237
Pythagoreans, their researches in physical science, 38; their constancy in investigating causes of phenomena, *ib.*; the pioneers of modern science, *ib.*
Pythias, Aristotle's wife, 12; his love for, 13
Pythias, daughter of Aristotle, 17

QUATREFAGES, his *Unity of the Human Species* cited, 195
Quiddity, one of the four Causes, 117. See Causes, Causation

RAMUS, cited, 2
Rathke, cited, 208, 275, 315; on the difference between oviparity and viviparity, 330; his observations on the Blenny, 332
Real Test, the criterion of Verification, 68; must supplement the Ideal Test, 80; necessity of, 82
Reason, Schelling on the absolutism of, 80
Réaumur, cited, 277, 353, 354; his observations on the Ephemeron, 329
Recollection, considered by Aristotle as distinct from Memory, 257

Redi, his couplet on the worship of Aristotle, 159
Reproduction, Aristotle on the power of, in females, 360. *See* Generation, Parthenogenesis
Reptiles, held by Aristotle to be bloodless, 276
Republic, Plato's, cited, 103
Respiration, Aristotle's ideas on, 174, 175, 176; the respiration of fish, 175, 176; A. on the process of, 177
Rest. *See* Motion
Ritter, cited, 6, 9, 140, 279
Robbe, Dr., his edition of Ammonius, 5
Robin, C., on embryology, 203; on the placenta, 216. Cited, 361
Robinet, his wild scheme on the origin of species, 187
Roger Bacon. *See* Bacon
Rohault, his definition of Motion, 127
Rondelet, on the male and female character of the Perch, 209; his work *De Piscis Marinis* quoted by Dufossé, 210
Rosmini, on the real weight of Aristotle's authority, 22; his estimate of A.'s philosophy, *ib.*
Rouget, cited, 208, 275, 345
Roulin, cited, 177
Rudolphi, cited, 210
Ruminating Fish, Aristotle's, 282; Milne Edwards's reference to, 283; Professor Owen's note on, *ib.*

SALAMANDER, an instance of the metamorphoses of animals, 213
Saverien, quotes Père Schot respecting the Planet Angels, 29
Scaliger, J. C., his opinion of Hermalaus Barbarus, 119; his palliation of Aristotle, 167; his edition of the *Hist. Animal.*, 269; finds no classification in it, 278; maintained that mice are generated from corruption, 361. Cited, 347, 367
Scarlet fever, Pliny on the phenomena of, 172
Scepticism, the chief element in true Method, 39; due to the Greeks, *ib.*; Aristotle on, 40; imperfectly practised by the Greeks, *ib.*
Schelling, on the absolutism of Reason, 80
Schleiermacher, cited, 109
Schleiden, cited, 296
Schneegass, on the aura seminalis, 356
Schneider, on Alexander's assistance to Aristotle, 15; his edition of the *Hist. Animal.*, 21, 269; his Latin version cited, 199
Schoolmen (the), their grand mistake, 70; employed a method on which all problems were insoluble, 71
Schröder van der Kolk, on the union between Soul and Body, 224. Cited, 261
Schuckhard, cited, 270
Schuyl, on Vegetable Life, 229
Schweigger, his fanciful explanation of ancient myths, 46
Scientific scepticism, its Greek origin, 39 Aristotle on, 40; imperfectly practised by the Greeks, *ib. See* Scepticism
SCIENCE, dawn of, 24; its gradual development, 24, 25; distinguished from "common knowledge," 26; the criterion or guarantee of, 33; its supposed origin in the East, 36; preëminently quantitative, 37; Pythagorean researches in, 38, 39; its dignity springs from disinterestedness, 42; cause of the hostility of theologians to, 43; Greeks the originators of, 44; cause of its eclipse in Europe, *ib.*; prolonged infancy of, 45; failure of the ancients in, 46; their failure owing to disregard of Observation and Experiment, 47; Playfair's verdict on the failure of the ancients, 49; Playfair inaccurate, 51; causes of the failure of the Greeks examined, 55; neglect of facts, not ideas, the cause of Greek failure, *ib.*; three modes of investigation, 57; Greek want of instruments, 58; source of the errors of the ancients, 60, 61; the law of progress in, 62; transcendental ideas of modern, 66; ancient and modern distinguished, 67; the absolute rule of, 69; the two criteria of Verification, *ib.*; definition of, 71; as distinguished from Metaphysics, 84, 93, 96; Kant's proposal to form an introductory science to Physics, 84; Whewell on the failure of the Greeks, 88; the successful method, 90; the primary requisition of science, *ib.*; meaning of the word "cause," *ib.*; disclaims attempts to penetrate secrets of causation, 91; seeks only the phenomenal and relative, *ib.*; its range and limits, 92; Copernicus cited, *ib.*; three stages of positive knowledge in, 96; continuous abandonment of unverified theories, 98; Plato's idea of, 103; Experience the true guide in, 111; danger of applying the true Method in Aristotle's time, 113; based on Inductive Syllogism, 115; fallacy of ancient

INDEX. 401

speculations, 115; Aristotle's scientific logic, 115, 116, 117; his four scientific causes, 117, 118; struggles against the popular horror of dissection, 160; conformity of ancient ideas with modern research, 185; curious illustration of ancient science, 300 ; summary of modern embryological science, 327 ; ancient and modern contrasted, 377 ; precision of modern, 378 ; personal equation, *ib.*

Sea Anemones, their bisexual structure, 209; Aristotle's classification of, 318

Secretion, moderation in, a cause of longevity, 267

Segni, his Tuscan paraphrase of the *De Animâ*, 221

Sensation, Aristotle on, 235, 238, 239, 252, 297; the judging faculty, 239; divided sensation, 252; the distinctions of, 297

Senses, Touch and Taste the primary, 243; other senses, 244, 246, 249, 251; Aristotle's treatise on, 246 ; A.'s analysis of Vision, *ib.*; of Taste and Smell, 249; of Hearing, 251

Sensibility, Aristotle's views on, 235, 236, 237

Serres, on the kidneys, 165; on the means of discovering the missing links in the chain of creation, 188; his *Précis d'Anat. transcendante* cited, 189; on the embryology of male and female organisms, 208; on the duality of organs, 315. Cited, 374

Severinus, cited, 176

Sexes, Aristotle on the differences of, 331; authorities cited on origin of, 367; Aristotle's hypotheses on, 368, 369, 370

S'Gravesande, on the differences of things, 117

Sharpey, cited, 216

Siebold. *See* Von Siebold

Skeleton, Aristotle's ideas of the homologies of, 157

Skin, Aristotle on the formation of the, 363

Sleep, Aristotle's treatise on, 258; his survey of, 258, 259; he asserts it to be the most active time of nutrition, 259; cause and natural aim of Sleep, 260; A.'s physiological explanation of, 260, 261, 262 ; compared to Epilepsy, 261; Kant on dreamless sleep, 265

Socrates, Aristotle alleged to have been a disciple of his, 5; cause of his repugnance to physical inquiries, 43

Solids, Plato's use of the five, 105

Sömmering, his defence of Aristotle respecting the seat of the Nerves, 168

Sonnenburg, on Aristotle's assertion as to the emptiness of the back part of the skull, 167. Cited, 219, 271

Soul, Descartes on the seat of, 83; Plato compares Man's soul to that of the universe, 106; Aristotle places its seat in the Heart, 120; first stage of its activity, 190; not equivalent to the ψυχή of Aristotle, 222; sensation the characteristic of, 224; doctrines on, *ib.*; Claudian Mammertus on the immaterialism of, 225 ; A. on the divisibility of, *ib.*; on the study of, 226, 227; Galen on the three kinds of, 233, 234; Aristotle's views on the immortality of, 233, 358; the "place of forms," 240

Space, useless discussions on the idea of, 131; Aristotle's profitless discussion on contraries in, 137, 138

Spallanzani, cited, 353

Species, Bonnet's and Robinet's schemes on the origin of, 187; Aristotle's views on, 293

Spectrum analysis, discloses metals in Sun's atmosphere, 70

Spencer, Herbert, his definition of Life, 230. Cited, 231

Sperm, whether derived from the whole body or only a part, 339, 340, 341; Aristotle's diagnosis of, 342, 343, 344; its physical nature, 356

Spermatozoon, description of, 352 ; figured by Andry and Gautier, *ib.*; Lallemand on its self-contained elements of development, 371

Sperm-cells, production of, 337

Speusippus, Aristotle pays 700*l.* for the works of, 8

Spinoza, on the hostility of theologians to physical science, 43. Cited, 79, 294

Spirit and Matter, Hegel's elucidation of, 81

Spix, cited, 167, 270; on Aristotle's standard of animal structure, 281; on A.'s wealth of facts, 290

Spleen, Aristotle's description of inaccurate, 165

Sponges, pronounced by Aristotle to be animals, 184, 193; Imperato's description of, 193; A.'s opinion adopted by the Moderns, *ib.*

Spontaneous Generation. *See* Generation

Spontaneous fission. *See* Monogenesis

Sprengel, cited, 159, 168; suggests that Aristotle may have dissected the human body, 168

26

Stagira, the birthplace of Aristotle, 6; its situation, ib.
Stagirite. See Aristotle
Stahl, on the functions of the Soul, 223; said to teach the same doctrine as Aristotle, ib.; on the Vital Principle, 228
Stahr, his article on Aristotle in the *Dictionary of Greek and Roman Philosophy* cited, 6
Stars, Aristotle's theory of their substance, 138, 139, 140
Statics, founded by Archimedes, 147, 379
Stenon, cited, 332, 333, 353
St. Hilaire, Barthélemy, his assertion of the accuracy of Aristotle's *Physics*, 46; his Introduction cited, ib.; on A.'s theory of Motion, 126; his version of the *Physics*, 128; his idolatry of A., 130; his translation of Aristotle's *Meteorology*, 143; his version of the *De Animâ*, 221. Cited, 112, 145
St. Hilaire, Geoffroy, cited, 183, 208, 218, 280, 319, 374; pronounces the chain of creation a chimæra, 188; his doctrine of the "unity of composition," ib.; on the development of the impregnated ovum, 215
St. Hilaire, Isidore, his eulogy on Aristotle, 155; quotes Buffon on the theory of gradation, 188; on hermaphroditism, 209; his wonderful goat, 285. Cited, 3, 23, 183, 190, 195, 207, 208, 270, 295, 309, 374
Stilling, cited, 113
St. Maur Benedictines, their *Literary History of France* cited, 32; their account of the auguries of the Druids, ib.; on the essence of the Soul, 225
Strack's translation of the *Hist. Animal.*, 269. Cited, 280
Subjective Method of interpreting Nature, 26, 34, 35; its influence, 35; contrasted with the Objective Method, ib.; arises from ignorance, 36, 63; relied on by the ancients, 49; its gradual relinquishment, 63; explanation of the preference for, ib.; the metaphysical phase of, 65; account of the Subjective and Objective Methods, ib.; error of Subjective Method tested, 81; Plato's frank avowal of, 103; its inability to measure physical forces, 300. See Objective Method, Ideal and Real Test
Sunderall, his *Die Thierarten des Aristoteles*, cited, 279
Sun's atmosphere, metals disclosed in, by spectrum analyses, 70
Swainson, on Aristotle's greatness, 270

Swammerdamm, his patient observations, 158; on the Heart as the great "cooking centre," 174; on the Ephemeron, 329. Cited, 220, 275, 353
Syllogism, Inductive, the basis of science, 115
Sylvius (Leboë), cited, 323
Syngenesis, ancient theory of, 353. See Generation
Syrian Mole. See Mole.

Taste, Aristotle on the sense of, 179. See Senses
Tauchnitz, edition of A.'s works, 22
Taurellus, his attack on Cæsalpinus cited, 2, 168, 228, 305, 333, 347
Telesius, cited, 2, 178; his *De Naturâ Rerum*, 177; his misconception of Aristotle's illustration of the Vital Principle, 232; held light to be visible heat, 248
Telescope, the, alleged to have been known to the ancients, 186; but theirs was a tube without a lens, ib.; supposed discovery of, by Roger Bacon, ib.
Tension, identical with *vis viva*, 123
Terror, its effect on animals, 302; its cause, ib.
Testacea, Aristotle on sight and hearing of, 287
Test (Ideal), placed above the Real by Aristotle, 68, 69; when subjectively true, ib.; must be supplemented by the Real Test, 80. See Real Test
Testes. See Organism, Generation, Embryology
Thales, cited by Whewell, 89
Thielmann, cited, 158
Theology: progress impeded by the theological conception of Nature, 31; its hostility to physical science, 43; its gradual approximation to science, 44
Theory (or Idea), its implied antithesis to Fact, 71, 74, 75; the real distinction, 75, 76, 77, 78; may be transferred from Metaphysics to Science, 84; or from Science to Metaphysics, 84, 85
Thermotics, value of the science of, 301
Thompson, Allen, cited, 351
Tiedemann, cited, 323
Tiraboschi, his *History of Italian Literature*, cited, 2, 118
Titze, his ingenious suggestion concerning the *Hist. Animal.*, 279
Timæus, Plato's, cause of the scientific extravagances in, 103; idea of the genesis, 104. Cited, 334, 335

Torpedo: weight of its eggs and of the developed young, 216
Torstrik, A., his recension of the *De Animâ*, 221; on the Intellect, 240
Touch, Aristotle on the sense of, 179. *See* Senses
Trendelenberg, his edition of the *De Animâ* cited, 118; on Aristotle's meaning of πόροι, 169. Cited, 240, 252
Treviranus, makes a separate kingdom of the Cryptogamic plants and Zoophytes, 188; his definition of Life, 221. Cited, 231
Truth, Hegel on the meaning of, 80; Descartes' erroneous criterion of, 83
Tyson, cited, 319

UNIFORMITY in Nature. *See* Nature.
Universals, importance attached to by Aristotle, 116, 117
Universe, Plato's idea of the creation of, 105, 106
Uterus, Aristotle's description of, 164, 165, 215, 334, 335, 336; error of the ancient anatomists respecting, 332, 333; Plato's description of, 335

VALENCIENNES, cited, 210
Vallisneri, cited, 352, 353, 354
Van Beneden, his *Mémoire sur les Vers Intestinaux* cited, 327
Vander Hooven's *Handbook on Zoology* cited, 295
Van Helmont, cited, 263; on the "poisonous quality of bull-beef," 303
Vatican, the ancient anatomical figures in, 161
Vegetal Soul, an existence *sui generis*, 30; Schuyl on vegetal Life, 229
Verany, cited, 197
Verification, the guarantee of Science, 33; the ruling principle of investigation, 57, 58; its process slow and difficult, 59; want of appreciation of amongst the Greeks, *ib.*; instance of Eratosthenes, *ib.*; A.'s carelessness of verification, 59, 171, 172; Haller's patient labours in, 60; instance of Müller, *ib.*; the criteria of verification, 68, 69; its immense applicability, 70; insolubility of all questions beyond it, *ib.*; instance of metals in the sun's atmosphere, *ib.*; future verification of propositions now insoluble, *ib.*; urgent demand for, 81; the principle of verification our best guide in Science, 96; the slow appreciation of, 377, 378

Vertebræ, varieties of in different animals, 85
Vertebral Theory, Aristotle's claim to, 186, 187
Vesalius, cited, 163, 167, 169, 332, 333; notices Aristotle's error in attributing eight ribs to Man, 165; first discovers the nature of the bone of the heart, 313
Vestiges of the Natural History of Creation, views of Meckel adopted in, 188
Vicq d'Azyr, on the objective interpretation of Nature, 31; on our natural horror at dissection, 162. Cited, 157, 190, 191, 320
Virboslai, Margaret, Countess, her extraordinary parturition, 374
Virtual velocities, the principle of known to Aristotle, 148
Viscera, Aristotle's diagnosis of, 310; the opinion of Democritus objected to by A., *ib.*; remarks on the viscera of the Apoda, 317; of molluscs and insects, 318
Vision, Aristotle on, 237, 246, 247; Newton on the sparks of the eye, 247
Vital Phenomena, Aristotle's idea of an ascending complexity in, 189. *See* Nature, Phenomena
Vital Principle, impersonation of, 87; results of its increased activity, 193; of plants and animals, 194; the nearest translation of Aristotle's ψυχή, 222; the nature of, 225, 226, 227, 228; "divided vitality," 228; Aristotle's conception of, 231, 232, 233; regarded by A. as a final cause, 234; the intellect of, 240
Viviparity. *See* Incubation
Vogt, cited, 197, 218
Vogt and Pappenheim, cited, 332
Von Baer, on the difference between the Vertebrate and Invertebrate types, 189; completed the discovery of the Mammalian egg, 213. Cited, 216, 295, 333, 353, 354, 357
Von Siebold, on Aristotle's acquaintance with the Cephalopoda, 199; his researches on the parthenogenesis of bees, 205
Vulpian and Philipeaux, on the importance of Verification, 60

WARMTH and Moisture, essential to growth and Life, 268
Wessling, his *Syntagma* cited, 169, 333
Whewell, Dr., cited, 49, 150; on the failure of Greek Philosophy, 52; his *History of the Inductive Sciences*

cited, 52 ; his conclusion as to the failure of ancient science, 53, 88 ; this conclusion examined, 53, 54 ; his *History of Scientific Ideas* cited, 55; on the first attempts to comprehend Nature, 88 ; on the employment of abstractions, *ib.*; on the propensity to seek for principles in the usages of language, 89 ; on Aristotle's subservience to language, *ib.* ; his reproach against Aristotle, 147; on the constitution of a classification, 278

Willis, his *Opera Omnia* cited, 169

Wimmer, cited, 142, 340, 346

Wolff, C. F., cited, 310, 354, 355

Wollaston, cited, 70

XENOCRATES, accompanies Aristotle on his visit to Hermias, 12; teaches in the Academy, 15

Xenophon, on the repugnance of Socrates to physical inquiries, 43

ZELLER, his *Philosophy of the Greeks* cited, 6, 118; on Ether as an element, 140

Zoology. *See* Animals, Plants, Generation, Biology

Zoophytes, plant-animals the second step in natural gradation, 192; examples selected by Aristotle, *ib.* *See* Plants.

THE END.

London: Printed by SMITH, ELDER and Co., Little Green Arbour Court, Old Bailey, E. C.

www.ingramcontent.com/pod-product-compliance
Lightning Source LLC
Chambersburg PA
CBHW030600300426
44111CB00009B/1048